THE TRAGEDY OF THE LOLLARDS' TOWER:

THE CASE OF RICHARD HUNNE

and its aftermath in the

REFORMATION PARLIAMENT, 1529-1533

THE TRAGEDY
OF THE
LOLLARDS' TOWER

I. THE CASE OF RICHARD HUNNE, with
its aftermath in

II. THE REFORMATION PARLIAMENT,
1529 - 33 : a review of events from the
downfall of WOLSEY to the birth of
ELIZABETH

by

ARTHUR OGLE, M.A.
RECTOR OF EAST ILSLEY, BERKS.

OXFORD

PEN - IN - HAND

DA335
H85
05
Cop2

*Made in England and
printed at The Blackmore Press, Gillingham, Dorset
by T. H. Brickell & Son, Ltd.*

To

the beloved memory

of

THOMAS HERBERT WARREN

President of Magdalen College, 1885 - 1928

I desire to thank the Master and Fellows of Corpus Christi College, Cambridge, for access to one of the manuscript treasures of their Library ; Mr. Geoffrey Barraclough, for help in deciphering the annotations on the margin of that volume ; the Secretary and staff of the Record Office for their kindness and help in getting up some volumes of State Papers from their war-time depositories so that I could examine them conveniently in London ; Dr. W. E. Campbell and Messrs. Eyre & Spottiswoode for allowing me to make free use of Dr. Campbell's modern version of More's dialogue ; And two historian friends, Professor Claude Jenkins and the Rev. J. M. Thompson, for reading this book in typescript and giving me valuable criticism and advice. Of the many scholars, past and present, into whose labours I have gratefully entered, I can here only name one, who has just passed away full of years and honours ; to the learning and judgment of Dr. A. F. Pollard all students of the period owe a lasting debt.

TABLE OF CONTENTS

PART I.—THE CASE OF RICHARD HUNNE

PART II.—THE REFORMATION PARLIAMENT, 1529-33 :
A REVIEW OF EVENTS FROM THE DOWNFALL OF WOLSEY TO THE BIRTH OF ELIZABETH

TABLE OF CONTENTS (*continued*)

Part I

THE CASE OF RICHARD HUNNE

Chapter I

INTRODUCTORY

The case of Richard Hunne occurred towards the close of 1514, when Henry VIII, an imposing young prince of twenty-three, had been about five years upon the throne. It occurred at what proved, though no one at the time suspected, to be a critical moment in history. The mediaeval order of Christendom, with the Papacy as its cementing bond, appeared to be impregnable. Wyclif had been long dead, and his body, as that of a condemned heretic, exhumed and burnt. The Wycliffite movement, as a public force, had been long and effectually suppressed, though obscure adherents of it, lingering in odd holes and corners, still engaged the attention of the authorities. Church and Crown were hand in glove, both nigh absolute in their respective spheres. And the powers of both were soon to be combined in one hand, that of Thomas Wolsey, who, as at once Lord Chancellor and Papal Legate a latere, was to rehearse the Supreme Headship, in all causes as well ecclesiastical as civil, which his masterful sovereign was presently to take over. No hint of that revolutionary transfer was discernible in 1514. Luther had not appeared in Germany, and Anne Boleyn had not appeared at Court. No bolt appeared to threaten from those blue skies under which the prelates, encouraged by a brilliant and benign prince, administered the agelong ecclesiastical system, and set their heel upon the few who dared impugn it. Yet within fifteen years of Hunne's death Germany had been convulsed by the Lutheran movement ; a proscribed English New Testament was being smuggled into England ; the King's marriage had become the question of the hour ; and there met the historic Parliament which, by a succession of rapid strokes, brought the papal authority in England to an end, and with it the unlimited power of Convocations and Church Courts to legislate for, and discipline, the " subject " laity.

11

THE CASE OF RICHARD HUNNE

What has history to make of this landslide of event? What, if anything, has the case of Richard Hunne to do with it? Historians, however they have differed as to the merits of the case, have been agreed in regarding it as significant in some sort. Certain, and important, is the belief of Hunne's fellow-citizens in London as to how he died. Less certain, but more important, is the question whether there was any real foundation for that belief. And that is the question which history has had to try, since it never came to trial before a judge and jury.

Unlike most of those who, at this period, were in trouble for heresy, Hunne was not quite a friendless and negligible person. He was a well-to-do merchant and freeman of London, whose character and opinions were sufficiently known. Arrested for heresy, he was confined, pending trial, in the Lollards' Tower, the Bishop of London's prison at the south-west corner of old St. Paul's. The Bishop's Palace stood opposite at the north-west corner. From the Lollards' Tower Hunne, on Saturday, December 2nd, 1514, was taken to Fulham for examination before the Bishop. Returned to prison, he was found on the following Monday morning in his cell, hanging. The discovery was at once communicated to the Bishop's chancellor, Dr. William Horsey, who had the custody of the Lollards' Tower and of prisoners therein confined. He, and other dignitaries of St. Paul's — High Mass having lately concluded — hastened to the Tower, and were doubtless horrified by what they saw. Hunne, a conscious heretic, had put an end to himself in order to forestall condemnation and the stake. A Coroner's jury was immediately impanelled. After examining Hunne's body and the state of the cell, they set aside at once the allegation of suicide; and, after an inquiry of some length, occupied in taking the depositions of those who could throw light upon the movements of the men concerned, they found a verdict of wilful murder against Doctor Horsey the Bishop's chancellor and two of his underlings. The accused men were duly indicted, but never tried; and the successful efforts of the authorities, ecclesiastical and lay, — prolonged for nearly a year,— to protect Horsey from being brought to trial, served only to confirm the belief of Hunne's

OLD ST. PAUL'S

with — at the south-west corner — the Parish Church of St. Gregory
and the Lollards' Tower

From the engraving by Hollar
Reproduced from the copy in the Bodleian Library

facing page 12

into his " Acts and Monuments." This tractate has been critically examined by Miss E. Jeffries Davis in a learned article on ' the authorities for the case of Richard Hunne ' in the English Historical Review for July, 1915. I give Miss Davis' conclusions, with certain comments of my own. She writes :—

" The question of its value as evidence is of some importance. One would be inclined to regard as of no value whatever the evidence of an anonymous pamphlet published more than twenty years after the events of which it treats."

But, it may be said, it was not until twenty years or so after the event that such a publication became in any way safe ; and that even then — as the compiler in his preface shows himself to be aware — the issue between the old order and the new, and between their respective partizans, was so much in the balance that it would have been in a high degree dangerous for any man to have put his name to it.

After citing several facts which tell in favour of its authenticity Miss Davis sums up as follows :—

" It thus seems not improbable that the tract is a collection of genuine documents, with a preface and marginal notes added by the compiler. But it cannot be assumed that even in his version, much less in those of Hall and Foxe, they are accurately printed ; and their statements, made at a time when the city was overwhelmed by a wave of excitement and party clamour, cannot be accepted without reserve. Hence the evidence of the tract is at best third rate." (Eng. Hist. Rev. July 1915, pp. 477 - 9).

I should not myself put it so low as that. If the tractate is, not improbably, a collection of genuine documents, and if, as is the case, there is nothing to show that they were garbled in the printing, they would seem to offer as good and full evidence as we could expect to have for any minor event of the period. And, be it re-membered, the death of Hunne was in itself a minor event, and only acquires a major importance through its apparent place in history. Moreover, it was the alleged facts as to the fate of Hunne which produced the ' wave of excitement ' in the City, and not the wave of excitement which produced the facts. The tractate

14

gives, not only the formal verdict of the jury, but a full statement of what they saw with their own eyes in the Lollards' Tower, along with the depositions taken from ten — some of them unwilling — witnesses ; and the facts so alleged are generally consistent, and only contradictory in the case of two incriminated persons who tried to establish an alibi by falsehood. Furthermore, we have the proved fact that the utmost efforts of authority, of " divers great lords spiritual and temporal and other of the King's honourable council," wholly failed to constrain the Jury to retract their verdict, or to silence the endeavours of the House of Commons to vindicate the integrity of the Jury. And, finally, it is hardly to be imagined that a responsible writer like Edward Hall, who about this time was Under Sheriff of London and would have access to the records of the Coroner's Court, would have inserted this tractate bodily in his Chronicle had there been any real question as to the genuineness of the documents it purported to reproduce. I therefore follow Dr. A. F. Pollard (' Wolsey,' pp. 35 - 6, note 3) in accepting this tractate as a straightforward record of sworn facts. Its acceptance would of course settle the question as to how Hunne came by his death. But the facts it contains have not been accepted by a contemporary like Sir Thomas More, who knew something of the circumstances at first hand ; and More has been followed by even more sceptical writers down to Dr. James Gairdner and Mr. Algernon Cecil in our own day. The human, and honest, mind is capable of strange vagaries ; and it still remains necessary to inquire whether the Coroner's Jury were in their right senses ; or whether, upon entering Hunne's cell, they suddenly — five and twenty of them — became somnambulists, and agreed upon an immediate, common and elaborate hallucination to which, for months of eventual wakefulness, they adhered through thick and thin. The investigation, as Dr. Pollard says, " almost rises to the level of detective fiction." And no one would add one more to the many attempts to solve the mystery without some hope of being able to raise it to the level of detective fact.

More, Hall, Harpsfield, Foxe, Bale, Fuller, Burnet, Creighton, Brewer, Gairdner, H. A. L. Fisher, and, most recently, Dr. A. F.

THE CASE OF RICHARD HUNNE

Pollard and Mr. Algernon Cecil, — a whole line of historical writers have examined the case, without reaching an agreed conclusion. The earlier writers in sympathy with the reforming movement accepted the conclusion of murder ; More and the apologists of the old order have been equally emphatic that it was a case of suicide. Such modern writers as incline to the theory of murder regard the case against Dr. Horsey as at best not proven. Some, like More the earliest, affect to discuss the case while ignoring the alleged evidence on which the indictment for murder was based ; others, like the latest, Mr. Algernon Cecil in his " Portrait of Thomas More," dismiss that evidence as a mere cock-and-bull story, unworthy of credence or serious consideration. It was this latter treatment of the matter which revived my own interest in the case. I first became acquainted with it many years ago while endeavouring to solve certain questions as to the early history of the Wycliffite Bible. I then, by accident, came across what I believe to be the crucial document in the case of Richard Hunne. It had lain for centuries unrecognised in the library of a Cambridge college. It was the manuscript copy of the Wycliffite Bible alleged to be Hunne's, and produced in evidence at his hurried post mortem trial for heresy held a fortnight after his death. Upon articles based upon the prologue of this Bible, Hunne was condemned as a contumacious heretic, his exhumed body was burnt, and any bodily evidence of murderous violence effectually obliterated. If I am right in the identification — and the evidence for it will be given in its place — then the document is important as throwing light upon the methods and motives of the prosecution, and so upon every other element in the case.

The facts in the case are fairly copious ; but they cannot be seen in their true light or given their true value without some knowledge of the contemporary mind and of certain elements in contemporary law. These elements of law now survive as little more than names and relics ; but it is necessary to see them as they were to men of Hunne's day, active realities, and possibly matters of life and death. Wriothesley in his Chronicle (1, 9), echoing the popular belief, says that Hunne " was made an heretique for suing a Praemunire." We have to see what was meant by Heresy, and by the writ of praemunire. We must know something also of the contemporary mind as regards the condition of the Church and Clergy ; what the lay people felt about the clergy, and what ground they had for feeling as they did. These matters, which lie, necessarily, upon the threshold of the inquiry, will be the subject of the following chapter.

Chapter II

WHAT WAS HERESY?

What was the sort of heresy with which the authorities in England had to deal in the fifteenth century, and the early years of the sixteenth? Briefly, it was adherence to the Wycliffite movement and Wycliffite doctrine, and the unlicensed reading of the Wycliffite Scriptures, with the consequent refusal to bow to " the determination of Holy Church," particularly in regard to image-worship, pilgrimages, praying to saints, compulsory auricular confession, and, above all, " the sacrament of the altar " and the dogma of Transubstantiation. This last was always the test question. What was it, and why did it become pre-eminent as a test of orthodoxy?

A then prevailing, but impermanent, philosophy distinguished between the " substance " of a thing and its " accidents," those externals cognisable by the senses, of sight, taste, touch and so on. It assumed that a " substance " and its sensible " accidents " are as separable in fact as they may be conceived to be in thought. Forgetful of the Apostle's warning against the " oppositions of science falsely so called," the Lateran Council in 1215, discovering in this doctrine a " scientific " explanation of the Presence of Christ in the Holy Sacrament, promulgated, as necessary belief for all the faithful, the dogma of Transubstantiation. It affirmed that as the words of Consecration were uttered by the priest the elements of bread and wine lost all substantive existence, and that nothing of them remained but their " accidents " of colour, shape, solidity, liquidity as visible and tangible abstractions. It affirmed that what was then alone present in " substance " upon the altar, under the " form " or " appearance " of bread and wine, was the Body and Blood of Christ ; and that this was the " very " Body which was born of the Virgin Mary, was buffeted, scourged, crucified, buried, raised from the dead and taken up into heaven in the sight of the Apostles ; and the Blood was the " very " blood which had trickled down the Saviour's brow, and coursed from the side which the soldier pierced and into which St. Thomas was invited to thrust his hand. Some such view had long been held as a permissible opinion, possibly true for such as could receive it. But to define it as of faith to be instilled by all the clergy into all the people was another matter. A doctrine postulating such physical intimacy of contact with the sacred Person of our Lord could only retain countenance if ministered by a priesthood of such personal sanctity as no great body of men have ever succeeded in maintaining for long. With a generally credulous and illiterate laity, it should have needed but little experience of human nature to foresee what such a doctrine was likely to become in the hands of an ill-recruited, ill-instructed, ill-disciplined clergy such as those of the later Middle Ages, by all the evidence, came increasingly to be. In their hands the doctrine was impressed with a bald downrightness, even a revolting crudity, of language which alone accounts for the significant phrase commonly current in regard to it. In an age when miracles were commonplaces of the popular mind, an ineffable mystery was converted into a familiar and recurrent miracle of routine ; and the priest, in celebrating the Sacrament, was popularly said to be " making Christ," " making " Him who, according to the Catholic creeds, was " neither made nor created " even by the Almighty Father. Upon the punctual working of this miracle of " making Christ " souls depended for their deliverance from perdition. Unless, on Sundays and holy days, the priest was at the altar to " make Christ," without doubt they would perish everlastingly. The priest, in every parish, became the one indispensable man. As the sole " maker " of Christ his person was sacrosanct ; by the law of Holy Church, he was amenable to no law but his own, and that at a time when the law of the Church, as a means of discipline, was falling into merited derision. As the one sovereignly necessary person his commands had to be obeyed, his demands on men, and sometimes women, met, his faults, and sometimes infamies, overlooked and condoned. The working effect of the doctrine was to set the clergy above the law, above their fellow-men, and, worst of all, above themselves. A further effect

19

was that the sacrifice of praise and thanksgiving, being clothed with a peculiar efficacy as an atoning sacrifice for the living and the dead, was established as a steady source of income. People would pay for masses which would avail to buy off the wrath of God and its consequences for themselves and the suffering souls in Purgatory. The more masses the more money, the greater the premium on superstition and the progagation of an unevangelical gospel of fear.* Very tardily and not, we may be sure, without some misery of spirit did Wyclif come to see all this. When he did, it was with his usual clarity of vision and trenchancy of action. He had come to see in Transubstantiation the very warrant and seal of a venal and irresponsible priestcraft : the very mine out of which men of the earth earthy won much of the merchandise that profaned the Father's House. With " weapons mighty through God to the pulling down of strongholds " he attacked it, his motive and purpose

---

* What that gospel meant we learn from Sir Thomas More's ' Supplication of Souls,' (English Works, 1557, pp. 337 - 8). The anguished Souls plead, not with God, but with any who can help them in a practical way by finding money for masses :
  "Finally, all our other friends and every good Christian man and woman, open your hearts and have some pity upon us. If ye believe not that we need your help, alas the lack of faith. If ye believe our need and care not for us, alas the lack of pity. For whoso pitieth not us, whom can he pity ? If ye pity the poor, there is none so poor as we that have not a bratte to put on our backs. If ye pity the blind, there is none so blind as we, which are here in the dark, saving for sights unpleasant and loathsome, till some comfort come. If ye pity the lame, there is none so lame as we, that neither can creep one foot out of the fire nor have one hand at liberty to defend our face from the flame. Finally if ye pity any man in pain, never knew ye pain comparable to ours, whose fire as far passeth in heat all the fires that ever burned upon earth as the hottest of all those passeth a feigned fire painted on a wall. If ever ye lay sick and thought the night long and longed sore for day while every hour seemed longer than five, bethink you then what a long night we silly souls endure, that lie sleepless, restless, burning and broiling in the dark fire one long night of many days, of many weeks, and some of many years together. You welter peradventure and tolter in sickness from side to side and find little rest in any part of the bed ; we lie bounden to the brands and cannot lift up our heads. You have your physicians with you that sometime cure and heal you ; no physic will help our pain nor no plaister cool our heat. Your keepers do you great ease and put you in good comfort ; our keepers are such as God keep you from, cruel damned spirits, odious, envious and hateful, dispiteous enemies and despiteful tormentors, and their company more horrible and grievous to us than is the pain itself and the intolerable torment that they do us, wherewith from top to toe they cease not continually to tear us."

entirely practical. In his ' Trialogus,' the treatise in which he brings the doctrine to the test of Holy Scripture and right reason, his examination of it begins as follows : " I maintain that among all the heresies which have ever appeared in the Church, there was never one which was more cunningly smuggled in by hypocrites than this, or which in more ways deceives the people ; for it plunders them, leads them astray into idolatry, denies the teaching of Scripture, and by this unbelief provokes the Truth Himself oftentimes to anger."* "Among all the heresies." Wyclif was not and never was on the defensive. He was himself the first English " malleus hereticorum," hammer of heretics ; and the fellow-priests who taught false doctrine and lived false lives were heretics to him. His vehemence in attack is that of a man who is not only devoted to the duties of his profession but jealous for its honour. He was a priest himself, as were all his chief lieutenants. He worked through the " poor priests " who espoused his cause. The Wycliffite movement, though it appealed to the laity and became for a time a power among them, was not, in origin or leadership, a lay movement. It was revolt of priests against a decadent priest-craft ; and when, some twenty years after Wyclif's death, the prelates felt strong enough to strike decisively at the priests who led it, its back was broken. By then its following among the laity had weakened. In his earlier polemic against the Papacy Wyclif had carried the layman with him ; he voiced what all felt. His attack on the Papacy as an institution gave them pause, for they saw nothing to replace it. In his rejection of Transubstantiation he went beyond their depth. Laymen had no understanding of the doctrine ; they took what they were taught on trust ; and felt that on a matter so nearly touching their life hereafter as well as, they were made to understand, their lives here, it was better to bow to " the determination of Holy Church," and take no risks. With

---

* " Inter omnes haereses quae unquam in ecclesia pullularunt, nunquam considero aliquam plus callide per hypocritas introductam et multiplicius populum defraudantem ; nam spoliat populum, facit ipsum committere idol-atriam, negat fidem Scripturae, et per consequens ex infidelitate multipliciter ad iracundiam provocat Veritatem." Wyclif, ' Trialogus,' bk. IV, cap. 2.

the repressive legislation of the early fifteenth century the risks became certainties. There had been a sudden shifting of the political scene. The violent cross-currents of politics under Richard II had favoured the growth of Wycliffism. In 1393, eight years after Wyclif's death, Parliament had passed the most formidable of the Statutes of Provisors. Three years later the Commons gave a hearing to a petition in which the entire Wycliffite programme of reform was pressed upon the attention of Parliament. But in 1396 the astute and resolute aristocrat Thomas Arundel became Archbishop of Canterbury. Impeached and banished a year later, he presently prevailed upon his fellow-exile, Henry of Lancaster, to make his bold and successful bid for the Crown. Henry, upon principles then recognised, was not next in succession. His throne rested upon parliamentary recognition, his own statesmanship, and the support of Arundel and the Church. The consequent alliance between Church and Crown boded ill for the Wycliffite party. Hardly was the new dynasty established than the first steps were taken to place all the services of the Crown at the disposal of the Bishops for the suppression of heresy. The statute " De haeretico comburendo " in 1401 made it the duty of the sheriffs to attend episcopal trials for heresy, and to receive from the Bishop's hands, and burn, the excommunicated convict. In order to clear the course for the Bishops and the attendant Sheriffs Arundel, in 1407, passed through Convocation a series of " constitutions " in which the whole range of Wycliffite activities was branded as heretical. For the obdurate offender there was only one punishment, death by burning. The measures of repression were completed by an Act of 1414, following upon the abortive outbreak of Sir John Oldcastle, Lord Cobham, the last of the Lollard lay leaders. By this Act magistrates and sheriffs were required to take the initiative in the detection and arrest of heretics, and to deliver them to the Bishops for trial, as well as to take delivery of them, when convicted, for burning according to law. The effect of these measures was immediate, and superficially final. The Wycliffite movement, which had stirred the conscience of a whole people for more than a generation, was driven underground ; and there for another century, in shapes more and more distorted by persecution, **it** smouldered sullenly and spread silently, flickering up from time to time, and having to be trampled down, in out-of-the-way places among obscure men deprived of responsible preaching and teaching, and cherishing their poor little fragments of the English Scriptures under threat of death. The well-meaning many, who had dallied with the movement but were already drifting away from it, went with the tide and gave no more trouble. Many others there were to whom the movement had brought something of the breath of life, and who could not in their hearts forsake it. Caring for truth much but life more, these took shelter in a cowed conformity, in which fear and self-contempt bred a bitter and ribald hatred of authority, to find vent at last, when times began to change, in the ferocious diatribe of Simon Fish. From time to time such men got into trouble by imprudent speech, and out of it by prudent abjuration. Not among these were the confessors found, the men who persevered unto the death. This heroic minority, though there were humble laymen among them, were mostly priests, who could understand the issues of truth at stake. The charges brought against them and others were more or less common form. They covered the general range of Wycliffite doctrine. The indictments were padded out with minor matters of dissidence, relating to image-worship, pilgrimages, Bible-reading and so on, matters of opinion for which no man need feel called upon to die. But in every important heresy trial the major and mortal charge related to what was, and could only be, a matter of conviction, the " sacrament of the altar " and the doctrine of Transubstantiation. The doctrine, to any man who took it seriously, was true or false, and there was no middle term. No compromise was possible on either side. The hierarchy, and the whole clerical order, defended it resolutely and ruthlessly ; for it was not only, to them, true, but the understood secret of their peculiar prestige and power. Many of the men who challenged it did not deny the Real Presence of Christ in the Sacrament. They affirmed, devoutly and positively, that the Body of Christ was present in the Sacrament under the form of Bread ; they were condemned for refusing to affirm that the Bread itself was no more than a form, an aggregation of "accidents" without any "subject," a simulacrum of nothing, instead of the plain Bread their plain senses showed it to be. Taking their stand upon the words of St. Paul, and upon our Lord's warning, in the 6th chapter of St. John, against the crude and carnal acceptation of words which "are spirit and are life," they denied the working of an otiose miracle by which "the Bread of Blessing which we break" should cease to be bread, or anything but a phantasmal assemblage of "accidents" incomprehensible by the sane mind. They rejected the doctrine not so much as untrue, but as untenable by the mind * ; and they preferred to die rather than, upon so grave a matter, to deny their own reason and the manhood that bade them be true to it. Their accusers were not concerned to explain the doctrine, but to constrain its acceptance. To them, in these heresy trials, it was not so much a doctrine as a touchstone of authority. The less explicable it was, the better it served as a touchstone of authority. The real crime of the so-called heretic was in being a rebel ; and the charge of denying Transubstantiation presented him with the stark choice between submission and death. That was why it was always the hanging or, of course, the burning matter. And that is why it is of importance in elucidating the case of Richard Hunne. For the fact is that the charge of rejecting Transubstantiation, the deadly charge, was not brought against Hunne while he lived, nor until there was only his dead body to answer it. In other words, the evidence against him while he lived was not such as to impel him to suicide.

---

* Their position does not appear to have differed from that held privately by Erasmus, as expressed in a letter to Pirckheimer on June 26, 1526. (Ep. 1717, ed. Allen, VI, p. 351) :

"Mihi non displiceret Oecolampadii sententia, nisi obstaret consensus Ecclesiae. Nec enim video quid agat corpus insensibile, nec utilitatem allaturum si sentiretur, modo adsit in symbolis gratia spiritualis. Et tamen ab Ecclesiae consensu non possum discedere, nec unquam discessi."

Erasmus accepted the Church's doctrine of Transubstantiation on the word of the Church just as Gardiner accepted the lawyers' doctrine of Praemunire on the word of the lawyers, though, in Gardiner's phrase, his "reason digested it not." See Gardiner's letter to the Protector Somerset, 14 October, 1547 : Muller, 'Letters,' p. 390, no. 130. Cf, Maynard Smith, 'Pre-Reformation England,' p. 504.

There was nothing against him like the damning case which would have ensured his death by legal process. To put an end to him, if he was held to deserve it, it was necessary to resort to other means.

There would seem to have been a marked difference between the heresy trials which occurred in the first half of the fifteenth century and those which followed in the early Tudor period. In the case of the former the accused were for the most part priests or friars whom the authorities were obliged to treat seriously, and who could answer the charges against them in argument. In these cases the first object of the trial appears to have been, as it always should have been, to convince and convert the offender, and to bring him to a conformable mind. In the trials of the Tudor period, on the other hand, the accused were mostly obscure lay malcontents ; and the proceedings against them have rather the character of summary police measures, in which there was little more then a perfunctory compliance with the forms of law. The charges against them were either so stereotyped or so extravagant that it is difficult to take them at their face value, or to determine what application they may have had to any particular case. As recorded, for example, in Archbishop Warham's Register, they seem to savour less of trials than of that process of ant-treading to which Sir Thomas More referred expressively in conversation with his son-in-law at a time when it began to look as if the heretics might one day be strong enough to turn the tables upon their persecutors. "Son Roper," said More, "I pray God that some of us, as high as we seem to sit upon mountains, treading heretics under our feet like ants, live not the day that we gladly would wish to be at league and composition with them, to let them have their churches quietly to themselves so that they would be content to let us have ours quietly to ourselves." (Roper, Life of More, p. 22).

Having seen what heresy was, it is important to remember what it was not. Criticism, apart from active disaffection, was not heresy. People might be critical of administrative abuses, of the practices of the Roman Court, and of the conduct of the ecclesiastical courts. Everybody was. It was not heresy to speak freely of the manners and morals of priests and monks and friars. Everybody did. It was not heresy to grumble audibly at tithes and dues and offerings, provided a man paid them. A man might say what he thought, in private, about his parson so long as he obeyed him and paid his dues and went to his " duties." But the limits of such criticism were well understood, and it was dangerous to transgress them. If a man spoke lightly of the sacraments and ordinances of the Church ; if he showed a dissident mind by not going to Confession and not attending Mass ; and if, above all, he gathered round him a knot of people likeminded and made himself a thorn in the side of his parish priest, he became suspect, and the authorities took a very short way with him. He would be arrested as a heretic and put on trial. He would be required to answer to certain articles ; and the only answer admitted, if he wished to save his life, was a confession, qualified or unqualified. He would then have the privilege of a first offender and be allowed to abjure on oath the errors imputed to him, swearing not to fall into them in future, and acknowledging the dire fate that awaited him if he did. He might then be released, subject to the performance of a more or less humiliating public penance, usually in the form of having to walk in the Sunday procession of his parish church clad in his shirt and carrying a faggot. And thereafter, for a term of years or for life, he might have to go about with a faggot embroidered upon his outer garment, and, in this convict garb, obtain work if he could among a people to whom heresy was a thing abhorrent. If — and such cases occur — in order to get work and bread in his mouth, he removed the faggot, or was persuaded by a would-be employer to do so, he might be re-arrested as a relapsed heretic, summarily convicted, and sent to execution. If a man had got himself regarded by the authorities as a mischief-maker who would give further trouble if he could and had merely abjured to save his life, his abjuration might afford him but a brief respite. His every movement would be watched, his every word reported. The Church, in her ubiquitous clergy in holy and minor orders, possessed a ready-made espionage system ; and, by the admission of Sir Thomas More himself, was none too squeamish as to the testimony she admitted in cases of heresy. The penal machine was so deadly, so certain in its operation, and, on occasion, so little embarrassed by scruple, that the only safe way was to keep well clear of it.

The general character of the Church's jurisdiction in heresy may be summarised in two words : it was charitable, and it was absolute.

Its primary purpose was charitable. A man's salvation depended upon his steadfastness in the Faith. To lapse from the Faith was to hazard perdition, and to incur it if the lapse was final. To fall away from the Faith was in the first place a crime ; but the object of the Church, in dealing with the crime, was not, primarily, to punish it, but to correct and convert the offender and bring him to a better mind. If, by argument and persuasion, that proved possible, the offender might be gently dealt with, and, if a penitent priest, even promised preferment. If, on the other hand, he remained obdurate, the Church, by her law, had no choice but to excommunicate him, and to " deliver him to Satan " and the sheriff " for the destruction of the flesh," if so be that his spirit might be saved even at the last. Under the ordeal of fire even the condemned convict might recant, and die absolved. In any case the charity which was wasted upon the heretic inured to the benefit of the Church's obedient children, whom the fire freed from his deadly contamination.

And again, the jurisdiction was absolute. No temporal court could impede or interfere with it. Certain matters of ecclesiastical cognisance involved questions of property and money which the temporal courts might claim the right to decide ; and pending their decision, proceedings in the ecclesiastical court might be stayed by writs of prohibition, and not these only. But heresy was an affair of doctrine, with which the temporal courts had no concern. No writ of any kind was issuable by any temporal court in stay of proceedings in a case of heresy. In heresy the jurisdiction of the Bishop or the Provincial Council was unfettered, unlimited and absolute. The temporal executive lent every support to the jurisdiction, and the temporal judicature stood entirely aside.

It is necessary to insist upon this because of a suggestion which has done not a little to darken counsel in considering the case of Richard Hunne. The suggestion is no more than that ; but it has the elusive vitality of a suggestion made, or countenanced, by a writer of weight and professed knowledge. And the writer is Sir Thomas More. More, in the " Dialogue " (English Works, ed. Campbell, II. 234-7) gives an account of certain curious and irregular proceedings held before a delegation of the Privy Council at Baynard's Castle. They purport to be an examination of the facts in the case of Hunne. More makes two brief allusions to the facts, but says exactly nothing of what they are. Instead, he describes at length, and with a wealth of comic detail, the examination of certain figures of fun, who are questioned by the lords with a queer blend of brow-beating and badinage. Two of these, a layman and a cleric, appear in the same interlude of burlesque.

" The temporal man that had reported it," — that " if Hunne had not sued the praemunire he should never have been accused of heresy," — " upon the mouth of the spiritual man, was a good worshipful man ; and for his truth and worship was in great credit. And surely the spiritual man was a man of worship also ; and well knowen both for cunning and virtuous. And therefore the Lords much marvelled, knowing them both for such as they were, that they should be like to find either the one or the other either make an untrue report or untruly deny the truth. And first the temporal man before the Lords in the hearing of the spiritual person standing by, said, ' My Lords all, as help me God and halidome, master doctor here said unto me (by) his own mouth, that if Hunne had not sued the praemunire he should never have been accused of heresy.' ' How say you master doctor ? ' quod the Lords, ' was that true, or else why said you so ? ' ' Surely, my Lords,' quod he, ' I said not all thing so ' but marye, this I said indeed, that if Hunne had not been accused of heresy he would never have sued the praemunire.' " Here is the suggestion. The cunning and virtuous cleric — a friend and partizan of the accused Horsey, as we are told elsewhere — falling in with the evident atmosphere of the proceedings, declares that he had said exactly the opposite of what the good worshipful layman averred, and used words suggesting that Hunne had sued the praemunire in order to delay or defeat the proceedings in heresy. More not only allows the suggestion to pass, but lends countenance to it by certain words of his own. He suggests — and his whole story savours overmuch of these forensic submissions — that Hunne's failure in the praemunire suit conduced to the desperation which led him, as an accused heretic, to put an end to himself rather than face the further stages of the trial. More, of course, as a finished lawyer, must have known perfectly well that, in whatever circumstances Hunne sued the praemunire, it could not have been to counter the charge of heresy ; and that the success or failure of his suit could not affect the issue, or his prospects on the charge of heresy, one way or the other. The writ of praemunire was a common law writ ; and nobody knew better than More that no court would consider its application to proceedings before the Bishop on a charge of heresy. More may have been persuaded on other grounds that Hunne had committed suicide ; but he is hard put to it to make a case for that conclusion in the face of the facts which had convinced the coroner's jury, and of which he is careful in the Dialogue to say nothing in detail. The countenance he apparently lends to the " spiritual man's " impossible suggestion is best explained as one of the legitimate shifts to which an advocate is driven when he has nothing better than suggestions to put forward.

As to which of these two, the layman or the cleric, was the honest man, the reader may judge. More, after his attractive fashion, represents both as honest men, the difference being that the cleric had all his wits about him, which is evident, whereas the layman was just a muddleheaded old fool, which is not so evident. Imagine a simple parallel in which A reports B as having said that one C had his head on his shoulders. B declares, in reply, that what he really had said was that C had his shoulders on his head. And More and the Lords accept B's version, and dismiss A and his possible story as merely subjects for indulgent mirth. The old layman was possibly flustered by the august presence, or hard of hearing, or slow of wit ; but having heard the words of his own story inverted, he said to the Lords :

" Lo, my Lords ; I am glad ye find me a true man. Will ye command me any more service ? "

WHAT WAS HERESY ?

" Nay, by my trouth," quod one of the lords, " not in this matter ; by my will, ye may go when ye will. For I have espied, good man, so the words be all one it maketh no matter to you which way they stand ; but all is one to you a horse mill and a mill horse, drink ere ye go, and go ere ye drink."

" Nay my Lords," quod he, " I will not drink, God yelde you."

" And therewith," More's story proceeds, " he made curtesie and went his way, leaving some of the lords laughing to see the good plain old honest man, how that as contrary as their two tales were, yet when he heard them both again, he marked no difference between them, but took them both for one because the words were one."

More's account of these proceedings at Baynard's Castle consists almost entirely of three such incidents, of which the above is the least farcical. That More, the most honest man and one of the ablest advocates of his time, should have tried to make some sort of a case out of such material, requires some explanation ; and it lies in the time and circumstances in which he wrote. These, and the whole story of Baynard's Castle, will be examined presently. For the moment it is sufficient to repeat that no temporal writ of praemunire or any other could hamper the Church's absolute jurisdiction in cases of heresy.

One office of charity the Church was careful to discharge. She left her children in no doubt as to the penalties incurred by so grievous a crime. They are summarised by the canonist Lyndwood in a gloss on one of Arundel's constitutions (' Provinciale,' ed. 1679, p. 293, " poenas in Jure expressas.") The heretic was excommunicate ipso jure. He was an outlaw to whom every obligation was dissolved. All legal acts were forbidden to him. He could hold no office civil or ecclesiastical. He could neither bequeath nor inherit. All his goods were confiscated. His sons, brothers and sisters had to forsake him. He lost all rights as father and husband. His very wife had to leave him, though she was bound to return if he made his peace. Condemned by the ecclesiastical judge as pertinacious and relapsed, and failing to sue for mercy before sentence, he was, as the Civil Law prescribed, to be condemned to death at the hands of (per) the secular power, and by it burned and " cremated by fire." And what was left of him was to have no Christian burial.

It might be supposed that for a crime which bore such dire penalties there would have been the fullest security for a fair trial. In practice there was not. In trials for heresy there were not even the safeguards which the common law provided in cases of treason. and murder (see Pollard, ' Wolsey,' p. 42 and note 1). A man's chance of a fair trial depended wholly upon the character of his judges and accusers. The law, no doubt, more often than not was honestly administered both in the letter and in the spirit. In dealing with an aggressive movement like Wycliffism, party spirit might often encroach upon the spirit of charity and justice, and the case be stressed against the accused. That was human nature, and calls for no special animadversion. It was otherwise when, as might easily happen, the law was deliberately abused for personal or party ends. If a man made an enemy of some important ecclesiastic ; if, worse still — let us suppose like Hunne — he took some action which was construed as an affront and threat to the whole clerical order, a charge of heresy offered a prompt and deadly means of retaliation. Perjury was a common vice of the age, and evidence to convict was always procurable. In the minor orders of the Church there was a horde of ne'er-do-wells who lived by their wits and worse, and who, as a contemporary Pope declared himself credibly informed, took orders for no other purpose but to escape the lay punishments for crime. Among these there were always men ready to act as informers and *agents provocateurs*, and to swear anything required. And the existence of this clerical underworld lends sinister point to a remarkable chapter in More's ' Dialogue,' in which his interlocutor complains of the ecclesiastical courts for accepting tainted evidence in cases of heresy. More not only admits the practice, but justifies it on grounds of necessity.

" The chief cause why in heinous criminal causes, as theft, murder, treason, and heresy, the law taketh such for witness as it will not accept in a matter of money or other contract made between two parties, is for that else all such crimes should pass forth unpunished, and thereby should the world swarm full of such mischievous people for lack of proof and trial in the matter, by cause that those which go about such an heinous deed as, coming once to knowledge, would bring them to a shameful death, do not use commonly to take a notary and honest witness with them to make an instrument thereof, as many men do and all men may do in a contract or covenant : but use to do it by stealth as covertly as they can. By reason whereof, reason moveth, and necessity compelleth (except ye would have all go to nought) to receive such records as they be wont to make of their counsel, which be, as ye wot well, none but such as they be themself." (Bk. 3, chap. 3 : English Works, II, 189).

It surely abates somewhat the force of More's " chief cause " that these heretics of his were not skulking thieves or lurking murderers, but men who asked for nothing better than freedom to commit openly the crime of reading Scripture in their mother tongue and holding for truth what they believed it taught them. It only remains to add that in his succeeding chapter he justifies the practice of the ecclesiastical courts in refusing to listen to rebutting evidence on behalf of the accused. This, with their admitted acceptance of tainted evidence against them, is sufficient to discredit these later heresy trials as having any conformity with what we now mean by justice. Their records consist of little more than the charges, and confessions which are seldom more than a recital of the charges ; and, from such study as I have been able to make of them, my impression is that, while some of them may be true, the truth of none of them can be taken for granted.

It is only when we understand these things and their approval by such a man as Sir Thomas More, that we can fully measure the magnitude of the victory won for thought and freedom by the men who gave their lives for Wycliffism and the Reformation ; or that we can assay the quality of thought which leads our sentimental mediaevalists, who enjoy the fruits of that victory in the security of their study chairs, to reprove and decry the men who died for it. *

---

* E.g. Dr. James Gairdner in his ' Lollardy and the Reformation.' Through half his first volume Dr. Gairdner directs a steady douche of cold water upon Wycliffism and all its works ; and then, on the evidence of Gascoigne and others, proceeds to show the inveteracy of the evils which Wycliffism had impeached

And of these the palm, for sheer faith and valour, must be given to the tiny band of sufferers who drew their inspiration from Wyclif. The many who perished in the Marian persecution had at least the knowledge that there was a great oncoming movement behind them, and that the candle they were lighting in England would not be put out. But their Wycliffite forerunners stand on a higher plane of heroism, with More himself. They died like More for a lost cause, but for the glory of human nature and its sovereignty of conscience. They stood up against, and withstood to the face and to the death, an ecclesiasticism which could put forth, upon occasion, a power as terrible, as tyrannous, and many times more established and secure, than that of Henry VIII. Some modern experience helps us to understand what the Mediaeval Church could be in her more sinister aspect. It is not uncommon to see a human face with different sides to it. One side appears all sweetness and charm, while the other side seems vacant of either. On one side of her the later Mediaeval Church appears as a firm, kind and tender Mother. On her hardfaced side she presents herself as an almost soulless embodied Authority, with little of natural goodness and feeling. She was, on this side, a European, supra-national totalitarian State, in which only one party was tolerated or suffered to survive. The clerical order was the omnipotent party organ, ramifying everywhere and dominating everyone. In the monks and friars she had her disciplined militia in their habits of black and white and brown and grey, corresponding to the variegated Shirts of modern days. And when threatened, or believing herself

and striven to remedy. Incidentally, in writing of what he calls " the fundamental basis of the whole Wycliffite philosophy," he says that " not only Wycliffe himself, but the whole of his followers, even to our own time, have rested their case entirely on Scripture, regarding it as the sole rule of faith without reference to ecclesiastical tradition or the teaching of the Church apart from Holy Writ," 1,191. And on the selfsame page he goes on to cite one of the contemporary opponents of Wycliffism, Thomas Netter of Walden, who charges Wycliffe with having " said that all holy Fathers since the first millenium were in error." Which means, of course, that on the testimony of his opponents Wycliffe acknowledged as authoritative the teaching of the Fathers for the first thousand years. The sort of holy Fathers whom Wycliffe rejected were those who, in the previous century, had burdened the Church with the dogma of Transubstantiation and with the papal theory exemplified in the pontificate of Boniface VIII.

to be threatened, by " undesirable elements," she could carry out a modern " purge," haling men in batches before lowering tribunals on charges of sabotaging the Faith. Except for the few souls which were stronger than her own, she could wring from them the same abject confessions of the like preposterous charges. And, before the more merciful dispensation of powder and shot, she could " liquidate " them finally by fire and faggot in the market square. If dissidence was only to be put down by war, she could proclaim a Crusade against it, and let fire and sword do the work of fire and faggot. The individual was lost if her punitive hand thought fit to close upon him. In her jurisdiction in heresy and her means of enforcing it the Church possessed, over the laity, an arbitrary power of life and death. And the laity not only tolerated, but approved and supported it ; they made themselves the instruments of its execution ; they accepted it as salutary, and their own safeguard against Hell. But the more complete their acceptance of it, the more certain, and perhaps the more sudden, might be their revulsion against it if the " men of Holy Church " who exercised it gave proof, in some signal and glaring case, that they could no longer be trusted to do so with honesty and justice. When More wrote the ' Dialogue ' in 1528 such a revulsion had plainly occurred, and the Lutheran influence percolating into England was giving it courage to find voice. Twenty years earlier, before Luther was heard of, there was little overt sign of it. If I am not mistaken, it dates from a certain Wednesday, December 20th, 1514, when the body of a freeman of London, Richard Hunne, was committed to the flames on the sentence of the Bishop Fitzjames, after having been found, sixteen days earlier, hanging, interrogatively, in the Lollards' Tower. Holy Church had run up against the City of London, and would be the first, though not the last, to learn what London, her common lawyers and her burgesses in Parliament, could do in overthrowing tyranny.

Having seen what heresy was and was not, there is a further question : what manner of men were they who were charged with the execution of these heresy laws, and what was their standing, and that of their order generally, in public repute ?

MEASURES AND MEN : DEAN COLET'S WITNESS

On this we have two pieces of contemporary evidence, neither of which is open to cavil. They come from two men who were ornaments of their age, strict with themselves, but both too conscious of their own frailties to be over-censorious of other men's failings. There is first the famous sermon delivered at the opening of the Convocation of 1512 by Doctor John Colet, the great Dean of St. Paul's. It was, of course, in Latin ; and was not at all the sort of discourse that Colet would have thought it right to address in English to a body of laymen. But the fact that it had no value as propaganda gives it absolute value as evidence. Perhaps no assemblage of clergy in any age has been told to its face so much conscience-smiting home truth. Colet speaks as " a man sorrowing the decay of the Church," and attributing it, without reserve, to the moral apostacy of the clergy. He stigmatises unsparingly their worldliness, their dissoluteness, and their unbridled greed of pelf and preferment. In one of the few passages which may be given without detaining the reader unduly, he speaks of the effect of that moral apostacy in alienating the laity.

" In this time also we perceive contradiction of the lay people. But they are not so much contrary unto us as we are ourselves ; nor their contrariness hurteth not us so much as the contrariness of our evil life, the which is contrary both to God and Christ. . . . . . "

" We are also nowadays grieved of heretics, men mad with marvellous foolishness. But the heresies of them are not so pestilent and pernicious unto us and the people as the evil and wicked life of priests ; the which, if we believe Saint Bernard, is a certain kind of heresy, and chief of all and most perilous. . . . The which reigneth now in the Church in priests not living priestly but secularly, to the utter and miserable destruction of the Church."

There is no need to make new laws, but only to provide that " once seeing we have a law, we live after the law."

" First, let those laws be rehearsed that do warn you Fathers that ye put not over soon your hands on every man, or admit unto holy orders. For there is the well of evils that, the broad gate of holy orders opened, every man that offereth himself is all where admitted without pulling back. Thereof springeth and cometh out the people that are in the Church both of unlearned and evil priests." . . . . . .

" Let the laws be rehearsed that command personal residence of curates in their churches. For of this many evils grow, because all things nowadays are done by vicars and parish priests, yea and those foolish also and unmeet and oftentimes wicked ; that seek none other thing in the people than foul lucre, whereof cometh occasion of evil heresies and ill christendom in the people."

" Let be rehearsed the laws and holy rules, given of Fathers, of the life and honesty of clerks ; that forbid that a clerk be no merchant, that he be no usurer, that he be no hunter, that he be no common player, that he bear no weapon ; the laws that forbid clerks to haunt taverns, that forbid them to have suspect familiarity with women ; the laws that command soberness, and a measureableness in apparel, and temperance in adorning of the body." . . . .

" Above all things, let the laws be rehearsed that pertain and concern you my reverend Fathers and Lords Bishops, laws of your just and canonical election in the chapters of your churches, with the calling of the Holy Ghost. For because that is not done nowadays, and because prelates are chosen oftentimes more by favour of men than by the grace of God, therefore truly have we not a few times bishops full little spiritual men, rather worldly than heavenly, savouring more the spirit of this world than the spirit of Christ " . . . .

" Let the laws be rehearsed, yea and that oftentimes, that take away the filths and uncleanliness of courts ; that take away those daily new-found crafts for lucre ; that busy them to pull away this foul covetousness, the which is the spring and cause of all evils, the which is the well of all iniquity." . . . .

" The clergy's and spiritual's part once reformed in the Church, then may we with a just order proceed to the reformation of the lay's part ; the which truly will be very easy to do if we first be reformed. . . . . Our goodness shall teach them more clearly to be good than all our teachings and preachings. Our goodness shall compel them into the right way truly more effectuously than all your suspendings and cursings."

Wherefore, if ye will have the lay people to live after your wish and will, first live you yourselves after the will of God " . . . .

" These are they, reverend Fathers and right famous men, that I thought to be said for the reformation of the Church's estate. I trust ye will take them of your gentleness to the best. And if peradventure it be thought that I have passed my bounds in this sermon, or have said anything out of temper, forgive it me ; and ye shall forgive a man speaking of very zeal, a man sorrowing the decay of the Church. And consider the thing itself, not regarding my foolishness. Consider the miserable form and state of the Church, and endeavour yourselves with all your minds to reform it."

To make its real impression the sermon should be read in full. It is given in Appendix C of the Rev. J. H. Lupton's ' Life of John Colet,' to be found in any public library. In reading it, some allowance must be made for the tendency of a preacher to stress the darker side of a situation which he passionately desires to remedy. No such allowance need be made for the balanced testimony of Sir Thomas More.

More's friend and Bishop, Cuthbert Tunstall, had succeeded Fitzjames in the see of London in 1521. He presently found, to his cost, that the only effect of buying up and burning prohibited books was to put money into the pockets of the producers and enable them to bring out new and better editions. Bethinking him of a better way, he licensed More to have and read the forbidden writings in order to confute them. The first and best — because the most reasoned and urbane — of More's apologetic works was his ' Dialogue concerning Heresies,' directed mainly against Tyndale and published in 1528. In it he set himself to vindicate Catholic faith and order. He held it, however, to be no part of his duty to defend the men and means by which that order was abused, to the scandal of all good Catholics, not least himself. His imagined interlocutor represents the contemporary ' man in the street ' ; More replies as ' the ecclesiastically-minded layman ' and something more, a devout Christian in whose soul the Catholic ideal shone with a steady light, which no human infirmity could becloud or sully.

In the 11th and 12th chapters of the Third Book of the ' Dialogue ' (ed. Campbell, II, 213 - 21) More addresses himself to the current strictures upon the clergy. His inquiring fellow-layman avers, and insists, that the clergy are a bad lot ; More deprecates over-censoriousness on the part of the laity ; they had need enough to look to themselves ; among the clergy there are many good ; and would God we all were better. And More concludes with some cogent reasons why the clergy, as a body, are no better than they are. As this matter, the character and repute of the clergy, is cardinal to a right understanding of the times, we may be thankful to have More's whole mind in regard to it.

Archbishop Arundel's designedly elastic constitution of 1407 had been so administered as to leave the laity with the rough-and-ready belief that all translations of Holy Scripture had been prohibited under dire penalties. Adverting to this, More makes his interlocutor utter himself as follows :—

" But surely the thing that maketh in this matter the clergy most suspect, and wherein, as it seemeth, it would be full hard to excuse them is this, that they not only damn Tyndale's translation (wherein there is good cause) but over that do damn all other, and as though a layman were no Christian man, will suffer no layman have any at all. But when they find any in his keeping, they lay heresy to him therefor. And thereupon they burn up the book, and sometime the good man withal, alleging for the defence of their doing a law of their own making and constitution provincial, whereby they have prohibited that any man shall have any upon pain of heresy. And this is a law very provincial, for it holdeth but here. For in all other countries of Christendom the people have the scripture translated into their own tongue, and the clergy there findeth no such fault therein. Wherefore either our people be worst of all people, or else our clergy is worst of all clergies. But, by my troth, for ought that I can see here, or perceive by them that have been elsewhere, our lay people be as good and as honest as be anywhere. And if any be otherwise, the occasion and example cometh of the clergy, among whom we see much more vice than among ourself. Whereas they should give us example of virtue and the light of learning, now their examples, what they be, we see. And as for learning, they neither will teach us but seldom, and that shall be but such things as pleaseth them, some glosses of their own making, nor suffer us to learn by ourself, but by their constitution pull Christ's gospel out of Christian people's hands, I cannot well see why, but lest we should see the truth." . . . .

More : " Your words, quod (quoth) I, be somewhat pugnant and sharp. But surely they prick somewhat more the men than the matter. For where ye touch in effect two things : one, the constitution provincial, by which ye think the clergy of this realm have evil prohibited all translations of scripture into our tongue ; another, the vice of the clergy in general ; the first point which indeed toucheth our matter, I can and will with few words answer you. But as for the other which toucheth the men, as where ye accuse the clergy in their persons of very vicious living as men much worse than ye say that we be, and yet as though their owne faults were too few, charge them with ours too, whereof ye call them the cause, in this point will I keep no schools with you, nor enter into disputations thereof, nor gladly meddle with the matter. For as I told you in the beginning, since we talk but of men's learning, I will not meddle of men's living, nor in that treating of this matter either praise or dispraise any man's manner, except some such as are for their heresies and evil doctrine cast out of Christ's church and through all Christendom damned and diffamed already by their own obstinate malice.

I wot well there be therein many very lewd and nought. And surely wheresoever there is a multitude it is not without miracle well possible to be otherwise. But now if the bishops would once take unto priesthood better laymen and fewer (for of us be they made) all the matter were more than half amended. . . . .

" Now they blame us : and we blame them : and both blameworthy : and either part more ready to find others' faults than to mend their own. For in reproach of them we be so studious that neither good nor bad passeth unreproved. If they be familiar, we call them light. If they be solitary, we call them fantastic. If they be sad, we call them solemn. If they be merry, we call them mad. If they be companionable we call them vicious. If they be holy we call them hypocrites. If they keep few servants we call them niggards.

If they keep many we call them pompous. If a lewd priest do a lewd deed, then we say, lo, see what sample the clergy giveth us, as though that priest were the clergy. But then forget we to look what good men be therein, and what good counsel they give us, and what good ensample they show us. But we fare as do the ravens and the carrion crows that never meddle with any quick flesh ; but where they may find a dead dog in a ditch, thereto they flee and thereon they feed apace. So where we see a good man and hear and see a good thing, there we take little heed. But when we see once an evil deed, thereon we gape, thereof we talk and feed ourselves all day with the filthy delight of evil communication. Let a good man preach, a short tale shall serve us thereof, and we shall neither much regard his exhortation nor his good examples. But let a lewd frere (friar) be taken with a wench, we will jest and rail upon the whole order all the year after, and say, lo, what sample they give us. And yet, when we have said, we will follow the same and then say we learned it of them, forgetting that we list not to hear and follow some other whose word or deed would give us light to do better, if we listed as well to learn the better as to follow the worse."

Here More indulges his readers with one of those racy asides which relieve the course of the Dialogue :—

" Indeed, quod he, because ye speak of light, they say that if a woman be fair, then is she young, and if a priest be good, then he is old. But yet have I seen a priest giving light to the people that was but very young.

(More) " Mary, quod I, God forbid else, ye may see that often an ye will.

" Truly, quod he, it is a pity that we see such light so seldom, being this wretched world in such darkness as it is. For I never saw it but once. Nor as it seemed few of the people neither. For in faith, they wondered as fast thereon as though they had never seen it before.

(More) " How happed that, quod I ?

Mary, quod he, it happed that a young priest very devoutly in a procession bare a candle before the cross for lying with a wench, and bare it light all the long way. Wherein the people took such spiritual pleasure and inward solace that they laughed apace. And one merry merchant said unto the priests that followed him, *sic luceat lux vestra coram hominibus.* Thus let your light shine afore the people.

(More) " Forsooth, quod I, it were pity but that an evil priest were punished. But yet it is as much pity that we take such a wretched pleasure in the hearing of their sin and in the sight of their shame. Good it is for them to look on their faults ; but for us were it better to look less to theirs and more unto our own. But surely many of us have such delight to hear of their harm, that it seemeth we be glad when one of them doth any such thing as we may have occasion to see them punished or had in derision. . . . . .

. . . . . " And (chap. 12) be a priest never so nought, albeit that he do some way much harm both to himself and other, yet this advantage take we by the privilege and prerogative of his priest-hood — beside the ministration of the sacraments unto us, the goodness whereof his noughtiness cannot appayre (impair) — that be he never so vicious and therewith so impenitent and so far from all purpose of amendment that his prayers were afore the face of God rejected and abhorred, yet, that sacred sacrifice and sweet oblation of Christ's holy body, offered up by his office, can take none empayring (impairing) by the filth of his sin, but highly helpeth to the upholding of this wretched world from the vengeance of the wrath of God, and is to God acceptable and to us as available for the thing itself as though it were offered by a better man, though percase his prayers joined therewith neither much profit other, nor the oblation himself, as with whom God is the more greatly grieved in that, being so bad, he durst presume to touch it.

" Marye," (interjects the other), " if this be thus, I marvel then why ye said right now that it were good to make fewer priests, that they might be taken only of the better, and the worse refused. For if their masses be so good for us, be themself never so nought, then seemeth it better for us to make yet more though they were yet worse, that we might have more masses.

(More) : " That reason, quod I, will not hold. For though God of his goodness, how bad soever the priest be, well accepteth the oblation of Christ's holy body for other folk, yet is he with that priest's presumption highly discontented. And we never ought to seek our own commodity with our neighbour's harm. And also we should, of our duty to God, rather forbear the profit that ourself might attain by a mass than to see his majesty disreverenced by the bold presumption of such an odious minister as he hath forboden to come about him. . . . . And therefore well shall the prelates do as much as they may to provide that God shall rather be more seldom presented with the pleasant present of the mass, than more offended with a displeasant messenger. And verily were all the bishops of my mind (as I know some that be) ye should not of priests have the plenty that ye have. The time hath been when there were very few in a great city ; and in a monastery of five hundred in one house, scantly would there four monks be bold to be priests. Then were all holy orders in high honour. Then find we that the degree of a deacon were a great thing, and of such dignity that when one of them went sometime in pilgrimage, he would not be knowen of his order, because he would not that folk should do him worship in the way. But as for nowadays if he be deacon, and priest too, he shall need to fear no such pride but rather rebuke and villainy. Which though it have happened by the lack of virtue among them, and decay of devotion among us, yet hath much of all this gear growen up by the mean of so great a number of priests and so familiar among us. Which thing must needs minish on our part reverence and estimation toward them which we never have but in things rare and scarce. Gold would not be set by if it were as common as chalk or clay. And whereof is there now such plenty as of priests ?

" In faith, quod he, there is more plenty of priests than of good men, and there be too many but if they were better chosen.

(More) : " Doubtless, quod I, there would be more diligence used in the choice, not of their learning only, but much more specially of their living. For without virtue the better they be learned the worse they be, saving that learning is good store against God send them grace to mend, which else it would be then haply too late to look for, specially if the proverb were true that ye spake of, that if a priest be good then he is old. But this is a very surety that it is not well possible to be without many very naught of that company whereof there is such a main multitude. The time was, I say, when few men durst presume to take upon them the high office of a priest, not even when they were chosen and called thereunto. Now runneth every rascal and boldly offereth himself for able. And where the dignity passeth all princes, and they that lewd be desireth it for worldly winning, yet cometh that sort thereto with such a mad mind that they reckon almost God much bounden to them that they vouchsafe to take it. But were I Pope . . . . .

" By my soul, quod he, I would ye were, and my lady your wife Popesse too.

(More) : " Well, quod I, then should she devise for nuns." . . . . . And here More takes up Colet's main theme.. . . . " And as for me, touching the choice of priests, I could not well devise better provisions than are by the laws of the church provided already, if they were as well kept as they be well made. But for the number, I would surely see such a way therein that we should not have such a rabble that every mean man must have a priest in his house to wait upon his wife, which no man almost lacketh now, to the contempt of priesthood, in as vile office as his horsekeeper.

That is, quod he, truth indeed, and in worse too, for they keep hawks and dogs. And yet, meseemeth, surely a more honest service to wait on a horse than on a dog.

(More) : " And yet I suppose, quod I, if the laws of the church, which Luther and Tyndale would have all broken, were all well observed and kept, this gear should not be thus ; but the number of priests would be much minished, and the remnant much the better. For it is by the laws of the church provided, to the intent no priest should unto the slander of priesthood be driven to live in such lewd manner or worse, there should none by admitted unto the priesthood until he have a title of a sufficient yearly living, either of his own patrimony, or otherwise. Nor at this day they be none otherwise accepted.

" Why, quod he, wherefore go there then so many of them a begging ?

(More) : " Mary, quod I, for (because) they delude the law and themself also. For they never have grant of a living that may serve them in sight for that purpose but they secretly discharge it ere they have it ; or else they could not get it. And thus the bishop is blinded by the sight of the writing ; and the priest goeth a begging for all his grant of a good living ; and the law is deluded ; and the order is rebuked by the priest's begging and lewd living, which either is fain to walk at rovers and live upon trentals, or worse ; or else to serve in a secular man's house, which should not need if this gap were stopped. For ye should have priests few enough if the law were truly observed that none were made but he that were, without collusion, sure of a living already.

" Then might it hap, quod he, that ye might have too few to serve the rooms and livings that be provided for them, except the prelates would provide that orders were not so commonly given, but always receive into orders as rooms and livings fall void to bestow them in, and no faster.

(More) : " Surely, quod I, for aught I see suddenly, that would not be much amiss. For so should they need no such titles at all, nor should need neither run at rovers, nor live in laymen's houses, by reason whereof there groweth among no little corruption in the priest's manners by the conversation of lay people and company of women in their houses.

" Nay, by our lady, quod he, I will not agree with you therein. For I think they cannot lightly meet with much worse company than themself, and that they rather corrupt us than we them."

So More, sorrowing over his own picture, is content to leave his supposed interlocutor with the last word.

More's picture, drawn though it is so decently and discreetly, does not appear to differ very much from that drawn, in ordurous detail, by the satiric tarbrush of Simon Fish.* More deplores what

---

* Author of the ' Supplication of Beggars.' (See Foxe IV., 656—64). I forbear to cite the ' Supplication,' because it seems to have become a habit to dismiss it summarily as " scurrilous " ; and I have no space to put before the reader a less inadequate estimate of one of the most remarkable and formidable writings of the time. It is true that the protesting down-and-outs whom Fish dramatises have no parlour manners and do not address the King in the language of the

Fish denounces, but the facts are substantially the same for both. What, in effect, does More tell us about the clerical order in his day ? The clergy are " a main multitude," among whom there must needs be " very many lewd and nought." Many of these good-for-nothings minister at the Altar, to the scandal of the lay folk and the ' discontentment ' of God. The laity no longer look to the clergy for serious teaching, or for good example of life and manners. The influence of the good has come to weigh for little against that of the evil. The old-time reverence for the clergy no longer subsists. A clerk on pilgrimage is less likely to be looked up to than to be looked down upon, more likely to meet with " rebuke and villany " than with respect and honour. Holy Orders themselves are in contempt among the very men who seek them. In old days men approached ordination with reverence and godly fear. Nowadays " runneth every rascal and boldly offereth himself for able " ; and that " with such a mad mind that they reckon almost God much bounden to them " for condescending to the priesthood. For the numbers of them, they are " such a rabble that every mean man must have a priest in his house to wait upon his wife, which no man almost lacketh now to the contempt of priesthood in as vile office as his horsekeeper." This indecent gate-crashing of the Sacred Ministry comes about because the good law designed to protect the church against clerical indigence is disregarded by the Bishops. The law requires that " there should none be admitted unto the priesthood until he have a title of a sufficient yearly living, either of his own patrimony, or other wise." But men are ordained upon

drawing-room : they call foul things and foul persons by the names they bear in popular usage. But it was not scurrility, so-called, that made the ' Supplication' formidable: it was its uncanny political clairvoyance, together with a power of terse and fierce invective rarely equalled in pieces of the kind. Colet and More write in sorrow : Fish, a brilliant young barrister embittered by enforced exile, writes in something more than anger. He gives voice to nothing less than that " deadly hatred " in which the House of Commons, in the draft of a famous document three years later and before a single step had been taken against " Rome," express their sense of the state of feeling then subsisting between clergy and laity (see below, pp. 314-15). Well may Professor Chambers say of More (' Thomas More,' p. 158) that " of all the heretical pamphlets he had most to dread that of Simon Fish." It was indeed the storm-cone of the coming revolution.

faked titles ; and the bishops, who must have been aware of the traffic as fully as More, take no care to inquire whether they are faked or not. The result is that numbers are ordained without any real visible means of subsistence. Some have to keep bread in their mouths by performing menial offices in laymen's households, " whereof there groweth no little corruption in the priest's manners." Others eke out an existence as starveling mass-priests, living " upon trentals," contracts for saying thirty masses for the dead on the thirty days after a man's demise. Others, a step lower, are " fain to walk at rovers," living by their wits and lapsing into vagabondage. " Or worse," says More, twice over. And this " or worse " refers to the criminal element who got themselves ordained in order to prey upon the community and plead their clergy in avoiding the common punishment for crime. Such is More's picture ; but it is not complete in the mind of the reader unless it is remembered that this order of men, immune themselves from the lay punishments for crime, possessed, through the laws of heresy, a power of life and death over a laity of whom the best could speak of them no better than did More and Colet.

More would have given his right hand to be able to say, with truth, that the current strictures against the clergy were slanderous and false. He knew, as Colet knew, that they were too well-founded, and he grieved over them as Colet grieved. Writing of them at all, it is not in him to muffle up the truth ; and he sets it down in the hope, doubtless, that more of the bishops will come to be of his mind, and take such steps as the law provides to restore the clergy to their old repute.

It is an old story that when a great and long powerful interest is threatened, and is conscious of being threatened, through its own forfeiture of public esteem, it will throw up men who will go to any length to enable it to keep its hold on power. The wise will strive, though belatedly and despairingly, to set their house in order ; but the others will strike out in panic defence, and stick at nothing to avert the consequences of their own recklessness : the result being, more often than not, to hasten the end of what they wish to pre-serve. We learn from Colet and More, to take their least unkindly critics, that the credit of the clerical order, at this period, was low, as low perhaps as it could well be ; too low to withstand any grave public shock ; so low that, in the eyes of men whose chief concern was to maintain their privileges, any grave public shock might shatter it irretrievably, and their cherished immunities along with it. Such a shock might be sustained if a reputable citizen of London, under examination for alleged heresy, was suddenly found hanging in the Bishop's prison : if a jury of his fellow-citizens, viewing the body and rejecting at once the imputation of suicide, concluded that the man had been foully done to death : if, in a full and searching inquiry, they collected evidence pointing to certain culprits, chief of whom was the Bishop's own chancellor and judge of the diocesan court : if then the Bishop, apparently to intimidate the jury and forestall its impending verdict against his chancellor, hurriedly mounted a formal trial for heresy over the dead man's body, proceeding, upon condemnation, to burn the body and obliterate the corporal evidence of crime ; and if thereafter, stampeding his brother-prelates into following his own reckless course, the Bishop, by every sort of manoeuvre and pressure protracted over a year, succeeded in inducing the Crown to deflect the course of justice, to ignore the Coroner, the jury and the evidence, to compound the felony, and to withdraw the case against the chancellor from open trial. Such proceedings leave behind them an exact and unrelenting memory. Bishop Fitzjames carried through his purpose, in spite of some determined efforts of opposition from the Commons then met in Parliament. But his success laid up for his whole order a terrible retribution in the Parliament next but one. The men who tried to get justice for Hunne and his memory could do nothing at the moment, but they had not long to bide their time. The tides of high politics were presently upon the turn ; and within fifteen years of these events there met, after an ominous interval, that fateful Parliament in which the whole edifice of clerical privilege and immunity came crashing down. In front of its Speaker sat an expectant and resentful Commons : and behind his Chair, we might imagine from the sequel, stood the ghost of Richard Hunne.

Chapter III

MORTUARIES AND PRAEMUNIRE :
THE INFANT'S ' BEARING-SHEET '

Among the fairly important people in London when the trouble arose about Hunne was the Italian, Polydore Vergil, then papal ' collector,' and later distinguished as among the earliest considerable historians of England. " Writing from London on March 3rd (1515) to Cardinal Hadrian at Rome and referring to Hunne's case " then being hotly debated in Parliament, Vergil " says the people were exclaiming, and would be raging, against the clergy, were not the king appeasing their fury " (Pollard, ' Wolsey,' p. 39).

Later, in his ' Anglicae Historiae, p. 645, (1555), Vergil interrupts his narrative of state affairs to give a half-page reference to the case of Hunne, of which he had a direct and personal memory. He says :—

" About the same time there arose in London a quarrel which had fatal consequences for its author. A certain Richard Hun, a tailor, lost an infant son ; whereupon the parish priest required from him, as is customary, the linen garment in which the infant had been wrapped when he was baptised. Richard on his part denied that anything was due to him, since it had not been the infant's property. The quarrel grew so hot between them that both went to law, and from litigation were carried away into crime, the priest being accused by Richard of having offended against that terrible law of praemunire, and Richard being charged by the priest with heresy, for which impious offence he was thrown into prison by Richard Fitzjames, Bishop of London. He remained there but a short time, for not long afterwards he was found by the gaoler hanging. When this came out in public and the knowledge spread through the city, it is a marvel to what outcries it gave rise, what lamentations it caused, people exclaiming against the impious and cruel officers of the Bishop, to have strangled an innocent man, an

especial father of the poor, for it was ever his way to give help
to the needy. The King took the matter very seriously, forthwith
ordering William Horsey, the Bishop's vicar - general, with the
gaoler and apparitor of the Bishop's court, to be taken into custody
(in vincula abripi), and an Inquest to be held. Which done, the
dead body was burnt ; and in the end William with his fellow
prisoners was freed from custody and discharged. But enough of
this digression."

The populace of London, who feared and hated heresy, and some
of whom knew and had cause to thank Hunne, believed that, in
Wriothesley's words, he had only been " made a heretic for suing a
praemunire," that is to say, as an act of reprisal. It was important
for the authorities to counter this belief ; and so, in the damnatory
formula pronounced at the trial over Hunne's dead body, Fitzjames
and his draughtsmen allege that in the recent Convocation Archbishop Warham, " out of vehement and violent presumptions of
heresy which he had against the same Richard Hunne desiring to
make due inquisition," took steps to have the offender cited before
him " to make answer upon the premises." The Archbishop's
purpose, " tam pium, tam sanctum et laudabile," fell through
because " the same Richard could not be apprehended." Fitzjames
then intervened and had him arrested ; but why the Bishop could
do what the Archbishop could not we are not told. In a subsequent
chapter dealing with the post-mortem trial the reader will be given
reason to think that nothing therein alleged as fact can be accepted
without corroboration. And for the allegation that Hunne was
already ' vehemently and violently ' suspect of heresy before the
trouble arose between him and the parson there is not a syllable
of corroboration.* And the suggestion bears its falsity upon its
face if we may believe what More tells us as to the circumstances
under which, and the temper in which, Hunne brought his suit.
From this we should gather that up to the time when Hunne was

---

* How could it be pretended that the Archbishop was powerless to arrest a
suspect who was actually defending a civil suit in his own Court of Audience,
and attempting to impeach the jurisdiction of that court by suing a writ of
praemunire against the plaintiff and the judge ?

thrown by Fitzjames into the Lollards' Tower he was a free man, going about his business, taking legal advice, talking freely among his friends, and looking forward to success in what he hoped, too rashly, might be an historic test case. More writes in the ' Dialogue ' (bk. 3, chap. 15) :

" And besides all this, considering that Hunne was — as they that well know him say he was indeed — though he were a fair dealer among his neighbours, yet a man high-minded and set on the glory of a victory which he hoped to have in the praemunire, whereof he much boasted, as they said, among his familiar friends that he trusted to be spoken of long after his days and have his matter in the years and terms called Hunne's case."

This is not the action of a man who is suspected or accused of heresy. It is that of a man whose record and conscience are good, and who believes himself to have nothing to fear. A man suspect of heresy, and in peril of arrest, would have had something more to think about than quarrelling with a parson over a twopenny-ha'penny bit of linen ; and no man so suspect would have been mad enough to provoke the clergy by suing the penal writ of praemunire against the process of a spiritual court. Nor could any man, taking legal advice, he left in doubt that, in cases of heresy, the jurisdiction of the spiritual court was absolute, and that, as has been shown in the previous chapter (pp. 27 - 9), no temporal court and no temporal writ could interfere with it in any way.

More, whose memory, in controversy, could be astonishingly short, returned to the matter a year later (1529) in his ' Supplication of Souls,' written in reprobation of Simon Fish's "Supplication of Beggars.' Apparently forgetting what he had written in the ' Dialogue,' and provoked by Fish's virulence to a like hardihood of assertion, More here declares :

" Now is it of truth well known that he was detected of heresy before the praemunire sued or thought upon," — this again without any evidence, — " and," he continued, " he began that suit to help to stop the other withal " ; and then, so short is his memory, he proceeds, within half a dozen lines, to contradict his own assertion by saying :

" it appeared clearly to the temporal judges and all that were anything learned in the temporal law that his suit of the praemunire was nothing worth in the king's law ; forasmuch as by plain statute the matter was out of question that the plea to be holden upon mortuaries belong to the spiritual court " (' The Supplycacyon of Soulys,' pp. 9 - 10).

So here, by More's own acknowledgment, it was the parson's suit for the mortuary and not the Bishop's suit for heresy that Hunne's suit for the praemunire was intended " to stop withal." This, of course, was tenable and credible ; and the law-books record an actual case in which the writ of praemunire had been invoked in connection with a mortuary suit rather more than a hundred years before (see Nelson, ' Rights of the Clergy,' ed. 1715, p. 414).

If the reader should be disposed to think that I have dwelt unduly upon these questions of priority, I can only say that it is largely because too little patience has been spent upon them that the truth about this case of Hunne has been indeterminate so long.

We may now ask, Who was this Richard Hunne, and what was the course of events which brought him to the Lollards' Tower ?

Hunne was a London merchant, living in the parish of St. Margaret's, Bridge Street, close to London Bridge. He was a free-man of the City, a liveryman of the Merchant Taylors' Company, and " of good substance," More says, " I think well worth a thousand marks," say £20,000 of our money.* More agrees that he was " a fair dealer among his neighbours," and adds, while trying to represent him as a guilty heretic, " Of his worldly conversation among the people I have heard none harm " (' Dialogue, bk. 3, chap. 15). The fact that he was prosperous and of good repute in itself goes far to negative the suggestion that he was a known heretic. Among the citizens of standing at this time there was no leaning towards real heresy. If Hunne had been known for a heretic, he would have been looked upon askance and his business

---

* Such estimates must be treated as more or less conjectural. Authorities differ as to whether Tudor monetary denominations should be multiplied thirty, or forty times.

would have dwindled to nothing. He doubtless shared to the full the critical spirit in which the citizens regarded the clergy, their exactions, and their ways in general ; but, as has been shown already (pp. 25 - 6), this lively, and sometimes acrid, criticism was not heresy, nor accounted heresy, nor talked of as heresy except in the parlance of those of the clergy for whom opposition of any sort smacked of heresy. Hunne passed among his neighbours for a good Catholic ; and on the great test question of orthodoxy, the doctrine of Transubstantiation, no charge — it is important by the way to note — was brought against him so long as he was alive.

His trouble arose in the autumn of the year 1514. October is the month mentioned by the chronicler Arnold. About that time Hunne had an infant son, Stephen, " at nurse in Middlesex," so Foxe says, " in the parish of St. Mary Matfilon," otherwise St. Mary's, Whitechapel. The child died when five weeks old. His body was taken to the church for burial ; and the parson, one Thomas Dryfield, demanded a mortuary in respect of the child.

Mortuaries were burial dues claimable by the parson, in parishes where their payment was customary, upon the death of a parishioner. They were paid in kind, and consisted of some more or less valuable article of property which had belonged to the dead person. Disputes about mortuaries were dealt with by the spiritual court ; but if the custom, or the reasonableness of the custom, was contested, the temporal court exercised the right to try the issue, and pending its decision, to hold up the process in the spiritual court by a writ of prohibition. Such writs of prohibition involved nothing more than a stay of proceedings, and caused no particular perturbation. But towards the middle of the previous century, about eighty years before Hunne's time, there occurred a development which roused, among the spiritualty, not merely perturbation but acute alarm. In cases where the common law was entitled to intervene, the common lawyers took to substituting, for the ordinary writ of prohibition, the formidable writ of ' praemunire facias.' This was the writ of summons directed to offenders against the highly penal Statutes of Provisors.

These Statutes had been devised to maintain the courts of Common

Law in the exercise of their jurisdiction in cases of patronage, asserted in England, despite the Canon Law, by the courts of the Crown. Any subject who " shall draw any out of the realm in plea whereof the cognizance pertaineth to the king's court, or of things whereof judgments be given in the king's court, or which do sue in any other court to defeat or impeach the judgments given in the king's court," was to be punished by outlawry, forfeiture of lands and goods and, imprisonment at the king's pleasure (27 Edward III, 1. c. 1, 1353). In the further Act, 16 Richard II, 2. c. 5 (1393), the penalties are applied, more explicitly, to such suitors " in the Court of Rome or elsewhere." In the little words " any other court," and " elsewhere," the Common Law judges were quick to discover no little meaning. Within them they brought* any special court operating under rules other than those of the Common Law ; the courts of the Admiral, the Marshal, the Constable, and even the Chancellor himself hearing suits in equity.

The ' writ of praemunire,' as it was called, — divorced from its statutory context, and with no regard to the subject-matter of ' provisions ' — came to be employed to restrain any of these courts conceived as exceeding its proper jurisdiction ; and anyone suing in such courts on a matter for which there was remedy at the common law, " fell into a praemunire," as the phrase was. In the earlier half of the fifteenth century this doctrine and practice began to be applied to the ' courts christian ' within the kingdom. The Bishops, their legal officers, and the practitioners in the ecclesiastical courts, were soon loud in protest. From the year 1434 onwards repeated remonstrances were made in Convocation. The use of the penal writs of praemunire in place of the customary writs of prohibition was challenged by the spiritualty as an unwarrantable innovation. By it, they protested, the Church's ordinary jurisdiction was " enormously damaged " (Wilkins, Concilia, III, 533 - 5). The ecclesiastical lawyers did not see how they were to carry on with Praemunire, like a sword of Damocles, hanging over their

* See Jacob, ' New Law Dictionary,' 8th ed., 1762, art. Praemunire, and Stephens ' Ecclesiastical Statutes,' I. 65, n. 1.

heads. As late as 1447 the whole clergy of the kingdom are petitioning the Crown against an interpretation of the statutes " too strange and too bitter," " too perilous and too unreasonable." After long and rather anguished effort the clergy secured, in 1462, an undertaking from the Crown that the use of the writs they held so grievous should be discontinued. In the latter part of the century the rival factions of the Roses were fighting out their quarrel, and questions of law and jurisdiction fell into the background. The common lawyers, however, maintained their principle ; and Coke records that in the 11th year of Henry VII (1496) " it was adjudged by the whole court that a suit in the ecclesiastical court within the realm for a temporal cause was in case of praemunire " (Inst. III, cap. 54) ; the common lawyers claiming the last word as to what was, and what was not, a temporal cause. But there was no further attempt to use the writ until it was made, some eighteen years later, by Richard Hunne.

The mortuary which the parson Dryfield claimed in respect of Hunne's dead infant, five weeks old, was the child's 'bearing-sheet.'* This minute and melancholy relic may have been of some value to the bereaved parents, but can have been of very little value to anybody else. Hunne, incensed by the demand and regarding it as just another instance of a parson's petty rapacity, refused it ; and was doubly incensed when Dryfield sued him for it in the ecclesiastical court, in this case the Archbishop's court of Audience. Hunne, as More tells us, was a man of substance and of spirit, and decided to teach the parson a lesson, ' pour encourager les autres.' He took, as More's account implies, legal advice ; and countered the parson's suit for the bearing-sheet by suing, in the King's Bench, a writ of praemunire against Dryfield and the judge before whom he brought his case. He must, under legal advice, have had some sort of warrant for suing the writ, and some sort of ground for hoping that his action might succeed.

What was this warrant, and this ground of hope ? The question

---

* Murray's Dictionary defines a ' bearing-cloth ' as a child's christening robe, and gives a reference to ' Winter's Tale,' act 3, scene 3, in which the Shepherd speaks of " a bearing-cloth for a squire's child."

merits closer attention than it has commonly received. Not a few confused and halting answers have been given to it, some of them coloured by the mistaken notion that the writ of praemunire was only available against suitors in the court of Rome.* An answer is none the easier for the fact that no record of these suits, either of Dryfield against Hunne or of Hunne against Dryfield, has survived. What came of them we can only deduce from the event.

In the absence of any record, we are thrown back upon what facts there are, and upon whatever sense we have of situation and motive. To arrive at any tenable solution, we have to consider how, the law being what it was and Hunne being the sort of man More tells us he was — " a man highminded and set on the glory of a victory," etc. — his mind might be expected to work.

The known facts are four in number : first, that Hunne refused the parson's demand for his baby's bearing-sheet upon a definite ground ; second, that he met the parson's suit for the bearing-sheet by suing a writ of praemunire against him ; third, that his action failed ; and fourth, that his fellow-citizens, with the one known exception of More, were unshakeably convinced that he was charged with heresy as a vengeful reprisal for having brought it.

First, Hunne refused to hand over the bearing-sheet upon a definite ground, that the dead baby had had no property in it. He thus raised an issue which had long been agitated among the laity, but never tried at law. Mortuaries were chattels, supposed to be taken of property belonging to deceased persons. And the laity were aggrieved at the clergy demanding them in respect of

---

* E.g., by Burnet, and, more recently, by Dr. Pickthorne. The latter says (Early Tudor Government : Henry VIII, p. 112) : " He tried to counter that by suing Dryfield in a praemunire, on the ground that the spiritual court, being held by the legate's authority, was a foreign tribunal, before which Englishmen were not bound to answer." The legate intended is no doubt Wolsey, but he was not made Legate a latere until four years later. The only legate who could possibly be in question was the Primate himself as ' legatus natus ' of the Holy See. The Court of Audience, before which, as More tells us, Dryfield brought his suit, was that in which the Archbishop was supposed, rather vaguely it would seem, to exercise his legatine jurisdiction ; and that may conceivably have been a factor, along with others mentioned in the text, in suggesting to Hunne and his advisers procedure by praemunire. (See Ollard and Crosse, ' Dictionary of English Church History,' art. Courts, p. 154).

persons, minors and married women, who, in law, could hold no property. The grievance was an old one ; and as long ago as 1367 Archbishop Langham had apparently intended to meet it by ordaining, in a Provincial Constitution, that if a woman died, her husband living, she should in no wise be compelled to the payment of a mortuary. (Lyndwood, Provinciale, p. 19). Lyndwood indicates in a note that he did not think much of this provision, a pretty plain intimation that the clergy, in the following century, were disregarding it. And a century later, after an Act of Parliament in 1529 had settled the question which Hunne had endeavoured to take to law, the lawyer Christopher Saint German writes :*

" And the cause why they," i.e. mortuaries taken in kind, " were taken away was forasmuch as there were few things within this realm that caused more variance among the people than they did when they were suffered ; for they were taken so far against the order of the king's laws and against justice and right, as shall hereafter appear. First they were taken not only after the death of the husband, but also after the death of the wife, which after the laws of the realm had no goods, but that it was taken of the husband's goods ; and they were taken also of servants and children as well infants as other," etc.

This, evidently, was the issue that Hunne meant to raise. This custom of claiming upon the supposed property of deceased persons who, in law, could have possessed no property, was on the face of it " unreasonable " ; and the temporal court could properly be moved to test its reasonableness.

But furthermore, suits for mortuaries in respect of such persons were so patently unreasonable, so manifestly " against the order of the king's laws and against justice and right," so a layman might think, that the spiritual court was exceeding its proper powers in entertaining them at all. And the now established procedure at common law against any court presumed to be exceeding its proper powers was by writ of praemunire. So Hunne might rightly be

* (A treatise concerning the division between the Spiritualty and Temporalty, chap. 9).

advised, and so he proceeded to act, suing the writ against the plaintiff Dryfield and impeaching the process of the spiritual court. The venture, he would be told, was not without hazard. The common law was conservative, and the Crown at the moment not less conservative ; and the judges of the King's Bench might hesitate about entering upon new ground and opening, not improbably, an old quarrel. But the experiment might succeed, and was worth trying. It if failed, Hunne could afford to be out of pocket ; and if it succeeded he would be looked upon as a benefactor by his fellow-citizens, and his name would go down in legal history in connection with " Hunne's Case." He no doubt felt hardly against Dryfield ; but his purpose in bringing a test case upon a long-vexed issue and doing so in the most challenging form, would not necessarily imply any special animosity against the clergy in general.

The clergy, not unnaturally, took a different view. In their eyes a presumptuous layman who, rather than hand over a valueless scrap of linen on the parson's demand, could invoke the writ of praemunire against a spiritual court, ranked himself at once as a dangerous malcontent. What Hunne had done was to resuscitate a spectre which had haunted them for years during the previous century, and which had cost them prolonged effort to lay. A man who would do that was, to their minds, a pestilent person, an enemy of their whole order, for whom any fate was too good. Holy Church, as we have seen, (pp. 25 - 6) had a ready and infallible weapon against persons who had come to be regarded in that light : and Bishop Fitzjames was not slow to apply it. He ordered Hunne's arrest on a charge of heresy, and consigned him to his prison in the Lollards' Tower, and to the custody of his chancellor Doctor William Horsey. Bishop and chancellor might be well assured that a search of Hunne's house and the cross-questioning of his neighbours would provide sufficient evidence to justify his arrest. The process in heresy did not begin for some time, the Bishop delaying it, as More tells us, until Hunne's suit for the praemunire had been disposed of in the King's Bench. This one example of the Bishop's prudence is recorded by More in his ' Supplication of Souls.'

" Albeit that he that was sued in the praemunire was nothing belonging to the Bishop of London before whom Richard Hunne was detected to heresy*, yet lest such as would be glad sinisterly to misconstrue everything toward the clergy might have occasion to say that the matter was hotly handled against him to force him to forbear his suit of the praemunire : the Bishop therefore did the more forbear till it appeared clearly to the temporal judges and all that were anything learned in the temporal law, that his suit of the praemunire was nothing worth in the King's law." (More, English Works, ' Supplycacyon of Soulys,' pp. 9 - 10).

At this point, while Hunne is awaiting the issue of his suit and his captors are waiting to deal with him as he deserved, it may be well to say a word about these latter.

Of Dr. Horsey, the Bishop's chancellor and vicar-general, little is known except that he had formerly been in some sort of obscure trouble with the secular authorities, and that afterwards, when his indictment for murder was eventually withdrawn, he faded out of London, and thenceforth flourished obscurely on various preferments in the far west, at Exeter and elsewhere.

Of Bishop Fitzjames More speaks as " a very wise man, a virtuous and a cunning." The ceremonious language of the time might apply that phrase to any man who was fairly able and intelligent. More, in his own mind, cannot have thought too highly of a prelate who had been the would-be persecutor of his own dear friend and master Colet ; or of whom his other master and friend Erasmus could write as one " who (to say nothing of his manners) was " a superstitious and stubborn Scotist," and " thereupon thought himself half a God. Of which sort of men, though I know some whom I will not call knaves, yet I never saw one whom I thought I might truly term a Christian. . . . . But when the old Bishop (for he was fourscore years of age) his hatred grew too high to be

---

* A passing reference to the fact that Dryfield's suit was brought in the Archbishop's court of Audience (see More, ' Dialogue,' bk. 3, chap. 15, ed. Campbell, p. 233). Fiddes, ' Life of Cardinal Wolsey,' p. 43, is mistaken in saying that the suit was brought " in the Court of the Bishop of London."

smothered, the fire broke out, and adjoining two other Bishops as wise and virulent as himself, he began to trouble Dr. Colet, exhibiting articles against him to the Archbishop of Canterbury, taken out of his sermons. . . . . The Archbishop, being well acquainted with Colet's excellencies, received the articles, but instead of being his judge became his advocate. Yet the old man's fury did not end so, but strove to incense the Court against him, especially K. Henry VIII himself " (" The Life of Dr. Colet, writ by Erasmus Roterdamus," 1661, pp. 75 - 6. Bodl.).

Erasmus is, no doubt, a prejudiced witness, for Fitzjames stood for all he least reverenced in the prelacy of the day. Fitzjames, to do him justice, was no bad representative of the prelates of his day. In his old age he was still a man of vigour and courage, ready to go any length in defence of his order and its privileges, and with the impetuous temperament which can sweep less truculent spirits along with it. From his own mouth and in connection with this case of Hunne, we have two pieces of evidence which show that there was little confidence or regard or love lost between him and his London flock. He was an able enough administrator, but apparently very little of a father in God.

Chapter IV

HUNNE EXAMINED AT FULHAM :
SATURDAY, DEC. 2, 1514

Hunne's attempt — to raise and remedy the standing lay grievance about mortuaries, as I believe it was — proved a fiasco. The old instrument ' Circumspecte agatis ' had recognised and affirmed the jurisdiction of the spiritual court in cases of mortuary : the King's judges declined to look beyond it, and dismissed the suit. Hunne's failure may have been due to a defect of procedure ; we cannot tell in the absence of records. But the rule of law was that a writ in stay of proceedings would not issue unless the custom, or the reasonableness of the custom, had first been disputed in the spiritual court* ; and Hunne, in haste to get to grips with Dryfield, may have overlooked this. For whatever reason, he failed ; and judgment against him for his baby's bearing-sheet would no doubt follow in the Court of Audience. His plight was not an enviable one. In a couple of months he had lost his child, his cause and his freedom. No longer " highminded and set on the glory of a victory," he had to consider, within four walls, how best to extricate himself from the meshes of the heresy law. He must have known, by this time, that he had committed, in the eyes of his gaolers, the unpardonable sin, the more heinous for being unavowable and unpunishable ; and that he could look for little mercy at their hands.

For the proceedings in heresy we have to depend upon Foxe's transcripts, taken, as he tells us (Acts and Monuments IV, 173) " out of the registers of Fitzjames, bishop of London, by the faithful

---

* See Stephens, ' Ecclesiastical Statutes,' I, 128, n. 1. " In Johnson v. Oldham (I Ld. Raym. 609) it was holden that a prohibition could not be granted to stay a suit in the spiritual court for a mortuary, without having denied the custom in the spiritual court." Holt, C. J. " A prohibition cannot be granted without a denial of the custom in the spiritual court, which is not done here " (y. 12 Mod. 416).

help and industry of R. Carket, citizen of London." The originals are wanting in the extant Register. At a later period the folios, while still unbound, may have been borrowed for some unknown purpose and never found their way back. They may yet be discovered, as other materials relating to the case have been discovered in quite recent days. We have to ask how Carket did his work. There is every reason to believe that he was as faithful as he was helpful and industrious. On certain particulars his transcripts printed by Foxe can be tested from other sources, and they prove to be precisely accurate. There is therefore no reason to doubt the value of the record as a whole.

It was on Saturday, December 2nd, 1514, that Hunne was taken from his cell to Fulham for his first — and last — examination before the Bishop. We may assume that he was no sooner in prison than his house was thoroughly ransacked and his servants and neighbours searchingly questioned. All procurable evidence against him would be in the hands of the Bishop on this December 2nd.

Six ' articles ' of charge were brought against the accused. Five out of the six are based upon alleged talk ; and all six are couched in the usual phrasing culled from the cruder Wycliffite writings. We have to look through them to the probable facts behind them. What strikes one first and most about them is their comparative flimsiness. They are here given, with observations in passing.

Articles objected against Richard Hunne.

1. That he had read, taught, preached, published, and obstinately defended, against the laws of Almighty God, that tithes, or paying of tithes, was never ordained to be due, saving only by the covetousness of priests."

No doubt Hunne had spoken irascibly about tithes, as many have done before and since.

2. " Item, that he had read, taught, preached, published, and obstinately defended, that bishops and priests be the Scribes and Pharisees that did crucify Christ, and damned him to death."

If Hunne had had anything to say against the clergy, he would probably have said it in less hackneyed terms. With his then imperfect experience, he could hardly have meant, prophetically, that there were men among the clergy who were as ready as the Scribes and Pharisees to cry ' blasphemer,' ' heretic,' in order to do an innocent man to death.

3. " Item, That he had read, taught, preached, etc. that bishops and priests be teachers and preachers, but no doers, neither fulfillers of the law of God ; but catching, ravening, and all things taking, and nothing ministering, neither giving."

These four lines might be taken as a rather masterly précis of what the bishops and priests had been told to their faces, two years before, by Dean Colet from the pulpit of St. Paul's. Such language if used, as it commonly was by Hunne and others, merely gave utterance to the " contradiction of the lay people " of which Colet spoke. It argues a singular want of prudence and humour that a body, already badly blown upon, should have advertised and augmented its discredit by exhibiting general charges of this kind. They might have been brought against anybody, and they impressed nobody.

It will be observed that none of the three above charges touches any Catholic ordinance or any article of the Catholic Faith.

The 4th and 5th articles may be taken together. They allege Hunne's active sympathy with a certain Joan Baker, who had been up before the Bishop some three or four years previously. It is a common feature of these heresy cases that A. is accused of sympathising with B., and B. of sympathising with C., and so on. Joan was charged with defending a certain " Lady Young," already burnt, as Hunne is charged with defending Joan.

4. " Item, Where and when one Joan Baker was detected and abjured of many great heresies (as it appeareth by her abjuration), the said Richard Hun said, published, taught, preached, and obstinately took upon him, saying that he would defend her and her opinions, if it cost him five hundred marks."

5. " Item, afterwards, where and when the said Joan Baker, after her abjuration, was enjoined open penance according to her demerits, the said Richard Hun said, published, taught, and obstinately did defend her, saying, ' The bishop of London and his

officers have done open wrong to the said Joan Baker, in punishing her for heresy ; for her sayings and opinions be according to the laws of God : wherefore the bishop and his officers are more worthy to be punished for heresy than she is."

The materials in the case of Joan Baker have been transcribed from the Bishop's Register by Miss E. Jeffries Davis, and printed as an annex to her learned article on ' The case of Richard Hunne ' in the English Historical Review, vol. 30, July, 1915.

Joan Baker lived, like Hunne, in the Parish of St. Margaret's, Bridge Street, or New Fish Street. Her husband, Gervis, is referred to as a " Citizen and taylor of London." Joan held, and was compelled to abjure, certain wayward opinions, chiefly connected with pilgrimages and image-worship. Presented with an imposing array of formal interrogatories, she acknowledged that she possessed the status and obligations of a Christian woman. Asked if she knew that she was defamed in her parish " upon certain errors and false opinions of heresy," she replied that she knew nothing of the kind ; but that if any such rumour or slander was abroad, it was because of the " evil talk and tales " of one " Odiam's wife and the curate of the said parish church of St. Margaret." It rather looks as if Joan's trouble arose out of a feud between her and Mrs. Odiam, in which the parson took the side of the rival termagant. There was a certain conventional Billingsgate in which ladies like Joan were apt to explode in any misunderstanding with the parson or other women more in favour with him. Whatever her opinions, Joan had the courage of them. Five out of the nine opprobrious things she is alleged to have said were said to the parson himself. The record reads as if the parson, ' sir ' John Cawood, had decided that Joan Baker was a nuisance in his parish, and must be silenced. As for Hunne, who doubtless knew the Bakers well, his active sympathy was probably with Gervis, for having a shrew of a wife who could not control her tongue and temper. He may well have thought of Joan as just a silly woman, whose offences might have been adequately met by a rating from the Bishop. He may have felt that to subject his friend's too voluble wife to " open penance according to her demerits " was unnecessarily harsh ; and even said that the Bishop and his officers, who could deal with such a woman in such a way, would look better bearing faggots in her place. He is alleged to have said that he would defend Joan's opinions — which could have been heard at any street-corner — at the cost of half his fortune, not a very likely remark for a man intelligent enough to make a fortune.

So much for Hunne, Joan Baker, and articles 4 and 5.

The above five articles, five-sixths of the entire charge, are chiefly significant for what they do not say. They contain no suggestion of erroneous opinion about " the sacrament of the altar," always the important count in any serious heresy trial. That his own parson, John Cawood, should have had nothing against him on that head is a fair proof that Hunne was a passably good Catholic, though critical of the clergy as were many good Catholics of the time.

The sixth and last article merits particular attention.

6. " Item, that the said Richard Hun hath in his keeping divers English books prohibited and damned by the law ; as the Apocalypse in English, epistles and gospels in English, Wickliff's damnable works, and other books containing infinite errors, in which he hath been a long time accustomed to read, teach, and study daily." (Foxe IV, 183 - 4).

This sort of charge, in much the same terms, was common form in these heresy trials ; and apart from some sort of detailed corroboration it is impossible to say what ground there was for it in any particular case. Had there been any ground for it in most of the cases, manuscripts of the Wycliffite Scriptures, in whole or part, must have been in very wide circulation ; and if so, even allowing for the many impounded and destroyed, we should probably have had many more than have in fact come down to us.

Furthermore, if " Wickliff's damnable works " had really been found in Hunne's possession, we should have had citations from them of far graver import than the comparatively trivial matter contained in the articles above rehearsed.

And finally — and to this the reader's attention is particularly directed — the express mention of certain fragmentary translations, " the Apocalypse in English, epistles and gospels in English," seems to exclude the notion that the most formidable of " Wickliff's damnable works," the complete Wycliffite Bible with its Prologue, was then in the hands of Hunne's accusers. Such a complete English Bible made a sudden appearance eight days later, after Hunne was dead. And a remarkable feature in the long literary history of the case is that neither to Foxe, nor to any of the many, and many famous, writers who have examined it, has it occurred to ask, Where was that complete English Bible on December 2nd, and why, if it was then in the hands of Hunne's accusers, was nothing said about it ?

Appended to these articles there is a declaration, written " with a contrary hand," ostensibly by Hunne. Foxe, who was apt to be a trifle disappointed if a likely martyr chose to make his peace, suggests a doubt as to whether Hunne wrote it at all. I see no reason for any doubt. There is nothing abject about the declaration. It contained a qualified admission, such as an honest man who was no heretic, and felt that he had had trouble enough, might quite honourably make. It read :

" As touching these articles, I have not spoken them as they be here laid ; howbeit unadvisedly I have spoken words somewhat sounding to the same, for which I am sorry, and ask God mercy, and submit me to my lord's charitable and favourable correction."

Attached to it in the margin was a note, " Hoc fuit scriptum manu propria Ricardi Hunne, UT DICITUR " : " this was written in Richard Hunne's own hand, AS IT IS SAID." Again the significant thing is what is not there. The declaration remained unsigned ; and Hunne, on his way back to the Lollards' Tower, may have pondered uncomfortably upon the purpose of his accusers in not allowing him to sign it. He must have written it with the intention of signing it ; and would certainly have signed it had he been allowed to do so. The sequel suggests a reason why he was not.

For the Bishop and his advisers, his chancellor Dr. Horsey in chief, the position, that Saturday afternoon, was not without embarrassment. Somewhat precipitately, as they would now realise, they had arrested a fairly well-known citizen, a member of one of the great City Companies, a man reputed for " a fair dealer among

C

his neighbours," of whose " worldly conversation " people had
" heard none harm." For some weeks they had kept him in prison.
Already they had treated him with a rigour which would arouse
indignation if the prisoner were ever free to tell the tale. They
had examined him that morning on all the evidence they had been
able to rake up. They knew, and he knew, how little it all amounted
to. He was not an ignorant person, to be intimidated by an array
of trivial charges dressed up in fearsome words. There was nothing
in them to bring a man to his death. And no man, however grave
his errors, could be brought to his death unless he obstinately
maintained them. And Hunne had not been obstinate. He had
indited a qualified admission, and submitted himself to the Bishop's
correction. Fortunately it had not been signed. Had he been
allowed to sign it, the law would have had to take its course. The
Bishop would have had to admonish him and, with a warning as
to the peril of any further offence, release him, enjoining upon
him some open penance. After the importance they had given to the
case, the penance imposed could not be a light one. At the least
he would be directed to walk in procession in his parish church
on certain Sundays, bearing a faggot. But there were difficulties.
That procedure was well enough in the case of the obscure and
friendless dissidents who were ordinarily brought before the Bishop's
court. But Hunne was a known man, whose fellow-citizens believed
him to be innocent, and nothing worse than the victim of clerical
spleen. To subject him to public humiliation in his own church
would merely bring odium upon themselves. It might lead to a
demonstration, perhaps broken heads. If the fellow were released
and remained himself innocuous, his name and cause would be a
rallying-point for disaffection. Others, emboldened by his example,
might venture where he had ventured, and might succeed where he
had failed. There were other possibilities, better unexpressed.
There was the Tudor equivalent of the Third Degree, none too gentle.
The rigour of his confinement might be increased. Already dispirit-
ed, his mind might be so worked upon that he might come to consider his case as desperate, and take for himself the short way out,
relieving his gaolers of further trouble. But that was uncertain.

The man was no fool, and no coward. He had lost his son, but he had a wife and two daughters, a name and a position, and something to live for. He would know that his life was so far in no danger from the law, if he were allowed the law. He would believe that his fellow-citizens had the will and the power to see that he had justice. A man, with hope, might endure much ; and his ordeal at worst could not be a long one. His case might be raised in the coming Parliament. The City was watchful, and was returning its members to the new Parliament in ten days' time (Pollard, Wolsey, p. 32). If Hunne should chance to die meanwhile . . . . . Time was pressing. The desperation of guilt would account for everything. There would be an inquest, but juries were juries. If any of the panel conceived suspicions, he would look at Hunne's body and keep them to himself. What jury would dare to brave the might of the Church, — and Realm. If anything went awry there was Wolsey, all-powerful with the King, with a career to make, vaultingly ambitious, not the man to have his pitch queered by untoward occurrences. A little management and a bold front, and there was nothing to fear. And no time to lose.

Within forty-eight hours of being returned to the Lollards' Tower, Hunne was found in his cell, hanging, with bodily marks, palpable to any jury, of having first been strangled and had his neck broken.

Chapter V

SUNDAY, DECEMBER 3RD : HUNNE DEAD

The programme adumbrated in these last passages was carried out with a swiftness and decision which suggest that the difficult situation, and the means of dealing with it, had been thought out beforehand. And this is borne out by the fact that on Friday, December 1st, the day before Hunne was taken to Fulham, dark, and not too secret, talk about Hunne's impending fate was circulating among the chancellor's underlings. Two of these underlings were indicted with him for Hunne's murder ; but the chancellor himself was the Bishop's underling ; and it is not to be supposed that the three worthies would have done what they did without the connivance, concurrence and promised protection of their respective principals.

Of these principals something must in justice be said ; and it glances, incidentally, at one of the more plausible arguments of Sir Thomas More. More represents it as unlikely that, having in his power a prisoner " so sore suspect and convict of heresy " as to " bring to him shame, and peradventure to shameful death also," Horsey, " if he hated the man," would have gone out of his way to kill him.* But this involves two assumptions, neither warranted. One is that Horsey, at the time of the examination at Fulham, had any such sufficient evidence against Hunne ; the other, that there was any question between them either of love or hatred. You tread on a cockroach in order to prevent the spread of cockroaches ; but you do not hate the cockroach. To Fitzjames and Horsey, Hunne was just a noxious creature, who had to be got rid of. If he could be goaded to suicide, well and good ; if not, ... It was their office to

---

* " This " (Hunne's suicide) " is, I say, much more likely to me than the thing whereof I never heard the like before, that the bishop's chancellor should kill in the Lollard's Tower a man so sore suspect and convict of heresy, whereby he might bring himself in business ; whereas, if he hated the man (for kill him he would not ye wot well if he loved him) he might easily bring him to shame, and peradventure to shameful death." Dialogue, bk. 3, chap. 15.

protect the people from the infection of heresy, and consequent damnation. They honestly believed — and this is the real marvel — that to fulfil that office they must preserve their power and privileges intact. Any man who impugned them, as Hunne had tried to do, must be crushed. They could therefore put an end to him without any qualms, or any after regret but for being found out, and put to the trouble, as ill-luck would have it in this case, the very serious trouble, of eluding the consequences.

In this chapter an attempt will be made to reconstruct the story of what happened, in and about the Lollards' Tower, on Sunday, December 3rd, the day after Hunne was brought back from Fulham. By midnight on that Sunday Hunne was dead.

The story is based upon the records of the Coroner's Inquest. The body was found on the Monday morning, December 4th, and the Inquest began on the morning of Tuesday.

Publication of the proceedings of Coroner's inquests was illegal ; and it was not until more than twenty years afterwards that the records of this historic inquest appeared in print as an anonymous booklet, four copies of which, two of them imperfect, are still extant. It was entitled, " The enquirie and verdite of the quest pannELD of the death of Richard Hune wich was founde hanged in Lolars tower." The contents of the booklet, with the exception of the preface and marginal comments, were incorporated in Hall's Chronicle, and thence transcribed into Foxe's " Acts and Monuments." The small verbal discrepancies between the versions are of no consequence. For convenience of reference citations will be given from Foxe's version, which is in every library. (See Miss E. Jeffries Davis in Eng. Hist. Rev. vol. 30, pp. 477 - 9).

In the Parliament of 1515, elected about the time of Hunne's death, Bishop Fitzjames made a determined effort to impeach and overthrow the verdict of the jury ; and the Commons made a no less determined effort to vindicate and maintain it. In the course of these contentions the Bishop produced what is referred to in the record as " my lord of London's book," a statement of the case on which he denounced the jury as " false perjured caitifs." The Coroner and jury, on their part, drew up a reasoned statement of the grounds on which they had arrived at their verdict ; and it is this reasoned statement, together with the more important depositions and a copy of their formal verdict, which is printed in the booklet. The authenticity of the record is in no real doubt. Dr. Pollard says (' Wolsey,' p. 36, note). " The theory of concoction has not been seriously or consistently maintained. There is no reason to suppose that it .' (the booklet) " was anything else than what it purported to be, i.e. the coroner's signed report of the proceedings in his court." The record is such as to defy invention ; the depositions bear one another out remarkably ; and there is no discrepant testimony except that of the two laymen incriminated, who tried to exculpate themselves by perjury, in one case admitted perjury.

The " dramatis personae " in this Grand Guignol of real life are :—

Dr. William Horsey, the Bishop of London's chancellor and vicar-general, custodian of the Lollards' Tower.

James, cook to the chancellor.

John Grandger, servant to the Bishop.

Charles Joseph, gaoler.

Peter Turner, son-in-law and assistant to Joseph.

Julian Littell, housekeeper to Joseph.

Master Porter, neighbour to Joseph.

" Baude " Barrington, cousin to Joseph.

Wife to Barrington.

A prostitute, name unknown.

John Spalding, bellringer and verger of St. Paul's, temporary gaoler, sometimes referred to as John Bellringer.

William Sampson, " John Bellringer's fellow," (colleague).

Dr. Thomas Head (Heede or Hed), Commissary to the Bishop.

Thomas Chytcheley, Tailor. (Witness).

Thomas Simondes, Stationer. (Witness).

John Enderby, Barber. (Witness).

Allen Creswell, Waxchandler. (Witness).

Richard Horsenail, " Bailiff of the Sanctuary-Town called Godsture (Good Easter) in Essex." (Witness).

Robert Johnson, Landlord of the Bell Tavern in Shoreditch. (Witness).

" Three bakers and a smith of Stratford."

Thomas Barnwell, Coroner of London.

John Bernard, Thomas Stert, William Warren, Henry Abraham, John Arborow, John Turner, Robert Allen, William Marler, John Burton, James Page, Thomas Pickhill, William Burton, Robert Bridgewater, Thomas Busted, Gilbert Howell, Richard Gibson, Christopher Crofton, John God, Richard Holt, John Pasmere, Edmund Hudson, John Aunsell, Richard Cooper and John Tynie, Members of the Jury.

Between dusk and daylight on these December days there were some fifteen hours of darkness. The sun rose about eight o'clock.

(The bracketed figures below give the pages on which the several items appear in Foxe, Vol. IV.)

The story may begin with Friday, December 1st. On that day, the day before he was taken to Fulham, there were already dark rumours about the fate in store for Hunne.

" The Friday before the death of Richard Hun, betwixt eight and nine of the clock in the morning, he," (the witness John Enderby) met with John Belrynger in Eastcheap, and asked of him how Master Hun fared ? the said Belrynger answered, saying, ' There is ordained for him so grievous penance that, when men hear of it, they shall have great marvel thereof." (195).

And, from the statement of the Jury, " the Friday before Hun's death, Peter Turner said to an honest woman, a wax-chandler's wife, dwelling before St. Mary's Spital gate, that before this day seven-night Hun should have a mischievous death. And, the same day at afternoon this Hun was found dead, the said Peter came to the same wife and told her that Hun was hanged, saying, ' What told I you ? ' (194).

" And James, the chancellor's cook, the Friday before Hun's death, said to five honest men that Hun should die or (ere) Christmas, or else he would die for him. And on the Monday that Hun was found dead, the said James came to the same men and said, ' What told I you ? is he not now hanged ? ' And we of the inquest

71

asked both of Peter Turner and of James Cook where they had knowledge that Hun should so shortly die ? and they said, ' In Master Chancellor's place, by every man., .'' (194).

With this may be read certain averments of the Jury based upon testimony not recorded.

" Moreover it is well proved that before Hun's death the said chancellor came up into the said Lollers' tower, and kneeling down before Hun, held up his hands to him, praying of him forgiveness for all that he had done to him, and must do to him." (191).

" Also before Hun was carried to Fulham, the chancellor commanded to be put upon Hun's neck a great collar of iron, with a great chain, which is too heavy for any man or beast to wear, and long to endure." (191).

It would seem that Hunne, when examined at Fulham on the 2nd, had already undergone some of the rigours of a Tudor prison.

On Saturday, the day after the above rumours are proved to have been afloat, Hunne was examined before the Bishop at Fulham, and taken back to his cell.

At four o'clock in the afternoon Charles Joseph was temporarily relieved of his duties as gaoler of the Lollards' Tower. In the coming affair Charles Joseph is the person to watch. He seems to have been much of the typical Tudor gaoler of drama and romance, a dissolute bully and blackguard, with stomach enough for any deed. Cast for any of the uglier work that might have to be done, an alibi had to be found for him. At six o'clock next (Sunday) morning, two hours before sunrise, he left home on horseback, rode out of London, and was not seen again — at home — till the following Wednesday night. His absence would have provided an effective alibi had he not been recognised in the early twilight of Monday morning, slinking in the neighbourhood of St. Paul's. Of him presently.

Meanwhile Spalding was on duty in his place.

" At four o'clock on the Saturday afternoon (194) " the chancellor called to him one John Spalding, bellringer of Paul's, and delivered to the same bellringer the keys of the Lollers' tower, giving to the said bellringer a great charge, saying, ' I charge thee to keep Hun more straitly than he hath been kept, and let him have but one meal a day; moreover, I charge thee let nobody come to him without my license, neither to bring him shirt, cap, kerchief, or any other thing, but that I see it before it come to him." (191).

An hour after, at five o'clock, as it was falling dark, Spalding saw the prisoner in his cell and "cherished him," that is to say, cheered him up and made him comfortable; and Hunne, grateful for a little human feeling, gave him a piece of salmon, left over no doubt from the midday meal, as a present for his wife. (194). And so ended Saturday.

The events of Sunday we learn from the depositions of Spalding, Peter Turner and John Grandger, "servant with my lord of London."

On Sunday Spalding visited his prisoner no less than eight times. At :—

9 a.m. he came and " asked him what meat he would have to his dinner? and he answered, ' but a morsel.' (194).

Later, he " went to the chancellor into the quier " (the choir of St. Paul's), and received the pious command to " take the penitentiary up to the prisoner with him, to make him holy water and holy bread." This he did, leaving the penitentiary, as directed, to minister to Hunne. (194). At

12 noon, he returned to the cell with Peter Turner, " and served the said prisoner with his dinner," telling Turner at the same time " that he would not come to him (Hunne) unto the morrow, for my lord had commanded him that the prisoner should have but one meal's meat of the day (194-5). He left Turner locked in with Hunne while he ate his dinner. At

1 p.m. he returned, let Turner out, and asked Hunne " what he would have to his supper? and he answered that he had meat enough. (194).

6 p.m., " After that he had shut Poules church doors " (195) — (Turner gave the time as 7. p.m.) — he returned with his " fellow " William Sampson, and brought the prisoner a quart of ale. (194).

In his deposition he swore, falsely, that " from the hour of six aforesaid unto twleve o'clock on the morrow " he came no more to Hunne's cell. (194).

Later at night Spalding, with (probably) Sampson, returned to the cell. They, " the keepers," set Hunne in the stocks, and subjected him to some form of maltreatment which tried him to the uttermost. What occurred came out in the deposition of Allen Creswell, waxchandler. " The said Allen saith, That John Grandger, servant with my lord of London, in my lord of London's kitchen, at such time as the said Allen was sering (cering) of Hun's coffin, that Grandger told to him that he was present with John Belringer the same Sunday at night that Richard Hun was found dead on the morrow, when the keepers set him in the stocks ; insomuch that the said Hun desired to borrow the keeper's knife : and the keeper asked him what he would do with his knife ; and he answered, ' I had lever kill myself than to be thus entreated.' " (195).

The ordeal over, Spalding obligingly left his knife with Hunne, and quitted the cell with Sampson and Grandger.

Later still at night, while having supper with Sampson at " Master Commissary's," — (the Bishop's Commissary was Dr. Head, and Sampson was probably one of his officers) — Spalding " remembered," — so he said, though it is difficult to believe that he can have forgotten, — " that he had left his knife with " Hunne ; " whereupon, by the counsel of Master Commissary, he went to the prisoner and fetched his knife, where he found the prisoner saying of his beads, and so the said deponent required his knife of the said prisoner, and the said prisoner delivered the knife to the said deponent gladly ; and so he departed for that night." This last, and his putting the incident of the knife on Saturday and not Sunday, are two of the proved falsities in Spalding's deposition.

Hunne, if he had been goaded for a moment to the thought of suicide, had overcome the temptation. He was alive in his cell and saying his beads. When Spalding and the knife returned, the Commissary, the Chancellor and others concerned were apprised that there was to be no suicide. There was nothing to be done but wait.

The man they waited for was on his way.

Some eighteen hours before, the gaoler, Charles Joseph, had left home, and ridden out of London, in the dark of the morning, to his cousin " Baude " Barrington's house at Neckhill. There he spent the day ; and there, that night, — as he swore until his alibi broke down — " he lay with a harlot, a man's wife." (193). In fact he took horse from Neckhill in time to reach his destination before midnight. He rode towards London as far as Shoreditch. There, by arrangement, he was met by his " boy " or son-in-law Peter Turner. He handed over his horse, " all besweat and all bemired," to Turner, bidding him take it to the " Bell " inn with a message that it was to remain there, saddled, throughout the night. Turner took the horse and gave the message : " Let my father's horse stand saddled, for I cannot tell whether my father will ride again to-night or not." (Deposition of Robert Johnson, landlord of the " Bell." (193)). Turner then rejoined Joseph, who continued his journey citywards on foot. Taking care not to go home, he made his way to the Lollards' Tower, where he was joined by two others. No time was lost. Close on midnight " John (Spalding) the bellringer bare up the steire (stair) into the Lollars' tower a wax-candle, having the keys of the doors hanging on his arm ; and I Charles went next to him, and master chancellor came up last : and when all we came up, we found Hun lying on his bed ; and then master chancellor said, ' Lay hands on the thief ' ; and so all we murdered Hun : and then I Charles put the girdle about Hun's neck ; and then John bellringer and I Charles did heave up Hun, and master chancellor pulled the girdle over the staple ; and so Hun was hanged." (192).

So, " of his own free will and unconstrained," Joseph confessed when, some time later, he was removed from sanctuary and examined for his purgation in the Tower of London. At this attempted purgation he produced Barrington's wife and the alleged harlot to testify to his honesty ; but abandoned his alibi when confronted with the evidence of Chytcheley and Simondes, who had chanced to see him lurking in their neighbourhood. (193).

The deed done, and the details of stage management hurriedly arranged, the three went their several ways. Dr. Horsey, the chancellor, is next heard of as present in the morning at High Mass in St. Paul's. (195). Spalding disappeared until midday, when " he met the chancellor, with other doctors " hastening to verify the tragic news brought to them by Turner — who, after a vain search for Spalding, had obtained the keys from his " fellow " Sampson — of what had happened in the Lollards' Tower. (194).

The adventures of Joseph make a fuller story.

He did not venture home " for fear of bewraying," as he afterwards said, that is, for fear of being seen and informed upon. He had to put in the night somewhere. He may have spent it with Spalding, who had access to the Cathcdral. Thence, by misadventure, he was seen emerging in the early twilight. He was recognised, there and thereabouts, by two people who knew him well. Thomas Chytcheley, tailor, deposed :

" The same Monday that Richard Hun was found dead, within a quarter of an hour after seven a clock in the morning, he met with Charles Joseph, coming out of Poules at the nether north door, going toward Paternoster row, saying ' Good morrow, Master Charles " and the said Charles answered, ' Good morrow ! ' and turned his back, when he was without the church door, and looked upon the said Chytcheley." And Thomas Simondes, stationer, further deposed :

" The same morning that Hun was dead, within a quarter of an hour after seven a clock in the morning, Charles Joseph came before him at his stall, and said, ' Good morrow, gossip Simondes ! ' and the same Simondes said, ' Good morrow " to him again ; and the wife of the same Simondes was by him ; and because of the deadly countenance and hasty going of Charles, the said Thomas bade his wife look whither Charles goeth ; and as she could perceive, Charles went into an ale house standing in Paternoster row, by the alley leading into the rood of Northern, or into the alley, whither (whether), she could not well tell." (193).

Three quarters of an hour afterwards (8 a.m.) he had reached the " Bell " at Shoreditch. " Charles," deposed the landlord Robert Johnson, " came booted and spurred about eight of the clock, and

asked if his horse was saddled ? and the servant answered, ' Yea.'
And the said Charles leaped upon his horse, and prayed the host
to let him out of his back gate, that he might ride out by the field
side ; which host so did." (193).

From Shoreditch he rode out again to Barrington's house
at Neckhill, (192), where he spent the rest of Monday, and pre-
sumably all Tuesday and most of Wednesday. On Wednesday
night he reappeared at home about supper time. The gaoler himself seems to have been an occasional gaol-bird — he had had word
that " divers sergeants " had been after him some days before,
(deposition of Peter Turner (194)) — so his woman-servant, Julian
Littell, had thought his absence sufficiently accounted for when told
that he was in prison. That night of his return he was in a cheery
and expansive mood. Jingling, no doubt, some ill-gotten coin, he
said to her, " It is merry to turn the penny," intimating that he had
been doing better business elsewhere. As it was not a case of prison
Julian, womanlike, was curious, the more so when, '" after supper,"
he " trussed up a persell of his goods," as if in preparation for
another departure, and with her help — it must have been a good-
sized parcel — " bare them into Mr. Porter's house to keep." By
then he had decided to take the woman into his secret. He might
need her help, and silence. What followed is best told in the words
of her deposition (192), as given in the statement of the Jury.

" Charles said to Julian ; ' Julian, if thou wilt be sworn to keep
my counsel, I will show thee my mind.' Julian answered, ' Yea,
if it be neither felony nor treason.' Then Charles took a book out
of his purse, and Julian sware to him thereupon. Then said Charles
to Julian, ' I have destroyed Richard Hun !' ' Alas, master,' said
Julian, ' how ? he was called an honest man.' Charles answered,
' I put a wire in his nose.' ' Alas,' said Julian, ' now be ye cast away
and undone.' Then said Charles, ' Julian, I trust in thee that thou
wilt keep my counsel.' And Julian answered, ' Yea, but for God's
sake, master, shift for yourself.' And then Charles said, ' I had
lever than 100 pound it were not done ; but what is done cannot
be undone.' Moreover Charles said then to Julian, ' Upon Sunday,
when I rode to my cousin Barington's house, I tarried there and

made good cheer all day till it was night ; and yet before it was midnight I was in London, and had killed Hun. And upon the next day I rode thither again, and was there at dinner, and sent for neighbours, and made good cheer.' Then Julian asked Charles, ' Where set you your horse that night you came to town, and wherefore came you not home ?' Charles answered, ' I came not home for fear of bewraying.' And then Julian asked Charles, ' Who was with you at the killing of Hun ? ' Charles answered, ' I will not tell thee.'

By Wednesday night it would be known that the Jury, who had begun their inquiry the day before, had put aside any suggestion of suicide, and were looking into what they believed to be a very foul murder. " Julian saith that upon the Thursday following Charles tarried all day in his house with great fear." On the Friday morning he ventured out early, and heard what turned his fear into acute alarm.

" Early in the morning before day, Charles went forth, as he said, to Paul's ; and at his coming in again he was in a great fear, saying hastily, ' Get me my horse ' ; and with great fear and haste made him ready to ride ; and bade Master Porter's lad lead his horse into the field by the backside," it being then daylight. " And then Charles put into his sleeve his mase, or masor, with other plate borrowed of Master Porter, both gold and silver ; but how much I am not sure : and Charles went into the field after his horse, and Julian brought his budget after him." (192).

For the next fortnight the fugitive lay low in some haunt, probably at Stratford. " Upon Friday in Christmas week following, Charles came home late in the night, and brought with him three bakers and a smith of Stratford, and the same night they carried out of Charles's house all his goods by the fieldside to the Bell in Shoreditch, and early in the morning conveyed it with carts to Stratford." (192).

Earlier that Friday, December 22nd, before this nocturnal furniture removal, Joseph had decided that it was time to take sanctuary. Richard Horsenail, Bailiff of the Sanctuary-Town called Godsture " (Good Easter) " in Essex, deposed

" That the Friday before Christmas-day last past, one Charles Joseph, sumner to my lord of London, became a sanctuary-man, and the aforesaid Friday he registered his name ; the said Charles saying it was for the safeguard of his body, for there be certain men in London so extreme against him for the death of Richard Hun that he dare not abide in London. Howbeit the said Charles saith, he knowledgeth himself guiltless of Hun's death ; for he delivered the keys to the chancellor by Hun's life. Also the said bailiff saith that Charles paid the duty of the said registering, both to him and Sir John Studley, vicar." (195).

At some later date Joseph was removed from sanctuary for examination in the Tower of London, and, his alibi having failed, made the confession above recorded, " of his own free will and unconstrained." Bishop Fitzjames affirmed, in an extraordinary letter to Wolsey, that his confession was " made by pain and durance " (196) ; but this, as Dr. Pollard points out (' Wolsey,' p. 38, note 2) " involves a charge against the constable of the Tower and the king's counsel who examined Joseph as well as against the coroner's jury," four of whom are named as being present, " with many other." (192).

Meanwhile Horsey, the chancellor, was in custody, that of his ecclesiastical superiors ; and Spalding, the bellringer, of whom nothing is recorded, would likewise be under arrest.

All this arose out of what the Coroner and his jury saw with their own eyes when they entered Hunne's cell on the morning of Tuesday, December 5th.

On the previous day, Monday, December 4th, " at the hour of eight o'clock in the morning," Peter Turner, who had to serve the prisoner with his one meal, looked for Spalding to obtain the keys. He " could not find him, and tarried until the high mass of Poules was done, and yet he could not find " him ; " and then one William (Sampson), John Belringer's fellow," produced Spalding's keys. Turner, knowing of his father-in-law Joseph's surreptitious return to London, had a shrewd idea of what he would find in the cell ; and, preferring not to go alone, took with him " two officers of my lord's, being sumners (summoners)." The three went up and found Hunne hanging, " his face to the wallward." Service in the Cathedral being over, Turner " immediately gave knowledge to the chancellor, whereupon the chancellor went up with the Master of the Rolls, and Master Subdean, with other doctors unknown, to the number of a dozen, and their servants." (195). These were duly shocked by what they saw. The heretic had added to his guilt the crime of suicide.

Nothing was disturbed in the cell until the following morning, except that a mulberry-coloured gown, which the Jury had " good proof " had lain on the stocks " at the going up of master chancellor into the Lollard's tower," had disappeared ; " whose gown it was we could never prove, neither who bare it away." (191).

A brief examination of the body, and of the cell, disposed of any notion of suicide. It was evident to the Jury that there had been foul play. " We found the body of the said Hun hanging upon a staple of iron, in a girdle of silk, with fair countenance, his head fair kemmed (combed), and his bonnet right sitting upon his head, with his eyes and mouth fair closed, without any staring, gaping, or frowning, also without any drivelling or spurging in any place of his body : Whereupon by one assent all we agreed to take down the dead body of the said Hun, and as soon as we began to heave the body it was loose . . . . ." (190). The arrangement of the noose was unconvincing. A stool, the one thing in the cell from which a suicide could have launched himself into eternity, was so standing that it could not have served the purpose. The " soft silken girdle " would not account for the abrasions upon Hunne's neck, or for the fact of his neck being broken. Out of his nostrils came a trickle of blood, " to the quantity of four drops. Save only these four drops of blood, the face, lips, chin, doublet, collar and shirt of the said Hun were clean from any blood." But " upon the left side of Hun's jacket, from the breast downward, two great streams of blood " were found. " Also within a flap of the left side of his jacket we find a great cluster of blood, and the jacket folden down thereupon." " Also we find in a corner, somewhat beyond the place where he did hang, a great parcel of blood." " Whereby it appeareth plainly to us all that the neck of Hun was broken, and the great plenty of blood was shed, before he was hanged. Wherefore all we find, by God and all our consciences, that Richard Hun was murdered. Also we acquit the said Richard Hun of his own death." (190 - 1).

The idea — first put forward by Fitzjames in his letter to Wolsey and impressed by certain writers since — that Horsey's complicity rested solely upon Joseph's confession, does not seem to have occurred to the Jury. They took the commonsense view that " Master William Horsey," having " had at his commandment both the rule and guiding of the said prisoner," the " murder could not have been done without consent and license of the chancellor." (191). They held that Joseph's stealthy departure from, and return to, London " was but a convention made betwixt Charles and the chancellor to colour the murder." (191). And they had therefore no difficulty in accepting Joseph's statement that Horsey took an active hand in the killing.

The inquest, begun on December 5th and 6th, was not concluded for some time. One of the most important witnesses, Julian Littell, Joseph's woman-servant, had taken sanctuary like her master. It was not until February 14th (see Eng. Hist. Rev. vol. 30, p. 479, note 14) that her evidence was taken on commission " within the chapel of our Lady of Bethlehem." Probably towards the end of the month the Jury returned their formal verdict, that

" William Horsey, of London, clerk, otherwise called William Heresie, chancellor to Richard bishop of London ; and one Charles Joseph,* late of London, sumner, and John Spalding of London, otherwise called John Bellringer, feloniously as felons to our lord the king, with force of arms against the peace of our sovereign lord the king, and dignity of his crown, the 4th day of December, the sixth year of the reign of our sovereign lord aforesaid, of their great malice, at the parish of St. Gregory aforesaid, upon the said Richard Hun made a fray, and feloniously strangled and smothered the same Richard Hun, and also the neck they did break of the said

---

* Joseph told Julian that the murder took place " before midnight " on Sunday, Dec. 3rd. The jury may have ascertained that the deed was done after midnight, and so give the date of death as Dec. 4th.

Richard Hun, and there feloniously slew him, and murdered him. And also the body of the said Richard Hun, afterward, the same fourth day, year, place, parish, and ward aforesaid, with the proper girdle of the same Richard Hun, of silk, black of colour, of the value of twelve pence, after his death, upon a hook driven into a piece of timber in the wall of the prison aforesaid, made fast, and so hanged him, against the peace of our sovereign lord the king, and the dignity of his crown. And so the said jury have sworn upon the holy evangelists, that the said William Horsey, clerk, Charles Joseph, and John Spalding, of their set malice, then and there feloniously killed and murdered the said Richard Hun in manner and form abovesaid, against the peace of our sovereign lord the king, his crown and dignity.

Subscribed in this manner :

Thomas Barnwell, Coroner of the City of London." (197).

Thereupon Fitzjames wrote an urgent, and rather abject, letter to Wolsey, not yet Chancellor or Cardinal or Legate, but already Archbishop of York and daily waxing in power. The letter must be one of the most extraordinary ever written by an English prelate. Later in Parliament Fitzjames denounced this particular jury as " false perjured caitiffs " ; but in this letter he roundly declared that "any twelve men in London " would be equally false to their oaths, and that no clerk, if brought before them, could look for a fair trial. The letter reveals both the character of the Bishop, and the state of public feeling in his diocese years before Luther was heard of. Fitzjames besought Wolsey to have the matter taken into the hands of the Privy Council, and the verdict of the jury annulled.* Here is the letter :

" I beseech your good lordship to stand so good lord unto my poor chancellor now in ward, and indicted by an untrue quest, for the death of Richard Hun, upon the only accusation of Charles Joseph made by pain and durance ; that by your intercession it

---

* " Indifferent persons of " the king's " discreet council " must surely mean the Privy Council, and not merely king's counsel learned in the law. We know from More that some committee of the Privy Council was actively concerned with the case.

may please the king's grace to have the matter duly and sufficiently examined by indifferent persons of his discreet council, in the presence of the parties, or (ere) there be any more done in the cause : and that upon the innocency of my said chancellor declared, it may further please the king's grace to award a placard unto his attorney, to confess the said indictment to be untrue, when the time shall require it ; for assured am I, if my chancellor be tried by any twelve men in London, they be so maliciously set 'in favorem haereticae pravitatis' (in favour of heresy) that they will cast and condemn any clerk,* though he were as innocent as Abel. " Quare si potes beate Pater, adjuva infirmitates nostras, et tibi in perpetuum devincti erimus' (Wherefore if you can, blessed Father, help our infirmities, and we shall be bound to you for ever). Over this, in most humble wise I beseech you that I may have the king's gracious favour, whom I never offended willingly ; and that by your good means I might speak with his grace and you : and I with all mine shall pray for your prosperous estate long to continue.

Your most humble orator, Richard London." (196).

Fitzjames of course knew that in the eyes of " any twelve men " of a High Court jury the evidence against Horsey would appear no less damning than to the twenty-four jurymen of the Coroner's Inquest ; and that the only thing to do was, by hook or by crook, to prevent the case from being brought to trial.

A remarkable authentication of Fitzjames' letter occurs in the records of the Corporation of London. From the minutes of the Court of Aldermen it appears that on April 17th a deputation, consisting of the Recorder, the Common Clerk and four Aldermen were (modern spelling)

" named and appointed by this Court to speak with the Bishop of London for certain perilous and heinous words as ben surmised by him to be spoken of the whole body of the City touching heresy specified in a Copy of a letter supposed to be written by the said Bishop." (Eng. Hist. Rev. vol. 30, p. 478).

The City, in fact, was watching Fitzjames and his manoeuvres

---

* " Any clerk " : see Pollard, ' Wolsey,' p. 38, note 3).

with jealous vigilance. There are indications of this from the very outset. One of Joseph's regrets upon having to take to flight was that he could turn no more dishonest pennies by informing against so-called heretics in London.

" Charles said to the said Julian, ' Were not this ungracious trouble, I could bring my lord of London to the doors of heretics in London, both of men and women, that be worth a thousand pound " ; and on his saying the same thing to Porter's wife " of the best in London," " Mrs. Porter answered, ' The best in London is my lord mayor.' Then Charles said, ' I will not scuse (excuse) him quite, for that he taketh this matter hot'." (193). This was within a few days of Hunne's death ; and when, or soon after, Fitzjames wrote his letter to Wolsey, the City members were active in Parliament on behalf of Hunne's children and the integrity of the jury.

The Bishop's letter was one of the first steps in a course of proceedings which occupied the time and passions of Convocation, Parliament and the Privy Council for a great part of the year 1515. They were concerned with large and long-debated matters of jurisdiction, and especially with a somewhat belated claim for felonious clerks to be exempt from trial before secular tribunals. Behind all these grave and general questions was, discreetly unacknowledged, the question whether a particular clerk, Dr. William Horsey, was to be brought to trial before the King's Bench. How this question was ultimately burked will presently be told. These august proceedings bring out, unmistakably, the historic importance of Hunne's case ; and the importance, therefore, of determining the truth about it, if that be possible.

Fitzjames, now engaged in a determined effort to nullify the verdict of the jury, had already, some three months before, made a bold attempt to anticipate and forestall it.

By the evening of Wednesday, Dec. 6th, it was known in London, and to the Bishop, that the jury were investigating a plain murder, and that the Bishop's chancellor, who had " had at his commandment both the rule and guiding of the prisoner " in the Lollards' Tower, was gravely implicated. The Bishop, foreseeing the unutterable scandal of a verdict against his chancellor, took measures with his usual reckless promptitude. Having failed to stage a plausible suicide, he and advisers fell back upon the expedient of continuing the process in heresy, and staging an elaborate and spectacular public trial in which Hunne would be condemned as a heretic post mortem. I am not aware of any previous case in which a dead man had been tried for heresy ; but Fitzjames was a man who made his own precedents. The proceeding, in any case, was impudently illegal. No man could be condemned to death for heresy unless he were contumacious and obstinately maintained his errors. Hunne had not been obstinate ; and there was no possibility of cross-examining his ghost to convict him of a change of mind. But what troubled Fitzjames was not the illegality, but the lack of evidence. Some form of law had to be observed ; and the kind of charges that were brought against Hunne at Fulham would have looked silly in a ceremonial trial carried through with every parade of pomp, and designed to impress opinion and silence clamour. The Bishop's object in mounting such a trial lies upon the surface. Counting, as such men will, upon the pusillanimity of the common man, he calculated that if Hunne were formally condemned as a heretic, and his body handed over to the secular arm for burning, the jury would not dare to proceed with their inquiry, and the whole matter would be allowed to drop. Any rumblings of lay opinion could be outfaced, and would soon die down.

But there was the old difficulty about evidence. Some weightier matter had to be provided. No heresy trial was of much importance or verisimilitude unless the accused could be charged with erroneous opinions about " the sacrament of the altar," a matter which had been conspicuously absent from the Fulham charges. As usual at need, and in the nick of time, the required evidence was forth-coming. By some means a complete copy of the English Bible with its unmistakably Wycliffite Prologue — also never mentioned at Fulham — came into the hands of the prosecution. In great haste, for there were only two or three days available, this lengthy Prologue was examined, and certain passages were marked for extraction as the basis of thirteen articles of charge. Among these

85

passages was one which, by a bold piece of garbling, could be twisted into a dogmatic denial of Transubstantiation. The ownership of the volume, and even the authorship of the incriminating passages and of the marginal annotations accompanying them, was to be attributed to Hunne. An elaborate programme of procedure for the forthcoming trial was drawn up. By the inclusion of the Bishops of Durham and Lincoln, and of Fitzjames' own suffragan the titular Bishop of Gallipoli, the tribunal was to be given the appearance of something more than a diocesan synod. The preacher at Paul's Cross on Sunday, Dec. 10th — just a week after the fatal Sunday in the Lollards' Tower — was given the necessary instructions. He announced :

" Masters and friends, for certain causes and considerations, I have in command to rehearse, show, and publish here unto you, the articles of heresy upon which Richard Hunne was detected and examined : and also other great articles and damnable points and opinions of heresy contained in some of his books, which be come to light and knowledge here ready to be shown.' " And therewith," says Foxe, " he read the articles openly unto the people, concluding with these words " :

" And masters, if there be any man desirous to see the specialty of these articles, or doubt whether they be contained in this book or not, for satisfying of his mind let him come to my lord of London, and he shall see it with good will." (186 - 7).

The challenge was a perfectly safe one, and everything was done to give the impression that the trial was to be open and aboveboard. It took place within the same week, on Saturday, Dec. 16th, in the Lady Chapel of St. Paul's. Besides the three Bishops abovementioned, there were present " six public notaries, his (Fitzjames') own register (registrar), and about twenty-five doctors, abbots, priors, and priests of name," with a concourse of lesser clergy whom Foxe, after his manner, described as " a great rabble of other common anointed catholics." There too were the Lord Mayor, Aldermen and Sheriffs of the City of London, doubtless, to judge from subsequent events, with a watching brief for their dead fellow-citizen. The forms were duly observed, and the incriminating articles duly recited. A portentous sentence of condemnation, opulent in the verbiage of ecclesiastical malediction, was duly pronounced, and the body, as that of a convicted heretic, delivered over to the secular arm. It was burnt at Smithfield on Dec. 20th, sixteen days after Hunne's demise.

But the solemn pageant was of no avail. This old-time Coroner's Jury were not the anticipated men of straw. Unintimidated and undeterred, they went on with their inquiry. They had got their hand upon a very big thing, and had no mind to let it go. The case of Richard Hunne had brought to a focus the long-growing distrust of these heresy trials. The lay people had become tired of hearing the cry ' heretic, heretic ' whenever a parson encountered opposition. That cry had been raised once too often, and had ended in murder. And the Jury, backed by the City, were resolved that the culprits, and especially the man whom they accounted the responsible culprit, Horsey the Bishop's chancellor, should be brought to book.

At this trial in the Lady Chapel of St. Paul's Sir Thomas More was present. More was satisfied that Hunne had been a guilty heretic, and was justly condemned, by what he there heard from the lips of the prosecution. Not having yet experienced, in his own person, the possibilities of human infamy, it never occurred to him to question whether what he there heard was true. Of that later.

Chapter VI

MURDER OR SUICIDE?
SIR THOMAS MORE IN THE ' DIALOGUE '

The reader is now in possession of the sworn facts in the case of
Richard Hunne ; and we have to see how those facts are dealt
with by Sir Thomas More, briefly in the ' Supplication of Souls '
and at length in the ' Dialogue concerning Tyndale ' (bk. 3, chap.
15). It is largely, one might almost say solely, in natural deference
to the authority of More that the truth about Hunne's case has
been so long in suspense, and that the alleged facts, to some writers,
have amounted to no more than a cock and bull story.

We have to consider what More said, what circumstances obliged
him to say, and what, if we can discover it, he really knew and
thought. To assume that what he said was all he thought is to do
less than justice to him as a responsible politician, working in a
world where one had to be circumspect. Politicians sometimes have
an undeserved bad name from the very fact of having a good
conscience. In time of war, and in critical times of peace, a man
who has regard for the public interest may not be free to utter
all his mind. Something has to be left for reading between the
lines.

If these considerations are valid, they have not been always
regarded in the use that has been made of More's authority.

We in our day, enveloped as we are in printed matter, are apt to
think of anyone commenting upon a past event as commenting upon
a printed record of it ; and one may be quite a long time checking
what Foxe wrote, and Hall wrote, and later authors have written, by
what was written by More before awaking to the fact that More
himself was the first person to write anything at all. It is therefore
worth while to collect the facts about this case of Hunne as they
would be known to us if we had nothing but More's account to go
upon. The undisputed facts, as More gives them, are these :

THOMAS MORE

Reproduced by courtesy of the Bodleian Library

facing page 88

That there was a London citizen named Richard Hunne, of good substance and of good repute :

That he was defendant in an action to recover a mortuary brought by a parson in the Archbishop's Court of Audience.

That, to scotch that suit, he sued a writ of praemunire against the plaintiff and the court.

That he was arrested on a charge of heresy, and confined in the Bishop of London's prison, in charge of the Bishop's chancellor.

That the process in heresy was suspended until his suit for the praemunire was disposed of, unfavourably to him.

That he was then examined before the Bishop.

That he was found hanging in his cell.

That his death was by the clergy imputed to suicide.

That a trial for heresy was held over his dead body in the Lady Chapel of St. Paul's, Sir Thomas More being present, with many others.

That he was condemned and his body burnt, and perhaps also his books, though that was uncertain.

That, meanwhile, a Coroner's Jury had inquired into the case and found that he had been murdered :

That they presently returned a verdict of murder against the Bishop's Chancellor :

That More believed them to be honest men who had found the verdict according to their consciences, though he himself could not subscribe to it.

That the matter was the subject of debate and contention, and led to further inquiry by a Committee or Commission of the Privy Council.

That there was an erroneous idea that the accused chancellor had sued for pardon as a guilty man.

That, in fact, he and " the others ' — the one and only reference to " the others " — had at length been duly arraigned on the Coronor's indictment before the King's Bench on the charge of murder.

That they pleaded not guilty.

That the Attorney General, for the Crown, allowed the plea and offered no evidence, the case, consequently, never coming to trial.

That the debate and contention were as active as ever when More wrote, some fifteen years after the event.

This outline of the case we should know from More if Foxe and Hall and the compiler of the booklet and the many writers who have dealt with the matter since had never written a line. But two things we should not know. We should not know a single thing about the evidence upon which the Jury found their verdict. And we should not know a single thing about the grounds upon which More himself was unable to subscribe to it, as he solemnly declared he was. He does indicate that there was some serious evidence against the chancellor, but only in a few general phrases which tell us nothing. All he says is :

" Of truth there were divers suspicious things laid against him, and all those well and substantially answered again for him. Howbeit, upon the telling of a tale often times, happeth that when all is heard that can be said therein yet shall the hearers some think one way and some another. And therefore, though I cannot think but that the Jury, which were right honest men, found the verdict as themself thought in their own conscience to be truth : yet, in mine own mind, for ought that ever I heard thereof in my life, as help me God, I could never think it."

But of the grounds of his dissent, not one word.

If this were all, we should be obliged to leave the case as a mystery, and More, professing complete knowledge of it and affecting complete candour in expounding it, as little less of a mystery than Hunne himself.

The mystery, as regards More, begins to disappear when we consider his own personal position, both at the time of Hunne's death and, some fourteen or fifteen years later, when he discussed the circumstances of it in the ' Dialogue ' and the ' Supplication of Souls'. More, in 1514, was a man of thirty-four, known as a scholar, a humanist, a wit, and a brilliant barrister in busy practice. He was Under Sheriff of London, presiding as judge in the Sheriffs' Court. He would be on friendly terms with all the civic dignitaries. He would be acquainted with Thomas Barnwell, the City Coroner.

As a privileged person he would have access to the records of the Coroner's Inquest. He tells us himself, and there is no reason to doubt, that he knew all about the case.

" So well I know it from top to toe that I suppose there be not very many men that knoweth it much better. For I have not only been divers times present myself at certain examinations thereof, but have also divers and many times sunderlye (separately) talked with almost all such, except the dead man himself, as most knew of the matter."

He was not only in a position to know the facts, but to form a balanced judgment upon them. He had a foot in both camps. He was intimate with the views and feelings of his fellow-citizens ; and, as a devoted layman, he would be impatient of unjust aspersions upon the clergy, and intolerant of any frivolous or malicious charge against so important a person as the Bishop's Chancellor.

In the years between 1514 and 1528 he had gone fast and far. He had won fame as a creative writer, the author of ' Utopia.' He had been knighted, and had served as Speaker of the Commons in the one Parliament, of 1523, that met between 1515 and 1529. He had held office as Under Treasurer, and as High Steward of the Universities of Oxford and Cambridge. In the inner circle of the royal Council, he was in close and constant attendance upon the King. In 1528 he was Chancellor of the Duchy of Lancaster, and within a year or so of succeeding Wolsey as Lord Chancellor of England. And every spare moment he was giving to apologetic writing, commissioned therefor by his friend and Bishop, Cuthbert Tunstall, who had succeeded Fitzjames in 1521. To this congenial work he brought all his learning, wisdom, wit and forensic skill. To the maintenance of the Faith he gave all his heart. In defence of the current ecclesiasticism he said what he could, vindicating its ideal, but, as we have seen in a previous chapter, with no great care to conceal what he felt about its squalid actuality. In the course of his task, he has to satisfy the minds of his readers about the vexed question of the fate of Richard Hunne, the old tragedy of fourteen years ago. He is here on difficult ground. He was convinced himself that Hunne had been a guilty heretic ; but he was in daily contact with many who held, unshakeably, the contrary conviction, and believed that Hunne was an innocent man who had had little justice in life and none at all in death. On the other hand, More had to argue to a brief, the brief given him by the Attorney-General when he withdrew the case from trial fourteen years before. A man was innocent until he was found guilty ; and the Crown, for reasons of its own, had seen to it that the chancellor was not found guilty, not allowing the case to go to trial. Horsey, therefore, was officially innocent ; and More, if he dealt with the matter at all, had to argue for the proposition that the charge against him was at any rate not proven.

Which is all he does.

The first thing to observe about More's treatment of the affair is that it is markedly different from that of Fitzjames, the impetuous old prelate whose precipitancy had occasioned the whole trouble. Fitzjames had declared roundly in Parliament that the Jury were " false perjured caitiffs." More does not say that. He says he took them to be " right honest men," who found their verdict according to their consciences. Fitzjames told the Lords that " Richard Hunne hanged himself, and that it was his own deed, and no man's else." More again does not say that. All he says is that it is more likely that he killed himself than that the chancellor killed him. And this presumption of probability he bases upon two grounds, one of which has been referred to already. It is that if Horsey " hated " Hunne, he would not, having evidence enough against him to ensure his undoing, have gone out of his way to kill him. But, in fact, neither the circumstances nor the evidence were such as to put Hunne in peril of his life ; and there was no question of Horsey " hating " Hunne ; there would be more excuse for him if there had been.

More's only other argument for the probability of suicide is best stated in his own words :

" Considering that Hunne was — as they that well know him say he was indeed — though he were a fair dealer among his neighbours, yet a man high-minded and set on the glory of a victory which he hoped to have in the praemunire, whereof he much boasted, as they said, among his familiar friends that he trusted to be spoken of long after his days and have his matter in the years and terms called Hunne's case. Which, when he perceived would go against his purpose, and that in the temporal law he should not win his spurs, and over that in the spiritual law perceived so much of his secret sores unwrapped and discovered that he began to fall in fear of worldly shame, it is to me much more likely that, for weariness of his life, he rid himself out thereof — which manner of affection we see not seldom happen, specially since the devil might peradventure join therewith a marvellous hope, of the which after happed, that the suspicion of his death might be laid to the charge and peril of the chancellor."

More here represents Hunne as a disappointed and desperate man, who was likely enough to do away with himself. The argument appears plausible until we look at it twice. No doubt, from the evidence given at the Inquest, a last-moment attempt was made, by semi-starvation and maltreatment, to drive the prisoner to desperation ; but there is nothing to show that the attempt had yet succeeded. Not long before Hunne's death the gaoler Spalding re-entered his cell, for the sixth time that fatal Sunday, in order to recover his knife. If Hunne had momentarily thought about the knife, he had thought better of it. Spalding found him " saying of his beads," not the behaviour of a man who is immediately contemplating the crime of suicide. And as to More's charitable surmise about the Devil, one knows not what to say of it. For consider what it means. A man, driven in desperation to suicide, calmly plans to stage a murder — of himself by others — and to manage the business of suicide so clumsily as to persuade a jury that his death was the work of bungling murderers. It is not in nature. Under the circumstances, one does not see how the Devil can have put such a suggestion into the mind of Hunne, or how anyone but the Devil, who can sometimes get within a good man's guard, can have put it into the mind of More.

And these two arguments, if the reader will believe it, are all in the way of real argument in the course of his lengthy fifteenth chapter. The chapter, as printed, extends to ten quarto pages, containing 423 lines. In the 24 lines of the concluding paragraph More states, quite clearly, his reason for believing Hunne to have been a guilty heretic. The other 399 lines, with the exception of one long paragraph of 55 lines, are concerned with the circumstances of Hunne's demise. In the course of them More states his own opinion ("I could never think it") that the Jury were mistaken in finding Horsey guilty of murder. But never by a single word does he betray his own belief, if he allowed himself to have one, as to how Hunne died. It would have been quite like More to disclaim having any personal belief at all, and to declare, with a quiet smile, that it was the business of the Jury or the Privy Council or the Attorney-General, but none of his. With a man destined to eminence in Tudor times such finesse had to become a habit if he was to be sure of keeping his head upon his shoulders. More was a master of it, and give a supreme example of it in his handling of the issue of the Supremacy when himself imprisoned in the Tower. There was nothing disingenuous about it. A wise man has no call, needlessly, to put himself in trouble, alienate his friends, or throw away his life. Murder or suicide, More leaves the question open. "Some shall think one way and some another." He urges the probability of suicide ; but the possibility of murder is not excluded, since there were "the other." By "the other" More refers, of course, to Charles Joseph and John Spalding, who were arraigned along with Horsey. More does not mention these worthies, or discuss their guilt or innocence. And, but for this one passing reference to "the other," we should not have known that any others were concerned in the affair besides the chancellor. It shows how little More chose to tell his readers of what he really knew. He has, however, to leave them with the impression that he has really told them something, and he does so in characteristic fashion.

In May, 1515, More left England on a diplomatic mission to Flanders. He was abroad for six months, during which his mind turned from the sombre shadows of the Lollards' Tower towards the golden dreams of his coming ' Utopia.' Before his departure, probably some time in March or April, he attended — as he implies, though he does not say so — an important meeting of some sort of commission of the Privy Council, held, no doubt, in response to Fitzjames' appeal for Wolsey's intervention. The preparations for this session were quite impressive. The " matter " (of Hunne and the chancellor) " was many times in sundry places examined."

" But specially," More proceeds, " at Baynard's Castle one day was it examined at great length and by a long time, every man being sent for before, and ready there, all that could be found that anything could tell, or that had said they could anything tell in the matter. And this examination was had before divers great lords spiritual and temporal, and other of the King's honourable council, sent thither by his highness for the nonce of his blessed zeal and princely desire borne to the searching of the truth."

This leads us to expect something of consequence to follow. What follows, and occupies no less than two-fifths of More's whole chapter, is a narrative of three episodes, comic interludes, each more farcical than the other. More makes his interlocutor advert to three items of idle talk, such as gather round such cases. He proceeds to dramatise these items of silly gossip, to clothe them with flesh and blood, gown and bonnet, and to present them to the Commission in the guise of witnesses. But witnesses like them were never on sea or land. They are obvious pantaloons, figures of fun, Aunt Sallies put up to be bowled down by volleys of raillery and ridicule. They are there to represent to the reader the complete frivolity of the matter which had brought suspicion upon the chancellor. They look as if the great lords temporal who presided had instructed their family fools to dress up, attend, make game of the proceedings, and offer themselves as butts for the judicial humour. They have no more semblance to life than puppets perched upon a ventriloquist's knees while their only creator, with grave face and immobile mouth and practised fingers manipulating the strings, makes them gesticulate and jabber absurdly to one another. And their only creator, it is charitable to suppose, was More himself. If such blithering personages had really been brought before the Commission, and allowed to occupy its time in the same proportion as they occupy of the pages of More, we could only conclude that these great lords spiritual and temporal and the rest were themselves parties to a barefaced attempt to simulate a serious inquiry, to throw dust in the eyes of the public, and to deflect the course of justice. Their purpose, no doubt, was to deflect the course of justice by bringing pressure upon the Coroner's Jury and inducing them to unsay their verdict. But their time, it may be presumed, was far too valuable to allow them to waste almost their whole session upon unsubstantial persons of this kind. It is better to suppose that More, by a variant of the old device of abusing the plaintiff's attorney, is ridiculing the plaintiff's witnessess, or the figures of burlesque whom he brings forward as witnesses. From his youth in Cardinal Morton's household he had been famed for his gift of merry make-believe. He saw no harm in it on suitable occasions, and even on occasions like this which were not so suitable. In a letter written to Erasmus little more than a year after Hunne's death, he says his friend knows he is " not so superstitiously truthful as to shrink from a little fib as if it were parricide." (R. W. Chambers, ' Thomas More,' pp. 119 - 20). More did not expect the few wise to take his fooling seriously, and it was well enough for the many who were not so wise. With his subtle mind and sensitive conscience, he was able to keep his balance on the tightrope of truth without ever coming down upon the wrong side of it. It was his way to turn the awkward corners of life — and death — with a pleasant jest ; and his gift of persiflage came in useful when he had to argue, as best he could, an almost impossible case. At the same time, a writer who entertains the reverence which an ordinary mortal must feel for More, cannot reproduce the passages which follow without some little compunction. These colloquies would be more amusing if one could forget their subject-matter. Even when an apologist is put to hard shifts, capering over a dead man's fate and memory is not very edifying. But if More, like other wits, was sometimes possibly lacking in taste, he was never lacking in sense ; and it is certain that these colloquies would never have been written if he had had the least prevision that the facts he was so careful to conceal, the facts produced at the Coroner's Inquest, would see the light within a very few years. More, in 1528, would have no such apprehension. The authorities had suppressed the case against Horsey ; and would see to it that the law which forbade the publication of the records of Inquests was not infringed. More could therefore write to satisfy the minds of people who could have no sure knowledge of the facts, nor were ever likely to have it. If their minds could be satisfied by tickling their ears, it was, from the point of view of a humourist and apologist hard-pressed for better matter, a salutary and pious work. Unfortunately these flights of Morian humour have been taken seriously by grave and eminent writers who have discussed them solemnly as a contribution to knowledge. It is solely for that reason that it is necessary to place them before the reader, in order that he may see for himself how irrelevant and, set beside the facts he knows already, even cheap they are.

Speaking of these colloquies a recent writer, not unperspicacious, has said that " after all we are getting, if not at the murderer of Hunne, at least at the table-talk of More." (Algernon Cecil, ' Thomas More,' p. 89). Let them be read then as examples of the table-talk of More, and of the art of telling nothing in several thousand words.

Episode 1.

" First, ye must understand, that because the coming together of the Lords from Greenwich to Baynardes castell for the trying out of the matter should not be frustrate, there was such diligence done before, that every man that aught had said therein was ready there against their coming. Where they began with the first point that ye spake of, as the special motion whereupon the kynges highness had sent them thither. Wherefore, after the rehearsal made of the cause of their coming, the greatest temporal Lord there present said unto a certain servant of his own standing there beside, " Sir, ye told me that one showed you that he could go take him by the sleeve that killed Hunne. Have ye brought him hither ? "

" Sir," quod he, " if it like your lordship, this man it was that told me so," pointing to one that he had caused to come thither. Then my lord asked that man,

" How say ye sir, can ye do as ye said ye could ? "

" Forsooth my Lord," quod he, " and it like your Lordship, I said

D   97 not so much, this gentleman did somewhat mistake me. But indeed I told him that I had a neighbour that told me he could do it."

" Where is that neighbour ? " quod my Lord.

" This man, sir," quod he, " bringeth (bringing ?) forth one which had also been warned to be there. Then was he asked whether he had said that he could do it.

" Nay, forsooth," quod he, " my Lord, I said not that I could do it myself ; but I said that one told me that he could do it."

" Well," quod my Lord, " who told you so ? "

" Forsooth, my Lord," quod he, " my neighbour here." Then was that man asked,

" Sir, know you one that can tell who killed Richard Hunne ?"

" Forsooth," quod he, " and it like your Lordship, I said not that I knew one surely that could tell who had killed him ; but I said indeed that I know one which I thought verily could tell who killed him."

" Well," quod the Lords at the last, " yet with much work we come to somewhat. But whereby think you that he can tell ? "

" Nay, forsooth, my Lord," quod he, " it is a woman, I would she were here with your Lordships now."

" Well," quod my Lord, " woman or man, all is one, she shall be had wheresoever she be."

" By my faith my Lords," quod he, " and she were with you, she would tell you wonders. For, by God, I have wist her to tell many marvellous things ere now."

" Why," quod the Lords, " what have you heard her told " (tell ?)

" Forsooth, my Lords," quod he, " if a thing had been stolen, she would have told who had it. And therefore I think she could as well tell who killed Hunne, as who stole a horse."

" Surely," said the Lords, " so think all we too, I trow. But how could she tell it, by the devil ? "

" Nay, by my truth, I trow," quod he, " for I could never see her use any worse way than looking in one's hand." Therewith the Lords laughed and asked,

" What is she ? "

" Forsooth, my Lords," quod he, " an Egyptian, and she was lodged here in Lambeth, but she is gone over sea now. Howbeit, I trow, she be not in her own country yet : for they say it is a great way hence, and she went over little more than a month ago."

Now, forsooth, quod your friend (More's interlocutor), this process came to a wise purpose, here was a great post well whittled to a pudding prick. But I pray you to what point came the second matter of him that had been in office under so many of the king's almoners that he knew by his own experience and proved that Richard Hunne had not hanged himself.

Episode 2.

Forsooth, quod I, he was called in next. And then was he asked whereby he knew it. But would God ye had seen his countenance. The man had of likelihood said somewhat too far, and was much amazed and looked as though his eyes would have fallen out of his head into the Lords' laps. But to the question he answered and said that he saw that very well ; for he saw him both ere he was taken down and after.

" What then ? " quod the Lords, " so did there many more which yet upon the sight could not tell that."

" No, my Lords, "quod he, " but I have another insight in such things than other men have."

" What insight ? " quod they.

" Forsooth," quod he, " it is not unknowen that I have occupied a great while under divers of the king's almoners, and have seen and considered many that have hanged themself, and thereby if I see one hang, I can tell anon whether he hanged himself or not."

" By what token can you tell ? " quod the Lords.

" Forsooth," quod he, " I cannot tell the tokens but I perceive it well enough by mine own sight."

But when they heard him speak of his own sight, and therewith saw what sight he had, looking as though his eyes would have fallen into their laps, there could few forbear laughing, and said,

" We see well surely that ye have a sight by yourself." And then said one lord merrily,

" Peradventure as some man is so cunning by experience of

99

jewels that he can perceive by his own eye whether a stone be right or counterfeit though he cannot well make another man to perceive the tokens ; so this good fellow, though he cannot tell us the marks, yet he hath such an experience in hanging that himself perceiveth upon the sight whether the man hanged himself or no."

" Yea, forsooth, my Lord," quod he, " even as your Lordship saith. For I know it well enough myself. I have seen so many by reason of my office."

" Why," quod another Lord merrily, " your office hath no more experience in hanging than hath an hangman : And yet he cannot tell."

" Nay, sir," quod he, " and it like your lordship, he meddleth not with them that hang themself as I do."

" Well," quod one of the Lords, " how many of them have ye meddled with in your days ? "

" With many, my lord," quod he ; for I have been officer under two almoners, and therefore I have seen many."

" How many ? " quod one of the lords.

" I cannot tell," quod he, " how many : but I wot well I have seen many."

" Have ye seen," quod one, " an hundred ? "

" Nay," quod he, " not an hundred."

" Have ye seen four score and ten ? "

Thereat a little he studied as one standing in a doubt, and that were loth to lie ; and at last he said that he thought nay, not fully four score and ten. Then was he asked whether he had seen twenty. And thereto without any sticking, he answered, " Nay, not twenty." Thereat the lords laughed well to see that he was so sure that he had not seen twenty, and was in doubt whether he had seen four score and ten. Then was he asked whether he had seen fifteen. And thereto he answered shortly, " nay." And in likewise of ten. And at last they came to five, and from five to four. And there he began to study again. Then came they to three ; and then, for shame, he was fain to say that he had seen so many and more too. But when he was asked, when, whom, and in what place, necessity drave him at last unto the truth, whereby it appeared that he never had seen but one in all his life. And that was an Irish fellow called Crookshanke, whom he had seen hanging in an old barn. And when all his cunning was come to this, he was bid walk like himself. And one said unto him that because he was not yet cunning enough in the craft of hanging : it was pity that he had no more experience thereof by one more.

Episode 3.

This episode — about the conflict of memory, and wits, between the " good worshipful " layman and the spiritual man who " was a man of worship also," — and the truth about the issue between them, has been fully given and examined above on pp. 28 - 30, to which one need do no more than refer the reader.

Passing from these patent absurdities, narrated at length, to the serious business of this important session, More disposes of it all in exactly thirty-one words, as follows :

" Of truth many other things were laid that, upon the hearing, seemed much more suspicious than these. Which yet when they were answered, always lost more than half their strength." Could there be a plainer demonstration of More's intention to tell his readers nothing ? Of these " much more suspicious " things he says nothing, not one word.

More himself, by the way, in an aside of apologetic candour, calls these episodes " trifles." Writing in 1528, he could not have imagined that, four centuries thence, the fate of Hunne would be still in debate, and that his sallies of evasive fun would be taken more or less for history by painstaking historians less impish than himself.

But why does More say nothing ? This raises the question of which More is so studious to withhold the answer, his own belief, if prudence permitted him to have one, as to how Hunne died. Be it remembered that with More there was a mile-wide difference between opinion and belief. Opinion might be right or wrong, and it might not matter either way. But belief was an affair of conscience, and had to be right, if a man's knowledge and judgment could make it so. If his argument for the probability of suicide was more than an opinion, an advocate's ' submission,' if he believed that Hunne had taken his own life, why could he not say so ?* What was there in his brief to prevent him saying so ? What need, indeed, of any brief at all ? If he believed that Hunne was guilty of his own death, what need to argue for the probability of Horsey being guiltless of it ? More says nothing because he could not get away from the sworn evidence. He might ignore it on paper, but he could not ignore it in his mind and conscience. The only thing to do, on paper, was to say nothing about it.

Whatever More's belief about the manner of Hunne's death, " there would no wise man, that good were, have any great doubt," after the evidence given in the Lady Chapel of St. Paul's, that he had been a guilty heretic. That was More's own undoubted belief ; and in his argument from probability, such as it is, there is imbedded a paragraph (the 55 lines above-mentioned, p. 94) which bears upon that belief, and calls for some examination. It relates to certain later disclosures to which More attached significance as confirming his belief.

" It happed that, as I remember, six or seven years after that Hunne was thus hanged, and his body burned for an heretic, there was one in Essex, a carpenter that used to make pumps, which had intended with other such as he was himself to do great robbery ; and, thereupon, was he brought into the court, where, by the commandment of the king's grace, a great honourable estate of this realm, and myself, had him in examination. Wherein, among other things, he confessed that he had long holden divers heresies which he said that his brother, being a clerk of a church, had taught both his father and him. And I promise you those heresies were of an

---

* He does say so in one sentence of his ' Supplication of Souls ' (English Works', 1557, p. 298) : " The fourth (loud lie) is that Doctor Horsey and his complices murdered him in prison ; for thereof is the contrary well known, and that the man hanged himself for despair, despite, and lack of grace." Here More is merely echoing Fitzjames, who had declared in the House of Lords that " Richard Hunne hanged himself, and that it was his own deed, and no man else's." (See p. 92). This sort of argument More, no doubt, thought good enough for Simon Fish, whose ' Supplication of Beggars ' he is attacking. For real argument, such as it is, we have to look to the ' Dialogue,' written under calmer circumstances the year before. The ' Supplication of Souls,' in the passages that concern Fish, is not much more than a competitive essay in asseveration and vituperation, by no means More at his best.

height. Then he showed us what other cunning masters of that
school he had heard read, and specially in a place which he named
us in London, where, he said, that such heretics were wont to resort
to their readings in a chamber at midnight. And when we asked
him the names of them that were wont to haunt those midnight
lectures, he rehearsed us divers. And among other he named
Richard Hunne. Whereof we somewhat marvelled in our minds,
but nothing said we thereto, but let him rehearse on all such as he
could call to mind. And when he stopped and could remember no
more, then asked we of them that he had named what they were and
where they dwelled. And he told us of some of them that were
convicted, and some that were fled, and some that were yet at that
time dwelling still in the town. And in the way, when we asked
him what man was that Hunne that he spake of, he told us his
person and his house. " And where is he now ? " said we. " Mary,"
quod he, " I went to Tournai ; and when I came thence again, then
heard I say that he was hanged in the Lollards' Tower, and his body
burned for an heretic." And thus there learned we, long after, that
Hunne had haunted heretics' lectures by night long before, which
we declared unto the king's highness as he had confessed. And his
highness, though he was sorry that any man should be so lewd, yet
highly did rejoice that the goodness of God brought such hid
mischief more and more to light. So after had we, by the king's
commandment, that man's brother in examination ; which did
indeed confess nothing, neither of the felonies nor of the heresies.
But yet his brother did abide by them, and avowed them in his face,
with such marks and tokens as it might well appear that he said
truth. And surely marvel were it if he would falsely have feigned
such heinous things against his own brother, his own father, and
himself, being thereto nothing compelled nor put either in pain or
fear. Now was the father dead, and other could we not come by,
whom we might further examine of that night school, saving that
he, which as I told you confessed this matter, showed us also at the
first time of one man in London taken for good and honest, which
was, as he said, a scholar also of his brother's in those heresies.
Which man for his honesty we forbare to meddle with till we should

have the other brother. Whom as soon as we had in hands, and that he was committed to the Marshalsea, this other man, which was, as I told you, detected unto us for an heretic and a scholar of his, came to me to labour and sue for him, pretending that he did it for charity. And forasmuch as we thought we could not fail of him when we would have him, we forbare therefore to examine him till we should have examined the other whom he laboured for. But then were we not aware in what wise we should be disappointed of him. For so mishapped it indeed that after his being at me to labour for him whose scholar in heresy he was detected to be, he was in his own house suddenly stricken and slain. And that wretched end had he. What conscience he died with, God knoweth, for I can tell you no further."

Nobody seems to have looked at this story at all closely ; but the more one does so, the queerer it becomes. This carpenter in Essex who made pumps is taken up for some offence not clearly defined, for having " intended with other such as he was himself to do great robbery." His offence, so far as we can make it out, was ' loitering with intent,' an ordinary Police Court matter, if police courts had existed in those days. Yet, " by commandment of the king's grace " no less, he is brought before an extraordinary tribunal, as if he had been a Buckingham, a great noble of the blood royal accused of high treason. He meets the secular charge against him, whatever it was, by deadly charges of heresy against himself, his father and his brother. What, if his mind were not deranged, could he possibly expect to gain by that ? He charged his brother, " a clerk of a church," with having conducted a " night school " for heretics in London, attended among others by Richard Hunne. This felonious carpenter " in Essex " is a mine of information about it. He gives, so it is said, the names, occupations and addresses of others who attended. Some of these persons had neither fled nor been convicted, but were " yet at that time dwelling still in the town." But none of them, singularly enough, could ever be " come by." The story, at this point, wears particularly thin. There was no householder in London who could not be " come by " if the authorities chose to lay their hands upon him. The allegation about the " night school " was steadily denied by the man's brother, and there is nothing to show that the denial was ever shaken, in the Marshalsea or outside it. How could a clerk of a church keep such a night school for any time without it becoming known to his neighbours and to the authorities ? How could he elude the vigilance of the Bishop's sumners ? Foxe searched Fitzjames' Register, and found not a trace of any of this, no proceedings or convictions of any sort. One of the people who could not be " come by " turned up himself, in order to say a good word for the imprisoned brother. Unfortunately, and notwithstanding his being so " good and honest," " he was in his own house suddenly stricken and slain. And that wretched end had he," before he could be examined. In fact, the carpenter's story remained uncorroborated at any point. The case does not appear to have been pursued to any conclusion. The father was dead, but of what became of the man or of his brother we hear nothing.

The following, for what it may be worth, is a conjectural reconstruction of this curious case.

It is an unhappy, but not an uncommon, experience that men who are not too strong in the head and are called up for military service, become badly unstuck as to their wits. I have known, intimately, two such cases, one in the last war and one in this ; such misadventures must be familiar enough to the medical authorities of the Army. Again it is a common experience for the mentally unstable to become obsessed by a " sensational " ' cause célèbre.'

This Essex carpenter who made pumps was with the then B.E.F. in Flanders in 1513, when Henry VIII crowned a successful expedition by the capture of Tournai. He remained with the English garrison of Tournai till shortly after the time of Hunne's death, returning to England with his mind seriously affected. From his station and his foreign service, it is unlikely that he can have known anything of Hunne or his habits. But the town was still full of the grim tragedy ; and his errant wits may have been switched in the direction of heresy by brooding morbidly over what he heard. He may have hung curiously about the Lollards' Tower, and stood gaping at Hunne's house near London Bridge, picking up enough about Hunne to impress More and a court some "six or seven years after." Heresy and heretics became the bee in his particular bonnet ; and when, some years later, he got into bad company and the hands of the law, he babbled largely of heretics and heresy, giving himself consequence as a holder of secrets. More, who at this time was a sleuth for heresy, got wind of him ; and, scenting important disclosures, convened an extraordinary tribunal to go into the case. The carpenter, finding himself in distinguished company, played up to the presence by scattering imputations of heresy right and left. He accused his dead father, his brother, and himself, with sundry others, none of whom, with possibly one exception, could ever be traced or "come by." The brother, the only other person ever examined, stoutly and steadily denied the whole thing. The sequel of the case, well, it had no sequel, so far as we are told. It appears to have fizzled out, the court concluding that the man was crazy, and that Master More, for once, had got hold of a mare's nest.

In fact, the only significant thing about this case is the significance it clearly had for More. Why does he seize so avidly upon the mention of Hunne's name as a belated confirmation of his belief that the man had been a guilty heretic ? More was a man of acute mind and scrupulous conscience. Was there some instinctive disquiet in the bottom of his mind that made him welcome the carpenter's revelations ? Was his relief at hearing them such as to obscure his sense of evidence ? Himself believing in Hunne's guilt, he had been exposed for years to a steady barrage of contrary conviction. A busy man, his mind can only have reverted to the case occasionally ; but when it did, some uneasy thoughts may have forced themselves upon it. Fitzjames and the others had declared roundly that Hunne "hanged himself, and that it was his own deed, and no man's else." More knew that that was going far beyond the certain truth. Had these same men been careful to keep within the truth in what they solemnly averred about Hunne in the Lady Chapel of St. Paul's ? True, More had seen them produce his Bible, and heard their precise and damning description of it. But why had that Bible not appeared before ? And where was it now ? Why all the mystery about it ? Why could he not learn whether it had been burnt with Hunne's body, or " secretly kept." And if the latter, why, in view of " so much suspicious rumour thereof," would the clergy not produce it ?

It is not to be supposed that More allowed his mind to harbour or dwell upon such questions. It would be too horrible to think that there was anything in them. It would have turned his whole being cold to think that Hunne had been the victim of a miscarriage of justice, more wicked than any crime alleged against himself. And yet, and yet ——— ?

This chapter may conclude by noticing More's reference to a popular notion that Horsey had sued for and obtained the royal pardon. The fact was different, though not very different in effect. More makes his interlocutor say :

" But I think verily for all this, there was great evidence given against the chancellor, for he was at length indited of Hunne's death, and was a great while in prison and, in conclusion, never durst abide the trial of twelve men for his acquittal but was fain by friendship to get a pardon. . . . . If he had not been guilty, he would never have sued his pardon."

" Yes," More replies, " right wise men have I heard say, ere this, that they will never refuse neither God's pardon nor the king's. It were no wisdom in a matter of many suspicious tales, be they never so false, to stand on twelve men's mouths where one may find a surer way." Surely a remarkable sentiment for a magistrate who, at the time of the event, was Under Sheriff of London, and, at the time of writing, soon to be Lord Chancellor of England. In the manner of a finished courtier — but with the mental reserves of a royal favourite who could tell " son Roper " that if his head could win Henry a castle in France, it should not fail to go, — More proceeds :

" For albeit there was never, I trow, brought in this world a prince of more benign nature " — Henry at the time was twenty-four — " nor of more merciful mind, than is our sovereign lord that now reigneth, and long mought reign upon us, whereby never king could find in his heart more freely to forgive and forget offences done and committed unto himself : yet hath his highness such a fervent affection to right and justice in other men's causes, and such a tender zeal to the conservation of his subjects — of whose lives his high wisdom considereth many to stand in peril by the giving of pardon to a few wilful murderers — that never was there king, I believe, that ever ware the crown of this realm, which hath in so many years given unto such folk so few (pardons). And therefore I make myself sure that in such a wilful purpensed heinous cruel deed as this had been if it had been true, all the friends that could have been founden for the chancellor in this world could never have gotten his pardon to pass in such wise, had it not been, that, upon the report of all the circumstances, the king's high prudence — which, without flattery, pierceth as deep into the bottom of a doubtful matter as ever I saw man in my life — had well perceived his innocency. And since I believe verily that if he had been guilty he never could have gotten in such an heinous murder any pardon of the king's highness, I dare make myself much more bold of his innocency now. For ye shall understand that he never sued pardon therefor ; but after long examination of the matter, as well the chancellor as the other, being indited of the deed, and arraigned upon the inditement in the king's bench, pleaded that they were not guilty. And thereupon the king's grace being well and sufficiently informed of the truth, and of his blessed disposition not willing that there should in his name any false matter be maintained, gave in commandment to his attorney to confess their pleas to be true without any further trouble."

The pith of this ceremonious passage lies in its four concluding words. What further trouble, we may ask ? Judicial trouble ? Obviously not. The case had been dragging on for over a year ; and it would have required but a few hours for a Judge to hear the evidence, point out its weaknesses, and instruct the Jury that they must give the three accused the benefit of any doubt. That done, Horsey would resume his duties as chancellor to the Bishop amid general sympathy ; Spalding would go back to his bellringing with a big tale to tell ; and Joseph, " celebrating," would have " sent for neighbours and made good cheer " in Baude Barington's house at Neckhill. But a surer way than standing on twelve men's mouths had to be found if, as was only too likely, the Assize Jury, with the sworn evidence before them, should see no choice but to endorse the verdict of the twenty-four jurymen of Coroner Barnwell's inquest. In that case there would be " further trouble " indeed. Spalding and Joseph would cause no further trouble, being duly hanged ; but Horsey would live on notorious as a clerk convict in perpetual custody ; there would remain an indelible blot upon the Church's justice ; the credit of the clerical order would receive another grievous blow ; the relations between the spiritualty and temporalty, already strained, might go from bad to worse ; and there was no telling what further trouble might ensue. Already the affair had occasioned an unconscionable amount of trouble. It had consumed no little of the time of the Parliament of 1515, summoned for quite other purposes. Bills had been introduced to restore to Hunne's children their father's property, forfeit to the Crown as that of a condemned heretic. There had been acrimonious debates about the integrity of the Jury, whom Fitzjames had denounced in the Upper House as " false perjured caitiffs." At Paul's Cross, in Convocation, and in the Privy Council, old and vexed questions about jurisdiction had sprung again into life, and brought the prelates and the King's Judges to open loggerheads. Wolsey himself had had to go down upon his knees before the King in order to patch up some sort of accommodation. By that splendid designate of fortune, who had no time to waste in his progress towards supreme power, the whole affair must have been regarded with vehement impatience. No sooner was Horsey released than Wolsey marked his displeasure by mulcting him to the tune of, in our money, some thousands of pounds, a quite arbitrary proceeding, but no more arbitrary than all the rest. Horsey had to compound, not of course for a felony, of which he was officially innocent, but for having been a first-rate public nuisance. He was further directed to wind up his affairs and put half a dozen counties between himself and London. More must have known these things ; but does not explain how they consisted with Horsey's innocence, or with his own laudation of the King's zeal for justice. More, a politician himself, was well enough aware of the strong political reasons for abandoning the case, for all his suave asseverations that it was abandoned upon its merits. More's opinion of the merits is clearly stated. " As for myself, in good faith, as I told you before, I never heard in my life — and yet have I heard all I ween that well could be said therein — any thing that moved me, after both the parties heard, to think that he (Horsey) should be guilty." That is an opinion, and we must take it as given. To More, in fact, the manner of Hunne's death was of no great concern ; some might " think one way and some another." What concerned him was that Hunne, a guilty heretic, was dead, and no longer able to infect the faithful. But his comparative unconcern as to the manner of Hunne's death depended upon his belief, no mere opinion, that the man had been a guilty heretic. And we may observe the difference in More's language when he is not merely expressing an opinion, but affirming a belief.

" Myself was present in Poules when the bishop, in the presence of the Mayor and the aldermen of the city, condemned him for an heretic after his death. And then were there read openly the depositions by which it was well proved that he was convict as well of divers other heresies as of misbelief toward the holy sacrament of the altar. And thereupon was the judgment given that his body should be burned, and so was it. Now this is to me a full proof."

In the following chapter we shall endeavour to see what, in fact, that " full proof " was worth.

NOTE TO CHAPTERS V AND VI
ON Dr. GAIRDNER'S TREATMENT OF THE CASE

Without detracting in any way from the debt which all students of the period owe to Dr. Gairdner, it may be permissible to point out some matters in which his treatment of the case is open to criticism. It is really necessary to do so, because his ' The English Church in the Sixteenth Century from the accession of HENRY VIII to the death of MARY ' has been a text-book in Theological Colleges and elsewhere for nearly half a century, and from it, no doubt, most of the present-day clergy have derived their views of these events.

Dr. Gairdner examines the case in chapters 3 and 4, pp. 25 - 50.

Dr. Gairdner's Treatment of the Case

1. He does not appear to be aware of the existence of the booklet, published about 1537 and containing the justificatory statement of the jury, which Hall incorporated in his Chronicle.

2. He speaks twice over (pp. 36 and 38) of " the discredited inquest " ; but his only ground for discrediting the inquest is that the record includes depositions obviously later than Dec. 5th and 6th. But, writes Dr. Pollard, (' Wolsey', pp. 35 - 6, n. 3) " nearly all the difficulties which Gairdner found so puzzling . . . arise from his assumption that the proceedings of the coroner's jury were necessarily completed on 5 - 6 Dec. when it was empanelled and viewed the body . . . The essential date . . . which is given in their records, is, like the date of acts of Parliament, the commencement of the proceedings, because the value of the evidence depends thereon . . . Hunne's case was one of peculiar difficulty, and the detailed account, published about 1537 . . . shows that the coroner's jury was still seeking evidence and taking depositions late in Feb., 1515."

Keilwey, too, on whom Dr. Gairdner relies in his 4th chapter, speaks expressly of an interval " between the time that the said Inquest was charged on view of the body of the said Hunne and before the said verdict (see below p. 148).

3. Dr. Gairdner speaks twice over (pp. 31 and 40) of " the sumner's extorted confession." But it is only Bishop Fitzjames, in his letter of appeal to Wolsey, who affirms that the confession was obtained by " pain and durance," and on this again Dr. Pollard writes (ibid. p. 38, n. 2) " The bishop was not present at Joseph's examination. Four of the coroner's jury, whose names are given ' with many others ' who were on oath and appointed to be present, testified that Joseph's evidence was given ' of his own free will and unconstrained.' Gairdner accepts the bishop's word against the jury ; but this involves a charge against the constable of the Tower and the king's counsel who examined Joseph as well as against the coroner's jury."

4. That the jury, Dr. Gairdner says, " had no notion of weighing evidences may be surmised even from one or two points in their finding — as, for instance, that about the stool on which Hunne could not possibly have balanced himself in order to hang himself. — It must have been still more difficult, one would think, for murderers by the aid of that " tickle " stool to hoist a dead body into such a position than it could have been for the living man to hang himself" (pp. 31 - 2). But the learned critic, might be the rude reply, had no more notion of reading evidences than, as he says, had the jury of weighing them ; for it is he alone who suggests the possible use of the stool in connection with the hoisting up of the body. How two men, with the body of a third between them, could make use of one stool, whether " tickle " or otherwise, in order to hoist it up, does not appear. Joseph's confession simply said, " and then John bellringer and I Charles did heave up Hunne, and master chancellor pulled the girdle over the staple, and so Hunne was hanged " (above p. 75).

5. Conceding that " Hall's ' Chronicle ' is, for the reign of Henry VIII, quite an invaluable source of information, being, in fact, a careful, orderly, and, in most things, a very accurate record of events," Dr. Gairdner adds : " But we must be on our guard against the author's bias, for his unfairness on some particular subjects goes the length of positive dishonesty " . . . " of his spite against ecclesiatical authority there is no doubt, and so good an opportunity did he find for gratifying it in connection with the death of Hunne, that he is not satisfied without devoting ten closely printed pages of his history to what professes to be a verbatim report of ' the whole inquiry and verdict of the inquest ' (p. 27). — This, however, (p. 29) " contains a large number of depositions and other documents, some of which are distinctly of later date than the inquest itself, and to embody them in what professes to be a verbatim report of that finding was a thing which admits of no justification." This would appear

to be put forward as an example of Hall's 'dishonesty'; but the imputation, if intended, rests upon nothing but Dr. Gairdner's mistaken assumption that the inquest ended on the dates given as those of its beginning.

6. Some statements on p. 30 appear to be involved and contradictory. "the verdict . . . accused by name Dr. Horsey, the Bishop of London's chancellor, Charles Joseph, his sumner, and John Spalding, bellringer, of wilful murder; and these persons were accordingly committed to prison. There Charles Joseph, 'by pain and durance,' was induced to accuse himself and the others." But all three were already in custody pending the verdict; and Joseph's confession was part of the material on which the verdict was based. "On this," Dr. Gairdner proceeds, "the Bishop of London (Richard Fitz-James) wrote to Wolsey, who had now become cardinal, begging his intercession, etc." But the verdict was returned towards the end of February, and Dr. Gairdner has said, sixteen lines earlier, that Wolsey "was only created cardinal in September."

7. In the opening of chapter 4, p. 41, we are told that " Hunne's case was almost immediately mixed up with another very important matter — the right of sanctuary "; but the rest of the chapter shows that the matter at issue was the immunity of clerks from secular jurisdiction, quite a different thing. The mention of sanctuary is no doubt a mere slip, but the following are points of substance.

8. On p. 43 Dr. Gairdner writes : " The question of the renewal of the act," — the temporary Benefit of Clergy Act of 1512 then expiring, — " came before Parliament again a year after Hunne's death, in the latter part of the year 1515. A bill with this object is mentioned in a list of agenda for the Lords on November 20th." But the question of the renewal of the Act, or the passing of a similar Act to take its place, had been before Parliament since February and March, and was the bone of contention throughout the two sessions. (See below, chap. VIII, and Appendix, pp. 162, 167-8).

9. In the earlier part of his chapter 4 Dr. Gairdner summarises Keilwey's report of the several conferences held in 1515 on the question of clerical immunity. On four occasions on which Keilwey lays stress upon the part, and sometimes the leading part, played in these conferences by members of the House of Commons, Dr. Gairdner ignores the Commons entirely, attributing all to " the Lords ", " the lay Lords ", " the Judges and Councillors spiritual and temporal " (pp. 44, 45 and 46). In one case, where the whole action was taken by members of the Commons, it is ascribed to the Lords (" After the lords had heard both sides ", etc. p. 44). The oversight here, together with that in the previous paragraph, means that the significance of these proceedings has been very largely missed.

10. Regarding the facts alleged by Hall as of little or no worth, Dr. Gairdner falls back upon the authority of Sir Thomas More. But his acceptance of More is quite uncritical ; and he gravely devotes three pages to quotation from the ridiculous stories with which More in the ' Dialogue ' endeavours to bemuse his readers. The fact may help to explain what might otherwise be puzzling, these curious passages of More. They go far to justify his faith as an inveterate humourist — " too much given to mocking," as Hall says — that one has only to make nonsense nonsensical enough and there will be no lack of judicious persons to embrace it as oracular.

Chapter VII

THE BIBLE 'SECRETLY KEPT'

More's fifteenth chapter has been examined at length in order to show how elusive and unsubstantial nearly all of it is. Those words, however, do not apply to its concluding paragraph, which is full of matter. In it More states unequivocally his belief, and his ground for the belief, that Hunne had been a guilty heretic.

" For surely at such time as he was denounced for an heretic, there lay his English bible open, and some other English books of his, that every man might see the places noted with his own hand, such words and in such wise, that there would no wise man, that good were, have any great doubt, after the sight thereof, what naughty minds the men had, both he that so noted them, and he that so made them. I remember not now the specialities of the matter, nor the formal words as they were written. But this I remember well, that besides other things, framed for the favour of divers other heresises, there were in the prologue of that bible such words touching the Blessed Sacrament as good Christian men did much abhor to hear, and which gave the readers undoubted occasion to think that book was written after Wiclif's copy, and by him translated into our tongue. And yet whether the book be burned, or secretly kept, I cannot surely say. But truly were the clergy of my mind, it should be somewhere reserved for the perpetual proof of the matter, (since) there hath gone so much suspicious rumour thereof. Which, as I believe, were all well answered, and the mind fully satisfied of any man, that were wise and good therewith, that once had overlooked, read, and advisedly considered that book."

The post mortem trial over Hunne's body in the Lady Chapel of St. Paul's has been already described on pp. 85 - 7 ; cf. 132 - 3. In this chapter an attempt will be made to follow the history of the English Bible that " there lay open " ; to account for its mysterious disappearance ; and to show that More, though of course he saw it, was not among those who had overlooked, read and advisedly considered it.

To do this I must ask the reader's indulgence for a brief excursion into autobiography.

Years ago, when prospecting in these fields, my attention was drawn to a certain adventurous thesis put forward in a then recent book, ' The Old English Bible,' by Dr. Francis Aidan Gasquet, afterwards Cardinal.

Dr. Gasquet maintained that the popular and learned tradition which, for five centuries, had ascribed the authorship of the first English Bible to Wyclif and his colleagues was wholly mistaken ; that any translation with which they might have been concerned had disappeared ; and that the versions printed as Wycliffite in the great edition of Messrs. Forshall and Madden in 1850 were none other than the " orthodox and authorised " versions of " our Catholic forefathers." Dr. Gasquet's summing-up is best given in his own words :

" I have no intention to deny that Wyclif MAY have had something to do with Biblical translations which we do not now possess. My concern is with the actual versions of the translated Scriptures now known to us. Two, and only two, such pre-Reformation vernacular versions are in existence. These have hitherto been ascribed unhesitatingly to Wyclif or his followers, and are known to all under the title of the Wycliffite Scriptures, as printed by Messrs. Forshall and Madden. It will be observed that the ascription of these translations to Wyclif is not based on positive testimony; but, when the case is looked into it really depends on the tacit assumption that there was no Catholic version at all. I desire, rather, to insist on this point, because to many it may seem more than strange that after the immense amount of labour that has been spent upon these manuscripts I should come forward with a theory that runs absolutely counter to the conclusions of many most learned and estimable men. But, if I mistake not, these same conclusions have been formed without any consideration of an alternative. Accordingly, no practical need has been felt by writers who have dealt with the subject to consider a number of facts, which in themselves constitute grave difficulties against the theory of the Wycliffite origin of these versions, and they have, in the circumstances naturally, perhaps, been allowed to lie dormant. But, as I have pointed out, there seems no possibility of denying the existence in pre-Reformation times of a Catholic and allowed version of the English Bible. At once, therefore, all these difficulties rise into life, and must be faced honestly if the truth is to be reached. For my own part, having looked into the matter with some care, I do not see how it is possible to come to any other conclusion than this : that the versions of the Sacred Scriptures, edited by Messrs. Forshall and Madden, and commonly known as Wycliffite, are in reality the Catholic versions of our pre-Reformation forefathers." (' The Old English Bible, pp. 154 - 5).

By certain previous work Dr. Gasquet had established a commanding reputation as an erudite, candid and disinterested scholar, albeit that his every word was directed towards persuading Englishmen that all that was done at the Reformation was a deplorable mistake. In his own field, that of mediaeval English church history, he seemed to bestride the learned world like a Colossus. His thesis, therefore, was received with the respect due to the eminence of the author ; and Sir F. G. Kenyon, for example, in his ' Our Bible and the Ancient Manuscripts,' pp. 204 - 8, discussed it with becoming gravity. Scholars who knew something of the subject at first hand were more than dubious ; but to a tyro like myself the argument, with its wealth of documentary references, seemed to enforce conviction. But I was interested in the matter and kept on reading round it, until it became plain that, by some strange mischance, Dr. Gasquet had completely overlooked — except for one quotation obviously at second-hand — the first document which an inquirer into the origin of these versions would have been at pains to study, the ' General Prologue ' prefixed by John Purvey to his revision of the books of the Old Testament. The passage in which Dr. Gasquet provided his own confutation is as follows :

" It is frequently asserted that all copies of the English Scriptures that fell into the hands of the ecclesiastical authorities were destroyed. Sir Thomas More says that "if this were done so, it were not well done ; but," he continues in reply to one who had asserted this, " I believe that ye mistake it." And taking up one case objected against him in which the Bible of a Lollard prisoner named Richard Hun, a London merchant, was said to have been burnt in the Bishop of London's prison, (sic) he says :

" This I remember well, that besides other things framed for the favour of divers other heresies there were in the prologue of that Bible such words touching the Blessed Sacrament as good Christian men did abhor to hear and that gave the readers undoubted occasion to think that the book was written after Wyclif's copy and by him translated into our tongue, and that this Bible was destroyed consequently not because it was in English, but because it contained gross and manifest heresy." — (By the way, the words from " tongue " onwards are not More's but Dr. Gasquet's).

" This is borne out by the account given by Foxe, who has printed from the Register of Fitzjames, Bishop of London, thirteen articles extracted from " the prologue " of Hun's " Great Book of the Bible." These were read to the people from the pulpit at Paul's Cross, and they were invited to come and examine the Bible for themselves in order to see that it contained these errors. If this list of articles can be relied upon, and there is no reason to distrust the account, it bears out Sir Thomas More's contention that this " great Bible " must have been a Lollard production, although we shall look in vain in the edition of Wycliffite Scriptures published by Forshall and Madden for any trace of these errors " (' Old English Bible,' pp. 128 - 9).

And there, in the various chapters of that Prologue, to which More referred, were every one of these thirteen articles, one by one and recognisably word for word. As I wrote later, the effect of Dr. Gasquet's argument was " to claim as a ' Catholic version of our pre-Reformation forefathers ' and ' the semi-official and certainly perfectly orthodox translation of the English Church,' an English Bible, such as was denounced, in the sentence of Bishop Fitzjames of London on the person and body of Richard Hunne, among books ' heretical ' and ' condemned by law.'" It was only necessary to print in parallel columns these thirteen incriminating articles and the passages from the Prologue from which they were textually drawn to put Dr. Gasquet's thesis beyond the pale of argument.*

There are two facts connected with this first English Bible for both of which there is sufficient evidence : first, that it was the work of Wyclif and his colleagues, second, that copies of it, or parts of it, were owned and used, under episcopal licence, by devout and orthodox persons during the century or so before the Reformation. Dr. Gasquet uses the latter fact to throw doubt upon, or deny, the former : a line of argument open to anyone sufficiently ignorant of, or indifferent to, the abundance of known facts.

There arose the question, By what species of scholarship had Dr. Gasquet managed to maintain an impossible proposition through so many learned pages ? That question I endeavoured to answer in two articles in the ' Church Quarterly Review,' (Oct. 1900 and Jan. 1901). In the limited space allowed me, these articles had to be purely destructive. They showed that, whatever were the questions connected with the origin and use of these versions, Dr. Gasquet had given no useful answer to them. The true answer I believed I knew ; but hoping to obtain some documentary proof of it, in prologues, marginal notes and other extraneous matter, I visited the great libraries of London, Oxford, Cambridge, Manchester and Dublin in order to examine the extant manuscripts. The search, in fact, did not yield very much, except an increased sense of the thoroughness and rigour with which the authorities, in the course of the fifteenth century, had seized and destroyed manuscripts of the Wycliffite versions containing, in notes and prologues, objectionable matter. But there was one manuscript in the library of Corpus Christi College, Cambridge, which I looked forward to seeing with particular interest. As described by Messrs. Forshall

* Dr. Gasquet's conduct in maintaining silence for some years and then (1908), without a word of alteration or justification, republishing a thesis which had been proved to be baseless out of his own mouth, provides one of the modern ' curiosities of literature.' It has been dealt with adequately by Dr. G. C. Coulton in some pages of his ' Mediaeval Studies, 1st ser. (1915), and his' Sectarian History,' pp. 5 - 8 (1937).

and Madden in the introduction to their printed edition of the Wycliffite versions, this manuscript (C. C. Coll. 147) — of the revised version complete with its General Prologue by the translator, John Purvey — contained marginal annotations said, in a note inserted by a later hand, to be in the handwriting of Geoffrey Blythe, Bishop of Lichfield and Coventry. Bishop Blythe was a contemporary of Bishop Fitzjames, and a colleague of his in Parliament and Convocation.

This folio volume was part of an old bequest of books which was jealously guarded in accordance with the will of the testator : but, by the courtesy of the authorities of the College, I was given full opportunity of examining it. It proved to be not only interesting but exciting. I had not been turning over the pages of the Prologue for ten minutes until I became aware that the volume had some sort of intimate connection with the case of Richard Hunne. I knew of course by heart the articles of charge which had been brought against Hunne ; and a brief inspection showed that some half of Bishop Blythe's marginal notes were attached to some half of the passages which had been summarised for the purposes of these articles of charge. It became important, therefore, to determine the character and purpose of these notes. They were not numerous in proportion to the length of the Prologue, which extends, in this manuscript, to 35 folio pages containing two columns apiece. Of the 70 columns Bishop Blythe's annotations appear on only 10 ; and on the first 36 columns there is only one. This is natural, because the Prologue consists mainly of a summary of the contents of the Old Testament, and the passages to which an orthodox bishop would take exception occur mainly in the latter half of it. Only three of the annotations are of any length. Two of these are attached to a passage (p. 30, col. 1) in which Purvey animadverts upon the University of Oxford ; and Blythe, in one of them, notes that if there were not in the University of Oxford theologians like great dogs baying against heresy, there would, without any doubt, through the whole kingdom of England be heretics like wolves devouring the whole Catholic Church. These longer notes are interlarded with reprobatory verses or parts of verses from the Vulgate Psalms ;

118

and the shorter notes on other passages consist mainly of such reprobatory verses.

As an example of these shorter notes we may take the very first, which appears on the margin of p. 2, col. 1. The text has " so it semeth opyn eeresie to seie that the gospel with his treuth and fredom suffisith not to salvacioun of cristen men without kepyng of ceremonyes and statutis of sinful men and unkunninge that ben maad in the tyme of Sathanas and Antechrist."

The Bishop notes : " latet anguis in herba " (a snake lurks in the grass) : " molliti sunt sermones ejus super oleum, et ipsi sunt jacula " (his words were softer than oil, yet were they drawn swords, A.V. and R.V. : Prayer Book version, his words were smoother than oil, and yet be they very swords (Ps. 55, v. 22). Douai version : His words are smoother than oil, and the same are darts. The passage in the text was adopted for the first article of the post mortem indictment against Hunne.

Another example may be given from the 5th article charged against Hunne, which reads : " That poor men and idiots have the truth of the holy Scriptures more than a thousand prelates and religious men and clerks of the school." To the original ('p. 19, col. 1) Bishop Blythe appends in the margin two tags from the Psalms :

" Disperdat dominus universa labia dolosa, et linguam magni-loquam," Psalm 12, v. 3, the Lord shall cut off all flattering lips and the tongue that speaketh proud things, A.V. (great things, R.V. Douai version, May the Lord destroy all deceitful lips, and the tongue that speaketh proud things. And Psalm 64, v.5, (Blythe's note), " firmaverunt sibi sermonem nequam " (They encourage themselves in an evil matter, A.V. (evil purpose, R.V.). Douai version, They are resolute in wickedness.

A similar note, with two other quotations from the Psalms, appears against the passage (p. 21, col. 2), a whole column long, summarised for the 10th article of charge against Hunne, which reads :

" He damneth adoration, prayers, kneeling and offering to images, which he calleth stocks and stones."

119

Bishop Blythe's notes upon the margin of the Prologue only number 12 all told.

The volume, which is without ornamentation, has the appearance of having been copied for one of the wealthier adherents of the Wycliffite movement in the early days, when it had an important following among the squirearchy. It had no doubt been impounded, during some heresy hunt, by Blythe himself, or by some predecessor in the See. The Bishops understood that the version itself was a perfectly honest rendering of the Vulgate ; and such a volume might be regarded as too interesting and valuable to destroy, though its inclusion of the uncompromising Wycliffite Prologue made it advisable to keep it under lock and key. Bishop Blythe, coming into possession of it or finding it in the episcopal library, had the curiosity to peruse it, and made notes upon the margin against the passages which most aroused his ire. The above description, though not exhaustive, gives a sufficient idea of the character of these notes. The notes themselves would appear to have had no particular purpose except to give vent to the Bishop's feelings.

But it is not these notes, BUT CERTAIN PEN-STROKES ACCOMPANYING THEM, and scored against certain other passages mostly adjacent to them, which connect this volume with the case of Richard Hunne. These marginal scorings are made with a very light pen, in contrast with Bishop Blythe's rather heavy penmanship. They have the appearance of mnemonic marks, made by a person going through the manuscript and noting passages to which, on subsequent perusal, he wished to recall his mind. There occurs, besides, another apparently mnemonic sign, consisting of three small and inconspicuous dots arranged as an inverted triangle. This dot-sign occurs on pages the margins of which are otherwise blank, and are such as might be made by a person working upon a borrowed manuscript and not wishing to deface it unnecessarily. And these pen-strokes and dot-signs appear against no less than eleven out of the thirteen passages summarised in the articles of charge against Hunne. What can it mean except that this volume, in the possession of Bishop Blythe, was lent for the purposes of the post mortem prosecution ? It that were so, it would account for the fact that no complete English Bible was produced or mentioned as belonging to Hunne at his examination at Fulham on Saturday, December 2nd, the day before his death.

There may now be put before the reader certain reasonable suppositions, along with certain demonstrable facts.

We may reasonably suppose that at the time of Hunne's death Bishop Blythe was up in London for the forthcoming Convocation and Parliament. He would hear at once of the event with which all London was astir. He would know, within two or three days, that the Coroners' Jury had put aside the suggestion of suicide, and that everything pointed to a verdict of murder against the men in charge of the Lollards' Tower, and chief among them the Bishop's chancellor. By the Wednesday or Thursday he would be apprised of Fitzjames' instant decision to forestall, and if possible prevent, the verdict of the Jury by instituting a formal trial for heresy over Hunne's dead body. And he would doubtless learn that the only difficulty was the lack of evidence commensurate in importance with the elaborate public trial intended. Detesting heresy as his annotations on the Prologue show him to have done, he might say to his brother of London : " I have in my possession a volume which may be of use to you. It is a complete copy of the Bible in English, with the notorious prologue which we have tried to suppress. I have myself noted some of the wickeder passages ; and the learned doctor who is getting up the case will have no difficulty in finding others. If he is pressed for time, my notes may be a useful starting point and guide. There can be no better use for a heretical writing than to convict a heretic, and I am glad to place this volume at your disposal.'*

---

* Was Bishop Blythe the sort of prelate who would be likely to lend himself to the course suggested ? Did he share Fitzjames' feelings towards heresy and heretics ? Four pages of his Register at Lichfield, fols. 98 a and b, 99a and 100 a, provide the answer. They show that in the winter of 1511, three years before the tragedy of Hunne, the Bishop was engaged in a determined drive against a numerous band of Wycliffites at Coventry. On eight given dates between the beginning of November and the end of January no fewer than thirty-six Coventry people, eleven of them women, were placed on trial. On six out of the eight occasions the examinations took place, sometimes before the Bishop himself, at Maxstoke Priory, a few miles out of Coventry and well

121

So much for supposition ; now for the facts.

The learned doctor in question, as Foxe informs us from Fitz-james' Register, was the Bishop's Commissary, Thomas Head, the same who had examined Joan Baker three years before (pp. 62 - 4), and on whose " counsel," three or four days before, the bellringer Spalding had returned to Hunne's cell (p. 74) to fetch his knife. It can hardly have been until the Thursday morning that Head began work upon the lengthy Prologue, and the articles of charge had to be culled from it in time for the preacher at Paul's Cross to " rehearse, show and publish " them to the people on Sunday morning. He had therefore to carry out his examination against time, and was glad to

away from possible sympathisers in the city. All the accused were convicted, compelled to abjure, and subjected to penance. A few weeks afterwards, in March, the Bishop pointed the moral of these abjurations by consigning to the flames — " delivering to the secular arm," in the legal euphemism — one Joan Warde, condemned as relapsed, she having abjured at Maidstone sixteen years before (August, 1495) and having then been branded (signata) with the letter H upon the left jaw in token of being an abjured heretic. The last of the eleven women convicted as above, Alice Rodney, was required, in penance, to bear a faggot at the burning of Joan Warde, and afterwards to carry it to a certain famous image of the blessed Virgin.

Of the thirty-six persons who abjured in 1511 Bishop Blythe, in 1519, had five men and one woman rearrested, confined throughout Lent at Maxstoke, condemned as relapsed, and burnt in Holy Week at the Little Park in Coventry, where a memorial Cross now stands. Foxe (vol. IV.) writes of them as " The seven godly martyrs of Coventry," the seventh being a glover named Wrigham, whose name does not appear among the 1511 abjurations. Another, Robert Silkeby, whose name does appear, evaded capture in 1519, but was arrested on his later return to Coventry, and burnt as a relapsed heretic in 1521.

The character of Bishop Blythe's notes on the margins of the Corpus ms. suggests that his interest in the volume, and his reprobation of certain passages in the Prologue, were fairly fresh. Can it have come into his hands during this drive against heretics at Coventry in 1511 ? Coventry was no more than a dozen miles from Wyclif's parish of Lutterworth, where such early copies of the English Scriptures were produced. So strong a body of humble survivors of Wycliffism at Coventry may have been held together by the secret possession of so precious a volume. Two of them, Thomas Fletcher and ' Johanna, wife of Richard Smith ' — the woman, by them a widow, burnt in 1519 — were separately charged in 1511, with the possession of " libros reprobatae lectionis." As the law had stood since Arundel's day, an unauthorised and unlicensed English Bible, complete like the Corpus ms., would be pre-eminent among " libros reprobatae lectionis." If such a book had been impounded by his officers in 1511, the Bishop of Lichfield and Coventry would naturally have it taken to his London house in order to exhibit it to his brother-prelates so valuable a find. And in that case Bishop Fitzjames may have been aware of its existence before misadventure compelled him to borrow it, or accept the loan of it, for pro-duction as evidence against Hunne at the post mortem trial.

avail himself of Bishop Blythe's notes, so far as they held out. His procedure can be followed transparently.

Beginning with the first chapter of the Prologue, he finds, on page 2, col. 1d, the first of Bishop Blythe's notes (see above, p. 119 " latet anguis in herba "). He draws one of his light pen-strokes against it ; and the noted passage presently appears in the indictment as

Article I. " First the said book damneth all holy canons, calling them ceremonies and statutes of sinful men and uncunning, and calleth the pope Satan and Antichrist."

He then turns over page after page, all blank, until he comes to page 19, where he finds three more of Blythe's marginal notes. These he scores ; and the three passages are presently summarised in the indictment as

Art. II. " Item, It damneth the pope's pardons, saying they be but leasings."

Art. IV. "Item, The said book saith that lords and prelates pursue full cruelly them that would teach truly and freely the law of God, and cherish them that preach sinful men's traditions and statutes ; by which he meaneth the holy canons of Christ's Church". And

Art. V. " Item, That poor men and idiots have the truth of the holy scriptures, more than a thousand prelates, and religious men, and clerks of the school."

Finding this 19th page so plentifully noted, Head reads it through, and happens upon two other passages which will serve his purpose, scoring one of them (p. 19, cols. 1c and 2b.) These two passages are condensed in the indictment as

Art. III. " Item, The said book of Hun saith, that kings and lords, called christian in name, and heathen in conditions, defile the sanctuary of God, bringing clerks full of covetousness, heresy and malice, to stop God's law, that it cannot be known, kept and freely preached " ; and

Art. VI. " Item, That christian kings and lords set up idols in God's house, and excite the people to idolatry."

Passing over the blank page 20 to page 21, Head finds, in col. 2c, a long passage to which Bishop Blythe has affixed two damnatory quotations from Psalms 50 and 36. He draws one of his sweeping pen-strokes down the whole column ; and the passage is presently summarised in the indictmant as

Art. X. " Item, He damneth adoration, prayer, kneeling, and offering to images, which he calleth stocks and stones."

Prospecting for himself over the same page 21, the doctor lights upon two other passages which will answer his purpose, col. 1b and d. He scores both in the margin, and their substance appears in the indictment as

Art. VIII. " Item, That every man, swearing by our lady, or any other saint or creature, giveth more honour to the saints than to the Holy Trinity ; and so he saith they be idolaters " : and

Art. IX. " Item, He saith that saints ought not to be honoured."

So far, on only 3 out of the 35 pages of the Prologue, all three bearing Bishop Blythe's annotations, Dr. Head has secured 9 out of his 13 articles. But he has not yet come upon the sort of passage which a prosecutor drawing up such an indictment would be most keen to discover, a passage on which to found a charge of erroneous belief about the sacrament of the altar, always the matter of most moment in any heresy trial. Continuing his research, he finds, on page 26, col. 2b, the material he requires. John Purvey, the author of the Prologue, is writing, at length and with the authority of Saint Augustine, on the interpretation of Scripture, and explaining when its words should be understood literally and when figuratively. The passage is so innocent that it had not occurred to Bishop Blythe as calling for animadversion.* But Head seizes

---

* The passage is as follows :

" Such a reule schal be kept in figuratif spechis, that so longe it be turned in mynde bi diligent consideracoun, til the expowyng either undirstonding be brought to the rewme of charite ; if eny speche of scripture sounneth propirly charite, it owith not to be gessid a figuratijf speche : and forbeedith wickidnesse, either comaundith profyt either good doynge, it is no figuratyf speche : if it seemith to comaunde cruelte, either wickidnesse, either to forbede prophit, either good doinge, it is a figuratijf speche. Crist seith, " if ye eten not the flesch of mannis sone and drinke not his blood, ye schulen not have lijf in you." This speche semith to comaunde wickidnesse either cruelte, therfore it is a figuratif speche, and comaundith men to comune with Cristis passioun, and to kepe in mynde sweetly and profitably, that Cristis flesch was woundid and crucified for us. Also whanne hooly scripture seith, " if thin enemy hungrith,

upon it as offering just the thing he wants. The word 'figurative' in connection with the sacrament of the altar had long been a red rag to the devotees of orthodoxy ; and the reverend doctor sees that by a piece of bold garbling this passage about 'figurative speeches' can be twisted into a downright denial of Transubstantiation. He therefore, in order not to deface the pure margin, affixes to the passage his other mnemonic mark, the inverted triangle of dots, which are hardly noticeable on the page. And when drafted into the indictment the passage is transmogrified into

Art. XI. " Item, He saith, that the very body of the Lord is not contained in the sacrament of the altar, but that men receiving it shall thereby keep in mind that Christ's flesh was wounded and crucified for us."

Years ago, when examining Dr. Gasquet's thesis and long before making any special inquiry into this case of Hunne, I observed the gross garbling which went to the making of this deadly article, and was satisfied, thenceforward, that there was no a priori presumption against Hunne having been murdered by the Bishop's chancellor. It seemed mere commonsense that men who were capable of lyingly defaming a dead man were perfectly capable of having killed him first. Whether they had done so or not was purely a matter of evidence.

Proceeding, Head finds, on turning to page 30, col. 1 a, b, c, d, a long passage beginning ' Alas, alas, alas,' in which Purvey deplores the shortcomings of the University of Oxford. Blythe occupied the whole margin of the column with two long notes, in the course of which he speaks of the Oxford theologians baying against heresy like great dogs. Head scores one of the notes, and summarises the whole passage in

feede thou hym, if he thurstith, geve thou drinke to hym," it comaundith benefice, either good doinge : whanne it seith, " thou schalt gadere togidere coolis on his heed," it seemith that wickidnesse of yvel wille is comaundid. This is seid by figuratijf speche, that thou undirstonde that the coolys of fijer ben brennynge weylyngis, either moornyngis of penaunce, bi whiche the pride of hym is mad hool, which sorwith, that he was enemy of a man that helpith and relevith his wrecchidnesse." General Prologue, (Forshall and Madden), chap. 12, pp. 44 - 5.

125

Art. XII. "Item, He damneth the university of Oxford, with all degrees and faculties in it, as art, civil, canon, and divinity, saying that they hinder the true way to come to the knowledge of the laws of God and holy Scripture."

Finally, he comes to the 15th and last chapter of the Prologue, extending to $9\frac{1}{2}$ columns, in which Purvey declares the purposes and principles of the men who had carried out the translation. Against a sentence on page 34, col. 2d which reads :

" Yit worldli clerkis axen gretli what spiryt makith idiotis hardi to translate now the bible into English, sithen the foure greete doctouris dursten nevere do this ? "

Head affixes his inconspicuous dot-sign, and summarises the whole chapter in

Art. XIII. "Item, He defendeth the translation of the Bible and the holy Scripture into the English tongue, which is prohibited by the laws of our mother, holy church."

So here we have eleven, out of the whole list of thirteen articles, distinguished by the Commissary's mnemonic marks.

What of the two articles VI and VII which are without notes or scorings ? They might reasonably be explained as last-moment additions, made on Head's final review of the manuscript. Article VI, recorded above p. 123, summarises a passage which is continuous with the passage summarised for article V, page 19, col. 2 a and b ; and the scoring against the latter may have been intended to apply to both. As to article VII, the original occurs on page 20, col. 2 b. In a final review when completing his draft, Head, on passing from page 19, from which he got five of his articles, to page 21, from which he got three, may have had his eye caught by the word ' Eroude ' on page 20, and summarised the passage there and then as

Art. VII. "Item, that princes, lords and prelates so doing be worse that Herod that pursued Christ, and worse than Jews and heathen men that crucified Christ."

It must be remembered that Head is not a leisurely scholar editing an edition for the press, but a law officer examining a lengthy document for the purposes of certain articles of charge, and with little time to do it in. As might be expected, there is a small number of notes and mnemonic marks which Head disregarded in his final review, as attaching to passages of minor significance. There are three such passages against which appear Blythe's notes and his own scorings ; one with his scoring only ; and four, on pages 3, 4 and 8, with his triangular dot-sign. But MOST of Blythe's notes and MOST of Head's mnemonic marks are attached to passages summarised for the indictment, eleven out of the whole thirteen.

What, we may now ask, is the inference to be drawn from these facts ? They cannot be accidental. The proverbial long arm would have to be wrenched out of its socket to account for them by any theory of coincidence. I submit that the only possible inference is that this volume in the Corpus Library at Cambridge is the actual volume produced in evidence against Hunne at the post mortem trial in the Lady Chapel of St. Paul's.

Just a week after Hunne's death, Sunday, December 10th, the preacher at Paul's Cross announced :

" And masters, if there be any man desirous to see the specialty of these articles, or doubt whether they be contained in this book or not, for satisfying of his mind let him come to my lord of London, and he shall see it with good will."

We do not know whether anyone availed himself of this invitation, but we do know one person who certainly did not. That person was Thomas More. If he had, and if " this book " were the volume we have been examining, he could not have been hoodwinked, as he completely was, by the description solemnly given of it in the Cathedral four days later.*

---

* In ' The Lollard Bible,' pp. 369 - 70, Miss Margaret Deanesly writes that this was " an offer of which Sir Thomas More must have availed himself." I can find no evidence whatever that he did.

" Sir Thomas More," we read further, " was present at his trial, and inspected his English Bible." This apparently refers to the post mortem trial. More was certainly then present and saw the Bible ; but, if this Corpus ms. was the Bible in question, he as certainly did not " inspect " it. One glance at the alleged passages of the Prologue would have been sufficient to expose the false description.

Miss Deanesly says elsewhere (ibid. p. 14, note 3) : " More was present at the examination of Richard Hun in the Tower in 1514." The only recorded examination of Hunne was before the Bishop at Fulham on the Saturday,

During my first visit to Cambridge, in 1901, I had the honour of dining with Dr. Montague James, then Provost of King's College. Knowing him as a great bibliographer, I mentioned to him my conclusion about the Corpus manuscript. Some years later, when compiling his catalogue of the Corpus Christi College Library and describing this manuscript of the Wycliffite Bible, Dr. James referred to the suggested identification. Later still it was called in question by Miss E. Jeffries Davis in her valuable article on Richard Hunne in the English Historical Review (vol. 30, July, 1915). In a footnote to page 480 Miss Davis writes :

" It has been suggested that a manuscript of that version now in the library of Corpus Christi College, Cambridge (see Dr. M. R. James's Catalogue, 1, 336) is the actual copy that belonged to Hunne, on the ground that certain passages marked, in a hand said to be that of Blythe, bishop of Lichfield and Coventry from 1503 to 1530, correspond to some of those collected by his accusers. But Blythe is nowhere mentioned (though other bishops besides Fitzjames are) in connexion with Hunne's case ; and Mrs. W. J. Harrison, who has kindly examined the manuscript for me, finds that the correspondence is by no means so exact as to warrant such a deduction. Some of the passages which are the originals of the thirteen articles in Foxe's summary are not marked, and there are marks against many which are not represented there. Hunne's Bible was popularly supposed to have been destroyed with his body, but More (Dyaloge, book 111, ch. xv.) states, " whyther the boke be burned or secretely kepte I can not surely saye."

In view of this objection, I paid a further visit to Cambridge, and spent a week in a minute examination of this manuscript. The results are given above. The correspondence is so far exact that Blythe's notes, or Head's mnemonic marks, or both, are attached to all but two articles out of the whole thirteen ; and their absence in the case of the two admits of explanation. There are marks,

December 2nd, and there is no record of More's having been present. If he had been, we should certainly have heard it from himself.

In writing specially about Hunne, it is necessary, and I hope not ungracious, to point out these slips in a most valuable book.

not " against many," but against a few passages which are not adopted for the articles ; but this is surely what one would expect. Head's scorings and dot-signs were made by the way, and he was not tied to every one of them in selecting matter for his final draft. The fact remains that most of Bishop Blythe's notes and most of Head's mnemonic marks are attached to passages summarised for the indictment. It is true that in Foxe's account of the post mortem trial derived from Fitzjames' register, Blythe's name does not appear among the bishops mentioned. But why should it ? If Blythe lent this manuscript for the purposes of the prosecution, and knew the use that was to be made of it, his absence would be sufficiently accounted for. And, of course, there is no proof that the English Bible first produced at the post mortem trial was ever Hunne's at all ; and if this Corpus manuscript was the volume in question, there is certain proof that it was never Hunne's at all.

In Elizabeth's time Archbishop Parker was greatly concerned about the disappearance and destruction of precious mediaeval manuscripts, and made efforts to recover as many of them as possible. Under stringent conditions for their safe custody, he bequeathed his collection to three Cambridge colleges ; and this manuscript was included in the portion of the bequest which came to Corpus Christi College. For nearly four centuries it had kept its secret.

And now for the conclusion of the whole matter. If, as I believe, and am confident no candid enquirer can help believing, this Corpus manuscript was the volume produced at the post mortem trial, the mystery surrounding it is perfectly explained. More's account of it, as it was described by the prosecution, is given twice over and is quite explicit. In the ' Supplication of Souls ' (English Works, p. 297) he writes :

" After which " — (that is, the failure of the praemunire suit)— the matter went forth afore the bishop, and he (Hunne) there well proved nought, and his books after brought forth, SUCH AND SO NOTED WITH HIS OWN HAND IN THE MARGENTS, as every wise man well saw what he was, and was full sore to see that

E   129 he was such as they there saw him proved." And in the ' Dialogue,' book III, chap. 15 :

" Myself was present in Poules when the bishop, in the presence of the Mayor and the aldermen of the city, condemned him for an heretic after his death. And then were there read openly the depositions by which it was well proved that he was convict as well of divers other heresies as of misbelief toward the holy sacrament of the altar." . . . .

" At such time as he was denounced for an heretic, there lay his English bible open, and some other English books of his, THAT EVERY MAN MIGHT SEE THE PLACES NOTED WITH HIS OWN HAND, such words and in such wise that there would no wise man, that good were, have any great doubt, after the sight thereof, what naughty minds the men had, BOTH HE THAT SO NOTED THEM, and he that so made them. I remember not now the specialities of the matter, nor the formal words as they were written. But this I remember well, that besides other things, framed for the favour of divers other heresies, there were in the prologue of that bible such words touching the Blessed Sacrament as good Christian men did much abhor to hear, and which gave the readers undoubted occasion to think that book was written after Wiclif's copy, and by him translated into our tongue."

More, sensible of the importance of the affair, made time to attend the trial. From his place in the general gathering, he heard the Bible which " there lay open " truly described as a Wycliffite production. He heard this prologue falsely described in terms of the mendacious 9th Article. He heard the volume falsely described as having belonged to Hunne. And he heard Bishop Blythe's notes upon the margins falsely described as in the handwriting of Hunne. Had he thought to go forward against the outgoing crowd and verify the description, a glance, the merest glance, would have shown him that these notes were not the work of a heretic, but of a man who detested heresy as heartily as himself. But why should he ? It would never occur to him to doubt the description so solemnly given, in the presence and hearing of the " very wise, virtuous and cunning " Bishop Fitzjames, by the reverend doctors in charge

130

of the prosecution. And as for the book as so described, it would be to More an unclean thing. He would have no desire to touch or handle or rest his eyes upon a volume on which a guilty heretic had fed his unhappy soul. So More departed with the rest, sorry but satisfied. The man, notwithstanding his fair dealing among his neighbours and his harmless conversation in the world, had been, in secret, a guilty heretic, who deserved death, whatever the manner of it. And when he came to write of the matter in the ' Dialogue ' fourteen years later, he did so in all good faith, making as little as possible of the evidence about murder, but firm in declaring that Hunne had been a guilty heretic, who merited death however he came by it.

But though, as he says, he knew the case " from top to toe," there was one thing he admits that he did not know. He did not know what had become of that book. He had reason to suspect that it had not been burned with Hunne's body, but " secretly kept." Whether that was so or not be could not " surely say." But, if not destroyed, he could not understand why " the clergy " did not produce it, " there hath gone so much suspicious rumour thereof." The puzzle that perplexed More need be no perplexity to us. They did not because they dared not. They dared not face Thomas More, and the consequences of the truth becoming known to More. So the book was " secretly kept " until times changed and it came, somehow, into the hands of Archbishop Parker and thence into the care of Corpus Christi College.

But More remained ignorant of the whereabouts of the book, and of the truth about what it most concerned him to know, whether Richard Hunne had or had not been a guilty heretic. And so he wrote, in 1528, with the authority of a perfectly honest man, but with no more than the authority of a man who, confident of knowing all the facts, had himself been impudently deceived.

Chapter VIII

THE COMMONS AND FITZJAMES

Immediately following upon the sentence, and on the same day, Fitzjames formally notified the Crown* " that We, Richard, by divine permission Bishop of London, duly and lawfully proceeding in the matter, lately raised, of an inquisition of heretical pravity against Richard Hunne, now deceased, of the parish, while he lived, of Saint Margaret, Bridge Street, London, within our jurisdiction : Have discovered and found, by facts deduced, exhibited and proved, and before us by the said Richard while living judicially confessed, that the said Richard was and is caught and guilty of the crime of heresy : And therefore the same Richard deceased, as a pertinacious or obstinate heretic, impenitent, guilty and convicted of the ɔrime of heretical pravity, We have condemned and excommunicated and his body We have pronounced and declared to be deprived of Christian burial (ecclesiastica sepultura) : And by our sentence as justice requires, him and his body or corpse, according to the canonical and lawful sanctions and the laudible custom of this your renowned realm hitherto used and observed in this behalf, We have committed and relinquished to the secular arm and power. Therefore We humbly pray your Majesty that whatever remains to do for the love of God and the conservation of the Catholic Faith you will graciously be pleased to execute. In witness whereof we have caused our Seal to be affixed to these presents. Given in our Palace in London the 16th day of the month of December in the year of our Lord fifteen hundred and fourteen, And of our Translation the ninth."

What remained to be done for the love of God and the conservation of the Catholic Faith was duly done at Smithfield four days

---

* Document found by Miss Eleanor J. B. Reid in the Record Office, Eng. Hist. Rev. vol. 30, July 1915.

later, Wednesday, December 20th, when Hunne's body was committed to the flames.

The post-mortem trial in the Lady Chapel was dignified by the presence of the Lord Mayor, Aldermen and Sheriffs. Doubtless present by invitation, it may safely be assumed that their presence was not merely one of ceremony. The man whose body formed the centre-piece of the solemn pageant had been known in his circle as a reputable citizen, and no heretic at all. He had been a liveryman of one of the great City Companies, and a man of whose worldly conversation his neighbours had heard none harm. Having given umbrage to the clergy and been arrested for heresy, he had been found dead in the Bishop's prison. The City Coroner and his Jury, then engaged upon the case, were making no secret of their conviction that the man had been the victim of murder, and that the Bishop's own chancellor had been implicated in the murder. If the proofs of Hunne's heresy were as damning as they were made to appear, if he had really been a pertinacious and obstinate heretic and as such foredoomed to the stake, what need was there to murder him ? What need for this spectacular trial at all ? Was Holy Church so punctilious about heresy that she needed to mount this trial, with its assemblage of ecclesiastical and civic dignitaries, merely in order to determine whether the dead man's body should be burnt or buried. Or was it the Bishop's hope that if the man was condemned as a guilty heretic nobody would dare to look further into the circumstances of his death ? If that were so, the Bishop was reckoning without a court more powerful than his own, the High Court of Parliament. At the moment attention was divided between the fate of Hunne and the forthcoming Parliament ; and the City had returned its members to the new House of Commons only four days before (Dec. 12th). Fitzjames might light the fires of Smithfield ; had he considered the possibility of their spreading to Westminster ? The Lord Mayor and his colleagues, between whom and the Bishop there was no love lost, must have watched the proceedings in the Lady Chapel with some such critical eye.

The new Parliament met on February 5th, 1515 ; and Dr. Pollard has drawn attention to its importance as follows ('Wolsey,' pp. 27 - 8) :—

"That Parliament has passed almost unnoticed in English history. 'In the whole course of its proceedings,' says the old PARLIAMENTARY HISTORY, 'we meet with nothing worth notice, except that tonnage and poundage was granted, and a subsidy.' Yet, apart from the fundamental issues raised therein, its records possess considerable matter of interest. It was the first parliament for which we have any regular record of attendance, the first in which we can therefore compare the summons to attend with the actual attendance, and ascertain whether, for instance, there was on any particular day, or throughout the session as a whole, a clerical or a lay majority in the lords ; and, with the possible exception of the parliament of 1523, for which we have scanty records, it was the last parliament in English history in which the spiritual lords outnumbered their secular colleagues."

This spiritual majority in the Lords was used consistently throughout the two sessions in order to frustrate a twofold endeavour of the House of Commons ; first, to obtain some sort of justice for the children and the memory of Richard Hunne, and secondly, to revive an Act which the Lords took the first opportunity to drop, the temporary Act of 1512, by which criminous clerks in minor orders were left subject to the ordinary lay punishments for crime. Simultaneously, the Commons were exerting all their influence with the King's Council to frustrate a bold attempt of Fitzjames and Convocation to put the clock back for generations in the matter of the " privilegium clericale." (See Appendix). As is plainly indicated in Robert Keilwey's account, the object of this attempt was perfectly palpable to contemporaries. It was to prevent a clerk in major orders, the Bishop's chancellor indicted for wilful murder, from being brought to trial.

It will be convenient to deal first with the proceedings in Parliament. To appreciate their significance we have to reverse our present-day mental picture of the relative importance of the two Houses. Through the latter part of Henry VIII's reign the Commons, owing to the King's needs and management, gained rapidly in consequence and authority ; though it was not until the end of the reign of Elizabeth that they drew level in importance with the House of Lords. At the beginning of Henry's reign they were still, what they had been throughout the middle ages, the minor element of the Legislature. All the effective organs of government were centred in the Upper House. The Bishops, the mitred abbots and the temporal peers occupied the parliament-chamber in the royal palace of Westminster, where sat also the judges and other elements of the King's Council out of which the House of Lords had developed. The Commons attended to hear the business propounded to them by the Crown, and then retired to their own meeting-place outside, in the Chapter-house of the Abbey, to deliberate in private : returning to make known their views and decisions through the mouth of the Speaker, who alone had audience in the parliament-chamber. They could assent, with more or less good grace, to the royal demands for money ; they could initiate bills, which might or might not gain a respectful hearing in the House of Lords. Where, as on the matters here in question, bills from the Commons encountered strong antagonism among the spiritual majority in the House of Lords, their fate was to be thrown out or shelved. The persistent presentation of such foredoomed bills during the two sessions of 1515 was significant only of the strength of feeling behind them. A position developed not unlike that which led to the passing of the Parliament Act in 1911, the Commons finding themselves repeatedly thwarted by steady stonewalling on the part of an immovable majority in the House of Lords. Their impotence and the opposing majority came alike to a dramatic end in the next Parliament but one.

The proceedings of this Parliament of 1515 have to be gleaned from the Journals of the Lords, the Commons' Journals dating only from 1547. The Lords' Journals give little more than the record of attendance, with the titles of bills before the House and a summary notice of their fate. But the record is sufficient to give a fair idea of what took place as between the two Houses.

The first session opened on February 5th ; and at their first meeting for the despatch of business, on the 10th, the Lords had before them the Criminous Clerks Act of 1512 (see Appendix). The prelates, in the last Parliament, had been persuaded to let the Act go through as a temporary measure. It had been " defended by Dr. John Taylor in an address to Convocation, of which he was Prolocutor, on 26th June, 1514 ; it was due, he said, to the brawling and dissolute life of the lower clergy." (Pollard, ' Wolsey,' p. 31). Withdrawing from clerical felons in minor orders the last vestige of " ecclesiastical liberty " in the shape of immunity from execution, its effects had been generally recognised as salutary. The lawyer Keilwey, whose narrative we are presently to examine, remarks that by this " good Act many common and horrible murderers and robbers were deprived of their clergy and executed to the great increase and advancement of the public good of all the realm, and to the great discomfort and fear of all such common murderers and robbers." Recent events, however, had made the prelates acutely sensitive on this matter of ecclesiastical liberty ; and one of them had just denounced the measure in an official sermon preached at Paul's Cross. (See below, p. 142). The measure expiring, the spiritual majority in the Lords took the first opportunity, on February 10th, of giving it its quietus. A month later, on March 10th, the Commons sent up a bill with the object of reviving it. It is described as " a Bill concerning Murderers and Felons not to be admitted to Ecclesiastical Liberty." It was read and dropped by the Lords two days later.

On April 2nd the Lords had before them two other bills sent up from the Commons. The first is described as an ' Appeal of Homicide ' ; and Dr. Pollard explains it by reference to an Act of Henry VII by which the widow or children of a murdered man " could in person or by proxy still bring an accusation or appeal of murder, within a year and a day, irrespective of the action of the crown." Some six weeks before, towards the end of February, the Coroner's Jury had returned a verdict of wilful murder against Horsey and his humbler henchmen. Fitzjames had promptly and piteously besought Wolsey on behalf of " my poor chancellor now in ward, and indicted by an untrue quest for the death of Richard Hun. , . . . that by your intercession it may please the King's Grace to have the matter duly and sufficiently examined by indifferent persons of his discreet council, in the presence of the parties, or (ere) there be any more done in the cause." It was evidently in response to this appeal that the proceedings took place at Baynard's Castle, of which More professes to give an account in some derisory pages of the " Dialogue " (see above, pp. 28-30, 97-101). More's story makes it plain that the purpose of these proceedings, before " divers great lords spiritual and temporal, and other of the King's honourable council," was to overawe the Jury and to discredit their verdict. The Bill of April 2nd, embodying the " Appeal of Homicide," was apparently a counter-move of the Commons against these irregular machinations. It was an intimation to the prelates in the Upper House that the Jury, in standing by their verdict, had the Commons behind them. The purport of the Bill may be gathered from " the words that the Bishop of London spake before the Lords in the Parliament-house," as recorded by Hall and Foxe. The Bishop declared that it was a bill " to make the jury that was charged upon the death of Hun true men ; and said and took upon his conscience that they were false perjured caitiffs. And said furthermore to all the lords there being, ' For the love of God look up this matter ; for if you do not, I dare not keep mine own house for heretics ' : and said that the said Richard Hun hanged himself, and that it was his own deed and no man's else ' ." Fitzjames' heat in Parliament was matched by the heat of feeling out of doors. Polydore Vergil, the London agent of the papal collector, writing on March 3rd to his principal in Rome, referred to " the amount of scandal that has arisen here ; and now especially on account of one heretic lately condemned to death by the Bishop of London, the people here and there exclaiming and now and then raging against the Clergy, (or would be) if the King's Majesty were not curbing their fury." (Eng. Hist. Rev. July, 1915 : Pollard, ' Wolsey,' p 39).

The King's desire to pacify public feeling appears in connection with the second bill which was also before the Lords on this April 2nd. It is described as " Pro liberis Ricardi Hune," for the children of Richard Hunne. Incidentally his family had been reduced to beggary by his condemnation as a heretic, his property being

137

thereby forfeited to the Crown. The Commons, obtaining the King's signature in token of his consent, promoted this bill to restore the property. The spiritual majority in the Lords, regarding it as derogating from Fitzjames' sentence, summarily threw it out.* On April 3rd we read, " The Lords decided that the bill of restitution to the children of Richard Hunne (though it was signed by the royal hand) should be rejected." (' Item, Domini decreverunt ut Billa pro Liberis Ricardi Hune restituendis (licet Regia manu signata sit) deliberetur," (Journals, 1. 41).

This first session ended on April 5th, the ' Appeal of Homicide being apparently among the sheaf of unagreed bills held over until the following session.

The seven months' recess produced events which led to another charge of heresy, over which the prelates were fated to burn their

---

* Some tardy justice was done in 1523, possibly connected with a desire of Wolsey to propitiate the House of Commons, which he was then importuning for a huge subsidy. Under date May 4th there is the record :

" Roger Whaplod and Margaret his wife, daughter of Ric. Hunne deceased. Grant to them and their executors for ever of all Hunne's lands and tenements, and all leases and deeds relating thereto."

L. and P. vol. III, part 2, 3062 (4).

In 1529 (Foxe, V, 27) there was an apparent attempt of the family to keep the case before the public in view of the meeting of Parliament.

" Roger Whaplod sent by one Tho. Norfolk unto Doctor Goderidge this bill following to be read at his sermon in the Spittle. ' If there be any well-disposed person willing to do any cost upon the reparation of the conduit in Fleet Street, let him or them resort unto the administrators of the goods and chattels of one Richard Hun, late merchant tailor of London, who died intestate, or else to me, and they shall have toward the same six pounds thirteen shillings and fourpence, and a better penny, of the goods of the said Richard Hun ; upon whose soul, and all Christian souls, Jesus have mercy'."

" For the which bill," Foxe records, " Whaplod and Norfolk were brought and troubled before the Bishop ; and also Dr. Goderidge, which took a groat for reading the said bill, was suspended for a time from saying mass, and also was forced to revoke the same at Paul's Cross ; reading this bill as followeth ", etc.

And among Cromwell's papers of uncertain date but calendared under 1540 (L. and P. vol. XV, 1029 (65) there is a " Petition of Margaret, wife of Richard Whaplod, one of the daughters of Richard Hunne, who was murdered. They have long been suitors to the King and Cromwell for aid, and have seven small children to support. Desire that Dr. Belhouse, Mr. Derbye, Rafe Fane and John Dearyng may be directed to hear and report upon the wrongs they have sustained ".

The paper is addressed to the Lord Privy Seal, to which office Cromwell succeeded in 1536.

fingers, the accused, on this occasion, being one of the King's own chaplains and councillors.

The proceedings in the second session, which opened on Monday, November 12th, are summarised thus by Dr. Pollard (' Wolsey,' p. 49) :—

" On Friday the 16th Warham, as chancellor, directed that bills, passed by the commons but not by the lords during the previous session, should be brought up for a conference on the following Monday between the two houses at their usual place for such purposes, the star chamber. What happened there we do not know, but next day two members, Sir Nicholas Vaux and Sir Thomas Hussey, brought up from the commons a memorandum on these suspended measures including the benefit of clergy bill. On the 22nd the lords gave this memorandum a first reading, and on the 24th committed it to Sir John Ernley, the attorney-general. Frequent adjournments to attend convocation took up most of the rest of the session, and nothing more was heard of the memorandum. The commons grew impatient : they passed the benefit of clergy bill a second time and sent it up on 14th December to the lords who gave it a first reading on the 17th. On the 20th the commons sent up another bill, concerning heresies ; it was read, with a note that the lords would consider it further. On the 21st convocation and on the 22nd parliament were dissolved."

Wolsey, for the past eighteen months Archbishop of York, had been made a Cardinal in September, and succeeded Warham as Lord Chancellor on the day the session closed. Having had enough of parliamentary contention, he advised the dissolution, and dispensed with Parliament altogether for the next seven years. The character of these contentions is indicated in notes appended to his records by Dr. John Taylor, Prolocutor and Clerk :—

" In this Convocation and Parliament the most dangerous seditions were raised between the clergy and the secular power over ecclesiastical liberties, a certain Friar Minor named Standish being the agent and instigator of all the mischief (omnium malorum ministro ac stimulatore)." (Wilkins, ' Concilia,' III, 658).

It was naive of Dr. Taylor to throw the onus upon Standish, who

139

only came into the affair when called upon, as one of his " spiritual counsel," to advise the King. The sequence of events makes it clear that the initiative, throughout these proceedings, is properly to be attributed to Bishop Fitzjames.

Dr. Pollard speaks of Fitzjames as " the heart and soul of the clerical party " ('Wolsey,' p. 41, note). He was that, and more. He had, in fact, made the party and provided it with a programme in order to pull his own chestnuts out of the fire. His position, on the eve of this 1515 Parliament, was not enviable. His chancellor was a fugitive in the Archbishop's household. His attempt to intimidate the Jury by the post-mortem trial had failed. Other efforts at dissuasion, of which we learn from both More and Keilwey, had equally failed. The Inquest, prolonged through the necessity of examining witnesses who had taken sanctuary, was shortly to conclude ; and Fitzjames knew, and all London knew, what the outcome was to be, a verdict of wilful murder against Horsey and " the others." And Fitzjames knew that if his chancellor, on the Coroner's indictment, were brought before the King's Bench, the verdict there, upon the sworn evidence, could be none other than that of guilty. If that took place, certain things would follow. Not only would the credit of the clergy be further impaired ; not only would the justice of the Church be indelibly besmirched ; but the awkward position would arise in which a convicted murderer would be handed over to the custody of his own unconvicted accomplice : since the public common-sense would entertain no doubt that if the Bishop's chief legal officer had murdered the Bishop's prisoner within thirty-six hours of his examination by the Bishop, the deed could not have been done without the connivance and concurrence of the Bishop himself. Means had to be found, by hook or crook, to prevent the case from coming to trial.

Fitzjames had two strings to his bow. He might, and did, appeal for Wolsey's intervention as soon as the Jury's verdict was known. Wolsey, however, though growingly powerful with the King, was not yet Cardinal or Lord Chancellor, and might not be powerful enough to interfere too openly with the course of justice. But agitation might reinforce appeal. There was the old question of jurisdiction, and the right of a temporal court to try a clerk at all. True that, by a long and gradual process, the courts of Common Law had established a secure position in relation to the criminous clerk. For generations they had not only ' convented ' the clerical felon, but tried and convicted him ; and, in latter days, had only handed him over to his Bishop with the stipulation that he was not to be freed by the too facile process of purgation (see Appendix). To challenge their jurisdiction, at that time of day, might seem to be a desperate expedient ; but Fitzjames was in a position in which " l'audace, l'audace et toujours l'audace " appeared an axiom of strategy. He was an old man in a panic, stubborn and intrepid, but he was no fool ; and can hardly have hoped, by anything he could do, to extrude the Common Law from the vantage-ground it had long held. But he might well hope, by raising these large questions of jurisdiction, to lay a smoke-screen of controversy and debate under cover of which his chancellor might escape, a hope which, in fact, was in the end fulfilled. A recent occurrence had played into his hands. Less than a year before (May, 1514) Pope Leo X, re-affirming in the Lateran Council the agelong prescription of the Canon Law, had pronounced that laymen had no jurisdiction over churchmen and that clerks were immune from temporal punishment. The Pope's word was law for ' men of Holy Church ' ; and Fitz-james knew that he had only to take his stand upon the papal bull, and his brother-prelates, whatever their view as to his own motives and whatever the misgivings among the more prudent, would be bound to follow him and march in step. Warham the Archbishop, who had lately protected Colet against him, he probably looked upon as an old sheep, and he had force enough himself to sweep the rest along with him. Among the prelates then in London for the coming Parliament and Convocation was Richard Kidderminster, Abbot of Winchcombe. Kidderminster, an active and reputable ecclesiastic of the day, had been one of the English delegates to the Lateran Council. A question which has been raised as to whether he had actually attended the sessions of the Council appears to be quite gratuitous. There is nothing to show that he had, and there is equally nothing to show that he had not ; and men of weight are not ordinarily appointed to such missions unless they are able and willing to discharge them. In any case it would be his duty to be cognizant of the decisions of the Council, and to give them currency in England so far as he could. He was an instrument ready to Fitzjames' hand.

Convocation was always opened with an official Sermon ; and it fell to Fitzjames, as Dean of the Province of Canterbury, to appoint the preacher. In appointing Kidderminster he would have no need to remind him of how gravely the Criminous Clerks Act, then about to expire, contravened the recent papal Bull, still less of how the practice of the English Common Law in conventing and convicting felonious clerks was contrary to the law of God and Holy Church. The Abbot accepted the commission with alacrity, and proceeded to make history at Paul's Cross.

The Abbot's discourse embraced two themes, which have not as a rule been sufficiently distinguished. He began with a root and branch denunciation of the Criminous Clerks Act, declaring that it was clean contrary to the law of God and the liberties of Holy Church : and that all who had had a hand in its making, including himself and his brother-prelates, had incurred the censures of the Church. He produced a decree, no doubt Pope Leo's recent decree, " in maintenance of his opinion, and," passing to the wider issue, " further said that by the same decree all Clerks who have received any manner of Orders, greater or lesser, are exempt from temporal punishment for criminal causes before the temporal Judge." The Sermon was thus a direct and open challenge to the established practice of the Common Law.

Now the position of the Common Law judges was strong enough for them to regard the Abbot's sermon as the mere ebullition of an inflated ecclesiastic, of which it would be foolish to take notice. But the newly elected House of Commons, with its City members, was indisposed to take so easy a view. In the Abbot's sermon they saw — and the narrative from which our information is derived makes it clear that they saw — the opening move in a covert campaign to get the Bishop's chancellor out of the hands of justice. And they were not without means of meeting it. Comparatively impotent in

Parliament, they had sufficient weight with the King's Council to secure that the issues raised by the Abbot should be taken up and thrashed out. If Fitzjames could appeal to the Council so could they ; and the Abbot had given them a first-rate fighting ground. By occupying it they would be pretty certain to embroil the prelates with the King and the Judges, and provide something of a counter-weight to the influence of Fitzjames. It is important to lay stress upon this action of the Commons because, in more than one recent and authoritative account of these affairs, little or no notice has been taken of it. It is entirely overlooked by Dr. Gairdner (English Church in the Sixteenth Century, pp. 43 - 50) ; and receives only one, and that the slightest, mention in Dr. Brewer's summary of Keilwey's narrative in the ' Letters and Papers of Henry VIII.' Yet the story without the Commons is like Hamlet without the Prince.

Our informant on these proceedings in the Council is Robert Keilwey, a barrister of standing and a younger contemporary of all the men whose actions he records. (See Pollard, ' Wolsey,' p. 44, note 2.) His narrative, with its touches of intimate detail, suggests derivation from someone who had borne an interested and leading part in these affairs, not improbably from Standish himself. That might well be ; for in 1518 Standish, to the disgust of the prelates whose schemes he had crossed, became Bishop of St. Asaph, and survived till 1535. Keilwey's story is included in a collection of law reports first published in 1602 ; but it is not iteslf, and does not profess to be, a law report. It is a memorandum of a series of conferences and debates which took place in the King's Council. It was the practice of those times, when principles of law were in dispute, to have them determined in such conferences, at which the Judges were present and reached decisions. Keilwey betrays something of the satisfaction of the common lawyer at seeing his rivals of the canon law discomfited ; but the facts he gives are not open to question. And, as to part of them, they are confirmed by another account, from another point of view, which has come down to us in the hand-writing of Wolsey's secretary.

It has been usual to give Keilwey's ' memorandum ' in more or less extended summaries ; but its effect is best seen in translation from the law French of the original. The translation which follows is complete, except that a passage, of some length and minor importance, is summarised in brackets. An incidental note of my own is introduced in double brackets. In the edition of 1688, which is usually cited, the story is quite unparagraphed, and appears in solid blocks of black-letter print in which it is difficult to see the wood for the trees. The successive episodes are here paragraphed, so that the reader may be better able to follow them stage by stage. Certain sentences, with their originals, are printed in italics, so as to emphasise a fact which has been sometimes overlooked, the part played by the House of Commons.

By the irony of events, the attempt of a layman to invoke the writ of praemunire against a parson and a court initiates a course of proceedings in which we see Bishop Fitzjames himself and his brother-prelates threatened with Praemunire, and reminded by the Judges of the precariousness of their place in Parliament : and the all-powerful minister Wolsey, for whose intercession Fitzjames had appealed, on his own knees before the King, interceding for himself, Fitzjames and the rest with earnest protestations and excuses. In view of the events so soon to follow, the story takes on the character of high drama.

Keilwey's Memorandum

PREAMBLE

Whereas it was enacted by the authority of Parliament held at Westminster the 4th day of February, the fourth year of our lord King Henry VIII, cap. 2, that murderers and robbers in churches and highways, and of men in their houses, should be deprived of their clergy, those who were in Holy Orders only excepted : this act of Parliament to continue until the Parliament then next ensuing, as by the same statute more plainly doth appear ; .... by force of which good Act many common and horrible murderers and robbers were deprived of their clergy and executed, to the great increase and advancement of the public good of all the Realm, and to the great discomfort and fear of all such common murderers and robbers ; And then

THE ABBOT'S SERMON

In the time of the next Parliament, that is to say, in the time of the Parliament held at Westminster in the 7th year of our lord the King, the Abbot of Winchcombe, in his service of St. Paul's Cross in London, declared openly that the said Act was clean against the law of God and the liberties of Holy Church : and said that all the makers of the same Act, that is to say, all as well spiritual as temporal who were parties to the Act, had incurred the censures of Holy Church ; and put forward a place of a decree made in maintenance of his opinion ; and further said that by the same decree all clerks who have received any manner of Orders, greater or lesser, are exempt from temporal punishment for criminal causes before the temporal judge, for he said that minor as well as major Orders are holy.

THE COMMONS AND TEMPORAL LORDS TAKE ACTION

Upon which matter our said lord the King, at the special request of his temporal lords and, in especial, at the diligent and effectual instance and labour of many honourable knights and divers other leading persons of the Commons House of Parliament .... " *a lespeciall request de ses temporall Seignors, et en especiall a le diligent et effectuall instance & labor de plusors honorables chivalers & divers auters substantiall persons del comen meason de Parliament* ' .... took to his spiritual counsel divers Doctors, as well divines as canonists ;

FIRST CONFERENCE AT BLACKFRIARS

the which spiritual counsel of the King and also the spiritual counsel of the Clergy, on a certain day assigned to them by the King at the house called Blackfriars in London, argued the matter before the Justices and temporal counsel of the King : at which time the matter was set forth ; and Doctor Henry Standish, doctor of divinity and also Warden of the Mendicant Friars in London, for the King said that the said Act, and also the conventing of clerks before the temporal judge for criminal causes, as had always been customary by the law of the land, could well stand with the law of God and with the liberties of Holy Church, and were contrariant in nothing : for they were things which promoted the public good of all the realm, which public good must be preferred in all the laws of the world.

Doctor ——— for the spiritualty, speaking on the other side, said that there was a decree made expressly to the contrary, which decree all persons of the Christian Religion are required to obey on pain of mortal sin : And so the conventing of clerks before a temporal judge for criminal causes is sin in itself.

Standish : God forbid ; for there is a decree that all Bishops should be resident in their Cathedral Church on each feast of the year. And we see well that the greater part of all the Bishops of England commonly do the reverse. And, for another thing, this decree about the exemption of clerks was never received here in England : for the contrary has always been done, as well at the time of the making of the decree as before and after. And so, being that the decree was never received here in England, therefore it is not binding.

To which, as to the said decree, no answer was given.

Nevertheless, the said doctor, for the Clergy, said that the exemption of clerks was made by the express commandment of our Saviour Jesus Christ in these words, ' Nolite tangere Christos meos ' ; against which commandment no usage to the contrary can stand ; for if any law be made or used which cannot stand with the law of God, that law is damnable in itself ; and therefore the custom of conventing clerks for causes of crime before the temporal judge is clean contrary to the commandment of God. So that it is sin in itself.

Standish : Those words ' Nolite tangere Christos meos ' were spoken by the prophet David in his Psalter, which was made more than a thousand years before the Incarnation of our Saviour ; but I assure you that you never found in your life, nor ever will find in any book, that those words were uttered or spoken by the mouth of our Saviour Jesus. And the reason which moved King David to put those words in the Psalter was that the greater part of the people at that time were unbelievers, and there was then but a small number who were of his sect, that is, who believed in the law of Moses and

146

in the Old Testament. And those who were of his sect he called
Christs ; and therefore he commanded the rest, who were unbelievers, that they should not touch or harm his Christs.

To which the said Doctor gave no reply. And yet it was he who
was the principal cause of the schism between the Spiritualty and
Temporalty touching the conventing of clerks before the temporal
judge, and took upon him to confound all those who held any
opinion to the contrary. But when he came to the arguments he
could say nothing to the purpose. Whereupon,

SOME OF THE COMMONS MOVE THE BISHOPS :
WITHOUT SUCCESS

Certain of the said Knights . . . . " *certaine des dits chivalers* " . . . .
when they had heard and perceived the said reasons on the one part
and on the other, moved divers of the Bishops that they should cause
the said Abbot to repair to the said Cross of St. Paul, and himself
openly renounce his said first Sermon ; to do which the Bishops
openly refused, and said that they were held by the law of Holy
Church to maintain the said opinion of the said Abbot in every part
of the said Sermon according to their power.

And so the matter rested for the time being, and further until
Michaelmas Term then next following.

A PARENTHESIS : HUNNE AND HORSEY

And at the same time one Doctor Horsey, chancellor to the Bishop
of London, found means that one Jo. Hunne of London, merchant,
was arrested on suspicion of heresy ; upon which the same Doctor,
by authority of his office, committed this same Hunne to the ward
and custody of one Joseph at the Bishop's prison called the Lollards'
Tower at Paul's in London aforesaid : between which Doctor
Horsey and Hunne there was bad blood (malice) beforehand by
reason of a praemunire then pending against the said Doctor at the
suit of this same Hunne. And then, one day in the morning, the
said Hunne was found hanging dead in his chamber in the said
Tower : whereupon the said Doctor and Joseph gave out that the
said Hunne had hanged himself by his silken girdle. Nevertheless,

within a short time after, the said Joseph the gaoler, perceiving that he and the said Doctor were suspected of the murder of the said Hunne, took sanctuary at Westminster. On which taking of sanctuary by the gaoler, and also upon many other great presumptions, as well the said Doctor as the said Joseph the gaoler were both indicted as principals in the murder of the said Hunne, and that by great and long deliberation and by a very important (' substantiall ') inquest taken by one of the Coroners of London on view of the body of the said Hunne. And in the meantime, that is, between the time that the said Inquest was charged on view of the body of the said Hunne and before the said verdict, the Bishops, perceiving that the said Jury intended to indict the said Doctor and Joseph for the murder of the said Hunne . . . . notwithstanding that the same Bishops had given them great deliberation and exhortation to the contrary . . . . , with these many great circumstances

STANDISH CHARGED WITH HERESY IN CONVOCATION

in Michaelmas Term, Anno 7, H. 8, the said Doctor Standish was summoned and compelled to appear before all the Clergy in the Court of their general Convocation on a certain day, by virtue of a citation addressed to him out of the same Court. On which day, when he appeared, they objected against him certain articles solely by word of mouth, according to the form as followeth :

First, whether it is lawful for a temporal judge to summon clerks before him in court ? ; and

Second, whether first orders are sacred orders or not ?

Third, whether a constitution ordained by the Pope and Clergy binds a region where a contrary custom has always prevailed ?

Fourth, whether a temporal prince can call Bishops to order when they fail duly to chastise (offenders) ?

And then, on another day, W. (Warham) Archbishop of Canterbury, by his own hands delivered to him in their full court of Convocation a bill of conclusions containing in itself the effect of the said first articles, and gave him a day to answer to the said conclusions specified in the said bill.

THE PRELATES' ACTION AGAINST STANDISH

STANDISH APPEALS TO THE KING

And the said Doctor Standish, perceiving by the bill, and by the manner of their conduct, that they bore him malice, and that their principal cause was no other than his opinion in maintenance of the temporal jurisdiction of our lord the King against the opinion of the said Abbot in his said sermon : And also he perceived further that they meant to use their great power to convict him of heresy, and that he was unable to resist their malice ; wherefore he came for help to our lord the King.

THE PRELATES EXPLAIN THEIR ACTION AGAINST STANDISH

And as soon as the Clergy perceived this, they made their excuse to our lord the King that they intended to do nothing against him (Standish) for anything that he had said or done against the said Sermon when he was of the counsel of our lord the King ; but they pretended that their quarrel and cause was by reason of certain lectures which he gave long after he was of the counsel of the King, that is, at Paul's and elsewhere ; in the which lectures he held opinions according to the form specified in the said bill of conclusions ; the which were clean contrary to the law and the liberties of Holy Church ; which thing they were bound to repress according to their power : And they prayed the King's assistance according to his Coronation Oath, and also to avoid the danger of the censures of Holy Church. And then

LORDS, COMMONS AND JUDGES TAKE COUNTER ACTION

the temporal Lords and Justices, at the prompting of those of the said Commons House of Parliament.... " *per ladvertisement de ceux del dit common meason del Parliament* " .... made like instance to the King to maintain his temporal jurisdiction according to his Coronation Oath : And also to help the said Doctor Standish in his great danger against the malice of the said Clergy ; for the principal matter of their bill against him and the matter of which the Abbot spoke in his said Sermon were all one in effect, for both were on the exemption of clerks.

THE KING CONSULTS THE DEAN OF HIS CHAPEL

Whereupon, when our lord the King had heard and perceived the said requests of both parties, the King summoned Doctor Veisey, the Dean of his Chapel, commanding him upon his faith and allegiance to tell him impartially the truth upon his knowledge and conscience, as to whether the conventing of clerks here in England before the temporal judges in criminal causes was plainly against the law of God and against the liberties of Holy Church, as those of the Spiritualty said, or not. Whereupon the said Doctor Veisey, after full consideration, answered our lord the King and said, on his faith and conscience and on his allegiance, that the conventing of clerks before the temporal judges, as had always been the custom in the realm of England, might well stand with the law of God and with the liberties of Holy Church, and showed the King divers considerations and reasons in maintenance of his opinion.

SECOND CONFERENCE AT BLACKFRIARS : STANDISH HEARD ON THE CHARGES OF HERESY

And then the Justices and all the King's Counsel spiritual and temporal, and also certain persons of the said Parliament House .... "*auxi certaine persons del dit Parliament meason*" ...., assembled by command of the King at the said house called Blackfriars in Ludgate on the same matter.

(A brief summary of the passage which follows. Standish, called upon to answer to the charges of heresy preferred by Convocation, affirms that " the conventing of clerks before the secular judge is not against the positive law of God " ; and that " the positive laws of the Church, whereof the contrary has been practised for 300 years, are only binding on those who receive them." He replies effectively to the contention of the spiritualty that the conventing of clerks before the temporal judge is a breach of the commandment ' Honour thy father.' Dr. Veisey " argued to the same effect," giving the conference the reasons he had already given to the King, and instancing the case of clerical marriage amongst the " East Christians," the Roman decree prohibiting such marriage never having been received in the Eastern Church. " Therefore, and a fortiori, the conventing of clerks here in England is permissible by reason of continual usage.")

THE JUDGES MAKE UP THEIR MINDS : PRAEMUNIRE

And then, that is, after the Justices had heard and fully considered all the reasons and arguments of both parts, that is, as well on the part of our said lord the King in maintenance of his temporal jurisdiction as on the part of the Clergy in maintenance of their spiritual jurisdiction, they reached the clear decision .... " ils fieront pleine determination " .... that all those of the said Convocation who were concerned in the said citation against the said Doctor Standish were in case of ' Praemunire facias,' &.

And further the Justices said that our lord the King might perfectly well hold his Parliament by himself and his temporal Lords and by his Commons quite without the spiritual Lords ; for the spiritual Lords have no place in the Parliament-chamber by reason of their spiritualty but only by reason of their temporal possessions, &.

((The conclusion of the Judges having brought matters to a head, there followed the final series of episodes)).

THE KING IN PARLIAMENT AT BAYNARD'S CASTLE

And then practically all the Lords spiritual and temporal, and many of the Knights and others of the Commons House of Parliament .... " et plusors des Chivalers et auters del common Meason del Parliament " ...., and also all the Justices and King's Counsel spiritual and temporal, assembled by command of the King at Baynard's Castle before the King himself to deal with the said cause. At which time

WOLSEY EXCUSES THE CLERGY

the Cardinal Archbishop of York* knelt before the King and, for the Clergy, said that to his knowledge none of the Clergy had ever meant to do anything in derogation of the King's prerogative ; and for his own part he said that he owed his whole advancement solely

* Wolsey had been raised to the cardinalate in September.

to our lord the King ; wherefore he said that he would assent to nothing that would tend to annul or derogate from his royal authority for all the world. Nevertheless, to all the Clergy this matter of the conventing of clerks before the temporal judge seems contrary to the laws of God and the liberties of Holy Church, the which he himself and all the prelates of Holy Church are bound by their oath to maintain according to their power. Wherefore, in the name of all the Clergy, he earnestly moved the King, for avoiding danger of the censures of Holy Church, to be content that the matter might be determined by our Holy Father the Pope and his Counsel at the Court of Rome.

THE KING'S CURT REPLY

Whereon our lord the King answered and said, " It seems to us that Doctor Standish and others of our spiritual Counsel have answered you sufficiently on all points."

BISHOP FOXE'S OUTBURST

At which the Bishop of Winchester answered our lord the King in these English words : " Sir, I warrant you Doctor Standish will not abide by his opinion at his peril."

Whereto the said Doctor answered in these words : " What should one poor friar do alone, against all the Bishops and the Clergy of England ? " As who should say that this was more for fear of their malice than for any good reason that they had or could have to the contrary.

ARCHBISHOP AND LORD CHIEF JUSTICE

And, after some consideration, the Archbishop of Canterbury, in the name of the Clergy, made like instance to the King, and said that in ancient times divers holy fathers of the Church had withstood the usage of the law of the land on this point, and some of them had suffered martyrdom in that quarrel.

And Fineux (Sir John Fineux, Lord Chief Justice) replying said that the conventing of clerks had been maintained by divers holy Kings, and many good holy fathers of the Church had been obedient and content with the usage of the law of the land in this point, which it is not to be presumed they would have done if they had believed or thought that it would be clean contrary to the laws of God, as you say nowadays.

And, for another thing, you have no authority by your law to bring anyone to answer for felony before you.

To which the Archbishop said that they had sufficient authority to bring them to answer ; and yet he did not say when or by what law.

And Fineux replying said, moreover, that in case a clerk was arrested by the secular hand for murder or felony, and then the temporal judge committed him to you according to your desire, you have no authority by your law, when he comes to you, to make determination for this murder or felony ; wherefore, to commit him to you, and when he comes you cannot deal with him, what intent or purpose would there be in sending him to you ?

To which no answer was made.

THE KING, CONCLUDING, ASSERTS HIS SOVEREIGNTY, AND REFUSES CONCESSIONS OR REFERENCE TO ROME

Whereupon our lord the King spoke as follows :—

" By the ordinance and sufferance of God we are King of England, and the Kings of England in time past have never had any superior but God only. Wherefor know you well that we will maintain the right of our Crown and of our temporal jurisdiction, as well in this point as in all others, in as ample a wise as any of our progenitors have done before us. And as to your decrees, we are well informed that you yourselves of the Spiritualty do expressly contrary to the words of many of them, as has been well shown to you by some of our spiritual Counsel : nevertheless, you interpret your decrees at your pleasure. Wherefor, consent to your desire more than our progenitors have done in time past we will not."

THE ARCHBISHOP'S FINAL PLEA

Whereupon the said Archbishop of Canterbury, in the name of the Clergy, made humble instance to the King that the matter might be held over until they could obtain a solution of the Court of Rome at their own costs and charges ; and if it might stand with the laws of God, they would be well content to be conformable to the Common Law of the land, &.

IGNORED BY THE KING

To which the King made no reply.

EPILOGUE. HORSEY AND STANDISH : A POLITICAL DEAL

Nevertheless, by reason of this motion they found means that the said Doctor Horsey should be preserved out of the temporal hands ; and he was in the household of the said Archbishop of Canterbury, in a way at liberty under colour of being a prisoner, until the great rumour of the said Hunne was to some extent abated, and they had made his peace with the King for the said murder ; and then he came privily into the King's Bench and surrendered himself prisoner to the Court ; and on that he was arraigned on the said indictment ' super visum corporis ' for the death of the said Hunne, and pleaded not guilty. And Ernley the King's Attorney (Sir John Ernley, Attorney-General) allowed the plea ; whereupon he was discharged ; and as to the said Doctor Standish, at the said last assembly before the King at Baynard's Castle the said Bishops promised the King, in part by his commandment and in part to do him pleasure, that he should be dismissed out of the Court of Convocation, and so it was done.

And note that every time the Bishops came before the King for the said matter, the said Doctor Standish was put aside, save at the very end of the last day.*

Such is Robert Keilwey's narrative. This last touch, and many other touches of intimate narration, seem to me to leave little doubt that it was compiled from material supplied by Standish himself. Nothing would be more natural than for Standish to

---

* (Keilwey, ' Reports d'ascuns cases,' Anno 7 Henrici octavi, 180 - 5, ed. 1688.)

preserve a record of proceedings in which he had borne so forward a part, and the importance of which was made more and more patent by subsequent events, events which he, himself a Bishop, survived distressfully to see. He lived to see the royal sovereignty reaffirmed formally in Acts of Parliament extending it to fields in which the boldest of the King's progenitors had forborne to trespass ; and his mind may well have gone back to that first assertion of sovereignty to which Henry had been provoked by the temerarious prelates of 1515. His thoughts may well have turned to Richard Hunne : and to the question whether it was worth while, for the sake of saving an incrimated clerk from trial, to stir such ' dangerous thoughts ' in the mind of such a King.

There survives in the Record Office another account of these proceedings in the handwriting of Brian Tuke, at that time Wolsey's secretary. It gives the story from the point of view of Wolsey and his fellow-prelates ; and shows that Keilwey had in no way overdrawn the perturbation produced among them by the warning of the Judges that in charging Standish with heresy they had put themselves " in case of Praemunire facias."

The document (' Letters and Papers of Henry VIII, vol. 2, no. 1314) evidently embodies the answer of the prelates to the Judges' warning. In a curious blend of assertiveness and submission, they make a lame and shuffling attempt to represent their action against Standish as having meant nothing in particular, and Standish himself as a person of no particular account. Their animus against Standish, whom they looked upon as a renegade, is undisguised. As to the details of their procedure, about which there seems to have been some dispute, they urge that their word should be taken against his. They admit having put to him certain incriminating questions ; but they plead that to question is not to affirm, and that in affirming nothing they had nothing offended. They protest their claim to speak their mind about Acts of Parliament, such as the Criminous Clerks Act, as freely as did the Parliament-men about the measures of Convocation. And, concluding rather plaintively, they " beseech the King, as they have ever been loyal subjects, nor impeached nor intended to impeach his prerogative, not to credit any sinister information against them, but suffer them to keep their Convocation as his predecessors have done."

They do not dispute the Judges' declaration that they sat in Parliament only by reason of their temporalities, and therefore in dependence upon the King's pleasure. Convocation, as to its summons and the duration of its sessions, was closely coupled with Parliament ; and the prelates seem to have been possessed with a serious fear that if their summons to Parliament was withheld, the royal writs of summons to Convocation, addressed to the Archbishops and through them to the lesser dignitaries, might be withheld likewise. In that case Convocation, the legislature of the Church, would cave in, an alarming prospect. But Convocation was not only a legislature, but the supreme court of justice in cases of heresy ; and its activities for a century past, and since the days of Wyclif, had mainly been concerned with the extirpation of heresy. And, in the course of these proceedings, they had seen a charge of heresy taken out of their hands, and the defendant examined and exonerated by the King's Council. That, of course, was exceptional, and due to the fact of his being one of the King's spiritual advisers. But it was a plain warning to the prelates of what might happen to their own peculiar jurisdiction if they went too far in impugning the jurisdiction of the Common Law. Hence this document, the deprecatory bleat of men who saw, too late, that they had been led by their bellwether, Fitzjames, to the brink of that barbarous precipice called Praemunire, and that it behoved them to draw back with all convenient speed.

The King, for his part, had no desire to embarrass their retreat. He had, as yet, no thought of disturbing the mediaeval order by which spiritualty and temporalty exercised something like co-ordinate authority in the governance of the lieges. Though not yet titular Defender of the Faith, he was a zealous son of the Church, and her protection was part and parcel of his own regality. He depended largely upon the prelates, as ministers and diplomatists, to carry on his government, and had no desire to see their order in discredit. At the joint parliamentary assembly at Baynárd's Castle he had affirmed his prerogative with sufficient distinctness ; and had given effect to it, and to the rule of the Common Law, by having Horsey, a clerk in Holy Orders indicted for murder, arraigned before the King's Bench. That done, he was content to placate the spirituality by directing his Attorney-General to proceed no further with the charge, and by allowing Wolsey to arrange the curious process of barter by which Horsey was exchanged for Standish and everybody's face was saved. Horsey and " the other," arraigned along with him, pleaded not guilty ; the Crown offered no evidence ; and the prisoners were discharged. We know from Keilway, and from More's derisory story (see pp. 28 - 30, 98 - 101) that some obscure efforts had been made to give colour to the idea that the case had been abandoned on its merits. But the reasons for its abandonment were obviously political. For over a year the death of Hunne and the fate of Horsey had given rise to agitation and recrimination of the bitterest kind. They had led to a pitched battle in Parliament between the Commons and the spiritual Lords. To reopen the case in the King's Bench, and to have the evidence which had satisfied the Coroner's Jury sworn to again before " any twelve men in London " — to borrow Fitzjames' words to Wolsey — would be to rekindle a blaze which the Government, that is to say the King and Wolsey, had every reason for allowing to die down. Hunne could not be recalled to life ; and having been, as the authorities had been led to believe, a guilty heretic, the manner of his death was not a matter which need be permitted to disturb the peace of the kingdom. From the point of view of the Government the question of Horsey's guilt or innocence was neither here nor there. In considering the course taken, we have to rid ourselves of the present-day notion of the course of justice as a thing inviolable, and not subject to influence or interference from the executive. In Tudor times, and long before and after, pure justice might at any time have to give place to the ' raison d'État.' The independence of the judiciary, secured in later times among the results of civil war and revolution, was still an achievement of the far future. At this time the Judges held office at the King's pleasure ; and where state policy was concerned, their duty to subserve that policy was taken for granted. There was, beside, the royal prerogative. If a man like

Horsey offended against the King's peace, he might be allowed to make his peace for reasons satisfactory to the King, and, more often than not, for a substantial consideration. Henry's father had instituted the Court of Star Chamber, an offshoot of the Council, in order to deal with " over-mighty subjects " or other persons against whom it was impossible or inexpedient to proceed by the ordinary course of law. The Star Chamber dealt with such offenders by committal to the Tower, or by more or less heavy pecuniary mulcts, or both. Such transactions might or might not be the subject of record ; and Simon Fish, in referring to two of them in his ' Supplication of Beggars,' does so with a cautious ' it is said.' One case is that of one of Wolsey's agents, Dr. Thomas Allen, who, for some obscure offence under the head of praemunire, had to pay five-hundred pounds. The other case is that of this man Horsey, who, " for him and his complices," had to pay a sum of six hundred pounds, a crippling fine and equivalent to about eighteen thousand pounds in our present-day money. It was said that Allen's fine went towards the building of the Star Chamber. We are left to speculate about the destination of Horsey's fine, if fined he was. Sir Thomas More in his ' Supplication of Souls,' written (1529) a year after the ' Dialogue,' — a piece in which the honey of the Dialogue gives place to vitriol — numbers this allegation of the fine among the series of " loud lies " which he attributes over-liberally to Simon Fish. In this case, however, More's denial is more oblique and less downright, though not less unsupported by evidence, than his other denials ; and he himself lends colour to the allegation by a suggestion, which he fathers gratuitously upon Simon Fish, that Horsey, not being likely to have had the money to meet the fine, was given his subsequent preferments so as to be able to reimburse the backers who had found it for him.* This

* What Fish says is : " The other (Horsey) (as it is said) paid six hundred pounds for him and his complices, which, forbecause that he had likewise fought so manfully against your crown and dignity, was immediately (as he had obtained your most gracious pardon) promoted by the captains of his kingdom with benefice upon benefice, to the value of four times as much ".
On this More writes : " We might and we would lay for the fifth (lie) the payment which he speaketh of, the six hundred pounds with which money he

seems to be in line with what Keilwey says about Horsey being
" in the household of the said Archbishop of Canterbury, in a way
at liberty under colour of being a prisoner, until the great rumour
of the said Hunne was to some extent abated, and they had made
his peace with the King for the said murder." It is not easy to
see how " they," his supporters, could have made his peace with
the King except by a liberal greasing of the royal palm. About the
fact of the fine Dr. Pollard (' Wolsey,' p. 51 and note 1), whose
judgment is of the weightiest, entertains no doubt. What is certain
is that Horsey had to leave London a broken man, broken in career
if not in pocket. He ceased forthwith to be Bishop's chancellor,
and had to relinquish his London preferments. He retained two
country prebends ; and in his subsequent life of thirty years he
became prebendary of Chichester and Wells and canon residentiary
of Exeter. He lived on till 1545, long enough to see his whole order
reap the full harvest of the ugly seed which he and his portentous
Bishop had helped to sow.

He was legally innocent, in the sense that he had not been tried
and found guilty ; but it is not clear that those who laboured for,
or assented to, his release regarded him as innocent in any other
sense. The treatment accorded to him was not that of an innocent
man. If Keilwey's story represents the view of Standish, and if
Standish's view was that of his associates, the King, the judges and
the temporal lords, it would seem that all of them regarded Hunne's
case as a case of murder, and Horsey as a man who needed to have
his peace made for the murder. And the stiffness and decision with
which the King and the judges withstood the pretensions of the
spiritualty in the matter of clerical immunity points to a perfect
understanding on their part that the large general question had

would men should ween that he bought his pardon. Wherein he layeth a good
great sum, to the end that folk, well witting that Doctor Horsey was not like
to have so much money of his own, should ween therewith that the clergy laid
out the money among them, and then gave him benefices whereof he might pay
them again. But this layeth he from himself, and sheweth not to whom, for
he saith it is said so. And yet were it no wrong that it were accounted his till
he put it better from him and prove of whom he heard it. Howbeit, sith there
is other store enough, we shall leave this lie in question between him and we
wot not here whom else."

159

been raised upon a particular, and a particularly bad, case. And the precipitancy with which the prelates gave ground in the face of opposition may have been due, not only to their awe of Praemunire, but to a sense, among the less reckless, that the occasion for reversing their action in 1512 and asserting the principle of immunity in its starkest form, had not been happily chosen. There was not much promise in standing for such a principle at a moment when, as everybody knew, its immediate application was to an eminent clerk then under indictment for what all the attendant circumstances made a peculiarly detestable crime.

In conclusion I may advert again to the passage in the ' Dialogue ' in which More, in the perfect manner both of courtier and special pleader, argues from Horsey's discharge to Horsey's innocence (quoted above, pp. 107 - 8). His ground in King Henry the Eighth's inexpugnable zeal for justice — that same justice which, within seven years of the time of writing, was to bring More's own head to the block. His bland argument from the royal passion for justice contains one rather fatal flaw. What applies to Horsey must apply equally to " the other," that mysterious " other " of whom More is studious to tell his readers nothing. The other was Charles Joseph, the gaoler of the Lollards' Tower, arraigned with Horsey and discharged along with him.* A year before, Joseph had been taken from sanctuary to the Tower of London, and there examined by king's counsel in the presence of certain members of the Jury and others. Having put forward a disreputable alibi which broke down, he thereupon confessed to the murder, and implicated Horsey as an active participant.

More knew these facts, or, being a privileged person, had the means of knowing them ; did know them if, as he says, he knew the case from top to toe. But he is writing, fourteen years after the event, for a public predisposed to the suggestion that the whole Hunne story had little in it but " many suspicious tales, be they never so false." Against mere " suspicious rumour " More's

* " The other " may be intended as a plural, and in that case would include the bellringer Spalding.

argument applied with telling effect ; but it crumbles completely on impact with the facts. Not a single fact sworn to at the Inquest does More so much as even mention. He indeed puts forward some lengthy and laboured nonsense as representing the evidence ; but one has only to compare it with the real evidence to see what sorry fustian it is. Though writing on the very eve of it, More could not foresee the rapid turn of events which made it possible, within a few years, for the justificatory statement of the Jury to appear in print : anonymously, owing to the continuing hazard of the times. In the tiny booklet in which it appeared, disinterested historians, despite its anonymity, have seen a plain tale which was not, and could not have been, the product of invention. " No doubt," writes Dr. Pollard (' Wolsey,' p. 36, note), " it was published as good propaganda. But there is no reason to suppose that it was anything else than what it purported to be, i.e. the coroner's signed report of the proceedings in his court." It is very certain that, had More anticipated its possible publication, he would have preferred the better part of silence in regard to the case of Richard Hunne. That he should have addressed himself to it, and employed all his forensic arts to make something of it, indicates that fourteen years afterwards, and within a year or so of the opening of the Reformation Parliament, the memory of the case, and the indignation it had aroused, were as fresh and fierce as ever.

APPENDIX TO PART I

BENEFIT OF CLERGY

In the fourth year of Henry VIII, 1512, there was passed a very remarkable Act of Parliament. It withdrew from clergy in minor orders, that is to say, from psalmists, lectors, acolytes, exorcists, all in orders below the degree of subdeacon, their agelong immunity from the ordinary law punishments for crime. This, the immunity from lay punishments for crime, is what ' benefit of clergy,' by this time, had come to mean. As such, it was not so much the law of the Church as a grudging concession to it, made in mitigation of its substantial overthrow by the courts of common law. It was a mere remnant and fag-end of the authentic ' privilegium clericale ' which Holy Church laid down for all Christendom, and for all Christian people, from Kings downwards.

By the ' privilegium clericale ' which the Church asserted, a clerk accused of felony or murder was to answer only to his Bishop. He could not even be brought before any secular judge. It was a question among the canonists whether a layman or the officers of the lay power could lay hands upon him even when caught in some criminal act. But the better opinion was that if a layman found a clerk interfering (' turpiter agens ') with his womenkind or committing some felony by which he himself was personally endamaged, he could forcibly deter and detain the offender. But the limit of that allowable detention was twenty hours. The accused had then to be handed over to his Bishop to be dealt with according to Canon Law, and tried by such process as was open to the spiritual court. But the spiritual court possessed no process by which it could try the facts. It could only proceed by ' compurgation.' The Bishop might put the accused to his " purgation," might call upon him to clear himself by his own oath and by the oaths of a few others who would swear to his credibility. And if, by perjury or otherwise, he could so clear himself, the Bishop had no choice but to release him. In the earlier Middle Ages, when ecclesiastical discipline was something of a reality, a notorious criminal who failed in his purgation might be excommunicated and degraded from his orders. And what was to happen to a felon so degraded and reduced to the status of a layman was one of the matters in controversy between Becket and Henry II.

At the time of this controversy two important things were happening at once. The decretals of a long line of Popes, genuine and other, were being digested into a great system of ecclesiastical jurisprudence, which was promulgated as law for the universal Church. Side by side with this, statesmen like Henry II and his ministers were laying the foundations of strong and orderly government in England on the basis of the indigenous Common Law. The Canon Law of the Church and the Common Law of England were diverse both in purpose and procedure. The primary purpose of the latter, — as it remained the primary purpose of all Kings and Governments until the advent of the recent motor age — was to protect the lives and limbs of the king's lieges and to secure them against killers and maimers of every sort. Henry could not see why the degraded ex-clerk who had committed murder should be suffered merely to walk abroad, and not be hanged like any other layman. Basing himself upon what he alleged to be the former custom of the realm, he claimed the right to hang the clerk degraded. Becket would have none of this, on the ground that it meant a double penalty for the one offence ; and the revulsion of feeling occasioned by the murder of Becket made it necessary for the King to withdraw his claim.

In the course of the century which followed upon the death of Becket the practice of excommunicating and degrading the criminous clerk — and so exposing him to the untender mercies of the Common Law, — appears to have been suspended. It was resumed, some two centuries later, in order to qualify clerks whose crime was adherence to Wycliffite doctrine, for burning by the secular arm. Holy Church, squeamish about allowing the sheriffs to hang her felons, was insistent upon their duty to burn her heretics. But meanwhile Archbishop Boniface (1245 - 1270) had prescribed

163

another way of dealing with the clerical felon. One of his 'constitutions' (1260) directs that every Bishop shall maintain one or two prisons, and that the criminal in orders, whose crime would have entailed execution had he been a layman, shall be kept in perpetual custody. The facility of purgation and the fragility of the Bishop's prisons ensured that this penal hospitality should not be an undue drain upon episcopal resources. Of how little account the process of purgation was held by the courts of common law is shown by a constitution of Archbishop Peckham, the successor of Boniface next but one. After a pointed warning given in Parliament four years before, Peckham ordains (1279) that

" Clerici pro suis criminibus detenti a publica potestate, et tandem pro convictis Ecclesiae restituti, non faciliter liberentur, nec perfunctorie pro eis purgatio admittatur, sed cum omni juris solennitate, et tam provida maturitate ut oculos merito offendere non debeat Regiae Majestatis, seu quorumlibet aliorum quos exagitat studium aequitatis." : that clerks in the custody of the public authority for their crimes, and at length restored to the Church for convicted, are not to be lightly set at liberty, nor is purgation for them to be admitted perfunctorily but with all solemnity of law, and with such full consideration as to avoid giving just offence to the eyes of the King's Majesty, or of any others who are concerned for the course of justice." Peckham's constitution points to a new procedure which had recently been adopted by the common law Judges, whose eyes had already been offended to some purpose. The Judges, as yet, are far from impugning the principle of the ' privilegium clericale ' ; they do not pretend to try the accused clerk, or even require him to plead. But they insist upon having him before them, and submitting the facts against him to the inquisition of a lay jury. If, upon the facts, the jury find him guilty, he is surrendered to the Bishop as a ' clericus convictus ' along with the documents in the case. The canonists insist that this word ' convictus ' is only a manner of speaking, since no one can convict him but the spiritual judge. They insist likewise, that the spiritual judge is in no way bound to take account of the findings of the secular court, though if these afford a presumption of guilt, the

Bishop, if he thinks fit, may put the accused to his purgation. If, by perjury or otherwise, he succeeds in his purgation, the Bishop has no choice but to release him. Still, this cautionary procedure of the common law had two effects. It gave some security that purgation in the Bishop's court should not be admitted " perfunctorily," or, that, if it was, the scandal of it should be evident. It had the further effect that the goods of the ' clericus convictus ' were forfeited to the Crown, and remained forfeit whatever the outcome of the proceedings in the Bishop's court. Against this practice — of confiscating the goods of the clerk convict notwithstanding his purgation — Archbishop Boniface inveighed in one of his many fulminatory constitutions. But the Common Law was like a deaf adder that stoppeth her ears. As time went on the secular judges viewed with ever more offended eyes the criminal enclave in which the Church insisted upon sheltering evildoers who, but for her protection, would have been summarily hanged. It is necessary to recollect who and what manner of men were too many of those who took, and remained in, minor orders. The laxity of the Bishops in admitting men to orders was a byword in the time of More and long before. Pretty well any man who had sufficient learning to stumble through his ' neck-verse ' if his neck was in danger, could get himself ordained. The criminal element present in every society were not long in discovering that the minor orders of the Church committed them to nothing in particular, and afforded a safe harbourage and anchorage for a career of crime. Two brothers might conspire to commit a felony. Taken red-handed, one of them, being wholly illiterate, would be convicted and hanged ; the other, having a tincture of letters and being possibly, though not necessarily, in minor orders, would plead his clergy ; and, after an inquiry into the facts by a lay jury, he would be handed over to the Bishop with the evidences of his crime. The Bishop, if he paid any attention to these — and he was not bound to do so by the Canon Law — might put the accused to his purgation ; and only an unthrifty knave, in planning a crime, would have neglected to provide himself with a few others likeminded, but not immediately in the hands of justice, who would back his own oath of innocence and swear to him as a reputable and credible person. And having so purged himself, he was free to depart the Bishop's presence, and with no care in the world but to replace the illgotten goods which, despite Boniface and purgation ' omni Juris solennitate,' remained forfeit to the Crown. That such a system should have survived so long is impressive testimony to the weight of conscience and authority behind it. Alive though they were to its present mischiefs, men retained a dim memory of times when secular Governments, at the feet of the Church, were only learning their business, and when the immunity of clerks from secular jurisdiction made for the defence rather than the defeat of justice. Those days were long past ; and, as time went on, the English courts of common law became more and more restive under their own impotence in the face of a privilege which was brazenly abused and made any common order of justice impossible. But it was not until the middle of the fifteenth century that the patience of the Common Law gave out, and that its foot was set decisively on this anarchic element in the law of Holy Church. Thenceforward the common law courts affect no reverence for the ' privilegium clericale,' and pay only the most displeasant deference to it. They not only arraign the criminous clerk, but try and convict him like any layman. Only after conviction is he suffered to plead his clergy ; and he is only surrendered to his Bishop " absque purgatione,' subject to the condition that he shall not be admitted to purgation, perfunctory or other. The Bishop, if he insists on sheltering the convicted felon, must keep him for life. The Judges, in so insisting, were giving effect to the unfulfilled promise, made by the prelates to a Parliament of Henry IV, that, in accordance with a constitution which they undertook, but failed, to make, a clerk convicted of petty treason or thievery and delivered to his Bishop, should be kept " safely and surely " and not suffered to " make purgation against the purport of the said constitution."

This slow, progressive, but finally drastic limitation of the ' privilegium clericale ' had been effected by the courts of Common Law. It was not until early in the reign of Henry VII, when the king and his ministers were bent upon making the law respected and supreme, that Parliament addressed itself to the problem of the criminous clerk. And its first essay, in 1488, was not directed against clerks properly so called, men who had actually received the tonsure. These retained intact their immunity from the ordinary lay punishment for crime, subject only to the requirement that if, after a first conviction by the lay court for felony or murder, they broke the Bishop's prison or otherwise regained their liberty, they should, upon a second conviction, produce their Letters of Orders in proof of their clergy and their right to go on claiming its privileges. The Act of 1488 was aimed at the lay criminal who had been suffered to enjoy the privilege of a clerk, and avoid the hangman, on account of his ability to read his ' neck-verse.' Even he retained his privilege on the first offence. But, as a means of identification in case he too broke prison and relapsed into crime, the Act prescribed that, at the time of conviction and before delivery to his Bishop, he should be branded by the gaoler " upon the brawn of the left thumb," the murderer with an M, thieves and other felons with a T.

This Act, like many others, produced unforeseen results. Shaven crowns were a sound insurance against branded thumbs ; — and the qualification for minor orders being of the slenderest, persons who meant to take up crime as a career took the obvious precaution to get themselves ordained. Within a generation Pope Leo X, in a bull issued at the instance of Wolsey, (Feb. 12th, 1516), declared himself to be credibly informed that in the kingdom of England people took the first clerical tonsure and minor orders, not with any purpose of proceeding to the higher sacred orders, but in order to be freer to commit excesses and crimes, to evade secular justice and obtain impunity : from which it results that " the crimes of ne'er-do-wells remain unpunished, clergyhood is besmirched and justice itself not a little hindered." (Pollard, ' Wolsey,' p. 31, note 1 ; Rymer's Foedera, XIII, 532 - 3). The evil had reached such dimensions that a Parliamentary attempt had been made to deal with it, four years before (1512), in the remarkable Act referred to at the beginning of this Appendix. Warham, Archbishop of Canterbury, and Bishop Fox of Winchester were both ministers of the Crown ;

167

and were alive to the scandal and mischief, both to Church and Realm, of allowing the Orders of the Church to become a sort of dug-out in which malefactors could take shelter and be safe from justice. They prevailed upon their colleagues in the House of Lords, in which the prelates at this period held a majority, to consent to a measure by which convict clerks in minor orders, all, that is, below the degree of subdeacon, were deprived of all remaining " benefit of clergy " and left subject to the ordinary lay punishments for crime. This, in view of what had gone before, was a revolutionary measure, the first of Henry VIII's reign ; but, unlike those which were to follow it twenty years later, it was very short-lived. Not all the prelates were like Foxe and Warham. Many, probably the majority, were fairly represented by Richard Fitzjames, Bishop of London, an able administrator with his face turned backwards, a smeller-out of heresy in any suggestion of reform. By him and his like the Act of 1512 must have been accepted with misgiving, as the thin end of perhaps an ominous wedge. It was, doubtless, to placate their scruples that the Act was made a temporary measure, to last only till the meeting of a subsequent Parliament.

That Parliament met on February 5th, 1515. A few days before its opening an official sermon had been delivered at Paul's Cross by one of the most reputable ecclesiastics of the day (see above, pp. 141 - 2). It was devoted to a downright, root and branch denunciation of the Act of 1512. He denounced it as an invasion of the liberties of the Church ; he declared, in strict accordance with Canon Law — as laid down by Lyndwood for example — that the distinction drawn in the Act between minor and holy orders was inadmissible ; that, by the law of Holy Church, no clerk, in any degree of orders, could be ' convented ' before any secular tribunal ; and that all concerned in the passing of the Act had incurred ecclesiastical censures. In these contentions he was supported, through prolonged debates in Parliament and Convocation, by all the prelates whose action he had impeached. For this sudden and complete change of front there is an explanation, and only one. The question, at the opening of the new Parliament in February,

1515, was not the general question whether accused clerks in minor orders should be convented before lay tribunals. It was the pressing and particular question whether a priest in Holy Orders, a Doctor of Canon Law, and no less a person than the Bishop of London's chancellor, Dr. William Horsey, indicted by a Coroner's jury, should be brought to trial in the King's Bench for the wilful murder of a freeman of London, found hanging in the Bishop's prison two months before.

Part II

THE REFORMATION PARLIAMENT
1529 - 1533

A REVIEW OF EVENTS
FROM THE DOWNFALL OF WOLSEY
TO THE BIRTH OF ELIZABETH

Chapter I

THE DAY, AND THE RECKONING
THE NEW PARLIAMENT MEETS : THOMAS
CROMWELL RETURNED FOR TAUNTON

November 3rd, 1529. On that day there met " the great organic Parliament, which began in 1529 and ran on to the spring of 1536 ; a Parliament which, both on account of its length and for the importance of its acts, may deserve the title of the Long Parliament of Henry VIII " (Stubbs, ' Seventeen Lectures,' p. 269). Its acts effected a revolution, the most far-reaching in our history.

It comes into this story because its very first act — Hall indicates that it was the first — was to settle by legislation the issue which Richard Hunne, to his own undoing, had endeavoured to raise at law, and for raising which, in the way he did, he had been, in the firm belief of his fellow-citizens, most foully done to death. This was only the beginning ; and it was followed by a series of measures in which those who believe in retributive justice may see, almost too inexorably, its stern hand at work. Some at least of the prelates whose memories went back to 1515, and who wrung their hands over the humiliation of the prelacy in 1532, must have wished to God that their dead colleague Fitzjames had never laid hands on Richard Hunne, and that they themselves had never had part or lot in the effort to shield Fitzjames' chancellor.

In reviewing the work of this historic Parliament we have to rid our minds of a notion which was formerly prevalent. A generation or so ago it was a commonplace with historians of the first repute that the House of Commons was packed, and packed with a purpose ; that it had little or no mind or will of its own ; and that its sole function was to assent to measures propounded and dictated to it by a despotic King. Later research has shown such views to be, in Dr. Pollard's words, " gross exaggerations " ; (Henry VIII,' p. 252) ; that the House was not packed and that there was no need to pack it ; that it could, and did upon occasion, manifest a very decided will of its own ; and that its concurrence with the King in action was due to a community of interest sufficient as the basis of a working alliance. We may no longer regard — and spoil the interest of the drama by regarding — the King as a sort of *deus ex machina* whose sovereign will can account for everything. The Commons, like every person and institution in the country, were reverential towards the royal person and authority ; but their action is not to be explained by tyranny on one side or servility on the other.

I propose to review the origins and earlier work of this Parliament, and of the man who from the outset led, and finally ruled it. I do so from the belief that though the Commons, as time went on, were drawn into positions which were less and less their own and more and more the King's and Cromwell's, their initial proceedings against the spiritualty were quite spontaneous, and actuated by a resolve to have done with grievances and wrongs of which the case of Richard Hunne was the best remembered, and most abhorred, example. We know, from its treatment in More's ' Dialogue ' written only the year before, that no circumstance connected with that case had been forgiven or forgotten. The probable temper of the forthcoming Parliament was known to the French Embassy. Less than a fortnight before its assembly the ambassador wrote : " It is not known yet who will have the Seal," that is, as Lord Chancellor in succession to Wolsey. " I expect the priests will never have it again, and that in this Parliament they will have terrible alarms."* With the brief exception of the session of 1523, which was wholly occupied with financial business, the Commons had not met for fourteen years. They were meeting now in the firm determination to renew the struggle from which they had had to retire defeated in 1515 (see pp. 135 - 9).

There is, in the first place, the question, Why was this Parliament summoned at all ? It seems a simple, even a simpleton's question,

---

* Future references to these calendared ' Letters and Papers ' will be given simply as, e.g. 1V, 6019.

which nobody of sense would trouble to ask. Does it not stand to reason that a Parliament which carried through a great consistent scheme of action marked by every evidence of design, was summoned and designed to do so ? So it seems to have been uniformly inferred. And yet, if we consider with attention what this Parliament did, and what was in the minds of those who summoned it, the two things begin to look discrepant. So discrepant that, to my mind, the measures which made this Parliament historic have the aspect of a wholly unforeseen by-product of the writs of summons. I cannot see how these measures, any one of them or all together, can have been within the contemplation of those, the Council and the King, who, in August, 1529, advised and directed the issue of the writs. After all, revolutions, however long prepared, have rather a way of beginning fortuitously ; and it may have been so in this case.

Take, for example, what is called the ' breach with Rome,' effected within the six-years lifetime of this Parliament. In August, 1529, the majestic lord who broke the bonds of Rome had no purpose of any breach with Rome, and was engaged, for several years thereafter, in a persevering effort to persuade Rome to break in his favour the bonds of matrimony. Again, the Parliament cannot have been summoned for any project connected with the Divorce ; not for more than four years was its assent required to any such measure ; and little less than three years after its summons, when the question of the Divorce was mooted in the House, the Commons were roundly told that the King's matrimonial troubles were no concern of theirs. The Parliament was not summoned to provide for the King's monetary necessities ; few of our Parliaments have been troubled so little with demands for money ; it was nearly three years before any such demand was made upon it, and even then the demand was withdrawn ; the money kept rolling in from other sources. Again, to take only the measures of the first session — Nov. 3rd to Dec. 17th — its seems unlikely that at a moment of political excitement and upheaval, when a great administration was foundering and a great minister falling, a new Parliament should have been summoned merely in order to enable the King to bilk his creditors, many of whom would be sitting in the two Houses. It is very unlikely that the temporal lords of the Council, preoccupied with their plans for the ruin of Wolsey, would have a thought to give to such things and persons as burial dues, probate fees, and pluralist and non-resident parsons. And it is altogether unlikely that the lords spiritual, intent as their lay compeers upon Wolsey's downfall, could have designed that the writs of summons should eventuate in the appearance of a House of Commons whose immediate action would be to retrench their own revenues, and to supersede their own ancient and exclusive authority in ecclesiastical legislation. Putting aside this conspectus of the impossible and the improbable, what have we left as a reason for summoning a new Parliament at this juncture? Nothing, apparently, but the lively fear, entertained by Wolsey's enemies in the Council, of the man whom they were about to bring to ruin. To the very day when, fifteen months later, they brought him, broken in body and broken in heart, to his death at Leicester Abbey, they were in dread lest, by some caprice of the King or incompetence of their own, the Cardinal should be restored to favour. Shortly before that event, as the imperial ambassador Chapuys reports, the King had flung out of the Council after an outburst of impatience at the bungling of his affairs. He had " said in a rage that the Cardinal was a better man than any of them for managing matters ; and repeating this twice, he left them " (IV, 6738). The incident may have precipitated the plot by which his enemies contrived his arrest for treason. In August the year before, when the Cardinal was tottering to his fall, they had but one thought. For a man of such commanding gifts, who had wielded so long such commanding power, there could be only one end. Disgrace was not sufficient ; for his enemies the only safety lay in his destruction. The only sure way of compassing his destruction was by attainder in Parliament. And that is the reason and, so far as I can see, the only reason why this Parliament was summoned at the moment it was.*

* Some authorities of weight have regarded the summons of Parliament as the King's " retort " to the Pope's ' advocation ' of his Divorce suit to Rome. But there are several reasons against this. First, it implies the existence of a

For nearly two years, and sorely against his own grain, the Cardinal had been exhausting the resources of diplomacy to obtain from Pope Clement VII the judicial annulment of the King's marriage. Clement, unfortunately, was not his own master. He was in the power, and for some time the actual prisoner, of the Emperor Charles V, Queen Katherine's nephew and her determined supporter ; and, with every reason for wishing to oblige the English King, he had every reason for not daring to do so. His only course was to play for time. At long last a Legatine Court, under the Cardinals Campeggio and Wolsey, was constituted to try the cause in England. On Monday, 21st June, 1529, both King and Queen appeared before it, the centre of one of the more pathetic scenes of history. The King was sanguine of the result, believing his cause to be as good as won. Campeggio, however, had come with secret instructions to drag out the time as long as possible, and in no circumstances to proceed to judgment. The King's hopes received their first blow when, on the 27th July, Campeggio announced that the Legates must follow the practice of the Roman Court and adjourn the proceedings to the opening of the ensuing law term in October. Hall tells us that the Dukes of Norfolk and Suffolk were

matured plan that could be put into operation at a moment's notice. The writs were issued within a fortnight of the prorogation of the Legatine Court, and the news of the actual advocation did not reach England till some days after that. Secondly, if the Parliament had been summoned with any such purpose, it would have been reflected in the measures to which it at once proceeded. These measures, though important in their implications, were of no great importance in themselves ; and, considered as a retort to Rome, they were so small as to have seemed merely spiteful and silly. Thirdly, the suggestion implies that these measures, such as they were, were promoted by the King ; whereas Hall, in his lucid and intimate narrative, makes it clear that the moving spirits were " the Burgesses of the Parliament " ; that the bills were drafted, at their instance, by " such " of their number " as were learned in the law " ; and that the King's part was that of a mediator and moderator, not fomenting the difficulties between the Commons and the Spiritualty, but doing his best to smooth them out.

Hall, as an " honourable and learned member " himself, cannot have been mistaken about the atmosphere of the proceedings.

The quarrel of the Commons with the Spiritualty was, at the outset at any rate, their own quarrel : and the King's chief interest in it, and in taking advantage of it, lay in the fact that if his personal quarrel with the Pope proceeded to a rupture, it would be useful to have had the Spiritualty in England subjugated beforehand.

at once despatched to the Court to insist upon an immediate sentence. Campeggio replied with a bland but firm non possumus.
Suffolk, the King's brother-in-law and crony, brought his fist down
upon the table, exclaiming : " By the Mass, now I see that the
old-said saw is true, that there was never Legate nor Cardinal that
did good in England " (Chronicle, II, 153). The King's disappointment was extreme ; and it was changed to fury on receipt of the
news that the Court was at an end, and that the cause, under pressure
from the Emperor, had been ' advoked ' to Rome. Towards
Campeggio the forms of courtesy were observed ; but Wolsey
was within reach of the King's wrath, and upon him it fell. His
enemies on the Council, in which his long isolation of eminence
had left him without one true friend, were quick to seize their
opportunity. Wolsey had so magnified his great offices of Legate
and Chancellor as to antagonise all the alternative elements of
power : the temporal lords whom he had thrown into the shade ;
the lords spiritual whose jurisdictions he had superseded ; the
common law judges resentful of his arrogations in Chancery, all
were ready to pounce upon him at the first sign of failure. Some
had already been busy ransacking the records of his administration
for articles of charge upon which to found a Bill of Attainder ; and
within a fortnight of the suspension of the Legatine Court, the writs
were issued for the necessary Parliament.

The project of Attainder in the end fell through because the King,
upon reflection, bethought him of a better way. He had no mind
himself to destroy Wolsey. Not yet the tyrant he was, under later
and baser tuition, to become, he could not be insensible of the long
and devoted service which had relieved him of the heavier burdens
of state, and left him the freer for the jousts and junketings in which
he and his prodigal Court delighted. Moreover, after nearly twenty
years of tutelage under the Cardinal, he was by no means so sure of
himself, or of his alternative advisers, as to feel safe in dispensing
with Wolsey altogether. Wrath yielding to calculation and spleen
to cupidity, he decided that the ends of justice would be sufficiently
served by humiliating the Cardinal, incriminating his Legacy, and
appropriating his palaces and possesssions. This could be very

simply and decently done by an indictment in the King's Bench for one or two specific breaches of the ' laws of Praemunire." Outlawry and forfeiture would follow as of course. Moreover, so many people, including the King himself, had been involved in, and profited by, the Cardinal's misdemeanours that any public defence, on his part, was greatly to be deprecated. It would be better if, by promises of lenity, he could be led to admit his guilt and sign away his goods. The King's second thoughts accordingly prevailed.* On October 8th, the opening day of the new law term, Wolsey, putting a brave face upon a disastrous situation, took his seat in the Chancery for the last time. On the same day the Attorney-General preferred the indictment against him in the King's Bench. Bitterly, for a prelate who believed, now as in 1515, that by the law of God no ecclesiastic could be convented before a lay tribunal, Wolsey, with the royal licence, appointed his attornies to represent him at the trial. On the 30th they appeared, and pleaded guilty on his behalf. Sentence followed ; and the Cardinal lay stripped of everything and at the King's mercy. The case against him had been heard and judged.

With one remarkable result. The new Parliament, which assembled four days later (Nov. 3rd) for its first session, assembled in a vacuum, with nothing of general consequence before it. Summoned by writs issued in August, its raison d'être had disappeared in the interval. The case against Wolsey had been dealt with otherwise and elsewhere. The rotund banalities in which the new Lord Chancellor, Sir Thomas More, adumbrated the programme of the session, but ill concealed the fact that there was no real programme at all.†

---

* " Henry", writes Chapuys the imperial ambassador, " had ' from the beginning determined that his case should not be brought before Parliament ; for, had it been decided against him, he could not, in face of such a decision, have pardoned him as he intended to do, and has since done, as I will relate hereafter ' ". Pollard, ' Wolsey,' p. 261.

† Hall reports him as declaring " that like as a good shepherd, which not alonly keepeth and attendeth well his sheep, but also foreseeth and provideth for althing which either may be hurtful or noisome to his flock, or may preserve and defend the same against all perils that may chance to come, so the King, which was the shepherd, ruler and governor of his realm, vigilantly foreseeing things to come, considered how divers laws before this time were made now by long

179

There being no Bill of Attainder, the articles against Wolsey were petering out in a mere petition from the Upper House praying for his perpetual exclusion from office. Relieved of any immediate concern with the Lords' gravamina against Wolsey, the Commons were free to address themselves to their own, and lost no time in doing so. " When the Commons were assembled in the nether House," writes Hall, " they began to common of their griefs wherewith the spiritualty had beforetime grievously oppressed them, both contrary to the law of the realm and contrary to all right." Among them, and not without a mandate from their constituents, sat the members for the City of London. Among them too, and towering above the rest in unrevealed capacity, sat a bold, and at the moment rather desperate, adventurer who, at the eleventh hour, had been returned to the House as member for Taunton. His name, ere long to be formidably known throughout the kingdom, was Thomas Cromwell.

Cromwell, now in middle life, was a man of no particular antecedents, and no prospects but such as he could make for himself. A Putney lad, with a scapegrace father and something, it would seem, of a scapegrace himself, he early went abroad in search of fortune. He spent some years of obscure adventure in Italy and Flanders. He tried his hand at soldiering and trading ; once at least he is known to have been in straits and glad to accept help ; a later waif of fortune, at Vienna and Munich, was not at times more down upon his luck, and resolute to surmount it, than this bit of English jetsam blown about upon the continent. Living by his wits and improving them to the uttermost, he picked up a first-hand knowledge of men and things. He learnt of life in the raw, without any colouring of convention or illusion. For him the world was not a place to learn to be good in, but simply to get on in ; his working religion was the main chance. His sojourn in Italy gave

continuance of time and mutation of things very insufficient and unperfect ; and also by the frail condition of man divers new enormities were sprung amongst the people, for the which no law was yet made to reform same ; which was the very cause why at that time the King summoned his high court of Parliament ; etc." Chronicle, 11, 164.

him a close-up view of Holy Church at the centre, and the impressions not uncommon among northerners whose faith was strained by that experience. There too, either from Machiavelli's 'Prince' (then circulating in manuscript) or from the general atmosphere, he seems to have imbibed the principles of renaissance statecraft at that time dominant.

Improved in mind if not in fortune, he returned to London early in the reign of Henry VIII. Marrying prudently, he made for himself a footing in the cloth trade, and throve apace. Taking presently, in addition, to the law, he is found in practice as a scrivener, a sort of attorney-cum-moneylender, with numerous and sometimes influential clients, whose trust and regard he seems to have held. An expert draughtsman, he is busied with indentures, leases, awards, 'obligations,' legal instruments of all sorts. His moneylending activities began to bring him connections among the impecunious great. In 1524 he becomes a member of Gray's Inn, and assumes the style and title of gentleman. Now a man of some substance, conscious of his powers, and ambitious of a public career, he found a seat in the Parliament of 1523. That Parliament, of which Sir Thomas More was Speaker, was wholly occupied, first in resisting Wolsey's intrusion in its debates, then in prolonged fencing with his staggering demands for money, necessitated by a forthcoming expedition to France. Of Cromwell's part in the Parliament, if any, there is no record. But there survives, in the handwriting of one of his clerks, the draft of a speech which he prepared for delivery. It is worth while pausing upon this speech for the light it throws upon Cromwell's mind. Noticeable throughout is its undertone of obsequious sarcasm. The subsidy demanded was £800,000, no less, not much less than twenty-five millions in our money. Assuming that its ostensible purpose, to make good in arms the royal title of King of France, is really in contemplation, Cromwell, while acclaiming to the full the laudability of the project, gives his own very humble reasons for regarding it as a foregone fiasco. The days of Agincourt are passed. The French, of course, will not stand up to an English army ; but they can bring it to ruin by harassing its communications. Three summers of such campaigning would exhaust the solid treasure of the kingdom, and we should have to fall back, as once before, upon a leathern currency. That opens up a prospect which no loving subject could contemplate without horror. The King, it was understood, was to accompany the expedition ; and if, which God forfend, his royal person should chance to fall into enemy hands, the French, who insisted upon having our gold for their wine, would not see themselves accepting our leather coin in return for their august captive. So does Cromwell apply the cold water of commonsense to the whole grandiose project. The speech exhibits the fruit of sane thought plentifully candied with flattery of unthinking folly. Careful in his language throughout, the speaker does allow his English downrightness to break out in one devastating aside. Among the proudest feathers in Henry's martial cap was the reduction of Thérouenne in the ' little war ' of 1512. The royal blood could always be set bubbling with complacency by the mention of Thérouenne. Cromwell, referring to the " importable charges " of such expeditions, recalls the King's " good experience in the winning of Thérouenne, which cost his highness more than twenty such ungracious Dogholes could be worth unto him " (Merriman, ' Thomas Cromwell,' I, p. 39). The speech concludes with a passage in which the simple-looking satirist gives way to the statesman. If England wants to annex anything, let her turn her mind to Scotland. The union of Scotland with the English Crown would deal a heavier blow to French power and policy than any possible invasion of France.

Plainly the man who so spoke, or wrote, was a political thinker of no mean order, and a parliamentarian of no mean gifts. Whether the speech was ever delivered we know not. Probably prudence kept it pigeonholed, the author contenting himself with some ironic impressions of life in Parliament given to a correspondent in Spain. In a letter addressed to John Creke at Bilbao he writes :

" Ye shall understand that by long time I amongst others have endured a Parliament which continued by the space of seventeen whole weeks : where we communed of war, peace, strife, contention, debate, murmur, grudge, riches, poverty, penury, truth, falsehood, justice, equity, deceit, oppression, magnanimity, activity, force,

' attempraunce,' treason, murder, felony, concili (ation ?), and also how a commonwealth might be edified and also continued within our Realm. Howbeit in conclusion we have done as our predecessors have been wont to do, that is to say, as well as we might, and left where we began." (ibid. 11, p. 313).

For a practical man whose time was money, seventeen whole weeks so spent would seem a poor investment. We might not be wrong in thinking that Cromwell's parliamentary ambitions were extinguished for the time being. When he next sought entrance into Parliament, it was not to make a figure but to save his neck.

In the years that followed to 1529 his career opens into broader waters. His command of law and business commended him to the Cardinal, who presently had important work for him to do. In those days every magnate had his own ' council,' a body of skilled advisers engaged in the management of his affairs. As time goes on, we find Cromwell being addressed as " counsellor to my lord Legate.' Of all the business which Wolsey had to delegate to his subordinates Cromwell was charged with the most invidious. Munificent at the cost of earlier and more pious founders, Wolsey had obtained bulls from the Pope empowering him to dissolve some score of minor monasteries and divert their endowments to the foundation of his new Colleges at Ipswich and Oxford. In the multifarious work connected with the dissolution of these religious houses from 1525 onwards Cromwell acted as agent in chief. By everything but an over-sensitive humanity he was perfectly qualified for the task. He had to see to the pensioning of their heads, the disposal of their inmates, the cataloguing of their lands and goods, the removal of their plate and furniture, the re-drafting of their leases, and the vesting of their property in the new foundations. It was work which an angel could not have carried through without causing much heartburning and distress ; and Cromwell was no angel. His curt and callous efficiency, which was all his own, and the venality which he shared with nearly everyone else — More seems to have been the shining exception — gave rise to murmurs and objurgations which reached the ears of the King, and drew down upon Wolsey a royal admonition as to the conduct of his agents. To the obloquy which his proceedings brought upon him Cromwell was fully alive and, with the law and the Cardinal behind him, wholly indifferent. Some twenty years of assiduity in business, with a pleasant accessibility to interested favours — nothing was too great or small for him to pocket graciously — had made him a man of wealth, with a handsome establishment in Austin Friars. But his prosperous skies were suddenly overcast ; with the Cardinal's ruin he had too much reason to apprehend his own ; his career and his accumulations were alike in jeopardy ; and there were rumours about of worse in store for him. (See Pole, ' Apologia ad Carolum Quintum,' p. 127).

Wolsey, on surrendering to the King his palace of York Place (Whitehall), had withdrawn to his manor-house at Esher. There, with such of his gentlemen and yeomen as had not taken service with the King, he remained for some weeks, the centre of a mournful and meagre household for which the barest necessaries had to be borrowed. One morning, "upon All-hallowne day", October 31st. the eve of All Saints, his devoted gentlemen-usher George Cavendish entered " the Great Chamber", and saw, " leaning in the great window," the familiar figure of Thomas Cromwell, unfamiliarly occupied. There he was "with a Primer in his hand, saying our Lady mattens, which had been a strange sight in him afore," Cavendish remarks, Cromwell being a man of parchments rather than of primers. With the transient superstition of the radically irreligious he was preparing himself, by unaccustomed devotion, for one of the critical moments of his life. Cavendish, on approaching, observed that his rather heavy jowl was moist with tears. Touched by his solicitude for their fallen master, or other occasion of concern, Cavendish hastened to offer words of comfort. " Why, Mr. Cromwell, " he said, " what meaneth this dole ? Is my lord in any danger that ye do lament for him, or is it for any other loss that ye have sustained by misfortune ? ".

Cromwell, who had no need to dissemble with Cavendish, is quick to disabuse him of the idea that he is grieving for any distresses but his own. " Nay, quoth he, it is for my unhappy adventure. For I am like to lose all that I have laboured for all the days of my life, for doing of my master true and diligent service.

" Why, sir, quoth I, I trust that you be too wise to do anything by my lord's commandment otherwise than ye might do, whereof you ought to be in doubt or danger for loss of your goods.

" Well, well, quoth he, I cannot tell ; but this I see before mine eyes, that everything is as it is taken ; and this I know well, that I am disdained withal for my master's sake ; and yet I am sure there is no cause why they should do so. An evil name once gotten will not lightly be put away. I never had promotion by my lord to the increase of my living. But," continues Cromwell, making a confidant of Cavendish, " this much I will say to you, that I will this afternoon, when my lord hath dined, ride to London and to the Court, where I will either make or mar or ever I come again. I will put myself in press to see what they be able to lay to my charge.

" Mary," says the good-natured Cavendish, " then in so doing you shall do wisely, beseeching God to send you good luck, as I would myself." (Cavendish, ' Life of Cardinal Wolsey,' pp. 169 - 71).

A gambler with fortune all his life, " make or mar," so Cavendish tells us, was a frequent phrase of Cromwell's. His talk about ' charges ' had been something of a blind. He was not a man to await attack, or blanch before adversity. Between the lines of his primer, we may well suppose, he had been conning a positive plan of action, pondered for some anxious weeks. He meant now to put it to the touch. That afternoon he rode to the Court, accompanied by one of his household, Ralph Sadler, a young man of twenty-two, who was to win distinction as a diplomatist in succeeding reigns. Arrived at the Court, Cromwell sought an audience with the Duke of Norfolk, Wolsey's arch-enemy and his successor in the leadership of the Council. Norfolk must have scrutinised narrowly the fallen Cardinal's right-hand man, who had ventured to approach him so boldly. Of what passed between them there is no record. We are left to imagine with what blend of apology and aplomb Cromwell managed to conciliate the Duke, and to commend himself as a man who might have his uses among " the King's servants " in the forthcoming Parliament. At any rate Norfolk was so far impressed by his unusual suitor as to promise to bring his name before the King. Before bowing himself out Cromwell handed to him ' a ring with a turquoise,' to be returned to him as a token if all went well. Leaving Sadler at the Court to await and report the outcome, he returned to Esher. At four o'clock the following day (All Saints, Nov. 1st) Sadler wrote to him as follows :

" A little before the receipt of your letter, I spoke with Mr. Gage at the Court, and, as you commanded, moved him to speak to the Duke of Norfolk for the burgess's room of the Parliament on your behalf, which he did. The Duke said he had spoken with the King, who was well contented that you should be a burgess, if you would follow the Duke's instructions. The Duke wishes to speak with you to-morrow, and has sent you as a token, by Mr. Gage, your ring with a turquoise, which I now send by the bearer. . . . It would be well for you to speak with the Duke of Norfolk as soon as possible, to know the King's pleasure how you shall order yourself in the Parliament House. Your friends would have you to tarry with my Lord there as little as might be, for many considerations, as Mr. Gage will show you. To-morrow night the King will be at York Place." (IV, App. no. 238).

We may be sure that on the morrow Cromwell attended punctually upon the Duke, and received the " instructions " he was expected to follow. The day after, Nov. 3rd, the supposed disciple of Machiavelli, and certainly one of the boldest political condottieri in our history, took his place in the new House as member for Taunton.

It is remarkable that the man who entered Parliament in this peculiar way should be the only member of the Commons, apart from the Speaker, of whose activities, in the opening session, we know anything. He was active in certain discreet endeavours on behalf of his fallen patron ; and there is more than a little reason to discern his hand in the measures which made the session memorable.

Chapter II

THE MEASURES OF THE FIRST SESSION
NOVEMBER 3rd — DECEMBER 17th

The Commons take action for the reform of the Church

Nearly all our knowledge of the proceedings of the session we owe to Edward Hall, rather patronisingly called " the chronicler." One absurdity which strikes the lay student of the period is the fashion, among certain historians, of discounting or dismissing the best testimony there is on the ground that the witness is " only Hall." Hall, in fact, was a man of culture, an eminent barrister, an under-sheriff of London, a member of this House of Commons, and quite a considerable man of letters. His foibles of opinion are on the surface, and easily allowed for. He could see no spot or blemish in the King, and aspired to a niche in history as the Boswell of his reign. On the other hand, he held no brief for the prelates and clergy, and was not disturbed by the measures of which they were the objects, or victims. His animus against the clergy, however, was only that of the Commons in general ; and it is part of the purpose of this book to show that that animus was real, and had real grounds. Hall's concern is not with opinions but with facts ; and he would have subscribed to the dictum of the famous editor that, while opinion is free, facts are sacred. His ' bias,' of which so much is made, was not of the kind to lead him to play fast and loose with facts. In his account of this opening session he writes as a witness, auditor and sharer in its proceedings ; and his story is consistent, simple and luminous. One thing he makes perfectly clear : that the action of the Commons was their own, and owed nothing to inspiration from outside. They meant to get certain things done and, not without effort, they got them done.

Hall begins with an account of the opening of Parliament and with a summary of the speech of Sir Thomas More, who had just succeeded Wolsey as Lord Chancellor. The speech makes rather hard reading, especially for those who can only see More upon a moral pedestal, above the ordinary canons of human criticism. Various attempts have been made to explain it, or explain it away. The least satisfactory, and the least consistent, is that which impugns the integrity of the narrator. In considering a man like More, who has become something of a legend, there is a natural temptation to save one's preconceptions by jettisoning the evidence. Dr. Brewer, for example, after discussing the speech with apparent acceptance and no little severity, appends a footnote stating that " Hall is the only authority for this speech," and suggesting that much or most of it may be " due to the active invention of the Chronicler." But Hall was among those who HEARD the speech. He was not so stupid as to mistake its drift, or to misreport an utterance which many about him would have heard and remembered. Himself an outspoken critic of Wolsey, he would not have dissented from More's strictures. With the reserves of a ceremonious lawyer who could not look lightly upon anything gilbertian in the make-up of a Lord Chancellor, he shared the general admiration for More. Writing of his appointment he speaks of him as " a man well learned in the tongues and also in the Common Law, whose wit was fine and full of imaginations, by reason whereof he was too much given to mocking, which was to his gravity a great blemish." What More is reported to have said of Wolsey on this occasion is regarded by Dr. Brewer as inconsistent with what Roper, writing long afterwards, records of his reference to him on another, then recent occasion ; " but Chapuys," the imperial ambassador, " writing on 8 Nov., five days after its delivery, gives a substantially similar account of the speech (Spanish Cal. p. 324)" to that given by Hall. (Pollard, ' Wolsey,' p. 256, n. 2).

Premising that, with its proper contexts and the mollifying effect of the speaker's personality, the speech may well have sounded better than it reads, More's words, as Hall summarises them, may be left to speak for themselves. After the introductory banalities above referred to (p. 179), which would be applicable to any Parliament at any time, More likened the King, there present in person,

to " a good shepherd," watchful over his flock ; " he resembled
the King to a shepherd or herdman for this cause ; for if a prince
be compared to his riches, he is but a rich man : if a prince be
compared to his honour, he is but an honourable man : but compare
him to the multitude of his people and the number of his flock,
then he is a ruler, a governor of might and puissance : so that his
people maketh him a prince, as of the multitude of sheep cometh
the name of a shepherd ; and as you see that amongst a great flock
of sheep some be rotten and faulty, which the good shepherd
sendeth from the good sheep, so the great wether which is of late
fallen, as you all know, so craftily, so scabbedly, yea and so untruly
juggled with the King, that all men must needs guess and think
that he thought in himself that he had no wit to perceive his crafty
doing, or else that he presumed that the King would not see nor
know his fraudulent juggling and attempts ; but he was deceived ;
for his Grace's sight was so quick and penetrable that he saw him,
yea and saw through him, both within and without, so that all
thing to him was open ; and according to his desert he hath had a
gentle correction ; which small punishment the King will not to
be an example to other offenders, but clearly declareth that whosoever hereafter shall make like attempt to commit like offence shall
not escape with like punishment."

So More, the humanist and until now a very minor minister,
allows himself to speak of the founder of Christ Church and the
foremost statesman of the age. The speech, at first sight, seems to
say little either for his genius or his generosity. But yet, if we
review the circumstances, it is difficult to see how, if he spoke at
all, he could have spoken otherwise. As Lord Chancellor he had
set his name to a series of articles, no less than forty-four, which
the Lords had drawn up as the basis of their projected bill of attainder. They were a miscellaneous hotch-potch of charges ; but their
general effect was to accuse Wolsey of having gone behind the
backs of King and Council, and tricked and cozened and deceived
them all. These were the " fraudulent juggling and attempts " to
which More refers. If he held these charges to be of weight, his
strictures, and his praise of the King's clemency in proceeding

against Wolsey for something less than treason, were very well deserved.* But More knew, at the time he spoke, that the articles against Wolsey were neither here nor there. For three weeks, from October 9th, the Cardinal's indictment for breaches of the ' laws of Praemunire,' — the matter of only one of the articles, the seventh — had been before the King's Bench. Three days before More spoke judgment had been given, Wolsey condemned, and the articles as a whole consigned to insignificance, except as a mere political manifesto. They were, as More and everybody else knew, neither the cause nor the occasion of Wolsey's downfall. His fate was that of the humbler person who is the subject of this book. Hunne, in suing the praemunire, and Wolsey, in failing to gratify the King in the matter of the Divorce, had been guilty of things that were unpunishable in law ; and they could only be brought within reach of the law by trumped-up charges, trumped-up in the sense that, whatever modicum of truth they may have had, they had nothing to do with the offenders' real offence. And there, I think, we have the explanation of More's difficult and laboured oratory. Deploring and detesting the whole business of the Divorce, he has, as Lord Chancellor, to pass public judgment upon a man whose real offence was his failure to carry through that very project. His speech seems touched with the embarrassment of a man who feels himself to be in a new, and more or less consciously false, position. And More's tragedy was that that position, initially false, became more and more false as time went on, and he found himself lending countenance and authority to a course of action against which his soul more and more rebelled. Not for two and a half years was he able, by resignation (May 16th, 1532) to extricate himself from that moral entanglement ; and by that time the revolution he dreaded was already half complete. More's heroic period begins with his committal to the Tower in April 1534. From then until the end, fourteen months later, he is living on the exalted plane of one facing death for

---

* Of these articles Wolsey, in a letter to Cromwell, says, " A great part be untrue, and those which be true are of such sort that by the doing of them no malice nor untruth can be justly arrected unto me, neither to the Prince's person, nor to the realm ". 1V. no 6076.

the testimony of what he believed to be the truth. On April 13th 1534, passing down river for the last time, " he took his boat towards Lambeth, wherein sitting still sadly a while," writes Roper, " at last he suddenly rounded me in the ear, and said, ' Son Roper, I thank our Lord the field is won.' " And some of the commiseration which has been given to More's last days might well be spared for those earlier years in which he held high office, and in which the field was still agonisingly in doubt. When the day of decision came, he chose what he had determined to be the better part, glorifying God by the death that could not be taken from him. Nearly six years earlier he had concluded his first speech as Lord Chancellor by directing the assembled Commons to retire and choose their Speaker.

" And because you of the Common House be a gross multitude and cannot speak all at one time, therefore the King's pleasure is that you shall resort to the nether House and there among yourselves according to the old and ancient custom to choose an able person to be your common mouth and Speaker ; and after your election so made to advertise his Grace thereof, which will declare to you his pleasure what day he will have him present in this place."

The Commons chose and presented their Speaker ; and then, having no Government business before them,* promptly got down to business of their own. Of that presently.

Meanwhile, in the intervals of business, the member for Taunton took occasion to do some effective lobbying on behalf of his former patron and, by the way, himself. The conditions were not unfavour-

---

* Hall says (Whibley's ed. II. 155 - 6) " the King called a Council of the chief of the nobles, to begin at Westminster the first day of October next ensuing, and also summoned a Parliament, to begin the third day of November then immediately following : and declared that the same Council should devise certain acts, necessary and needful to be passed at the said Parliament, for reformation of certain exactions done by the clergy to the lay people." This looks something like a Government programme : but Hall, in his ordered account of the session (pp. 163 - 71) makes it clear that the original bills were " drawn," in fact, by certain members of the Commons learned in the law, at the instance of " the Burgesses of the Parliament." Two of the bills originating in the Commons were ultimately re-drafted by the Council (p. 169) in order to make them less unpalatable to the protesting prelates ; but these were the only bills, except that for the remission of the King's debts, which the Council seems to have had any hand in " devising " or revising.

able. Wolsey had other friends and servants in the House. The Commons represented those elements in the nation which the Cardinal's administration had antagonised least. Always understanding and generous in personal matters, the House had listened, probably with no great favour, to the Chancellor's unsympathetic oration, and was not undisposed to hear what could be said on the other side. And Cromwell could say it without much misgiving. After his second colloquy with Norfolk on November 2nd he had returned to Esher, and told Cavendish the good news of his entry into Parliament. " He came again," says Cavendish, " with a pleasant countenance, and said to me that he had once adventured to put in his feet where he would be better regarded or ever the Parliament were finished. Then talked he with my lord'" Wolsey, who had good news of his own to give. After Cromwell had left for the Court, the household at Esher was knocked up in the dead of night by Sir John Russell and a troop of horsemen, who had ridden from London in a drenching downpour on a private mission from the King. Russell had been charged to deliver to Wolsey a ring in token of the King's sympathy and regard. So Cromwell knew that he could say something for the Cardinal without risk of the royal disfavour. " After his talk," continues Cavendish, " he rode again to London, because he would not be absent from the Parliament," which was to meet the following day. " There was nothing done against him," Wolsey, " in the Parliament house, but he sent to my lord to know what answer he might make in his behalf ; insomuch that there was nothing alleged against my lord but that he was ready to make answer thereto ; insomuch that at the length his honest estimation and correct behaviour in his master's cause grew so in every man's opinion that he was reputed the most faithful servant to his master of all other, wherein he was greatly of all men commended. Then was there brought in a bill of articles into the Parliament house to have my lord "— so Cavendish writing long afterwards says mistakenly —"condemned of treason". The " bill " in fact had ceased to be a penal measure ; it was now nothing more than a portentous petition praying for Wolsey's perpetual exclusion from office. It was debated in the Lords ; and in December, when the session was more than half over, it was communicatcd for their information to the House of Commons. But, though Cavendish's recollection was at fault as to the nature of the " bill " when it reached the Commons, there is no reason to reject his statement that it led to a debate which gave Cromwell his great opportunity. The undelivered speech which he prepared for the Parliament of 1523 (see above, pp. 181 - 2) enables us to imagine the force and address with which he took advantage of it. Against the bill, such as it was, " Mr. Cromwell inveighed so discreetly, and with such witty persuasions and deep reasons, that the same could take no effect". The bill, in short, was 'ordered to lie on the table', which was all it was ever meant to do ; and Cromwell thenceforward had the ear of the House.

But already, there is good reason to believe, he had made a place for himself as something more than an impressive debater. A few weeks before, he had entered the House under a heavy cloud ; but the cloud was quickly dissipated. The House, bent upon certain action, discovered in the member for Taunton a colleague who was able, with complete facility, to translate passion into policy, and a common impulse into the clauses of a bill. The three important bills of this session are, in content and principle, so much of a piece with later legislation which is known to have been inspired by Cromwell as to afford a strong presumption, apart from other evidence, that he had an active part in their drafting.

I propose, on the authority of Hall — who is the only authority there is — to re-tell the story of this session : partly because its proceedings were in some sense a sequel to the case of Richard Hunne : partly because the legislative Reformation in England cannot be understood coherently if the setting of these proceedings is misconceived. As to the authority of Hall, it seems to me arbitrary and absurd to dismiss it on the ground of bias, unless it can be shown that his bias, so-called, was not that of the Commons in general. In point of fact Hall's feeling reflected accurately the feeling of the Commons, and that feeling is required to account for their action. Hall, who sat in the House and was in immediate touch with all that occurred, lends no countenance to the notion

G

that these measures, influenced or inspired or dictated by the Court, were an initial stage in a preconceived plan, on the part of the King, to humiliate the clergy and prepare the way for a breach with Rome. Over a year later, and not till then, there are signs of such a plan germinating in the mind of Cromwell. But Cromwell's sole preoccupation, when he entered Parliament in November, 1529, was to save and re-make his own career. An ill-considered outsider, it was by identifying himself with the mind of the House and placing his singular talents at its disposal, that he established a footing which, in course of time and with the backing of the Court, became an ascendancy. That he felt much personal warmth about the initial measures of reform to which he lent his powers, it is unnecessary to suppose. But he was perfectly capable both of simulating zeal himself and of stimulating zeal in others ; while at the same time his feeling about disorders in the Church, of which experience had given him an intimate knowledge, was less of indignation than of contempt, the contempt of an efficient person for a system of things which was at once ramshackle and abusive. To Cromwell the strength of feeling in the Commons was merely a political fact, to be turned adroitly to account.

" When the Commons were assembled in the nether House," writes Hall, " they began to common (commune) of their griefs wherewith the spiritualty had beforetime grievously oppressed them, both contrary to the law of the realm and contrary to all right ; and in especial they were moved with six great causes."

In enumerating the " six great causes " which were dealt with in the three bills ensuing, Hall gives some idea of the debate they occasioned, and of the turbid volume of complaint which poured forth when the creaking floodgates began to give way.

" These things before this time might in no wise be touched nor yet talked of by no man except he would be made an heretic or lose all that he had ; for the Bishops were Chancellors, and," as Simon Fish had protested, " had all the rule about the King, so that no man durst once presume to attempt anything contrary to their profit or commodity."

" But now, when God had illumined the eyes of the King," —

whose eyes, so far, had not been illumined by much but his infatuation for Mistress Anne, though the eyes of the malcontent laity
were brightening with the possibilities which might emerge if that
infatuation persisted, and the King, baffled in the effort to obtain
the annulment of his marriage at Rome, should finally take the bit
between his teeth and the law into his own hands — " and that
their subtle doings were once espied, then men began charitably to
desire a reformation, and so at this Parliament men began to show
their grudges."

" Whereupon the Burgesses of the Parliament," including, of
course, the members for the City and Londoners like Cromwell
who sat for country constituencies, " appointed such as were
learned in the law being of the Common House, to draw one bill
of the probates of Testaments, another for Mortuaries, and the
third for non-residence, pluralities, and taking of Farms by spiritual
men."

" The learned men took much pain . . . " That Thomas Cromwell
was among the learned men appointed to this drafting committee
is not a matter of conjecture. Among the documents in the Record
Office is a portion of a preliminary draft, calendared by Dr. Brewer
as " corrected by Cromwell " and headed by him, " Concerning
an order to be taken and set in the spiritualty." (IV. 6043 (7)). It
enumerates among abuses to be remedied

1. The taking of fees by the parsons ministering " the sacraments and sacramentals of Holy Church," including those taken
for burial.
2. Excessive charges for the proving of wills.
3. Other excessive charges in the spiritual courts.

The draft was evidently prepared with a view to the measures of
this first session. The amendments to the draft either modify
certain intemperate expressions in the language of the original
draft, or by removing redundant words make its meaning clearer.*
The draft is exactly of the same character as Cromwell's more
famous draft of the ' Supplication of the Commons against the

---

* This summary was kindly sent to me by the Record Office.

Ordinaries ' presented, more than two years later, in the parliamentary session of 1532.

To continue with Hall : " The learned men took much pain, and first set forth the bill of Mortuaries . . . " Nothing could show more clearly what was in the mind and memory of the House than this their first action. It was to strike at, and abolish, the long-standing abuse by which mortuaries, supposed to be taken of the property of the deceased, were exacted in respect of infants and married women under coverture who, in law, could hold no property. Against that abuse, and the attempt to practice it against his five-weeks-old baby, Richard Hunne had risen in protest, a protest which cost him his liberty and his life. His fate, so his fellow-citizens believed, had been attended with every circumstance of atrocity. Had there been any pretence to have justice done about it, the matter might have blown over, and have faded out of mind. But the evil impression the affair created had been fixed indelibly by the determined and successful effort of the spiritualty to prevent any sort of justice being done. Had the memory of the case needed revival, it would have been revived by the attempt of Sir Thomas More, writing in the ' Dialogue ' a year before, to put some better face upon it. The fate of Hunne, and the denial of justice in connection with it, had aroused opinion to the pitch of reprobation at which men say to themselves and to one another, ' Never gain ' ; and now the Commons, defeated in the Parliament of 1515, were meeting with the resolve that no infamy of the kind should ever be possible in future.

Part of the preamble of the Mortuaries Act recites : " Forasmuch . . . (2) as also for that such mortuaries or corse presents have been demanded and levied for such as at the time of their death have had no property in any goods or chattels," etc.

And the Act provided, " That for no woman being covert baron, nor child, ne for any person not keeping house, any manner mortuary be paid, ne that any parson, vicar, curate, parish priest or other, ask, demand or take, for any such woman, child or for any person not keeping house dying or dead, any manner thing or money by way of mortuary."

For the rest, no mortuaries in kind were to be demanded any longer. They were commuted for moderate money payments graded according to the personal estate of the deceased. The penalty for demanding any sum in excess of the scale laid down by Parliament was to be the forfeiture of the overcharge and a fine of forty shillings, say £50 in our money. And no demand at all was to be made in respect of householders who died worth less than ten marks, persons, as we might say, below the income-tax level.

The Mortuaries bill, Hall proceeds, " passed the Common House, and was sent up to the Lords.

" To this bill the spiritual Lords made a fair face, saying that surely priests and curates took more than they should, and therefore it were well done to take some reasonable order ; thus they spake because it touched them little" the bill being aimed at " parsons and vicars," whom, says Hall, it " sore displeased."

" But within two days after," he continues, " was sent up the bill concerning probates of Testaments," limiting drastically the fees for probate levied in the metropolitan and diocesan courts. It dealt, says Hall, summarising the debate in the Commons, with " the excess fines which the Ordinaries took for probate of Testaments : insomuch that Sir Henry Guilford, Knight of the Garter and Comptroller of the King's House, declared in the open Parliament on his fidelity that he and other, being executors to Sir William Compton, knight, paid for the probate of his will to the Cardinal and the Archbishop of Canterbury a thousand marks sterling " — some twenty-thousand pounds in our money ; " after this declaration were showed so many extortions done by Ordinaries for probates of wills that it were too much to rehearse."

At this Probate bill " the Archbishop of Canterbury in especial, and all other Bishops in general, both frowned and grunted, for that touched their profit ; in so much as Doctor John Fisher, Bishop of Rochester, said openly in the Parliament chamber these words, " My Lords, you see daily what bills come hither from the Common House, and all is to the destruction of the Church. For God's sake see what a realm the kingdom of Bohemia was ; and wher the Church went down, then fell the glory of the kingdom. Now with the Commons is nothing but ' Down with the Church,' and all this meseemeth is for lack of faith only."

The Bishop's diagnosis was quite mistaken, and his speech did not improve matters. With less of malignity, but with no more sense of the real situation, the Bishop was libelling the House of Commons just as Fitzjames had libelled the citizens of London fourteen years before. The Commons were unimpeachably ortho- dox ; and they were moved, not by lack of faith, but by lack of patience with an order of men who habitually raised the cry ' heretic, heretic ' and ' lack of faith ' at any lay suggestion of reform. The House, taking umbrage at the Bishop's imputation, and fearing lest " his slanderous words would have persuaded the temporal lords to have restrained their consent from the said two bills," deputed their Speaker, with thirty other members, to protest to the King. " The King was not well contented with the saying of the Bishop," and summoned him, with the Archbishop and six other bishops, to his presence ; and Fisher explained that it was the kingdom of Bohemia and not the Commons whom he had charged with lack of faith, " which blind excuse pleased the Commons nothing at all."

" After this divers assemblies were kept between certain of the Lords and certain of the Commons for the bills of probates of Testaments, and the mortuaries. The temporalty laid to the spirit- ualty their own laws and constitutions, and the spirituality sore defended them by prescription and usage ; to whom an answer was made by a gentleman of Gray's Inn : ' the usage hath ever been of thieves to rob on Shooter's Hill : ergo, is it lawful ? ' With this answer the spiritual men were sore offended, because their doings were called robberies ; but the temporal men stood still by their sayings, in so much the said gentleman said to the Archbishop of Canterbury that both the exaction of probates of Testaments, and the taking of Mortuaries, as they were used, were open robbery and theft. After long disputation the temporal Lords began to lean to the Commons ; but for all that the bills remained unconcluded a while."

The only gentleman of Gray's Inn whom we know to have taken an active part in the work of this session was Thomas Cromwell.

Cromwell could cringe or hector, be suave or brutal, as occasion called. The interjection, by which the time-honoured principle of usage was brushed aside by a reference to the usage of thieves on Shooter's Hill, is Cromwell at his most truculent. It could only have been made by a man who sensed already that, with the Commons at his back, he might have the clergy at his mercy.

At this point Hall interpolates a paragraph to explain what it was that induced the King himself to lean to the Commons in their controversy with the prelates. It relates to the only bill of the session which can be regarded as having been " devised " by the Court.

" In the mean season there was a bill assented by the Lords and sent down to the Commons, the effect whereof was that the whole realm by the said act did release to the King all such sums of money as he had borrowed of them at the loan in the fifteenth year of his reign (as you have heard before). This bill was sore argued in the Common House ; but the most part of the Commons were the King's servants, and the other were so laboured to by other that the bill was assented to.

" When this release of the loan was known to the commons of the Realm, Lord so they grudged and spake ill of the whole Parliament ; for almost every man counted it his debt, and reckoned surely of the payment of the same ; and therefore some made their wills of the same, and some other did set it over to other for debt, and so many men had loss by it ; which caused them sore to murmer, but there was no remedy. The King, like a good and a discreet Prince, seeing that his Commons in the Parliament House had released the loan, intending somewhat to requite the same, granted to them a general Pardon of all offences, certain great offences and debts only except ; also he aided them for the redress of their greves against the spiritualty, and caused two new bills to be made indifferently, both for the probate of Testaments and Mortuaries ; which bills were so reasonable that the spiritual lords assented to them although they were sore against their minds ; and in especial the probate of Testaments sore displeased the Bishops, and the mortuaries sore displeased the Parsons and Vicars."

'C'est le premier pas qui coute'; and Cromwell, who was a master of affairs, had doubtless impressed it upon his colleagues that if, at any cost to their own pockets and popularity, they could enlist the King's help in putting through their initial measures, any further measures of the kind — such as those which were mooted in their later 'Supplication against the Ordinaries' — would have an easier passage. That the Commons who, in subsequent sessions, stoutly and successfully opposed the King's wishes in the matter of the Wardships Bill, should have agreed, in the first session, to this wholesale cancellation of the King's debts, is sufficient witness to the strength of their feeling, and to their determination, in renewed conflict with the prelates, not again to suffer defeat.

There followed the third bill, directed against pluralism, absenteeism, and clerical trading for profit. Existing pluralists were to retain not more than four benefices. For the future a parson accepting a second benefice was ipso facto to vacate the first, as in fact the old canon law required. Exceptions were made in favour of the chaplains of various grades of dignitaries, civil and ecclesiastical. Incumbents were not to absent themselves from their benefices for more than a month at a time, or for more than two months altogether in the year.

"After these Acts thus agreed," Hall proceeds, "the Commons made another Act for pluralities of benefices, non-residence, buying and selling and taking of farms by spiritual persons; which Act so displeased the spiritualty that the priests railed on the commons of the Common House and called them heretics and schismatics; for the which divers priests were punished.

"This Act was sore debated above in the Parliament chamber, and the Lords Spiritual would in nowise consent. Wherefore the King, perceiving the grudge of his Commons, caused eight Lords and eight of his Commons to meet in the Star Chamber at an afternoon, and there was sore debating of the cause; in so much that the temporal Lords of the Upper House, which were there, took part with the Commons against the spiritual Lords, and by force of reason caused them to assent to the bill with a little qualifying; which bill the next day was wholly agreed to in the Lords'

House, to the great rejoicing of the lay people, and to the great displeasure of the spiritual persons."

The Pluralities Act had one or two features in common with later legislation in this Parliament. Its preamble, for example. It reads :

" For the more quiet and virtuous increase and maintenance of divine service, the preaching and teaching the word of God, with godly and good example giving, the better discharge of curates, the maintenance of hospitality, the relief of poor people, the increase of devotion and good opinion of the lay fee toward the spiritual persons, ... Be it enacted," etc.

This reads like a first essay in the composition of those unctuous prefaces by which later statutes were introduced. It suggests, ' Aut Cromwell aut nullus.'

The Act too was remarkable in prescribing a heavy pecuniary penalty for anyone who, in the language of the ' Praemunire ' statute, should " procure or obtain, at the Court of Rome or elsewhere, any licence " to contravene the Act. It was probably this feature which aroused most opposition among the prelates and clergy. The freedom to drive a coach and horses through the law of the Church by procuring licences and dispensations from Rome was so ingrained in the system that nobody could see how to carry on without it.

To conclude this survey : the three measures of this opening session were at once moderate and revolutionary. They were moderate in enacting reasonable reforms ; they were revolutionary in doing so without regard to the Church and her Convocations, a matter, to the clergy, of bitter but fruitless complaint. In this they struck the key-note of the legislation which followed.

I have examined the proceedings of this opening session with some fulness because their customary treatment seems to me to call for reconsideration. Our historians have tended to read into the story of this session, beginning in November, 1529, impressions derived from later sessions in 1532 and onwards. Far too much has been made of the " subservience " of this Parliament, and far too little attention has been given to the real weight of the lay grievances against the clergy which had been accumulating since the early days of the reign, and especially since the time of Richard Hunne. The action of the Commons in dealing at once with certain old and obvious grievances has been interpreted, after the manner of Bishop Fisher, as an " attack on the Church " ; and, in default of any sufficient apprehension of the real grievances, the obvious way of accounting for this immediate and sudden " attack " was to attribute it to the royal initiative, the opening measures of the Commons being regarded as an initial stage in a preconceived plan aimed at putting successful pressure upon the Pope or, failing that, at the subversion of the papal authority.

As a fair modern example of the treatment which seems to me to require amendment, I give the reader two passages from Dr. H. A. L. Fisher's ' Political History of England, 1487 - 1547.' As a one-time pupil of that great teacher, I do so, of course, with every respect.

" January 15, 1532, was fixed for the opening of the next session of Parliament. . . . In the previous year the King had led the on-slaught on the Church " ; — (a reference to the involvement of the Clergy in the guilt of ' Praemunire,' and their forced acknow-ledgment of the King's ' Supreme Headship ') — " the attack was now to be entrusted to the Commons. The Praemunire of 1531 was to be followed by a great parliamentary campaign against ecclesiastical legislation and jurisdiction. Both manoeuvres formed part of a common plan, the object of which was to intimidate the Pope, to enrich the Crown, and to subject the Church. It is probable that both phases of the plot owed something to the inventive genius of Cromwell." (Fisher, pp. 110 - 11).

This states the position as it stood in the beginning of 1532, though it is more than doubtful if even then there was such a ' common plan ' or ' plot ' in the sense that the Commons were conscious parties to it. The ' manoeuvres ' were those of the King and Cromwell, who were using the anti-clerical sentiment of the Commons for their own purposes.

But the following passages relate to the position as it stood more than two years earlier, in November and December 1529. They convey the impression that the position of 1532 was at least inchoate in 1529.

" In summoning Parliament to his aid Henry was doubtless aware that a genuine feeling existed in many parts of the country, and more especially in the capital, against the claims and conduct of the spiritualty. " Nearly all the people here,' wrote Chapuys on December 13, 1529, ' hate the priests '; and this hatred was no passing outburst of petulance" (ibid. p. 292). (Dr. Fisher here quotes Saint-German at length on the causes and extent of the ill-feeling). " To the anti-sacerdotal elements in the spirit of his people Henry now made appeal. He had not decided to break with the Pope ; indeed his anxiety for the support of papal authority may be gauged by the audacity and magnitude of the plan which he conceived for extorting it. Still less did he contemplate any alteration in the foundations of religious belief. But he was of opinion that his cause was good, and that the Pope might be frightened into concessions by the menace of the withdrawal of the English obedience to Rome. Experience had proved that the pleas of the English envoys weighed light in the balance against the sword of the Empire. It was time to show that the English nation was behind the King, that the clergy were as submissive to his will as the Parliament, and that the attack upon the Roman position in England had seriously begun. (p. 294).

" It was generally understood (p. 297) that Parliament was summoned to deal with the ' enormities of the clergy ' . . . . . The Commons at once proceeded to fall upon the abuses of the Church."

After an account of the measures of the opening session Dr. Fisher continues (pp. 299 - 300) :

" The attack against the outworks had succeeded. The Pope, whose power of licensing pluralities had been limited, might now know that the King was in earnest ; the Church might learn that the King was powerful ; and the Commons might congratulate themselves upon having worsted the priests in the first engagement. In his management of parliamentary business Henry showed no little dexterity. . . . . . When Parliament was prorogued on December 17 the first step had been taken towards the subjection of the clergy."

" Whether or no the matter should go further, whether the power of the Pope should be abolished and the Church subjected to the uncontested control of the monarchy, was an issue depending upon the action of the Curia in the great matrimonial cause."*

The implication of all this is that the ' common plan ' or ' plot ' which, in the minds at any rate of the King and Cromwell, was plainly afoot in 1532, was set afoot, with the King as prime mover, in the opening session of the Parliament more than two years earlier. I can discover no mite of evidence that it was. The suggestion is wholly at variance with the account of Hall, who makes it clear that it was the House of Commons who took the initiative, and that the House went to extreme lengths, even to the extent of incurring unpopularity by agreeing to the cancellation of the King's debts, in order to obtain the royal support in overcoming the opposition of the prelates. The suggestion, too, is inconsistent with the then position of Thomas Cromwell, whose, it is generally agreed, was the mind behind the ' common plan.' In 1532, and for more than a year before, Cromwell was in close and secret contact with the King, so close and secret that the foreign ambassadors, watchful and well-informed, were unaware of it until a year later. But in November, 1529, Cromwell was only known to the King as an ill-reputed servant of the fallen Cardinal, and a last-minute suppliant to the Duke of Norfolk for a seat in Parliament. The " instructions " which he received from the Duke on the day before Parliament met can only have been a general instruction to vote with ' the King's servants ' on any matter, such as the Loan Cancellation Bill, that concerned the Crown. Cromwell, in that first session, was pre-occupied, not with the King's business, but with his own. He had told Cavendish that he " had adventured to put in his feet where he would be better regarded or ever the Parliament were finished." That pledge to himself he amply fulfilled or ever its first session was finished. In our own time we have seen a self-confident newcomer establishing himself, by a maiden speech, as a candidate for the Front Bench ; and it was by the same insistent evidence of capacity, perhaps by the same fluent, suave, amusing insolence backed by

* See Appendix II.

ability of the first order, that Cromwell made himself a power in the House. His prestige as a parliamentary leader gave him immediate standing with the Court. Parliament, in fact, did not meet again for more than a year (January 1531) ; but circumstances might have called for its resumption at any time, and in that case Cromwell's services would be invaluable. By the end of the session he is a marked man ; and within a month or so of the prorogation he is writing to one of his agents abroad with the confidence and elation of a made man. Stephen Vaughan replies on February 3rd 1530 (IV, no. 6196), speaking of his gladness to learn how Cromwell's business had succeeded, and warning him against overmuch elation. " You now sail in a sure haven. A merry semblance of weather often thrusteth men into the dangerous seas, not thinking to be suddenly oppressed with tempest, when unawares they be prevented and brought in great jeopardy." Cromwell, who was nothing if not worldly-wise, can hardly have needed his friend's caution.

At this point it may be well to clear the ground by reference to a contemporary writing which bears upon these matters. The notion that the measures of this Parliament were all parts of a precon-certed scheme which was present from the outset to the minds of the King and his advisers, is quite an old one. Its earliest and most energetic exponent was Cardinal Pole. Years afterwards when in exile (1539) Pole addressed his ' Apologia ' to the Emperor Charles V. It is a violent rhetorical philippic denouncing Henry VIII and his counsellors, more especially Thomas Cromwell. In the events of the previous ten years Pole sees the development of a co-ordinated plan, destructive and detestable, and in inspiration diabolic. Having no great respect for the King's intelligence, and seeing in the plan a complete and sudden reversal of the policy pursued under Wolsey, Pole regards it as having been put into the King's mind by somebody else, some ' nuncius Sathanae,' some emissary of the Devil, whom he presently identifies as Thomas Cromwell. He has to account to himself for the sudden emergence of Cromwell as a central figure upon the stage. It was easy to account for the rise of Wolsey ; but how came it that a low-born attorney, without backing of Church or University, could attain an ascendancy which enabled him, in a few brief years, to carry through a revolution ? Pole's conclusion is that Cromwell bought his way to power by propounding, in some (unspecified) moment of royal dejection, a great subversive plan which promised satisfaction for the King's dearest wish. He gives what he calls a ' summa ' of the plan, and puts into the mouth of Cromwell a rhetorical ' oratio,'* in which Cromwell may be supposed to have presented it to the King. But Pole was a truthful person ; and he is careful to guard against the notion that this piece of imaginative reconstruction is more than what it pretends to be, a statement of his view as to what might have happened and probably did. He insists, however, that it contains nothing of mere invention. " I can affirm," he says, " that there is nothing in it of anymoment " (alicujus momenti) but what he has heard at one time or another either from Cromwell himself (eo narrante) or from those who were in his confidence (vel ab illis qui ejus consilii fuerunt).† This is all intelligible and straightforward. It is likely enough that from 1533 onwards, when the progress of his policy was assured, Cromwell made no great secret of his own part in its inception. There was nothing particularly original in it. The material of it was in the air. What Cromwell did was to precipitate this floating material into a policy, and carry it out, as opportunity offered, with unwavering purpose.

---

* Dr. Cyril Bailey, who agrees with my reading of Pole's ' Oratio,' has kindly supplied me with the following translation :—
"I should not say what I have said, if I admitted that in this speech I had followed the usual custom of historians and writers of dialogues. When they attribute an appropriate speech to some historical personage, even though it was never actually delivered, they like it to appear that the speech fulfils their duty in writing history and in claiming to speak the truth. I am certainly not following their example now ; I am not inventing a plausible speech which might have been delivered by the Devil's Nuncio, and presenting it as though he really delivered it. No, this is not my procedure : but I do claim truth for my account, even though perhaps in the manner and arrangement I have adopted I cannot maintain that I have reproduced the actual words which he used ; for I was not present. But this much I can claim, that there is nothing of any importance recorded in the speech I have written, which I have not been given to understand either from his own account or from those who shared his policy ; these hints were given me bit by bit and on different occasions, and I have put together a summary of them. I am far from having thought out a plausible speech by my own wits, but had it all from their lips, and therefore present it as the truth."

† Apologia ad Carolum V, Brixiae, 1744, p. 123.

Some commentators, however, have speculated about the occasion on which this supposed ' oratio ' was put before the King. Canon Dixon, for example, (' History of the Church of England,' I. p. 50. n.) actually places it at the time of Cromwell's visit to the Court to ' make or mar,' the visit of which Cavendish tells the story (above, pp. 184 - 5). Canon Dixon writes :

" A more momentous interview never took place than that which followed, when these two men " (i.e. the King and Cromwell) " first looked at one another. Cromwell had not studied in vain to penetrate the secret mind of princes, when for the first time he knelt before the formidable despot who was to use him, to enrich and ennoble him, to delegate to him his own highest functions, and then to cast him out to infamy and death. His cunning was deep, his resources and ability considerable, his boldness great ; but it would have been well for him and for his country if he had never matched those ordinary qualities against that unscrupulous will and that remorseless heart."*

Canon Dixon wrote before the documents were calendared ; or it must have been clear to him, from Sadler's letter of November 1st (above, p. 22) that Cromwell's sole communication with the King at this juncture was through the Duke of Norfolk. It follows that the " momentous interview " so movingly described never in fact took place at all. It would have been indeed the extreme of temerarious folly for a man without personal or, at the time alleged, political standing, to have approached the King, enlarged upon

---

* So, more tentatively, but toying with the same idea, writes Dr. Gairdner (art. ' Thomas Cromwell,' D.N.B.). " Yet it was apparently at this very time, just after Cardinal Wolsey's fall, that he found means of access to the King's presence and suggested to him that policy of making himself head of the Church of England which would enable him to have his own way in the matter of the divorce, and give him other advantages as well. So at least we must suppose from the testimony of Cardinal Pole, writing nine or ten years later." (cf. Gairdner, ' The English Church in the Sixteenth Century,' p. 101).

Professor Merriman (' Life and Letters of Thomas Cromwell, I, 91) places the supposed colloquy with the King a year later, " at the time of Wolsey's death," (Nov., 1530). I cannot find that Pole himself gives any indication of date whatever. Looking back, in 1539, over the occurrences of the previous decade, Pole states in substance what really did occur over a course of years, but so dramatises and foreshortens the process of its occurrence as to give a false impression of premeditation and concertedness.

the 'timidity' of his veteran counsellors, propounded a great revolutionary scheme involving certain turmoil within the kingdom and grave risk of trouble from abroad, and expected the King to embrace it forthwith and spend several years thereafter in putting it into execution. Neither then, nor at any later time, was Cromwell capable of folly upon that scale. No man, so bold in action, was ever more careful to feel his ground.*

* Professor van Dyke, in the course of an examination of Pole's 'Apologia' (American Historical Review, vol. IX, July 1904, pp. 696 - 724) writes :

"It is impossible to compare carefully the 'Apologia' with the 'Pro Unitatis Defensione', and Pole's letters between 1532 and 1539, without a suspicion rising almost to certainty that in this rhetorical invective against Cromwell he is telescoping in a very misleading way events long separated," (p. 712). And, he concludes : "Thomas Cromwell was no 'Martyr of the Gospel'. But the diabolically inspired disciple of Machiavelli is a creation of the excited imagination of Pole. And the mysteriously sinister atmosphere which modern writers have borrowed from Pole to throw round their portraits of one of the most capable of English statesmen is not the light of history " (p. 724.)

Chapter III

1530. THE DISTRESSES AND DEATH OF WOLSEY :
THE WHOLE CLERGY INDICTED FOR
' PRAEMUNIRE '

As has been seen, Cromwell's services in Parliament were likely to be of value to the Court ; but his services were more immediately valuable in another direction. Cromwell had all Wolsey's business at his finger ends ; and the Cardinal's surviving preferments, revenues, and the endowments of his Colleges at Ipswich and Oxford all lay open to pillage. Throughout the year 1530, until Wolsey's arrest for treason in November, we see Cromwell acting in a double character. He poses, perhaps with such a measure of sincerity as his own interests would allow — for Wolsey's restoration to favour was for some time a possibility — as the Cardinal's assiduous and devoted servant at Court, endeavouring to save his fortunes from further wreck ; and, at the same time, he has to lend himself to the schemes of the King and courtiers who regarded Wolsey's survival, for the time being, as a golden opportunity for picking his bones. Cromwell, meanwhile, has no official status whatever ; he merely acts as go-between, mutual friend and honest broker, who happens to possess the necessary knowledge and aptitude.

The bracketed numbers which follow are those of the documents calendared in the ' Letters and Papers of Henry VIII,' vol. IV, part 3. Wolsey had been condemned in the King's Bench on Oct. 30th, 1529 (6035). On November 18th he was granted a patent of protection during the King's pleasure (6059). On the following February 12th he was given a general pardon (6213). On the 14th he received a patent of restitution to the Archbishopric of York, with a gift of " money, goods and chattels " valued at over £6,000, no unhandsome provision (6214). He had had to resign into the King's hands the rich abbacy of St. Alban's and the revenues of the see of Winchester, retaining only a pension of a thousand marks out of the latter. Until the end of March he remained at Esher and Richmond, as close as he was permitted to the Court. In April he was rusticated to his northern diocese, and resided, for his few last months, at his dilapidated manor of Southwell, the builder of palaces incurring suspicion by his efforts to render his habitation weatherproof (6545). Meanwhile Cromwell is operating at the Court, ostensibly on Wolsey's behalf. One of Wolsey's letters in June is addressed " To my right trusty and well-beloved counsellor and servant Thomas Cromwell " (6484). In undated letters Wolsey writes to him as " mine only comfort," and " mine own good, trusty and most assured refuge in this my calamity " (6203 and 6204). Early in the year we find Cromwell dispensing, on Wolsey's behalf, pensions to Court favourites out of the revenues of Winchester (6181). The surviving records afford only indications of what is happening ; but a significant instance occurs in June. On June 1st Sir John Russell writes to Cromwell :

" The King has granted the Lord Chamberlain," (Lord Sandys) " 100 marks yearly out of the lordship of Farnham as keeper of the castle, and he desires Cromwell to make him out a patent, and to send him a form of a letter how the King should write to Wolsey for his consent, and for his sign and seal ; and to tell him whether Wolsey or the chancellor of Winchester has the seal. . . ."" After you left the King, his Grace had very good communication of you " (6420).* On June 4th Cromwell, always expeditious in such matters, receives a letter in which Sandys " thanks him for his trouble about the letter and patent, which he has received by

---

* Is it supposable that this tentative expression of the King's approval could have been uttered of a man who, for already some seven months, had been of the King's most intimate counsel, and was actually the inspirer of the royal policy, as Pole, and those who attach weight to his belated maunderings about Cromwell, would have us believe ? Pole was out of the country at the material time, that is, from October 1529 to July 1530 ; he went abroad again in January 1532, and never felt it safe to return during Henry's reign. He can have known no more than anybody else of any intimate relations between the King and Cromwell. Even sharp-sighted diplomatists like Chapuys, who were on the spot and whose business it was to be well-informed, were not aware of Cromwell as a power behind the Throne until the spring of 1533. How could Pole have been any wiser ?

Cromwell's servant, the bearer. Returns it engrossed, and asks him to send it to the Cardinal, and solicit the patent " (6435). On June 17th Sandys writes again thanking him for his promise about the expedition of the King's letter for the sealing of his letter to Wolsey (6460). In an undated letter (6226) Wolsey bids Cromwell " take boldness unto you, and be not afeared to board his Grace " ; and in another letter, doubtfully dated August 10th, he " begs him to continue his efforts in Wolsey's behalf, and do the best in his power to make my lord of Norfolk (reasonable). As Cromwell has such opportunities of access to the King's presence, he may from time (to time set) forth his causes " (6554).

It becomes pretty plain that it is over the débris of Wolsey's fortunes that Cromwell is climbing his way into the royal closet. This becomes more evident from July onwards, when the first definitive steps were taken towards the confiscation of the endowments of Wolsey's colleges, of which Cromwell knew more than anyone else. From the first it was seen that these endowments were in jeopardy as a result of Wolsey's so-called attainder. On December 29th, 1529, a fortnight after the prorogation of Parliament, Thomas Russhe, another of Wolsey's agents, writes to Cromwell :

" At my departure from London, at the Horse Head without Aldgate, I found Mr. Audeley " (the Speaker) " ready to ride homeward, and accompanied him to Colchester. . . . . He thought the King would take all the monasteries suppressed, as my lord Cardinal's forfeiture dated from the first time of his offence, and that all leases would be void. If so, let me know to come and sue remedy, lest any grant pass the King " (6110, cf. 6061).

This legal doctrine, that the Cardinal's forfeiture ' dated from the first time of his offence ' was evidently overlooked when the original indictment was preferred against Wolsey in the King's Bench on October 9th. He is then charged with having " on 27 July 21 Henry VIII (1529) conferred upon James Gorton, clerk, the parish church of Stoke Gylford, Surrey, Winchester diocese, void by the death of Andrew Swynne, although Robert, prior of St. Pancras, Lewes, was the true patron " (6034). But somebody had the wit to point out that if Wolsey was charged with, or induced to plead guilty to, an offence which was only three months old, the amount of loot accruing to the Crown would be insignificant. Accordingly, eleven days after, on October 20th, the Attorney-General preferred another bill of indictment, in which Wolsey was charged with having " on the 2 Dec. 15 Henry (1523) conferred the parish church of Galbye, Leicester, Lincoln Diocese, void by the death of Ric. Woderoffe, on John Alyn, LL.D. now Archbishop of Dublin, although the master and brethren of the hospital of Burton St. Lazer, Leicester, were the true patrons " (6035). By this device, charging the Cardinal with a specific offence against the ' law of Praemunire,' not three months before his prosecution, but three months after his appointment as Legate for life six years before, the whole of the monastic lands destined for the endowment of Wolsey's colleges were brought within the scope of the forfeiture. So that when, on July 14th 1530, commissions were appointed in twenty-seven counties " to make inquisition concerning the possessions held by Thos. cardinal arch-bishop of York," this " 2 Dec. 15 Henry VIII, when the Cardinal committed certain offences against the Crown," was the date on and from which the inquiries are to proceed (6516). The date has a further important significance, which will be noticed in due course. It bears upon the suggestion, insinuation, assumption — for it was in reality never anything more — that the tenure of the Legacy was in itself illegal.

During these last four months, from July to October 1530, Wolsey is in an agony of distress over the impending fate of his colleges. He writes to the Chief Justice of the King's Bench, begging him " to consider, as a merciful judge, that though I am the first great prelate that ever was convicted in the praemunire for using of the authority of the Legate de latere within this realm, and percase by the severity of the law the same may extend as well to me as to the lands of my said poor college " (in Oxford), " yet forasmuch as I have so humbly submitted myself and, as God be my judge, I never used the said authority contemptuously or maliciously, intending to do thereby anything that should be either to the derogation of the King's dignity, majesty royal, jurisdiction, or laws ; great pity it were that to these poor innocents the sharpness and rigour of the law should be ministered. It may please you, therefore, in the way of charity, by your great wisdom and goodness, to be a mean to attemper this said severity with mercy, clemency and compassion, — And the rather it may please you thus to do for the old amity that hath been betwixt us ; and that in the erection and foundation of the said college I have used as well your said advice and counsel as of the residue of the judges,"— (6575).

What the law was ,or was made out to be, is indicated in a letter addressed to Wolsey about the same time (August 22nd) by Dr. John Higdon, Dean of the College :

They " have searched the College muniments in Oxford and London whether they might lawfully justify or not. Were assisted by Edmund Knyghtley ; and after long deliberation, concluded that the common law will not help us in this case, because your donation to the college is not effectual, but void in law ; ' forasmuch as ye, being seized in the lands of the houses suppressed in fee simple only, and to no use expressed in the King's deed of gift unto your Grace, was in danger of praemunire what time ye granted the said lands unto the college ; and all the judges agreeth that the praemunire must have relation not only from the judgment given, but from the first act done contrary to the same. Wherefore, because your Grace used your authority legatine, and thereby was in case of the statute of provisions before the donation made unto your college, they say that the donation now standeth at the King's pleasure " (6579).

The college at Ipswich was doomed from the first. On October 4th its head, Dr. William Capon, writes to inform Wolsey that on September 19th a commission, one member of which was Cromwell's colleague Thomas Russhe, " gave verdict that by reason of the praemunire committed by your Grace, as they allege, all our lands were forfeited to the King " (6663). The fate of the Oxford College — now Christ Church — hung in the balance, only the Lord Chancellor More and Stephen Gardiner, the King's secretary, showing any disposition to preserve it (6679). As for Cromwell, he was in no position to do anything but subserve the King's pleasure, whatever that might prove to be. In a letter dated July 12th he writes to Wolsey :

213

" As touching your colleges, the King is determined to dissolve them, and that new offices shall be found," that is, new title-deeds drawn up, " of all the lands belonging to them newly to intitle his Highness, which be already drawn for this purpose. But whether his Highness, after the dissolution of them, mean to revive them again, and found them in his own name, I know not. Wherefore I entreat your Grace to be content, and let your Prince execute his pleasure."

In the same letter Cromwell pointedly tells the Cardinal that " this soliciting his cause hath been very chargeable to him, and he cannot sustain it any longer without other respect than he hath had heretofore. I am 1000 pounds worse than I was when your troubles began." There is no doubt a measure of truth in this. Cromwell was a wealthy man ; and it was worth his while to spend largely in making good his footing at the Court by services to all parties. His servant Sadler writes expressing Cromwell's disappointment with Wolsey's response.

The above is taken from some records of correspondence in the possession of Jesus College, Oxford. It includes summaries of two very significant letters exchanged in October, shortly before the Cardinal's arrest for treason. Cromwell writes :

" I am informed your Grace hath me in some diffidence, as if I did dissemble with you, or procure anything contrary to your profit and honour. I much muse that your Grace should so think, or report it secretly, considering the pains I have taken, etc. Wherefore I beseech you to speak without feigning, if you have such conceit, that I may clear myself. I reckoned that your Grace would have written plainly unto me of such thing, rather than secretly to have misreported me, etc. But I shall bear your Grace no less good will, etc. Let God judge between us. Truly your Grace in some things overshooteth yourself ; there is regard to be given what things ye utter, and to whom, etc."

In reply

" The Cardinal strives to clear himself to Cromwell, protesting that he suspects him not, and that may appear by his deeds, for that he useth no man's help nor counsel but his, etc. Indeed, report hath been made to him that Cromwell hath not done him so good offices as he might concerning his colleges and his archbishopric ; but he hath not believed them ; yet he hath asked of their common friends how Cromwell hath behaved himself towards him, and to his great comfort, hath found him faithful, etc. Wherefore he beseecheth him with weeping tears to continue steadfast, and give no credit to the false suggestions of such as would sow variance between us, and so leave me destitute of all help, etc. (6076).

These last letters were exchanged within a month of the Cardinal's arrest for treason on November 4th (1530).

In the preceding pages it has been shown that Cromwell's facility of access to the King in the summer of 1530, on matters connected with Wolsey's affairs, coincides in time with the first definitive steps taken for the liquidation of Wolsey's colleges, and for the complete or partial confiscation of their endowments. It coincides in time also with a very remarkable discovery. It was the discovery that all the prelates and clergy of the kingdom, to the number of thousands, by recognising Wolsey as Papal Legate, were implicated in Wolsey's guilt, had incurred the penalties of Praemunire, and were liable to forfeiture of lands and goods and to imprisonment at the King's pleasure.

There is nothing overt or documentary to connect this discovery — not made until eight months or so after Wolsey's condemnation — with Thomas Cromwell. But then there would not be. It was not yet Cromwell's business to arrange agenda for the Privy Council, of which he was not a member (cf. V. no. 394 : August 1531). At this time he was a mere member of Parliament who happened to have business about the Court. But a discreet aside, a word dropped in the right quarter, among the greedy crew who surrounded the King. was quite enough to set such a project in motion. It had, of course, to be carried through by the King and Council. There is nothing, I repeat, to connect the project with Thomas Cromwell except its character, its impudence, its politic rapacity, and its implicit contempt for its intended victims. It bespeaks the pettifogging attorney in excelsis, lurking about the purlieus of the Court.

To weigh adequately the enormity of the proceeding, we have to consider what it was of which the Cardinal had been found guilty. On this Dr. Pollard is explicit, and his view of the matter is historically sound. He writes (' Wolsey,' pp. 245 - 7) :

" The condemnation of the most powerful impersonator of papal jurisdiction in England by a simple and almost routine process in the court of king's bench is so crucial an episode in the development of the English constitution that it requires closer examination. The conventional statement that Wolsey was condemned for being papal legate is legally so absurd that it can be dismissed in a few words. It was no offence by any law then obtaining in England to be papal legate. Every Archbishop of Canterbury or York for centuries had been a papal legate — even Cranmer took the title in 1532 ; English law drew no distinction between a *legatus natus* and a legate *a latere* ; and the specific statute under which Wolsey was condemned (16 Richard 11, c. 5) makes no mention of legates at all. It appears, indeed, impossible to condemn anyone in any English law-court for ' being ' anything at all . . . . . To say that Wolsey was condemned for being a papal legate is as meaningless as to say that a policeman, condemned for taking bribes, is condemned for being a policeman. It was not for being a legate that Wolsey was condemned, but for what he did as a legate : . . . . . He was not accused of exercising legatine powers, but of ' purchasing ' bulls from Rome and illegally exercising his powers under those bulls in such a way as to usurp the legal rights of others by making presentations which did not belong to him, ... "

This is all very well, and all very true ; but " the conventional statement that Wolsey was condemned for being papal legate," legally absurd as it may be and is, has full warrant in the words of the indictment. The words of the indictment are not less explicit.*

* The actual words — kindly extracted for me by the Search Department of the Record Office from the Controlment Roll (K.B.), Michaelmas Term 21 Henry VIII — are these :

" Quidam tamen," i.e. notwithstanding 16 Richard 11, c. 5, " reverendissimus in Christo pater Thomas permissione divina apostolice sedis de latere legatus presbiter cardinalis Ebor. archiepiscopus Anglieque primas premissorum non ignarus machinans tam dominum regem nunc et coronam suam regiam de

They charge Wolsey with " having procured bulls from Clement VII to make himself Legate, contrary to the statute of 16 Ric. 11 ; which bulls he published at Westminster, 28 August, 15 Henry VIII, and thereupon assumed and exercised the office of Legate " ; . . . . . So it appears that Wolsey was indicted for being Legate, confessed by his attornies the offence of being Legate, and was condemned for being Legate under the statute of 16 Richard 11, although, as Dr. Pollard truly says, that statute " makes no mention of legates," and contains in fact no single word which bears upon Wolsey's misdemeanours at all. The indictment proceeds : " by virtue of which

hujusmodi placitis et placitorum illorum cognicione ac sua jurisdiccione regia in ea parte quam prelatos et alios tam seculares quam ecclesiasticas personas de suis jurisdiccionibus libertatibus et presentacionibus deprivare et expellere: quasdam bullas apostolicas a sanctissimo in Christo patre et domino domino Clementi divina providencia nuper illius nominis papa septimo ut idem cardinalis continue infra hoc regnum Anglie commorans per ipsum sanctissimum in Christo patrem legatus de latere in hoc regno Anglie et alia loca (sic) ei adjacen' efficeretur prout de facto per easdem bullas effectus et prefectus est et jurisdiccione ac auctoritate legativa infra hoc regnum Anglie durante vita sua fungeretur habere et gaudere posset impetravit Quasquidem bullas apostolicas idem cardinalis postea scilicet vicessimo octavo die Augusti anno regni dicti domini regis nunc quinto decimo ad et usque villam Westmonasterii in comitatu Midd' deferri jussit et procuravit ac easdem bullas apostolicas adtunc et ibidem publicavit pronunciavit et legi fecit necnon auctoritatem nomen dignatatem et jurisdiccionem legati de latere predicti nuper pape adtunc et ibidem super se ambisiose assumpsit ipsisque a predicto xxviii die Augusti hucusque infra hoc regnum Anglie continue usus gavisus fuit et exercuit : infra quodquidem tempus, scilicet secundo die Decembris anno regni domini regis nunc quinto-decimo supradicto, prefatus cardinalis pretextu bullarum apostolicarum predictarum pariter et auctoritate coloreque et umbraculo dicte jurisdiccionis sue legatine apud villam Westmonasterii in comitatu Midd' ecclesiam parochialem de Galbye in comitatu Leicestr' Lincolniensis diocesis per mortem Ricardi Woderoffe tunc ultimi rectoris ecclesie illius adtunc vacantem, cujusquidem ecclesie magister et fratres hospitalis Sancti Lazari de Burton' Lazer in comitatu Leicestr' sunt et dicto secundo die Decembris fuerunt verus patronus, reverendo patri Johanni archiepiscopo Dublinensi in Hibernia, tunc dicto Johanni Alyn' utriusque juris doctori, contulit et donavit, ac ipsum Johannem Alyn' in realem possessionem ecclesie predicte poni fecit et procuravit, quiquidem Johannes Alyn' eisdem mediis et auctoritate ecclesiam illam ut rector ejusdem ecclesie per longum tempus possedit et eadem ecclesia gavisus fuit . . . . . .".

In Wolsey's formal pardon (see Rymer, VI, part 2, p. 146) he is forgiven " omnes et omnimodas Transgressiones IN ACCEPTATIONE aut circa Executione officii Legationis de Latere.".

In all the three material documents, the indictment, the pardon, and the first of the Lords' Articles, it is assumed and asserted that Wolsey's offence — against 16 Richard 11, c. 5 — consisted primarily in having " purchased " (impetravit) bulls to make himself Legate.

(office), on 27 July, 21 Henry VIII, he conferred upon James Gorton, clerk, the parish of Stoke Gylford, Surrey, Winchester diocese, void by the death of Andrew Swynne, although Robert, prior of St. Pancras, Lewes, was the true patron " (IV. 6035). This, and the earlier case of interference with the lawful rights of patrons cited as having occured on 2 December, 15 Henry VIII, were offences punishable by forfeiture and imprisonment, not under the alleged statute of Richard II, but under the statutes of 25 and 27 Edward III, in 1350 and 1353. In fact, the indictment charges the Cardinal with two offences, one real and the other imaginary. The real offence, that of encroaching upon the lawful rights of patrons, was indictable under these statutes of Edward III ; the other, that of ' being,' and ' having assumed and exercised the office of Legate,' was no offence in law and was not indictable under any statute whatever. How came it then that it was charged as an offence under a statute which " makes no mention of legates at all ? " The answer is simple, and not flattering to the Attorney-General who preferred the indictment and to the Lord Chief Justice who admitted it and gave sentence upon it. The independence of the judiciary had still to be fought for ; and the Judges, in matters that concerned the Crown, still regarded themselves as instruments of the royal will. The charge against Wolsey of ' being ' papal Legate merely condensed the first of the articles of impeachment produced against him by the Lords. Its appearance in the indictment was simply a brazen — and in its way successful — attempt to incorporate the opening paragraph of a political manifesto within the body of the law. The first of the Lords' articles recites certain large expressions from the statute 16 Richard II, c. 5. The statute, in actual fact, is directed specifically against two things : first, papal excommunications of English prelates who execute the judgments of the royal courts in matters of patronage, and, second, papal translations of bishops without their own or the King's assent. By such proceedings, it declares, " the crown of England, which hath been so free at all times that it hath been in no earthly subjection, but immediately subject to God in all things touching the regalty of the same crown, and to none other, should be submitted to the Pope, and the laws and statutes of the realm by him defeated and avoided at his will, in perpetual destruction of the sovereignty of the King our Lord, his crown, his regalty and of all his realm, which God forfend." The words do not impeach the general exercise of the papal authority, whether direct or legatine. But the words are " lifted " out of the statute into the first of the Lords' articles as follows :—

" Where your Grace and noble Progenitors within this Realm of England being Kings of England, have been so free that they have had in all the world no other Sovereign, but immediately subject to Almighty God in all things touching the Regality of your Crown of England ; and the same Preeminence, Prerogative, Jurisdiction, lawful and peaceable possession, your Grace and noble Progenitors have had, used and enjoyed, without interruption of business therefor, by the space of two hundred years and more ; whereby your Grace may prescribe against the Pope's holiness that he should not nor ought not to send or make any Legate, to execute any authority Legantine, contrary to your Grace's Prerogative within this your Realm : Now the Lord Cardinal of York, being your Subject and natural Liege born, hath of his high orgallous and insatiable mind, for his own singular advancement and profit, in derogation and to the great emblemishment and hurt of your said Royal jurisdiction and Prerogative, and the long continuance of the possession of the same, obtained authority Legantine : By reason whereof he has not only hurt your said Prescription, but also by the said authority Legantine hath spoiled and taken away from many Houses of Religion within this your Realm much substance of their goods, and also hath usurped upon all your Ordinaries within this your Realm much part of their jurisdiction, in derogation of your Prerogative, and to the great hurt of your said Ordinaries, Prelates and Religious." (Fiddes, ' Life of Wolsey, Collections, p. 173).

The first of the seventeen signatories to this and the other forty-three articles was the Lord Chancellor, Sir Thomas More : and the last was the Lord Chief Justice. It was open to the latter, as a politician in the Lords, to put his name to whatever ' tendentious ' proposition he pleased. But it was none the less his duty, when such a proposition came before him in the King's Bench as part of

an indictment purporting to be legal, to direct the Attorney-General
to strike it out, as having no warrant either in the suggested statute
of Richard II or in any other.   So far from doing this, he admitted it,
and gave judgment against Wolsey in terms of it.   What Dr. Pollard
justly describes as " legally absurd," " meaningless," " impossible,"
he nevertheless did.   He condemned the policeman for being a
policeman, and so prepared the way for fining everybody on the
beat.   He sentenced Wolsey for " having, contrary to the statute of
16 Ric. II, assumed and exercised the office of Legate " ;   and so
laid open the door to the ingenious continuator who presently discovered that Wolsey, having committed the crime of being Legate,
the whole clergy of England, having recognised him as Legate, were
involved in the crime, and might be required to purchase their
pardon by an enormous ransom.   It was as if the modern Minister of
Health had made some Regulation from which an aggrieved subject
appeals to the Court.   The Court decides that the Minister's action
is ultra vires, and awards the complainant damages.   It further proceeds, under some irrelevant statute, to declare the Minister's office
to be illegal, and to provide the legal ground for mulcting the County
Councils, the District Councils, the Parish Councils and all the rate-
payers of the kingdom to the tune of three millions sterling for having
recognised him as Minister.   In view of the sort of law on which the
forfeiture was demanded from the clergy, it can only be described as
daylight robbery on the grand scale.   To Thomas Cromwell, if he
was the author of it, it would not appear particularly flagitious.   If
he shared the opinion of the House of Commons that the gains of
the clergy were largely ill-gotten :   if he was the " gentleman of
Gray's Inn " who had told the Archbishop to his face that mortuaries and probate fees " as they were used were open robbery
and theft," he would regard the clergy as fair game for plunder.
The judgment of the King's Bench in Wolsey's case had opened
the way.   For whatever sins the clergy had committed, that judgment had provided the instrument of retribution.   The worst and
best remembered of those sins had been their mishandling of
Richard Hunne.   And it is not a little curious that the uncle, Richard
Fitzjames, Bishop of London, had done the wrong, and that it was

the nephew Sir John Fitzjames, Chief Justice of the King's Bench, who plaited the whip wherewith to scourge it.

The original idea may have been comparatively modest, merely that of laying under contribution certain well-to-do ecclesiastics who had had business with the legatine court. Calendared under June, 1530, we have (6488) " Memoranda of indictments against the Bishops of Coventry and Lichfield, Norwich, St. Asaph, Ely, Bangor, Rochester, Bath and Wells, and Chichester, Martin abbot of Bury, Edward Fynche archdeacon of Wilts, Edmund Froceter dean of Hereford, the abbot of Waltham Holy Cross, John Abbot of St. Peter's, Westminster, and Giles Hakluyt subdean of Salisbury." These are subsequently noted as having been pardoned " by virtue of the Act of Parliament." But the scheme speedily assumed a larger scope. The only " fautors and abettors " of Wolsey's real offence under the indictment were the two incumbents, Gorton and Allen, who had profited by his illegal ' provisions.' But the fautors and abettors of his imaginary offence in being Legate could be made out to be the whole clergy of England who, willingly or otherwise, had recognised his authority. The project was so impudent and rapacious that it had to be managed with the utmost circumspection. There is only one reference to the preparations for it in the surviving correspondence, and that is in a letter from Cromwell to Wolsey. It is noticeable that the inception of the scheme immediately preceded the final steps for the destruction of Wolsey, and that its accomplishment was immediately followed by Cromwell's elevation to the Privy Council. If the plan was inspired by Cromwell, it is not necessary to attribute to him, at least at the outset, any deep-laid purpose. It need have been nothing more than a bold device for gaining favour with the King, and for replenishing the royal coffers without recourse to Parliament. And it would obviously have a smoother passage if Wolsey was out of the way. From Michaelmas the Cardinal was at Cawood, preparing for his enthronement at York on November 7th. He had summoned the Northern Convocation for the same day. For reasons of policy, as he had explained to Cavendish, he had confessed his own guilt. The confession had been won from

221

him by promises of lenity which had been very scantly fulfilled.
Presiding in the Northern Convocation, it would now fall to him,
not only to declare himself under a load of guilt to which his own
conscience had never subscribed, but to tell the prelates and clergy
of his province, whose hearts he had begun to win, that they were
all involved in his guilt, and must purchase the King's pardon by
a heavy fine. A worm will turn, and the Cardinal of York had not
always been a worm. A man can only die once ; and overmuch
provocation might produce another Becket in the north. But it
needed no heroics on Wolsey's part to make the situation hazardous.
Cromwell, through long acquaintance, had taken very accurately
the measure of the southern clergy ; but there was no saying what
the men of the north might do. It is noticeable what pains were
taken, both in the case of Wolsey and of the clergy in general, to
avoid any real trial at law.* The process was the same in both
cases ; to bring a grave and intimidating charge, and to invite the
supposed culprits to ransom themselves by a heavy forfeiture. The
authors of the scheme, whoever they were, were fairly confident
that the Southern Convocation would submit to intimidation ; but
they were not so sure of what might happen in the north ; and
plans were made to exact proportionate contributions from individual clergy in the north if the Convocation of York should prove
recalcitrant (see Gibson, Codex, 1, pp. 91 - 2). The obvious way
to discourage such opposition was to strike down the Archbishop
and leave the province headless. There were, of course, other wheels
within wheels. " The Duke, the lady, and the father have not
ceased since then," — that is, since the King's reported outburst
in the Council against the incompetence of his advisers, see above,
p. 176 — " to plot against the Cardinal : especially the lady, who

---

* C f. Stephen's Commentaries on the Laws of England, 7th ed. 1874, vol. IV,
p. 169, note y.
   " The terrible penalties of a *praemunire* are denounced by a great variety of
statutes, yet prosecutions upon a *praemunire* are unheard of in our courts.
There is only one instance of such a prosecution in the State Trials ; in which
case the penalties of a *praemunire* were inflicted upon some persons for refusing
to take the oath of allegiance in the reign of Charles the Second. Haig, State
Trials, vol. II, p. 463."

does not cease to weep and regret her lost time and her honour, threatening the King that she would leave him, in such sort that the King has had much trouble to appease her ; and though the King prayed her most affectionately, even with tears in his eyes, that she would not speak of leaving him, nothing would satisfy her except the arrest of the Cardinal. It was pretended that he had written to Rome to be reinstated in his possessions, and to France for its favour, and was returning to his ancient pomp, and corrupting the people." So writes the imperial ambassador Chapuys when Wolsey, under arrest for treason, was lying upon his deathbed at Leicester (Nov. 27th, 6738).

Three months before (Aug. 18th, 6571), Cromwell had written to Wolsey a disarming letter. He assured him that, notwithstanding the reference to praemunire in the preamble, " the finding of certain offices " (inquisitions as to title, etc.) " respecting the bishopric of York " did not portend a further chapter of spoliation. " Take patiently the finding of these offices, and on return order shall be taken that you are not molested in your revenues. The Dean and others " (of the Oxford College) " have had a favourable answer from the King touching your colleges, of which offices shall be found. I expect to get 1000 marks at the audit for Winchester . . . "

" You are much bound to God that you have obtained the good wishes of the people in those parts, and the report of it here has augmented the good opinion of many towards you ; yet, notwithstanding, your charitable demeanour is misinterpreted here by your enemies. Yet follow all such things that shall stand best with the pleasure of God and the King. Some allege you keep too great a house, and are continually building. I beseech you, as I have often done before, to consider the times, and refrain from all building more than necessity requires."

And he continues in a strain as alien to his proper nature as his former pious meditations at Esher :

" I thank you for the geldings you have sent, and think you happy that you are now at liberty to serve God, and banish all vain desires of the world, which bring men nothing but trouble and anxiety. Wherefore, in mine opinion, your Grace being as ye are, I suppose ye would not be as ye were to win a hundred times as much as ever ye were possessed of."

Cromwell was not a natural hypocrite, and this last passage should have put Wolsey on his guard.

There followed in October the exchange of letters (see above pp. 214 - 5) in which Cromwell, not without a touch of masterful resentment, repels Wolsey's passing doubts about the whole-heartedness of his service, and to which Wolsey replies in an endeavour to placate him.

Cromwell's last letter is dated October 21st (6699). Curiously irrelevant to the approaching tragedy, it is very far from suggestion that the recipient is to be arrested for treason within a fortnight. Cromwell refers to certain ominous legal documents which have " lain three months in the Chancery ; howbeit your Grace shall be so provided for that ye shall be out of all doubts for all the King's officers in the mean season." Asks for some office under Wolsey for his kinsman Dr. Karbott. Though somewhat simple in appearance, believes he will do well if put in trust. I hope you will also be good lord to your servant Nic. Gyfforde, when anything falls that may do him good. Though young and somewhat wild, he is disposed to truth, honesty and hardiness, and will love your Grace with all his heart. " If anything fall, I beseech your Grace to remember my scholars in Cambridge, and both they and I shall pray to our Lord Jesu Christ to preserve you in long life, good health, with increase of honour." Then comes the one reference to the project against the clergy, of which Wolsey had somehow got wind. Slipped in between references to the Emperor and the German princes, it seems studiedly casual.

" The Emperor will be at Cologne in the Feast of . . . . . without fail. The parliament is prorogued until the 6th day of January. The prelates shall not appear in the praemunire. There is another way devised in place thereof, as your Grace shall further know. The princes of Almayne can ne will not agree to Emperor. Written for lack of . . . in haste, the 21st of October."

Cromwell writes as a man who has ' inside ' information, which he means to impart piecemeal or not at all. The other " way devised " was no doubt that of levying a block fine through the Convocations in the polite guise of a subsidy, a cunning device which had three advantages ; it would humiliate the clergy as a body by making them subscribe to their own spoliation ; it would save the Law Officers and the Courts an infinity of trouble ; and it would guard against the real danger that some prelate or parson, not wholly pusillanimous, might protest his innocence, demand a trial at law, and perhaps explode the whole enterprise.

On Friday, November 4th, within less than a fortnight after receiving Cromwell's last letter, the Cardinal Archbishop of York was arrested at Cawood for high treason ; and two days afterwards he began his journey towards the Tower.

From the moment of his disgrace his wisdom would have been to eschew high politics altogether, to devote himself to his diocese and province, and to have become, in due time, a far from negligible power in the north. But his passion for great affairs, his hopes oi restoration to great office, were irrepressible ; and for months he had maintained a private, and not too prudent, correspondence with Rome and with the imperial and French ambassadors. When the time arrived it was not difficult, with the help of an informer, to give this correspondence, which was known to the Court, the colour and twist required to make it appear treasonable. The necessary informer was found in the person of Wolsey's trusted physician, an Italian named Agostini, who had acted as intermediary in these communications. As a member of Wolsey's household, this man was well known to Cromwell, who had rendered him, for stiff fees, certain legal services some months before (6374, May 10th). When, on November 4th, the Earl of Northumberland arrived at Cawood to carry out the arrest, he was accompanied by Walter Walshe, of the King's privy chamber. Walshe, apprehending Agostini, hustled him into Wolsey's presence with the words, heard and recorded by Cavendish, " Go in, traitor, or I shall make thee." The comedy was kept up by sending Agostini forward to London with his feet shackled beneath his horse's belly, traitorwise. The next we hear of him is in a despatch from Chapuys written on November 27th :

" Since they have had the Cardinal's physician in their hands, they have found what they sought for. Since he has been here, the same physician has lived in the Duke of Norfolk's house like a prince. He is singing the tune as they wished him " (6738).

" De Vaux", writes Chapuys on 27th November, " told the Venetian ambassador that by the physician's own confession the cardinal had solicited the pope at Rome to excommunicate the king and lay an interdict on his kingdom, unless he immediately dismissed the lady from Court and treated the queen with proper respect. By which means he hoped to cause a rising throughout the country, and in the midst of the confusion seize again the reins of government". (Pollard, 'Wolsey', pp.296-7).

The actual charges remained hearsay. The ambassadors could obtain no certain knowledge of them, still less the people. The Cardinal having died on the 29th., there was no need to produce or prove them. Their character may be judged from the pains that were taken to prevent their coming to light. Public opinion was by no means defunct ; and Wolsey had not governed the kingdom for some fifteen years without giving his countrymen a shrewd idea of what he was likely to attempt and do. At a moment when the immediate object was to mulct the whole Clergy of England under cover of the shakiest sort of judge-made law, it was inadvisable to risk turning opinion in their favour by publishing preposterous charges against a dead man, long the most illustrious of their Order. Accordingly the informer, Agostini, was required to enter into a heavy bond — a copy of which survives in the handwriting of Wriothesley, Cromwell's confidential secretary — to keep his mouth shut for the time being. We have (6763)

"A recognisance of Mr. Doctor De Agostinis, Venetian, in the sum of £100 to be paid to the use of our sovereign Lord the King at Christmas next ; on condition that if he keep secret all such matter as is mentioned in a book written with his own hand concerning the late cardinal of York, and presented by him to my lord of Norfolk, president of the Council, this recognisance shall be void ; otherwise it is to stand in full force. Hampton Court, 11 Dec. 22 Hen. VIII ".

226

THOMAS CROMWELL

Reproduced by courtesy of the Bodleian Library

facing page 226

THE WHOLE CLERGY INDICTED FOR PRAEMUNIRE

About the same time, in this same December, the Attorney-General laid an information in the King's Bench against the whole Clergy of England for having offended against the "statutes of Praemunire" in recognising "the late Cardinal of York" as Papal Legate.

In the following month, January 1531, there occurred two events connected apparently with the same chain of circumstance. The clergy, in the Convocation of Canterbury, were faced with a demand for a hundred thousand pounds — some three millions in our money — by way of composition for their supposed offence ; and Thomas Cromwell, hitherto a person with no official standing whatever, was sworn of the Privy Council.

Chapter IV

A PARENTHESIS ON 'PRAEMUNIRE'

It may be for the convenience of the reader if the following observations, instead of being relegated to an appendix, are here interpolated, both as a commentary upon the fall of the Cardinal and as an introduction to the impending fate of the clergy. The importance of the matter may justify some fulness of treatment.

The process by which, in the minds of the Tudor lawyers and in the text of the Statute of Appeals in 1533, the authentic Statute of Provisors, 16 Richard II,c.5, was translated into the phantasmal " Statute of Provision and Praemunire", was not a little remarkable. It was effected by the omission, and systematic disregard, of five or six little words.

The real statute of Richard was directed against two specific exercises of the Papal authority which were held to derogate from " the regalty of our lord the King ". They were, first, the making of " divers processes " and the pronouncement of " censures of excommunication " against English prelates for executing the judgments of the King's courts in questions of patronage ; and, second, the arbitrary translations of bishops within or without the realm and with or without their own consent and the King's, thus depriving the King of necessary counsel, and conveying the treasure of the kingdom abroad. These things are being done ; "AND SO", says the statute, "the crown of England, which hath been so free at all times that it hath been in no earthly subjection, but immediately subject to God in all things touching the regalty of the same crown, and to none other, should be submitted to the Pope, and the laws and statutes of the realm by him defeated and avoided at his will, in perpetual destruction of the sovereignty of the King our lord, his crown, his regalty, and of all his realm, which God forfend".

The penalties of the statute — outlawry, forfeiture and imprisonment, as laid down in Edward III's statutes of Provisors —are enjoined against any who "purchase or pursue ; or cause to be purchased or pursued, in the court of Rome or elsewhere, ANY SUCH translations, processes,.and sentences of excommunications, bulls, instruments or other thing whatsoever which touch the King, against him, his crown, and his regalty, or his realm, AS IS AFORESAID".

"ASCUNS TIEUX translations, processes et sentences de excommengementz bulles instrumentz ou autre chose qeconqe qe touche le roi nostre seignur encountre luy sa corone et regalie ou son roialme COME DEVANT EST DIT ".

The words "OTHER THING WHATSOEVER"— or "ANY OTHER THINGS WHATSOEVER ", as in the translation in Stephens' ' Ecclesiastical Statutes',— are in evident apposition to the nouns preceding them, "any such translations, processes, etc", and are governed by the words "any such" and limited by the words "as is aforesaid".

In the Statute of Appeals, 1533, the limiting words ANY SUCH — AS IS AFORESAID are omitted, and, by the loosest sort of paraphrase, the "pains, penalties, and forfeitures ordained and provided by the Statute of Provision and Praemunire, made in the sixteenth year of the reign of the right noble prince King Richard the Second" are represented as being incurred by "such as attempt, procure, or make provision to the see of Rome, or elsewhere, FOR ANY THING OR THINGS, to the derogation, or contrary to the prerogative or jurisdiction of the crown and dignity of this realm".

By this device King Richard's Statute of Provisors, designed to limit the papal authority vis-a-vis the King in two defined particulars, was made to remove any limit to the exercise of the royal authority vis-a-vis the Pope upon which the King and the judges, or the King in Parliament, might agree. For example, it might be used to make the tenure of the Legacy illegal when the object was to ruin and rob the Legate ; and thereafter, to make its recognition illegal when the object was to flummox and fleece the whole clergy of England.

229

A PARENTHESIS ON 'PRAEMUNIRE'

The effect of the perversion of the Statute of Provisors was far-reaching. In the ecclesiastical sphere it gave the King the means of making himself absolute, and paved the way for a political absolutism — Divine Right and the rest — which it required a Civil War and a Revolution to overthrow. In it was implicit the Supreme Headship. It gave a sort of statutory charter to the royal prerogative, "that undefinable term", as Bishop Stubbs calls it (Const. Hist. 11, p. 561). Its operation tended to be as undefinable as the prerogative it was made to guard. Its secrets were supposed to reside within the bosom of the King, or beneath the bonnets of the judges. The clergy pleaded or clamoured in vain for a definition of it, so that they might know how to keep out of trouble. Praemunire — a word properly applied to the writ of summons, loosely applied to the penalties, but not commonly applied to the Statute until Tudor times — was not so much a statute as a superstition, a sort of spring-heeled Jack of pretended legislation, lurking in the shadows, appearing suddenly, bounding over the tombs of clerical pretension, sending everybody scuttling for safety, and disappearing as suddenly as it came.

In pre-Tudor times the Statutes of Provisors, so far from being regarded as a reinforcement of the prerogative, were looked upon, ordinarily, as an inconvenient clog upon it, King and Pope uniting in collusive action to side-track and circumvent the statutes. As Bishop Stubbs says :

" The whole history of the statute of provisors is one long story of similar tactics, a compromise between the statute law and the religious obedience which was thought due to the apostolic see ; by regarding the transgression of the law simply as an infraction of the royal right of patronage, to be condoned by the royal licence, the royal administration virtually conceded all that the popes demanded ; the persons promoted by the popes renounced all words prejudicial to the royal authority which occurred in the bulls of appointment, and when the king wished to promote a servant he availed himself of the papal machinery to evade the rights of the cathedral chapters. This compromise was viewed with great dislike by the parliaments ; in 1391 the knights of the shire

230

threw out a proposal to repeal the statute of provisors, which had lately been made more rigorous, although the proposal was supported by the king and the duke of Lancaster ; but they allowed the king until the next parliament to overrule the operation of the statute " (Const. Hist. 11, pp. 633 - 4).

This passage relates to bishoprics ; but as late as the beginning of Henry VIII's reign royal licences were being granted to override the statutes in regard to papal provisions to ordinary benefices. Rymer records three such licences, the third of which was granted on the 23rd November, 1514, shortly before Hunne was found hanging in the Lollards' Tower. By this time the formula in which the statute of 16 Richard II was mis-cited had become stereotyped. The citation in the first of these licences (7th August, 1512, Foedera VI., pt. 1, p. 36, cf. pp. 86 - 7, 3rd edition) is word for word the same (with only a difference of tenses) as that which appears in the Bill of Indictment against Wolsey on the 9th October, 1529. In both the limiting words " such . . . . as is aforesaid " are omitted, and the statute of Richard given an unlimited scope. With them also is omitted the word " translations," relating to one of the two specific purposes to which the statute of Richard was directed. Its inclusion in the established formula might have set the inquisitive layman wondering and inquiring what the statute of Richard — the so-called " Statute of Provision and Praemunire " as it is cited in Henry VIII's Statute of Appeals (1533) — really said and did. Some eighty years before the date of these licences the notion of 16 Richard II, c. 5 as a general statute in maintenance of the royal prerogative and the King's courts of common law must have been current among the common lawyers ; for only so can we explain their attempted use of the writ of praemunire in restraint of other courts than their own, and especially the church courts within the kingdom, an innovation against which the spiritualty made vehement protest.*

For myself, I have a difficulty in following the consensus of

---

* See above, chap. 3, and Ogle, *The Canon Law in Mediaeval England*, pp. 166 - 75.

authority which discovers certain " statutes of Praemunire " as distinct from the statutes of Provisors, and finds some difference between them as to origin and purpose. For instance, in a footnote to Tanner, ' Tudor Constitutional Documents,' p. 18, " The first Statute of Provisors was passed in 1351, and the second in 1390. The first Statute of Praemunire was passed in 1353, and the second in 1393." And Bishop Stubbs (Const. Hist. 111, pp. 353, 356) writes :

" The great statute of provisors, passed in 1351, was a very solemn expression of the national determination not to give way to the pope's usurpation of patronage. . . . The history of the statute of praemunire starts from a somewhat different point, but runs parallel for the most part with the legislation of the subject of provisions. It was intended to prevent encroachments on and usurpations of jurisdiction, as the other was framed for the defence of patronage."

But, so far as I can see, the distinction is without a difference : for the jurisdiction which all the statutes were designed to defend was the jurisdiction of the King's courts in defence of patronage, and no other province of jurisdiction whatever. That, and that alone, was the field in dispute. The writ of praemunire had no context except the statutes of Provisors ; it, and the penalties foreshadowed by it and loosely called after it, were relative to the " provisor," his fautors and abettors, and no one else. To give " praemunire " a being of its own, a substantive existence apart from the provisor, is to admit and endorse the very perversion which it was sought, by systematic misquotation of 16 Richard II, to establish as honest law, and as a general statute for the maintenance, and indefinite expansion, of the prerogative. It was to create an offence of praemunire, based upon a suppositious " statute of Provision and Praemunire," the revolutionary sea-change suffered, at the hands of Tudor lawyers and draughtsmen, by Richard's conservative statute of Provisors.* In the statutes

* There is, in the Record Office (S.P. Henry VIII, vol. L : cf. L. and P. V, no. 722 (3) a contemporary ms. translation of the Statute in which the limiting words " any such . . . . as before is said " are accurately given. The paper is endorsed in the hand of Lord Chancellor Audley ; and it would seem to show

" things whereof the cognizance pertaineth to the king's court,"
.... " plea whereof the cognizance pertaineth to the king's court,
or of things whereof judgments be given in the king's court " (27
Edward III, st. c. 1) ; " causes whose cognizance and final discussing
pertaineth to our lord the king and his royal court " (38 Edward III,
st. 2) ; " churches, prebends and other benefices of holy church,
to the which they " — that is, " our lord the king and all his liege
people," — " had right to present, the cognizance of plea of which
presentment belongeth only to the king's court of the old right of
his crown " (16 Richard II, c. 5) : their whole context shows that
these expressions refer, not to jurisdiction in general whether papal
or royal, but to the particular branch of jurisdiction in dispute
between the common-law courts of England and the court of Rome,
the Jus Patronatus, the law relating to Patronage. The matter was
in substance quite simple. " The holy church of England was
founded in the estate of prelacy " (25 Edward III, c. 6), and its
bishoprics and benefices had been endowed by the sovereigns and
other lay founders, who exercised, as such, rights of patronage and
presentation. These were valuable temporal rights, and so, in
England, were within the cognisance of the temporal courts, the
king's courts of common law. When, in the course of the thirteenth
century, the Popes took, on an extensive scale, to reserving the
bishoprics and benefices of the church for their own nominees,
often non-resident aliens, trouble arose. Patrons claimed, in the
temporal courts, their lawful rights of presentation ; and the
common law courts, refusing to be ousted from their traditional
jurisdiction in defence of those rights, called upon the King in
Parliament for help in maintaining them. Hence the successive
statutes " de Provisoribus et aliis " concerning Provisors and others
(that is to say, their aiders and abettors), who trafficked in and
" purchased " " provisions," those anticipative nominations by the
Court of Rome, to the prejudice of the lawful patrons and of the
jurisdiction in patronage of the King's court. Such persons were

that Audley and the group of lawyers and politicians who were concerned in
these affairs had the words of the Statute plainly before them, and could not be
blind as to their meaning.

cited to appear and answer for themselves by the writ of
" praemunire facias," by which the sheriff was directed to
FOREWARN them to " stand and be at the law." The word
" praemunire " properly applied to the writ. Thence, by our habit
of giving a compendious nickname to things which are too much of
a mouthful to express at length, it became attached as a loose label
to the penalties prescribed by the statutes. To " fall into a
praemunire," to be " in case of praemunire," meant to render
oneself liable to the penalties of outlawry, forfeiture and imprisonment enjoined by the statutes " concerning Provisors " against
" people of the king's ligeance " who, being charged with pursuing
or purchasing " provisions," and suing processes in connection
therewith, in the court of Rome or elsewhere to the endamagement
of the rightful patrons and of the jurisdiction thereon of the king's
court, and being summoned to answer by the writ of "praemunire
facias," failed to prove that they were not guilty. But there was
no distinctive offence of Praemunire ; the offence was that of being
a Provisor, a ' provision ' dealer in and with the Roman Court.
Experimented as a legal device by the common lawyers of the
previous century, the ' statute of Praemunire,' as a developed
political weapon, was in substance a Tudor invention, first given a
spurious parliamentary hall-mark by citation in the Acts of Pardon
(1531), and as ' the Statute of Provision and Praemunire ' in Henry
VIII's Statute of Appeals in 1533. If the position taken in the
preamble of this latter statute had been true, and if Richard's
Statute of Provisors (1393) had said what the Tudor lawyers said it
said, there would have been no need for any Statute of Appeals at
all ; since the writ of praemunire could have been invoked against
anybody whatever who had recourse to the court of Rome for any
cause whatever. The authors of the statute of Appeals inevitably
gave themselves the lie in drafting it. In the same Act and in the
same breath they acknowledge Richard's statute to be of limited
scope, while invoking it as an instrument of the prerogative which
could be brought into play, without limit, " FOR ANY THING
OR THINGS."

The reader will follow these affairs the better if he remembers that, owing to the comparative strength of the English Crown and the comparative maturity of the English Common Law, England, in these matters of jurisdiction, had something of a place of her own among nations of the Roman obedience. Well before the Popes could act effectively as " universal ordinaries " administering in the Roman Court a fully developed Canon Law, the King's courts and the common lawyers in England were dealing with questions of patronage. When told by the rising schools of canonists that such questions were properly of ecclesiastical cognisance, they turned a deaf ear, went on with their business, and declared as bluntly as the barons at Merton, " We wo'nt have the laws of England changed." At the same time, and in order that the ecclesiastical lawyers might not suffer unduly in prestige and pocket, the latter were allowed to assume the lucrative jurisdiction in testamentary causes, which, according to their Canon Law, were no concern of theirs. The maintenance by the King's courts in England of their old jurisdiction concerning patronage was a sore stumbling block to the Popes ; but while able, by diplomatic means, to get round the " execrable " statutes which defended it, they were quite unable to secure their repeal.

It is fair to acknowledge that Henry VIII's lawyers, in omitting the limiting words " such . . . as is aforesaid " in their citation of Richard II's statute of Provisors (16 Richard II, c. 5), have been followed by some very authoritative modern works. The same omission occurs in the summary of the statute in Holdsworth's ' History of English Law,' 1, p. 586 ; and in Tanner, ' Tudor Constitutional Documents,' p. 17 : the latter rather surprising, because the reference is to Gee and Hardy (' Documents illustrative of English Church History,' p. 125), who give the text of the statute accurately and in full. The " come devant est dit,' as is aforesaid, is likewise omitted in Lodge and Thornton, ' English Constitutional Documents, 1307 - 1485,' p. 313. These omissions are of course due to the apparent unimportance of the words in question. They do seem unimportant until it is realised that by their omission the most important of the statutes of Provisors could be wrested from its defined purpose, and the writ of praemunire turned into an all-round weapon of the prerogative which could be swivelled at will in ANY required direction, and brought into action, in the ecclesiastical sphere, " FOR ANY THING OR THINGS."

Lest the views here stated should seem to savour of singularity and be suspect as newfangled, it may be well to add that precisely the same point as to the wording of Richard's Statute of Provisors was made and pressed by the Clergy in Convocation just upon five centuries ago. In a petition to the Crown in 1447 they say, " it was ordained . . . . that no man should purchase, nor pursue, nor make to be purchased or pursued in the said court of Rome, or other places, any suit, process, sentences of cursing, instruments, bull, or any other things whatsomever they be touching the king, his regalie or his realm of England in the wise aforesaid ; the which words, that is to say, any such process, sentences of cursing, and also the words ' in the wise aforesaid ' owen to be noted " (Wilkins, ' Concilia,' III, pp. 555 - 6). The words ' owen to be noted ' seem an excess of moderation. It was partly, no doubt, because the contention of the clergy was seen to be unanswerable that Edward IV, in the course of a charter granted to them in 1462, enjoined " that no Ordinary, or spiritual judge or any other prosecuting his own cause in the ecclesiastical or spiritual court should be in any manner burdened, inquieted, harassed or otherwise molested by the writ of ' Praemunire facias ' for the prosecution or decision of any cause to be determined in the spiritual court and begun within the realm ; and that neither judge, nor prosecutor nor defendant nor their counsel should fall into any penalty contained in the statute ' de Praemunire facias ' " (ibid. 111, pp. 584 - 5). It is apparent that by this time Richard's statute ' De Provisoribus ' was coming to be called by the name of its distinctive writ ; but that could not create a distinctive statutory offence called praemunire, apart from and over and above the defined offence of trafficking in provisions. Praemunire indeed seems to have been nothing more than a piece of legal propaganda, " built up " by a steady insistence upon certain big words in Richard's statute of Provisors, and a steady disregard of certain little words which conditioned them. No doubt the common lawyers, in their effort to control other jurisdictions, felt the need of such a weapon, or they would not have resorted to such shifts to get it.

NOTE

The above chapter was written before my attention was drawn, by a reference in Dr. Pickthorne's book ' Early Tudor Government : Henry VIII,' to an acute and learned article by Mr. F. W. Waugh on ' The Great Statute of Praemunire ' which appeared in vol. 37 of the English Historical Review (1922), pp. 173 - 205. The article begins :

" The so-called statutes of *praemunire* are among the most famous laws in English History . . . . But when the student, anxious to know precisely what the statute (of 1393 : 16 Richard II, c. 5) contained, and what it was designed to effect, turns for light to the works of modern historians, he finds himself faced by a perplexing variety of opinions."

Mr. Waugh's own reading of the statute coincides entirely with that given above. He stresses the preamble and the two specific mischiefs against which the Act was directed ; he stresses the enacting words " Such . . . . . as is aforesaid," pointing back to the mischiefs set forth in the preamble. He points out, I believe for the first time, that, these mischiefs ceasing almost immediately to be felt as mischiefs, this act directed against them fell into virtual oblivion for something like a generation, such controversy as there was centring round the previous statute of provisors passed in 1390. The reappearance of the act, and its adaptation to new uses, Mr. Waugh connects, conjecturally, with the quarrel between Duke Humphrey of Gloucester and Cardinal Beaufort early in the reign of Henry VI. At that time, he says, " conditions were extraordinarily favourable for the misinterpretation of the statute." The common lawyers, casting about for a means of controlling rival jurisdictions, especially the Courts Christian within and without the realm, discovered that with a judicious blue-pencilling of the statute of 1393 and a heavy stress upon its affirmations of the prerogative, they had a ready instrument to their hand. " As long as any respect was shown for the wording of the statute, it gave the temporal authorities few powers that they would not have possessed without it. . . . . The statute of 1393 did not seriously threaten the established relations between church and state until the king's courts took to ignoring, not merely the preamble, but certain words in the enacting part, words of restrictive force which might yet be omitted without destroying grammar or sense. Once the preamble was disregarded, the words " tieux " and " come devant est dit " ceased to have much apparent weight, and at some date unknown disappeared from writs citing the statute ; even when their full significance was overlooked, they might have served as reminders that the range of the measure was not so wide as the courts assumed. But it was more serious still when the statute was cited as covering everything which touched the king, his crown, regalty or realm, the words ' against him,' awkwardly inserted in the original text after the word ' king,' being left out. Thus the writ of praemunire in vogue in 1529 makes the penalties of the statute apply to those who pursue in the court of Rome or elsewhere, or bring into the realm, or receive, notify or in any way execute within the same realm any processes, sentences of excommunication, bulls, instruments or other things whatsoever which touch the king, his crown, regalty or realm. The pistol was already primed, and first Wolsey and then the whole body of the clergy put up their hands when it was levelled at them. No other act would have served the King's ends so readily. It is doubtless true that on any conceivable interpretation of the statute the clergy might have contested Henry's allegation that they had broken it by recognising Wolsey's legatine authority. But the grasp of the statute was wide — who but the king's justices could say how wide ? — terrible punishments (partly unknown) awaited those who fell into its clutches ; and the clergy feared their fate too much to make a stand for their deserts." (E. H. R. vol. 37, pp. 203 - 5).

These closing sentences are as far as Mr. Waugh felt called upon to go in characterising a subtle, but none the less monstrous, legal perversion, the production of an ' Act ' that never came out of Parliament.

Chapter V

" PRAEMUNIRE " AND " SUPREME HEADSHIP "

After an interval of a year — during which the King's main concern had been to collect opinions from foreign Universities in favour of his Divorce — Parliament reassembled for its second session on January 16, 1531.

A few days later the Convocation of Canterbury met for the most catastrophic session in all its long history. It had first to determine its attitude towards the charge of praemunire which had just been preferred against the whole clergy of the kingdom. How are we to account for the utter want of spirit with which the clergy in Convocation met that charge, thinking only of acknowledging their guilt and haggling over the amount of their ransom? By clergy, in this connection, we must understand the prelates, of greater and lesser degree. The rank and file, with their exiguous representation in Convocation, could have little say. They were unconscious of any crime but that of having been Wolsey's contemporaries ; and some months later (Sept. 1st), in the course of some riotous protests in the chapter-house of St. Paul's, the London parsons told their unpopular bishop Stokesley that they had " meddled never with the Cardinal's faculties," and that such prelates as had should pay the forfeit. (Hall, II, pp. 200 - 1). No one seems to have thought of questioning the law, as laid down in the King's Bench judgment upon Wolsey. No one seems to have challenged the right of Convocation to plead guilty on behalf of the clergy, or to negotiate for their pardon. The Bishops were not the men to make head against the King. With the exception of Fisher of Rochester all the more prominent were or had been in the royal service as ministers or diplomatists. They were, for the most part, the selfsame men who had followed Bishop Fitzjames in the Parliament and Convocation of 1515. They had shown no lack of spirit on that occasion. They had heard Fitzjames denouncing a London jury as " false, perjured caitiffs." They had followed Fitzjames and the Abbot of Winchcombe in raising the large question of clerical immunity in order to save Fitzjames' chancellor, indicted for murder, from secular justice. When one of the King's ' spiritual counsel ' Standish, since to their disgust made Bishop of St. Asaph, argued against them, they had formally charged him with heresy. They had hurriedly drawn in their horns when the Judges, by way of rejoinder, began to talk of praemunire, and when the Chief Justice, Sir John Fineux, intimated that the King, if he chose, could perfectly well hold his Parliament without them, an open threat to Convocation itself. The man who had interceded for them on that occasion, the rising young Primate of York, having gathered to himself an exceeding weight of glory only to lose all, was now not two months dead. Fifteen months had elapsed since his fall from power. Relieved of the incubus of his legatine pretensions, the bishops had felt a carefree satisfaction in his overthrow, without a thought that it might involve their own. They were now face to face with that formidable regality of which they had provoked the young King to talk so roundly in 1515. " By the ordinance and sufferance of God We are King of England, and the Kings of England in times past have never had any superior but God only " (see above p. 153). Then the King, notwithstanding his warning words, had held in with them on the whole ; and the House of Commons, in its effort to get justice for the memory and children of Richard Hunne, had been defeated. Now the prelates found themselves caught between two fires, between a grasping King and an unforgetful and implacable House of Commons, not to speak of some doctrinal cross-fire from some Lutheran scholars in the Universities. They had no time to think of the merits of the case, or of the justice of the charge, or of anything but propitiating the King at whatever cost. Their submission, like Wolsey's, was dictated by policy ; they felt, like Wolsey, that they had less to fear from the King than from Parliament. The King's favour was essential if they were not to encounter more such sessions as the first. In the effort to make the best terms possible, they offered forty thousand pounds, a sum which we may multiply by thirty.

The King would have none of it ; his gracious pardon could only be had for a hundred thousand. The Commons had purchased the King's support by cancelling his debts ; the prelates, in agreeing finally to the royal demand, doubtless hoped to outbid the Commons and have the King with them in any further controversy. They did not realise that the Londoner whose parliamentary carpet-bag was labelled Taunton, and who had made himself instantly a power in the House, was already at the King's elbow and in possession of the King's ear ; and that henceforth, under his discreet and resourceful management of both, King and Commons would be working in close collaboration.

The sorry business of the ransom was no sooner disposed of, as they imagined, than the prelates were faced with a further complication. The ransom was to be disguised as an ordinary subsidy, to which the clergy had been constrained by sheer gratitude. By the first week in February (1531) the draft of the grant had been completed, and submitted to, and considered by, the Privy Council. On February 7th (or possibly before) certain of the judges and king's counsel were closeted with the Archbishop " secreta communicatione." They required the acceptance by Convocation of certain novel " articles," which, by a neat process of ' invisible mending,' had been stitched into the preamble of the grant. By one of them the clergy, in enumerating the occasions of gratitude which had dictated the grant, were to make express mention of the King's benignity in pardoning their offences against the " statutes of Provisors and Praemunire." By another the clergy are made to acknowledge that it is by the King's protection against unspecified " fear and peril " that they are able to serve the King's people and the cure of souls committed to him. But the daunting article was the first, by which they are to acknowledge the King as " the only Protector and Supreme Head of the English Church and Clergy." This last demand, coming when it did, has every appearance of having been somebody's afterthought. Whose, we may well ask ? It would have been quite in the manner of Thomas Cromwell to signalise his advent to the Privy Council by some obsequious

241

advice, such as nobody else was at all likely to give.* The Clergy were smarting under the lash of praemunire. What better opportunity could there be to put an end to the old ambiguity of jurisdictions, to make good the King's old boast of having no superior but God, to show that he was, and meant to be, entire master in his own house, and to require the clergy to recognise that fact by their own solemn attestation. There was, as Cromwell would not be slow to see, a certain grim consistency in tacking on the demand for the recognition of the Supreme Headship to the act of forfeiture which the clergy were being compelled to execute. So far as regards the clergy, Praemunire, as fabricated and formulated by the Tudor lawyers, had made the King absolute ; he could fine or imprison " for any thing or things " which he and his judges might declare to be in derogation of the prerogative. What Praemunire was actually doing de facto the recognition of the Supreme Headship would acknowledge as being done de jure. How did the prelates themselves regard the demand ? It might be merely declaratory, a clumsy and offensive affirmation of the supervision and control in ecclesiastical affairs which the sovereigns had exercised from the time of the Conquest, a control compatible with the recognition of the papal authority in general. But why affirm it just now, and in such terms ? What extraordinary notion was in the King's mind, and finding expression in so extraordinary a phrase ? " Supreme " might pass ; but " Head," and " Head of the Church," even if it be only the English Church ? The Eternal Father had given the Son " to be the Head over all things to the Church, which is His Body, far above all principality, and power, and might, and dominion, and every name that is named, not only in this world, but also in that which is to come " (Eph. 1, 21 - 3) ; Supreme Head, in fact. And here was a philandering King with a floundering conscience arrogating the sacred appellation to himself. The name was to be anathema to Papist and Calvinist alike ; and towards the end of the century the judicious Hooker is writing twenty pages to make

---

* If this surmise were correct, it might offer such foundation as there is for the ' oratio ' which Pole puts into the mouth of Cromwell (above pp. 205 - 8).

it — or the memory of it, for the judicious Elizabeth had very wisely dropped it — less intolerable to devout Anglicans like himself. But there it was, and what did the King mean by it? What did he mean, in another article of these required acknowledgments, by talking of having committed to him " the cure of souls "? These phrases, so suddenly sprung upon them and demanding their assent, what did they portend? Were the old fast colours of spiritual and temporal running into one another, so that no man should know where he was, and the course of duty become a blur? Was Caesar, albeit Defender of the Faith, claiming what belonged to God, and to the Church of God, and to the ministers of the Church, and to their hitherto acknowledged jurisdiction? How much of the agelong order was the phrase " Supreme Head " adapted, possibly intended, to lever up? Faced with such questionings, there was only one thing for plain men to do. It was to request the King, with all duty, to clarify his demand ; and, meanwhile, to vote no penny of the hundred thousand pounds, praemunire or no praemunire, pardon or no pardon. Other men in other days, when the clergy as a body believèd in themselves and their people as a body believed in them, would have done so without hesitation. The question now at issue was not one of cash but of creed, of which the prelates were guardians. They had now the greatest opportunity that had been offered to them since the days of Runnymede. The Crown was strong, but not strong enough to have put the kingdom under a royal interdict. By one act of faith and courage the Bishops, led by a successor of Langton, could have brought the King to reason, confounded the Boleyn faction, and re-established their failing credit with the people, who hated the Boleyn and were all for the injured Queen whom she was aiming to supplant. It was not to be. The children had come to the birth and there was no strength to bring forth. The two men in Convocation who commanded reverence, Archbishop Warham and Bishop Fisher of Rochester, were old and spent : capable still of belated protest, but not of timely and intrepid action. Stokesley's predecessor as Bishop of London, Cuthbert Tunstall, might have had enough clearness and presence of mind to rally opinion and inspire conduct ;

243

but he had been translated, some two years earlier, to the Northern Province and the see of Durham. Firm leadership there was apparently none. The Archbishop brought before Convocation " the matter of the articles added to the preamble," giving it to be understood that without their acceptance the vast sum they had agreed to forfeit would not after all avail for their pardon. " The notion of the King's Supremacy," says the sober record, " did not commend itself (haud bene placuit) to the prelates and clergy, so they wished it to be modified." For three sittings discussion went on with the king's counsel as to " how they might bend the King's mind towards expressing that article in milder terms (mollioribus verbis)." By way of easing matters and quieting qualms the King, whose obsession with " the lady " had bereft him alike of dignity and humour, intimated, through " the lady's " brother, that he would be content to be acknowledged as Supreme Head " post Deum," after God. This, he said, was his last word. Its effect was rather to confirm, than to allay, misgivings. " At length on the eleventh day of February " — it is noticeable with what hustle and haste the whole affair was carried through — the Archbishop put forward a formula which, as he supposed, would save everybody's face and commit nobody to anything. The King was to be acknowledged as Supreme Head " quantum per Christi legem licet," so far as may be by the law of Christ. The proposal was received in silence. The Primate, feebly anxious for a decision of some sort, observed that silence would appear to mean consent. " Then," exclaimed the anonymous Voice which is often decisive upon such occasions, " we are all silent." And so, in glum unanimity, the affair went through, the Lower House accepting the decision of the Upper. It remained only to embody it in a formal act, from which no circumstance of ignominy was wanting to embitter its memory to those who took part in it. The ransom had to be dressed up in the form of a voluntary subsidy extorted, not by fear of the hobgoblin of Praemunire, but by a grateful sense of the King's manifold merits and services to the Church. He had in fact, under cover of allegations of law too shoddy to submit to argument in court, inflicted upon the clergy a callous outrage which would compel many of them, so they said, to sell their sacred vessels. None the less, Convocation is made to be eloquent of their gratitude. Most illustrious Majesty had deserved so well of them that his services were " above all praise, beyond all thanks, or any services to requite, still less gifts and rewards of theirs to recompense." In earlier days, sparing no labour of pen or expense in war, he defended the Universal Church, whose humblest members we are, against her enemies ; and so stoutly and invincibly as to earn an eternal glory of name and fame, as well as to open for himself the way to Heaven and make straight his pathway thereunto. And apart from these elder services by which he has bound to himself the whole Church of Christ in general, and more particularly us his subjects, in a perpetual obligation, so just now the crowd of adversaries, especially Lutherans, conspiring for the destruction of the English Church and Clergy — whose singular Protector, Only and Supreme Lord, and, so far as may be by the law of Christ, even SUPREME HEAD we acknowledge his Majesty to be — his most wise Majesty, as became the devout Defender of Faith and Church, has, by his labours, zeal, reasonings, counsels, yea, by his edicts and authority, dealt such knock-down blows (taliter contudit et repressit) that their boldness has begun to cool off (quod illorum audacia coepit refrigescere)," etc., etc. (Wilkins, III, 742).

So, — though the full implications of the great surrender did not unfold themselves until a year later, when the Spiritualty, on the complaint of the Commons and the demand of the King, gave up their right of independent legislation, — the die was cast. The great Fact went down before the great Fake ; Magna Carta succumbed to Praemunire ; and all that Langton and the barons had meant by the English Church being free and having her rights entire and her liberties undamaged, all of it had perished in a parenthesis. And all because what had long been the most powerful estate of the realm, lording it over God's heritage and answering to none, suddenly found itself without support, without a voice to speak for it in the City or the House of Commons, and driven to retain what authority it had on the King's terms and at the King's pleasure.

245

Such is the strange story as told, necessarily, from the standpoint of later times and in the light of later history. But we are fortunate in being able to tell part of it from the standpoint of a day-to-day onlooker, the Emperor's ambassador Chapuys, whose duty it was to learn, and accurately report, what happened.

Parliament had met on January 16th, On the 23rd Chapuys writes to Charles V :

" Nothing has yet been said in the estates concerning the affair of the Queen. They have been occupied with police arrangements against plague, and also what is considered to be the principal cause of this assembly, to exact a composition from the clergy who heretofore acknowledged the legation of the Cardinal, and whom the King, as I wrote to your Majesty, pretends to be liable to a confiscation in bodies and goods. Though the clergy know themselves innocent, seeing that it was determined to find fault with them, they offered of their own accord 160000 ducats, which the King refused to accept, swearing that he will have 400000, or that he will punish everyone with extreme rigour ; so that they will be obliged to pass it, though it will compel them to sell their chalices and reliquaries.

" About five days ago it was agreed between the Nuncio and me that he should go to the said ecclesiastics in their congregation, and recommend them to support the immunity of the Church, and to inform themselves about the Queen's affair, showing them the letters which the Pope has written to them thereupon, and offering to intercede for them with the King about the gift with which he wishes to charge them. On coming into the congregation they were all utterly astonished and scandalised, and, without allowing him to open his mouth, they begged him to leave them in peace, for they had not the King's leave to speak with him, and if he came to execute any Apostolic mandate he ought to address himself to the archbishop of Canterbury their chief, who was not then present. The Nuncio accordingly returned without having public audience of them, and only explained his intention to the bishop of London their proctor (Stokesley), who said he would report it. But he will beware of doing so without having the King's command, for he is the principal promoter of these affairs."

January 31st.

" The clergy, in spite of the aid the Nuncio desired to give them, who has remonstrated strongly with the Council, have made a composition with the King, of 400000 ducats payable in five or six years. Now that he has thus bled them, the King shows them favour, and puts them in hope of restoring their liberties, which were taken away at the last Parliament," (a reference to the measures of the first session).

February 14th.

" Since my last letters, the clergy have withdrawn the offer of money of which I wrote, because the King demanded that in case he or any of his allies made war they should be bound to advance the said moneys without waiting the said five years, and also because the King would not grant them what had chiefly induced them to make the gift, viz. the restoration of their old liberties and exemption from praemunire ; and, thirdly, because the King declared to them the importance of the said law of praemunire to guard himself from being misunderstood ; which law no person in England can understand, and its interpretation lies solely in the King's head, who amplifies it and declares it at his pleasure, making it apply to any case he pleases, the penalty being confiscation of bodies and goods. At last, after a good deal of negotiation, the matter has been settled, that the King shall not press them for payment before the expiration of the said five years, and that of the three demands of the clergy they should have that of the exemption, and nothing more......

" The thing which has been treated to the Pope's prejudice is that the clergy have been compelled, under pain of the said law of praemunire, to accept the King as head of the Church, which implies in effect as much as if they had declared him Pope of England. It is true that the clergy have added to this declaration that they did so only so far as permitted by the law of God. But that is all the same, as far as the King is concerned, as if they had made no reservation : for no one now will be so bold as to contest with his lord the importance of this reservation. This Act has very much astonished the Queen, who, seeing that the King is not afraid to commit such enormities, notwithstanding the promises which

247

have been made to the contrary, which were only to lull suspicion, has no doubt that now the King's lady is as much delighted as if she had gained paradise."

February 21st.

" The Act has been passed against the Pope, of which I wrote in my last. It has been drawn up in these words : ' Hujus cleri et ecclesiae Anglicanae dominum ac protectorem singularem, ejusque unicum summum ac supremum caput, quantum per legem Christi licet, regiam Majestatem agnoscimus et confitemur.' By this his Holiness will perceive the truth of what I have always told the Nuncio and written to Mai, that his timidity (doulceur) and dissimulation would not only prejudice the Queen's interests, but his own authority. . . . If the Pope had ordered the Lady to be separated from the King, the King would never have pretended to claim sovereignty over the Church ; for, as far as I can understand, she and her father have been the principal cause of it. . . . There is none that do not blame this usurpation, except those who have promoted it. The Chancellor (Sir Thomas More) is so mortified at it that he is anxious above all things to resign his office. The Bishop of Rochester (Fisher) is very ill with disappointment at it. He opposes it as much as he can ; but, being threatened that he and his adherents should be thrown in the river, he was forced to consent to the King's will. And it may be taken for granted, since the prelates have not dared to stand out against it, and have thus destroyed the Pope's authority, that, being commanded to proceed in the Queen's affair, they will do what they are bid, especially considering the coolness shown by the Pope. . . . The Nuncio has been with the King . . . . The Nuncio then entered on the subject of this new papacy made here ; to which the King replied that it was nothing, and was not intended to infringe the authority of the Pope, provided his Holiness would pay due regard to him, and otherwise he knew what to do."

March 8th.

" The clergy are more conscious every day of the great error they committed in acknowledging the King as sovereign of the Church, and they are urgent in Parliament to retract it ; otherwise, they say, they will not pay a penny of the 400000 cr. What will be the issue no one knows."

The issue was in suspense for two years longer, during which the Supreme Head continued to acknowledge the papal authority by keeping his case before the Roman Court.

One might hazard a guess that the notion of the ' Supreme Head ' was not, in origin, the King's at all. It looks like the crude impro-visation of someone, say Thomas Cromwell, who was accustomed to the use of religious language without any sense of what it meant to the religious ear. However that may be, the King once committed to the formula, it became sacrosanct ; nothing less would serve, notwithstanding the trouble, the not inconsiderable trouble, it subsequently cost him in explaining it, or explaining it away. The idea developed in two stages. In the first and negative stage it meant that the clergy, in the last resort, should bow to the King's, and to no other or opposing authority. This they had already been obliged to do in the former controversies about papal " provisions." The King claimed to be Supreme Head, not of the Church, but " of the English Church and Clergy." And the two terms in this ex-pression could be understood as synonymous. When men in those days spoke of the Church and Churchmen they commonly meant ' men of Holy Church,' the clerical order. We have relics of that usage in our common speech, as when people speak of a person's ' going into the Church,' or ' the Church ' being one of the liberal professions. The King's own explanation, given, not ungraciously, in a long and argumentative letter to the protesting Convocation of York, is decisive as to his original intent. " Therefore, albeit ' Ecclesia ' is spoken of in these words touched in the proem, yet there it is added ' et cleri Anglicani,' which words conjoined restrain, by way of interpretation, the word ' Ecclesia,' and is as much as to say the Church, that is to say, the Clergy of England " (Wilkins, ' Concilia,' III, pp. 762 - 5). So defined, the Supreme Headship could, and for two years longer did, co-exist with the papal author-ity. It was not until 1533 that the second stage was reached, and the Supreme Head began to expand positively in order to fill the administrative and judicial vacuum created by the elimination of

the Court of Rome. The King, having broken with Rome, had to
provide for immediate exigencies by acting as " papa alterius
orbis," with Thomas Cromwell as the royal legate de latere. This
was an emergency arrangement ; and Elizabeth, when her time
came, was able to re-assert her father's Supremacy while eschewing
its extravagancies of name and act. She was content to be over all
persons and in all causes, as well ecclesiastical as civil, within her
dominions supreme. Henry had meant no more originally ; but
in the King's assumed title men so opposite as Thomas More and
Thomas Cromwell saw very much more : Cromwell what, for his
own sake, he hoped for, More what, for the sake of Christendom,
he feared for. Colleagues for a year longer in the royal service,
both could see well ahead of the King, both knowing him better
than he knew himself.

The pardon of the clergy had to be embodied in a parliamentary
bill. When it came before the Commons they refused to pass it.
This was not from any graceless wish to keep the clergy under the
harrow of Praemunire ; it was a precautionary measure of their
own. So far as their intelligence could grasp the position, it seemed
clear that if the clergy as a body were criminally responsible for
having breathed the same air as Wolsey, so, not less, were the laity.
It was true that the King had not thought of drawing an indictment
against the whole nation ; but this impossibility, as a later political
philosopher thought it, was quite, so thought the faithful Commons,
within the royal compass ; and it was as well to be on the safe side.
They therefore refused to accept the bill of pardon for the clergy
without a like bill — except that it cost the beneficiaries nothing —
in favour of the laity. The King seems to have been a little non-
plussed by this excess of caution on the part of the Commons. The
whole quaint story, which is not without an important moral, is
best read in the quaint narrative of Edward Hall :

" When the Parliament was begun the 6th day of January, the
pardon of the spiritual persons was signed with the King's hand and
sent to the Lords, which in time convenient assented to the bill and
sent it to the Commons in the lower House ; and when it was read,
divers froward persons would in no wise assent to it except all men

were pardoned, saying that all men which had anything to do with the Cardinal were in the same case. The wiser sort answered that they would not compel the King to give them his pardon, and beside that, it was uncharitably done of them to hurt the clergy and do themselves no good ; wherefore they advised them to consent to the bill and after to sue to the King for their pardon ; which counsel was not followed, but they determined first to send the Speaker to the King or (ere) they would assent to the bill ; whereupon Thomas Audely, Speaker for the Commons, with a convenient number of the Common House, came to the King's presence, and there eloquently declared to the King how the Commons sore lamented and bewailed their chance to think or imagine themselves to be out of his gracious favour, because that he had graciously given his pardon of the Praemunire to his spiritual subjects and not to them ; wherefore they most humbly besought his Grace of his accustomed goodness and clemency to include them in the same pardon.

" The King wisely answered that he was their prince and sovereign lord, and that they ought not to restrain him of his liberty, nor to compel him to show his mercy ; for it was at his pleasure to use the extremity of his laws, or mitigate and pardon the same ; wherefore, sith they denied to assent to the pardon of the spiritual persons, which pardon he said he might give without their assent by his great seal, he would be well advised or he pardoned them, because he would not be noted to be compelled to do it ; with this answer the Speaker and the Commons departed very sorrowful and pensive ; and some light persons said that Thomas Cromwell, which was newly come to the favour of the King, had disclosed the secrets of the Commons, which thing caused the King to be so extreme.

" The King like a good Prince considered how sorrowful his Commons were of the answer that he made them, and thought that they were not quiet ; wherefore of his own motion he caused a pardon of the Praemunire to be drawn, and signed it with his hand, and sent it to the Common House by Christopher Hales his Attorney, which bill was soon assented to. Then the Commons lovingly thanked the King, and much praised his wit, that he had denied it to them when they unworthily demanded it, and had bountifully

granted it when he perceived that they sorrowed and lamented "
(' Chronicle,' II, pp. 183 - 5).

We have heard in our day of Welsh wizardry ; but there must
have been some sort of weird wizardry about Henry Tudor to make
Englishmen behave to him in this fashion. The incident, however,
is more than curious. It points to a difference of moral outlook
between those days and ours. In those days conscience, for the
ordinary man, moved wholly within the orbit of law. The " open
vision " of truth and right which was to be brought by the open
Bible — for which Wyclif had striven and Tyndale was striving at
the moment — within reach of the common man, was not yet ; the
modern era in which law, with more or less of a time-lag, would
conform itself to the demands of a growing and developing public
conscience, was still to come. For moral rule men had only the law
of the land and the law of Holy Church ; and right or wrong was
what the law allowed or disallowed. An act might be regrettable,
deplorable, detestable ; but you could not go the length of calling
it wrong if it came within the law. So, on this occasion, the Commons, provided their immediate pardon was assured, were ready to
incriminate themselves and the laity in general on a preposterous
charge : their sense of its absurdity being lost in their sense of its
enormity as coming, reputedly, within the law. That was why a
man like Cromwell, who knew how to manipulate and rig the law,
could become so speedily such a power in the land. It was why
Henry's victims upon the scaffold, one after the other, paid homage
to the law under which they suffered, and to the impeccable tyrant
in whose name it worked. It was why the fate of Richard Hunne
excited more, and more lasting, public reprobation than any of the
more distinguished killings of the reign. It was not that he was
done to death, but that he was done to death without process of
law, and that the pretence of trying him after death was looked
upon as an indecent pantomime. There was all the difference in
the world between dying legally under the hand of the executioner
and being murdered by one's gaolers, and gaolers who could shelter
from justice behind their privilege. The prime exemplar of this
legal conscience, the most superstitious devotee of law as law, was

252

the King himself. Passionately anxious to marry Anne Boleyn, he was not less passionately anxious really to marry her, that is, to do so according to law and after the legal annulment of his marriage with Katherine ; and the Pope being the final judge, Henry, for no less than six years, spent untold sums and every device he knew, in the effort to secure a papal sentence in his favour. When at last his patience gave out and he went through a form of marriage with Anne (Jan. 1533), he hastened to put himself right with the law by making a new set of laws of the required pattern. In general, the restiveness of his people stopped short of revolt because he could always make out a plausible case, and was always careful to keep within the law. Under Cromwell the forms of law became the toolbox of tyranny.

The reference to Cromwell, in the above passage from Hall, as suspected of disclosing to the King the secrets of the Commons, is significant. Since the beginning of the Parliament in November, 1529 the Commons had looked upon Cromwell as eminently their man ; now, in January, 1531, some " light persons " among them were inclined to suspect that he was becoming rather too much of the King's man.

So far we have been considering the first measures of the Parliament of 1529 ; the first step in the ascent to power of Thomas Cromwell ; and the first action taken, through the enforced acknowledgment of the King's Supreme Headship, to reduce the clergy from the status of an ' imperium in imperio ' which they had held throughout the Middle Ages. It remains only to consider the corollary of this last, which took place a year later, and is known as the " Submission of the Clergy."

But meanwhile, and at this point, it may be well to set forth a position which the facts appear to warrant. During the first half of the six-years life of this Parliament, that is, from November, 1529 to the end of 1532, three policies, and not one, are discernibly at work. They are concurrent and overlap, but they are plainly distinguishable. There is, first, the policy of the House of Commons: to put a limit to the privileges and immunities of the clergy, and to assert for the laity some voice in the making and execution of the ecclesiastical laws which governed them. In carrying out that policy the Commons required no prompting either from King or Court ; and they found in Cromwell a new ' parliamentary hand ' who was ready and able to throw their purposes into shape, and to manage their affairs in committee and conference. Secondly, there was the policy of the King : to gratify his passion and his desire for a male heir by marrying Anne Boleyn, and to do so in due course of law, after obtaining from the Pope the annulment of his marriage with Katherine. This had been Wolsey's policy, and the King hoped to succeed in it where Wolsey had failed, and persevered in it long after his new and coming adviser Cromwell had seen it to be a wan hope. The King's policy at this stage was wholly conservative, though it was shot through with hints and threats of a radical solution. The policy of the Commons was moderately radical, though the prelates and clergy regarded it as radical in the most opprobrious sense of that word. But the only revolutionary policy was that which remained discreetly undisclosed in the bosom of Thomas Cromwell. It was that of developing the newly recognised Supreme Headship so that, if matters drifted to a deadlock between King and Pope, the former could take over from the latter with no great ado, the clergy, as a possible centre of opposition, being immobilised beforehand. The approach had to be made with caution because, at the period under review and until the end of 1532, neither King nor Commons were prepared for decisive action against the Pope. Not the King, because his case was still *sub judice* before the Roman Court, and the resources of diplomacy, as he still had hope, were not yet exhausted. And not the Commons, because a breach with the Pope would mean a break with the Emperor and the interruption or loss of the all-important trade with Flanders ; not to speak of the pretty certain fact that their wives, to a woman, were all for the Pope in refusing to be cajoled or bullied into pronouncing against Katherine. But Cromwell had no need merely to mark time ; for the Commons were ready and eager to go forward with their action against the clergy begun in their first session ; and we shall see what use they made of the opportunity when it was given them in the session of 1532.

254

That session opened on January 15th, nearly a year after the acknowledgment of the Supreme Headship on the previous February 11th. Meanwhile the King's ' great matter,' descending to lower levels of meanness and monotony the further it proceeded, dragged its slow length along and the name of England in the mud. The credit and consequence which Wolsey, by energetic participation in the affairs of Europe, had gained for his country, was quickly dissipated. All other interests gave way before the ' great matter ' of the so-called Divorce. England had ceased to be a good European ; her King, the erstwhile pattern of princely magnificence, was coming to be ranked abroad as a rebel and a renegade. The Turk might be tearing at the vitals of Europe ; but all it meant to Henry was some useful embarrassment for the Queen's imperial nephew and partizan. England, perhaps, might help the Pope to save Christendom from the infidel if the Pope would enable her King to marry by pronouncing that, after twenty years of reputed wedlock, he had never in fact been married at all. Henry, of course, had a legal case ; he always had : but he was at pains to destroy it, from every point of view but that of law, to destroy it especially in the eyes of his Queen, by his open courtship of her long-headed rival. Throughout 1531 the question of the venue was uppermost. The King contended that neither the peace, nor what he called the " privileges," of his kingdom would permit him to obey the papal citation to plead at Rome ; the appellant Queen, supported by the Emperor, insisted that nowhere but at Rome would her cause receive justice. Lawyers, archivists, diplomatists worked like beavers upon the case : but it made no headway because, on one matter, Pope and King were in complete accord. Both desired to drag out the time as long as possible, the King in the hope of avoiding an adverse judgment, the Pope in the hope of avoiding the necessity for any judgment at all. Clement vacillated in the fond and feeble hope that, as he said in May, " time will cure it " (V, no. 256). Meanwhile the Queen maintained her ground with an exasperating faultlessness of demeanour. Apart from consenting to renounce her wifehood, her daughter's legitimacy, and her right to justice before the supreme tribunal, she was submission and

255

dutifulness itself. Early in June a daunting attempt was made to shake her resolution. Headed by the Duke of Norfolk, a delegation of nobles and prelates over thirty strong, intruded upon her at an indecently late hour, " about 8 or 9 at night, as she was retiring to rest " ; only to find themselves and their pleas and blusterings reduced to ignominy by Katherine's steadfastness, integrity and mother-wit. (V. no. 287). The record leaves one marvelling how a prince, undeniably brilliant and reputedly able, could have lived with such a woman for twenty years without discovering which was the better man. " In the end," writes Chapuys to the Emperor, " Norfolk and Wiltshire, by way of excuse, wished her to understand that they were not the promoters of these affairs, and that they did not apply themselves to it further than what they heard men of the long robe say. And so they left without uttering another word, though the bishop of London was very much urged to speak ; but when he had heard the Queen's reasons, he had not the courage. As for the most part of the rest, if they had the liberty of speaking their thoughts, they would have inclined to the Queen's side ; but as they could do no more, they testified their inclinations by showing the satisfaction they had at the Queen's answers, and they secretly nudged one another when any point touched the quick. Among these was the secretary, Dr. Stephen (Gardiner), who at the commencement unravelled these affairs, but is now very much suspected by the Lady. Some said they had worked hard, and counselled long, and devised fine plans, but were confounded by a single woman, and all their designs turned topsyturvy. Of these was Guildford, the Controller (of the Household), who said it would be the best deed in the world to tie all the doctors who had invented and supported this affair in a cart, and send them to Rome to maintain their opinion, or meet with the confusion they deserve. When the said Duke and others came to the King, who was waiting for them in great anxiety to hear of their success, they told him what had occurred. On which he said he was afraid it would be so, considering the courage and fantasy of the Queen ; but it would be very necessary to provide other remedies. And on saying this, he remained very pensive." (V, no. 287). Even " the said Duke," who was, in this matter of the divorce, the King's most consistent jackal, had been provoked into saying, a short time before, that " it was the Devil, and nobody else, who was the inventor of this accursed dispute " (May. V. no. 238).

Meanwhile the astute merchant-lawyer who sat for Taunton, and who had just been rewarded (Jan. 1531), for certain obscure but important services, with a seat on the Privy Council, was careful to keep clear of the whole unpromising business.* A new man, he saw that while the Emperor's forces overshadowed Rome, nothing was to be done by chaffering with the Pope upon the ancient lines. He was content to wait for the day, still some two years ahead, when the royal suitor, contemning the court, would take the law into his own hands, and require the help of Parliament, and of a practised parliamentary hand, in measures to meet the papal anathemas. Leaving foreign affairs, which had come to mean little but the affair of the Divorce, to others more committed or less intelligent, he set himself to master the domestic business of the kingdom. He makes himself intimately acquainted with the multifarious sources of the royal revenue, and sets them forth in a six-page " memorial to the King's Highness " (V. no. 397). He is the man to see that no penny accruing to the Crown from fees, fines, forfeitures, feudal incidents and what not, is lost to the Exchequer. He has, for some strange reason, perhaps for his extensive and peculiar knowledge of ecclesiastics, the sort of fingers to which ecclesiastical affairs inevitably stick ; and all the proper patronage of the Crown, and all the Crown could acquire through persuasion

---

* Dr. Friedmann (' Anne Boleyn,' 1,145) gives Chapuys as authority for the statement that Cromwell was " the only councillor who did not take part in the long discussions about the validity of her (Katherine's) marriage."
    Writing in an earlier passage (1,134) of " the spring of 1531," Dr. Friedmann says : " It was at this most critical juncture that Anne found an able and faithful ally in Thomas Cromwell." This seems to rest only upon the assumption — in my belief mistaken — that the anti-clerical measures with which the Commons and Cromwell were concerned at this time were directed towards facilitating the divorce. Cromwell, of course, served Anne's purposes in serving the King's ; but I question whether he was ever her ally in any other sense. He showed no unreadiness to throw her over when he found her credit failing, and arranged with complete callousness for her destruction when he saw the King had done with her.

or pressure, passes through Cromwell's hands. Though the newest recruit to the Council, it is "to his trusty counsellor Thomas Cromwell" that the King addresses his "instructions" as to the business, some of it connected with the next session of Parliament, "to be declared to the Council, and undelayedly put in execution this Michaelmas term, 23 Hen. VIII" (ibid. no. 394). With all this he retains his foothold in commerce and the law. He conducts, with ease, an extensive correspondence, and all the business arising out of it. High and low, rich and poor, one with another, everybody with a cause to plead or an axe to grind, seems to have recourse to Cromwell. His correspondents write with friendliness and appreciation, and, as often as not, substantial tokens of goodwill. Everywhere he makes useful friends, and nobody is allowed to feel the powerful grip within the velvet glove. He has the gift of organising and delegating work ; he is well served, and knows how to reward service ; his clerks and underlings are men of quality, more than one of whom attained to rank and fortune and high office in the state. He himself is not ambitious of office ; his goal is power, and it is sufficient for him to have the King's ear. Visibly he is merely a force in occasional sessions of Parliament, and a steady but unobtrusive influence in the Council. His public appointments, such as they were — Master of the Jewels, Clerk of the Hanaper, etc. — make comic reading when measured against his real and growing influence and authority. His chosen part will be to "produce" the coming drama and direct it off-stage ; the revolution he effected will be in substance complete before the foreign ambassadors, informed and watchful, begin to be aware of him.

Not the least interesting of the letters addressed to Cromwell at this period — its date is November 3rd, 1531 — is one from Richard Kidderminster, the estimable old ex-Abbot of Winchcombe, the same who, sixteen years before, when Cromwell was starting in business as a struggling clothier, had been used to pull Bishop Fitzjames' chestnuts out of the fire (see above pp. 141 - 7). He asks "Master Thos. Cromwell, councillor to the King," "not to impute his neglect of writing to obliviousness or negligence, but to his great age and sickness. Intends to supply by hearty prayer for his welfare the omission of his duty in writing. The increase of Cromwell's honour and authority, of which he daily hears, is more to his comfort than he can express. He desires credence for the cellarer. Cromwell's labours and kindness will be considered by the abbot and convent. Winchcombe, 3 Nov." (V. no. 510).

Chapter VI

PRELATES AND HERETICS, 1531

Apart from the quiet progress of Thomas Cromwell, the chief interest of the year lies in the action of the prelates. Smitten alike in pocket and in conscience by the Praemunire, the price of their pardon and the enforced acknowledgment, incidental thereto, of the King's Supreme Headship, they seem, by a sort of curious atavism, to have turned to the harrying and burning of ' heretics ' as a means of recovering themselves and the situation. As Bishop Fisher had said, the " Church " — meaning by that the clerical order with its privileges and immunities — was in danger ; and the prelates thought to save it by refurbishing the old weapons drawn from Archbishop Arundel's armoury of repression. In repressing Wycliffism Arundel, with the Crown and Parliament firmly behind him, had used those weapons with effect. His successors, in the beginning of 1531, were too flustered in their wits to consider how those weapons were likely to serve with the lay elements in Parliament openly hostile and a Crown whose support grew more and more precarious with every month that the Divorce business dragged along. They, and, it must be said, their zealous lay coadjutor Lord Chancellor More, completely mistook the quarter from which the real danger threatened, and took the surest means to draw it upon themselves. In rekindling the fires of Smithfield which, during Wolsey's long period of control, had ceased even to smoulder, the prelates were challenging elements of opinion of whose full weight and volume they seem to have been unaware. The ruder was the awakening when, in the spring session of the following year (1532), they had to meet a frontal attack, by a perfectly orthodox House of Commons, upon the laws of heresy and upon the " Ordinaries," the Bishops and their chancellors, commissaries and vicars-general, who executed them. That attack led, directly and quickly, to the great constitutional instrument known as the " Submission of the

Clergy " : by which the prelates and Convocations gave up their powers of independent legislation, and the ecclesiastical ' imperium in imperio,' which was the distinguishing mark of the Middle Ages, was brought, in England, to an abrupt end. The constitutional principle of the Reformation had been established, and the power of the clergy to maintain themselves or, as was soon to appear, the Supreme Pontiff, against the Crown and Parliament, had ceased to be.

The pursuit of heresy even to the death, which began again in 1531, was really a throw-back to the early days of the reign and to the episcopate of Fitzjames. That portentous prelate died in 1521, and, until about that date, intermittent burnings took place to his order, and to the order of his worthy fellows, Longland of Lincoln and Blythe of Lichfield and Coventry. Fitzjames was succeeded in London by Cuthbert Tunstall, a humanist and a clement person, who knew that in the new age of printed books heresy might be argued out, but could not be burnt out. For that reason he had given the necessary licence to Sir Thomas More to have and read Lutheran books in order to confute them. He understood as well as Wolsey the nature of the times, and the impolicy of making martyrs if it could anyhow be helped. During his tenure of London, terminating, after Wolsey's fall, in his translation to Durham in 1530, prosecutions for heresy took place from time to time, but pains were taken, especially with the most notable of the accused, to prevent their being carried to extremity. Tunstall's earnest, fatherly, even affectionate patience in the endeavour to save ' little Bilney ' — of whom presently — from himself and from the stake makes one of the brighter pages in the darkling annals of repression. In his reliance upon persuasion Tunstall was of one mind with the Cardinal Legate. Unlike his more devout successor in office, Wolsey, Lord Chancellor since 1515, had no disposition to be active as an inquisitor, or to turn York Place, as More turned his house and garden at Chelsea, that storied Academe, into a pallid semblance of the Holy Office. As Legate a latere he could and did impose some check upon the untimely zeal of persecuting prelates. In his great foundation at Oxford he embodied his belief that the remedy for heresy was learning, and not burning.* On his fall, his slackness against heterodoxy was numbered among his offences. The forty-third of the Lords' articles of charge against him recites the complaint of certain Bishops in Parliament that two of them, unnamed, had been checked in a proposed anti-Lutheran drive in the University of Cambridge. " The Lord Cardinal, informed of the good minds and intents of the said two Bishops in that behalf, expressly inhibited and commanded them in no wise so to do. By means whereof the same errors, as they affirmed, crept more abroad and took greater place ; saying furthermore that it was not in their defaults that the said Heresies were not punished, but in the said Lord Cardinal ; and that 'twas no reason any blame or lack should be arrected to them for his offence. Whereby it evidently appeareth that the said Lord Cardinal, besides all other his heinous offences, hath been the Impeacher and Disturber of due and direct Correction of Heresies, being highly to the danger and peril of the whole Body, and good Christian People of this your Realm " (Fiddes, ' Life of Cardinal Wolsey,' Collections, p. 178). In point of fact, during the decade when Tunstall ruled in London with Wolsey ruling in all England, no lurid glow appeared over Smithfield, or the Lollards' Pit at Norwich, or Little Park at Coventry ; the mortal fires remained unlit. During that decade Lutheran books, smuggled in by merchants and mariners, found a ready market, notwithstanding the ban of authority and their ceremonial burning at Paul's Cross. Lutheran opinions " crept abroad " among the scholars at Cambridge, and in a less degree at Oxford ; and there was at least a dawning of the idea that religious debate could be carried on without the argument of fire and faggot. But no sooner was the Cardinal's hand removed than the habit of

---

* The concern and energy which Bishops Fitzjames, Longland and Blythe before him, and Stokesley, Nix and Veysey after him, put into the harrying of heretics Wolsey put into the founding of his colleges at Oxford and Ipswich. Dr. Pollard writes (' Wolsey,' p. 214) : " While the records of his legatine court teem with cases of penance, confession, abjuration, and imprisonment, there is no instance of the extreme penalty being inflicted during Wolsey's legacy by the cardinal himself, his commissaries, or the diocesan synods whose jurisdiction he effectively superseded."

coercion resumed its sway. Within four months of his fall from power, one Thomas Hitton was burned at Maidstone. It was not, however, until the violent fluttering of the dovecotes in the spring of 1531 that the prelates in Convocation, chagrined by the enforced acknowledgment of the Supreme Headship, betook themselves incontinent to a field of action in which their own headship was acknowledged as supreme, and applied the rigour of the law once more to those who were " detected " to them as heretics.

Their first essay in that kind was not fortunate. It might have been designed to recall men's minds, if they had needed recalling, to the case of Richard Hunne. It was nothing less than condemning a dead man for heresy, digging up his body, and handing it over to the secular power for burning. It would almost seem as if the prelates had sought to cover their confusion over the ' supreme head ' affair by an act of pure bravado ; for the deceased convict had been a man of standing, and high sheriff of his county. William Tracy, a Gloucestershire squire, had made a will which made enough history for it to figure importantly in Hall's Chronicle. It was customary in those days for a man, when making his will, to include in it a solemn confession of his faith. Tracy did so as follows :

" First and before all things I commit me unto God and to His mercy, believing without any doubt or mistrust that by His grace and the mercies of Jesus Christ, and by the virtue of His passion and of His resurrection, I have and shall have remission of my sins and resurrection of body and soul ... There is but one God, and one mediator between God and man, which is Jesus Christ :—And therefore will I bestow no part of my goods for that intent that any man should say, or do, to help my soul ; for therein I trust only to the promises of God " ; . . . . .

This, doctrinally, was the substance of the will, and of the heresy for which its deceased author was condemned. It is taken from Hall's " true copy of his will, for the which, as you have heard before, after he was almost three years dead, they took him up and burned him " (' Chronicle ' II, pp. 225 - 7).

Squire Tracy, in inditing this will, had probably no thought but of delivering his own soul ; he can hardly be supposed to have meant to make trouble for his heirs and executors. He overlooked the fact, however, that the will would have to be proved in the ecclesiastical court. The attempt to obtain probate led to its appearance before Convocation. On February 25th (1531), a fortnight after its acceptance of the ' supreme headship,' " Convocation proceeded to examine the will of Will. Tracy, and condemn the author of it as a heretic " (V, no. 928). The matter came up in subsequent sessions, and further steps were taken with a deliberation which suggests some dubiety in the minds of those responsible. The final order for the exhumation of Tracy's body was not given until May 13th, 1532, midway between two catastrophic dates which fell within the same week : the 10th, when the King's Almoner laid before Convocation the royal demand for the surrender of their powers of free and independent ecclesiastical legislation, and the 15th, when Convocation closed its own chapter of mediaeval history by bowing to the demand. " Handed over for the fire " by the ecclesiastical authorities, — I borrow the phrase from the canonist Lyndwood, and cite it in refutation of the idle pretence that Holy Church was not responsible for the burnings, — *the secular power, in the person of the sheriff, received the body, and had it duly burnt. But presently we find the secular power taking note of the matter from a cooler angle. The condemnation and the burning had been carried out in strict accordance with law, except in one particular. The chancellor of the diocese of Worcester, Thomas Parker, who had directed the exhumation under mandate from the Archbishop, had done so without procuring a warrant from the Crown which, rightly or wrongly, was presumed to be requisite. Such errors of omission, affecting clerics and involving cash, came within the purview of that unofficial and nondescript, but very effective, department which was being " run " semi-privately by Privy Councillor Cromwell. Under date 15th January, 1533, we have a

---

* Ponderandum esse quod relapsis poenitentibus solum conceditur sacramentum Eucharistae, non autem Extremae Unctionis : quia sacramentum Extremae Unctionis non adaptatur relapsis etiam poenitentibus quia relapsi TRADUNTUR INCENDIO." ('Provinciale,' p. 296, 'sententialiter declaretur.')

letter written by Richard Tracy, the dead man's son and heir, to a friend who might be in touch with Cromwell. It is calendared as follows :

" You know the great trouble I have had about my father's testament, and the great and abominable worldly shame done unto his kindred in burning his rotten bones, which was dishonourable also to the gentlemen of the shire, as he had been high sheriff, and had held commissions from the late and the present kings. Hears the principal actor will be punished for it, but there were other accomplices. If they are found guilty, the king will profit £1000 by revoking grants to them ; and it will be a great benefit to Gloucestershire, as he can show Master Cromwell, to whom, as he hears, the King has committed the matter. Will not write about it, but will come to London within four days of Candlemas, and show the matter to Cromwell. Asks his correspondent, if he has such acquaintance with Cromwell, to stay the matter till then. Ex aedibus nostris, 15 Jan. (VI, no. 40).

Hall reports the sequel, which took place later in the year.

" The King, hearing his subject to be exhumate and burnt without his knowledge or order of his law, sent for the chancellor and laid the high offence to him ; which excused him by the Archbishop of Canterbury which was late dead ; but in conclusion it cost him three hundred pound " — some thousands in our money — " to have his pardon " (' Chronicle,' 11, p. 225). Cromwell, who disapproved of burnings and still more of folly, doubtless felt a sardonic satisfaction in levying this fine upon the luckless chancellor, who according to Dr. Gairdner, " seems besides to have lost his place." It was an ill time for too zealous chancellors. The incident shows that the spiritual and secular powers, no longer working hand in glove as in the days of Arundel, were now tending to get across one another.

The prelates, however, unable to discern the signs of the times, followed up their action against the dead Tracy by burning three live people before the end of 1531.

The first was a man whose case requires more than passing mention because it illustrates the peculiar character of the process in heresy, and goes far to explain why, some months later, the House of Commons formally impeached that process, and proceeded, within three years, to the unprecedented step of regulating it by Act of Parliament so as to bring it more into conformity with secular canons of justice. For very different reasons of course, the case aroused as much public interest as that of Richard Hunne, and received much the same measure of controversial treatment in More's ' Dialogue.'

Thomas Bilney, graduate of Cambridge, scholar, priest and preacher, was burnt as a relapsed heretic in the Lollards' Pit at Norwich on August 31st.

This was the summary end to a process which had begun five years earlier. Bilney had been delated to the authorities in 1526. On that occasion Wolsey, who, as Legate, could override diocesan authority, took the case in hand. " This man," writes More (' Dialogue,' bk. 3, chap. 4) " had also been before that accused unto the greatest prelate in this realm, who, for his tender favour borne to the University, did not proceed far in the matter against him. But accepting his denial, with a corporal oath that he should from that time forth be no setter forth of heresies but in his preachings and readings impugn them, dismissed him very benignly ; and of his liberal bounty gave him also money for his costs." But Bilney's preaching still gave umbrage, especially to the friars, who delated him again in 1527. This time the Cardinal took the matter more seriously, and Bilney was brought before a legatine court, Wolsey himself presiding at the opening session, with the assistance of Archbishop Warham and no less than eight other Bishops. Having set the case in motion with all solemnity, the Legate withdrew on the plea of State business, leaving the further conduct of the proceedings to Bishop Tunstall ; not, one imagines from the sequel, without a plain hint to Tunstall that Bilney, whatever his belief or misbelief, was not a man to burn.

In point of fact Bilney's misbelief, if any, was of the mildest. He was not even a Lutheran, in the sense of having borrowed anything from Luther, or of accepting Luther's doctrine about the Sacrament of the Altar, the great test question, about which Bilney's orthodoxy was so little suspect that he was never even examined upon it. He tells his own story in one of his letters written to Tunstall at the time of the trial. Oppressed with the burden of his sins, he, like the woman in the Gospel, had suffered many things of many physicians and was nothing bettered. The ignorant doctors, the unlearned confessors, who had prescribed for him fastings, watchings, purchases of indulgences and masses, had left him low in spirit and poor in purse.

" But at last," writes this mature priest, " I heard about Jesus." His friends at Cambridge were seeing Jesus with new eyes, through the new Latin into which Erasmus had rendered the New Testament. Drawn by the fame of its Latinity — " rather than by the Word of God, for at that time I knew not what it meant " — he bought a copy. " At the first reading, as I well remember, I chanced upon this, to me most comforting, sentence of Paul in I. Tim. 1 : ' It is a true saying, and worthy of all men to be embraced, that Christ Jesus came into the world to save sinners : of whom I am chief." Here was the message of hope and assurance which his soul craved. " After this, the Scripture began to be more pleasant unto me than the honey or the honeycomb." His passion was to bring to others the comfort wherewith he himself had been comforted of God. " Therefore with all my whole power I teach that all men should first acknowledge their sins and condemn them, and afterwards hunger and thirst for that righteousness whereof St. Paul speaketh : the righteousness of God, by faith in Jesus Christ, is upon all them which believe in Him ; for there is no difference ; all have sinned and lack the glory of God, and are justified freely through his grace by the redemption which is in Christ Jesus ' ; which whosoever doth hunger or thirst for, without doubt they shall at length so be satisfied that they shall not hunger and thirst for ever.

" But, forasmuch as this hunger and thirst were wont to be quenched with the fulness of man's righteousness, which is wrought through the faith of our own elect and chosen works, as pilgrimages, buying of pardons, offering of candles, elect and chosen fasts, and oftentimes superstitious : and finally all kind of voluntary devotions (as they call them) ; therefore, I say, oftentimes I have spoken of those works, not condemning them (as I take God to my witness) but reproving their abuse ; making the lawful use of them manifest even unto children ; exhorting all men not so to cleave unto them that they, being saturate therewith, should lose all taste for Christ, as many do ; in Whom I bid your fatherhood most prosperously well to fare." (Foxe, IV, p. 633 - 6).

Such was the extent of Bilney's "heresy." The popular — and very profitable — recourse to saints and their shrines tended to draw away men's minds from the one true Mediator who alone could give peace with God. If, as the Baptist had proclaimed, Jesus was the Lamb of God, who taketh away the sins of the world, what room was there for the doctrine of the friars that burial in the cowl of St. Francis remitted the four parts of penance ? Such questions brought the friars upon Bilney's track ; and so, on November 27th, 1527, he stood on trial before the Legate and his imposing array of Bishops.

The proceedings lasted until December 7th, and resolved themselves into a strange duel between faith and charity : between Bilney's faith in the gospel he had preached and his utter refusal to renounce it or admit it to have been heretical : and Tunstall's charity — and prudence — in refusing to allow him to doom himself to immediate death by persistence in denial. If Bilney had been Tunstall's own son, the Bishop could not have laboured more anxiously and patiently for his life. The critical moment occurred towards the close of the sitting on December 4th. Here is the story in the words of the Bishop's Register :

" And then the said Reverend Father the Bishop of London advised him to consider with himself whether he would return to the unity of the Church and renounce his opinions : and bade him retire and consider with himself in private (in loco remoto) ; and so he withdrew for half an hour. Then, on Master Bilney's reappearance, the said Reverend Father the Bishop of London interrogated him anew as to whether he would return to the Church. His answer was : ' Justice and Judgment be done in the name of the Lord.' And again admonished and exhorted as above, he said as before, "Judgment be done.' Interrogated as to whether he could show why he ought not to be pronounced guilty of heresy, he answered : ' This is the day that the Lord hath made : let us rejoice and be glad in it.' Interrogated again as to whether he knew or wished to show cause why he ought not to be declared guilty of heresy, he answered again, ' Justice and judgment be done.' Then, interrogated by the same Reverend Father, he acknowledged that he was convicted by witnesses of the crime of heresy ; and then, after consultation, the said Reverend Father the Bishop of London, removing his cap, spoke as follows :

" In the name of the Father and of the Son and of the Holy Ghost, Amen. Let God arise and let his enemies be scattered," crossing himself on the forehead and breast. And then, with the express consent and counsel of the said Reverend Fathers, the said Reverend Father, in a loud voice, pronounced the said Master Bilney, present and seeing and hearing the premises, (guilty) as follows : " I, with the counsel and consent of all my brethren present, pronounce thee, Thomas Bilney, upon several articles accused, detected and convicted of heresy, and " — (here delivery to the secular arm should have followed in due course, but the Bishop concluded) :—" for the remainder of the sentence we shall consult until to-morrow." (Foxe IV. Appendix : from Tunstall's Register).

Bilney's life was hanging by a hair.

When the morrow came he showed some disposition to temporise. He declared that he had no wish to be a stumbling-block to the Church. He asked leave to produce witnesses on his own behalf, averring that he could produce thirty in his favour for one against him. The plea was disallowed as inadmissible in law. He asked for time to consult with friends and advisers, and this was granted to him not ungenerously. At long last, on the 7th December, he agreed to sign a prescribed form of abjuration after examining it carefully.

This form of abjuration enabled Tunstall and the court to avoid sending him to the stake ; but it came in for the severest animadversion from Sir Thomas More, writing in the ' Dialogue ' a year or so later (1528). More regarded it as almost, if not quite, without precedent, and felt and said that the court, in accepting it, had strained the law almost to breaking point in favour of the accused. For in fact, as More saw clearly, Bilney had been allowed to abjure the heresies imputed to him without any express acknowledgment of ever having held them, or of penitence for having done so. More's expressions are notable as indicative of his own mind as well as of the facts. More is arguing against his supposed inter- locutor that, so far from having been hardly dealt with, " the man we speak of " — More does not mention Bilney by name — had received undue favour from the court.

" I would fain wit who had right if he had wrong, although there had been used to him more rigour a great deal than there was ?"

' Why, quod he, what devil rigour could they more have showed for the first time, than to make him abjure and bear a faggot ? '

' Yes, quod I, some man had liefer bear twain cold in his neck, than have one bear him hot on a fire at his feet.'

' In faith, quod he, they could not have done that to him at the first time.'

' No, quod I, not if he willingly returned to the church, knowledg- ing his fault, and ready to abjure all heresies, and penitently sub- mitted himself to penance. And else, if he prove himself obstinate and impenitent, the church neither is bounden nor ought to receive him, but utterly may forsake him and leave him to the secular hands. But now was he so obstinate that he would not abjure of long time. And divers days were his judges fain of their favour to give him, with sufferance of some his best friends and whom he most trusted, to resort unto him. And yet scantly could all this make him submit himself to make his abjuration. And finally were they fain, for saving of his life, to devise a form of abjuration whereof I never saw the like, nor in so plain a case never would, were I the judge, suffer the like hereafter.'

' What manner of abjuration was that ? quod he.

' Mary, quod I, his abjuration was such that he therein abjured and forsware all heresies, knowledging himself lawfully convict. But whereas they be wont to confess in their own abjuration that they have holden such heresies and be guilty thereof, that would he do in no wise ; but as clearly as his fault was proved, and by as many, yet would he not, to die therefor, confess himself faulty . . ."

And now if I should prove you that his judges showed him such favour, I fear me lest I should therewith somewhat seem to charge them that they had done, though not wrong, yet very near wrong, the favour appearing to be showed, if not against the law, yet at the leastway the law, for favour, so far stretched forth that the leather could scant hold . . . . . .

' I will not say that his judges did wrong. But surely methinketh I may well say that they showed him great favour in that they received him to penance without the confession of his fault. And I think verily that it was a favourable fashion of abjuration, and so strange that the like hath been very seldom seen, if ever it were seen before.' (Dialogue,' ' bk. 3, chap. 5 : English Works, 11. pp. 195—202).

As a matter of law, More's strictures were entirely justified. His austere and rigid mind, where heresy was concerned, could entertain no consideration of policy in dealing with a heretic. He should have the law, the whole law, and nothing but the law. But Wolsey and Tunstall were practical statesmen ; and they found themselves struggling in the toils of the heresy law more anxiously than their own prisoner. Bilney, " standing to his conscience," (in his own phrase), was indifferent to death ; but neither Wolsey nor Tunstall was indifferent to the consequences of burning a man who was a light and power in Cambridge, and who, for his austerities, his charities, his transparent holiness of life, was recognised by all who knew him as of the very salt of the earth. Had the process in heresy admitted of an acquittal, the solution might have been more straightforward ; but in practice it did not. That process was a self-acting machine which, once set in motion, went on working to its inevitable end. A wise and clement Bishop, pestered, say, by a crew of mischief-making friars, was little less helpless than his own prisoner when once caught between its cogs. Let me remind the reader once again (see ante pp. 31 - 2) what that process was. Either by the Bishop's officers or by the civil magistrate for delivery to the

Bishop, a man was arrested upon information given. He was not confronted with the informers, whose identity was concealed as long as possible. He was confronted instead with a set of " articles," drawn from a ready-made schedule, covering the ordinary heads of heresy, and selected for their supposed relevance to the case. Sworn, and closely examined upon these, he was expected to incriminate himself. If he failed to do so, the informers were introduced in the guise of witnesses. They might be persons of sufficient credit, or of none. As we have seen, and shall see, the acceptance of tainted testimony in heresy cases was formally defended by More and the Bishops. No disrepute on the part of a witness was any bar to the acceptance of his testimony against a person on trial for heresy. The evidence for the prosecution having been given, the accused was not suffered to produce rebutting testimony. His own denials went for nothing. There was nothing before him but to abjure the errors imputed to him, acknowledging his guilt, with an abject expression of penitence. There followed the infliction of a humiliating public penance — bearing a faggot at procession in church or during the sermon at Paul's Cross or elsewhere — with, perhaps, a term of imprisonment at the Bishop's pleasure, and, certainly, a lifetime of miserable surveillance in which a man had to watch every step and weigh every word for fear of rearrest and execution as a " relapse." If, like Bilney on that Dec. 4th., he maintained on oath his plea of not guilty, the law, as rightly interpreted by More, left the Bishop no choice but to hand him over to the secular power for burning. No deadlock was possible except perhaps, momentarily, in such a unique case as that of Bilney, where the accused man, rather than forswear his real gospel or admit it to be heretical, was prepared to die, and where the Bishop, and his principal the Cardinal Legate, were not prepared to let him if the law which claimed his life could anyhow be circumvented. More might look sourly upon the device adopted, but it saved the situation. What he calls " a favourable fashion of abjuration " was as follows :

" I, Thomas Bilney, priest, — intend by the grace of God here-after ever to persevere and abide in the true doctrine of Holy Church, and do detest and abjure all manner of heresies and articles following, whereupon I am now diffamed, noted, vehemently suspected, and convicted,: that is to say,

That men should pray only to God and to no saints.

Item, that Christian men ought to worship God and no saints.

Item, that Christian men ought to set up no lights before images of saints.

Item, that men do not well to go on pilgrimages.

Item, that man in no wise can merit by his own deeds.

Item, that miracles daily showed be wrought by the devil by the sufferance of God.

Item, that no Pope hath such power and authority as Peter had except he be of like purity of life and perfection as Peter was.

And in these articles and all other I here expressly consent unto our mother the holy church of Rome, and the apostolic doctrine of the same " ; etc. (Foxe, IV. Appendix from Tunstall's Register).

Bilney is here made to abjure the errors of which he had been " diffamed, suspected and convicted ", but the holding of which, as appears both from More's story and from the Bishop's Register, he flatly and firmly denied throughout. It is unnecessary to suppose, however, that those who had listened to some of his sermons and gave evidence against him, were conscious of false witness. It is difficult for a popular preacher, inveighing against the abuse of a thing, to prevent the ill-instructed or the ill-disposed from imagining that his invectives are directed against the thing itself. More constantly urges throughout the " Dialogue " that the abuse of a thing is no argument against the thing itself. Bilney solemnly affirmed in his letter to Tunstall that he had oftentimes spoken of pilgrimages to the shrines of saints and other ' voluntary devotions ', " not condemning them (as I take God to my witness) ", but reproving their abuse. Yet, when he repeats that affirmation on oath before the court, More can do no better than write of him as a hardened and unrepentant perjurer. The handling of Bilney in the ' Dialogue ' did not augur well for the fairplay reputed heretics were likely to receive when it became More's duty, as Chancellor and magistrate, to arrest and examine them.

Legally an abjured heretic, Bilney had to fulfil his penance.

He was ordered, humbly and penitently, bareheaded and carrying a faggot, to lead the procession in St. Paul's on the following day, and so to stand throughout the sermon at Paul's Cross or elsewhere ; to remain in prison until released by the Lord Legate or other his Ordinary ; and never thenceforward to preach " in any place or church " unless by special licence of the Apostolic See or the Legate or his own Ordinary. Breach of this last element in his imposed penance would involve his rearrest and summary execution as a relapsed heretic.

After more than a year's imprisonment in the Tower Bilney was suffered to return to Cambridge ; and there the story is taken up by his devoted friend and disciple, Hugh Latimer. In a sermon delivered years later when such as he were freer to write and speak, Latimer owned his own debt to Bilney.

" Here," he says, " I have occasion to tell you a story which happened at Cambridge. Master Bilney, or rather saint Bilney, that suffered death for God's word's sake, the same Bilney was the instrument whereby God called me to knowledge. For I may thank him, next to God, for that knowledge that I have in the word of God ; for I was as obstinate a papist as any was in England, insomuch that when I should be made bachelor of divinity, my whole oration went against Master Philip Melancthon, and against his opinions. Bilney heard me at that time, and perceived that I was zealous without knowledge ; and came to me afterwards in my study, and desired me, for God's sake, to hear his confession. I did so, and, to say the truth, by his confession I learned more than afore in many years."

Bilney, on trial before Tunstall in 1527, had been persuaded to purchase respite by a sort of compromise, hardly realising what was before him. His life at Cambridge, after his release from the Tower, was one of misery and self-reproach. In two other passages Latimer tells that story :

" That same Master Bilney, which was burnt here in England for God's word's sake, was induced and persuaded by his friends to bear a faggot at the time when the Cardinal was aloft and bare the swing. Now when the same Bilney came to Cambridge again a whole year after, he was in such anguish and agony that nothing did him good, neither eating nor drinking, nor even any other communication of God's word ; for he thought that all the whole Scriptures were against him, and sounded to his condemnation ; so that I many a time communed with him (for I was familiarly acquainted with him) ; but all things whatsoever any man could allege to his comfort, seemed to him to make against him. Yet for all that afterwards he came again. God endued him with such strength and perfectness of faith that he not only confessed his faith in the gospel of our Saviour Jesu Christ, but also suffered his body to be burned for that same gospel's sake which we now preach in England."

And again, in a sermon preached before the boy King Edward : " I knew a man myself, Bilney, little Bilney, that blessed martyr of God, who, what time he had borne his faggot and was come again to Cambridge, had such conflicts within himself (beholding this image of death) that his friends were afraid to let him be alone. They were fain to be with him day and night, and comfort him as they could ; but no comforts would serve. And as for the comfortable places of Scripture, to bring them unto him, it was as though a man would run him through the heart with a sword." (Foxe, IV., 641—2).

It seems to have been in the spring of 1531, when the Bishops were moved to renewed action against heresy, that Bilney's trouble of spirit reached its crisis. His soul was charged with a saving gospel about which he was forbidden, under pain of death, to open his mouth. Late one night, so it was told, he bade farewell to his friends in Trinity Hall, telling them, in the prophetic words of our Lord, that he was going up to Jerusalem. His Jerusalem was Norwich and the Lollards' Pit. His renewed activities were speedily known. In March his name was before Convocation, along with those of Crome and Latimer. Latimer, who had declared for the King in the matter of the divorce, was now a Court chaplain, and could look for protection. For Bilney, the abjured ' heretic ', there was none. Wolsey was dead ; Tunstall was far away in the north. Had Richard Nix, the blind old Bishop who was nearing the end of his inglorious reign at Norwich, been disposed to mercy, the law would not have allowed it. The sentence on a relapsed heretic, and his delivery to the secular arm for burning, was a matter of routine. Bilney wished to die as he had lived, a good Christian and a good enough Catholic. He begged to be released from the ban of excommunication, and to receive absolution and the Holy Sacrament. His plea, after some hesitation, was granted ; and an attempt was made by the authorities to represent his edifying end as in the nature of a recantation. When about to address the people at the stake, a paper, supposed to be a ' bill ' of revocation, was thrust into his hand by Dr. Pellis, the Bishop's chancellor, by whom he had been sentenced. A bystander, one Curat, an alderman of Norwich, averred that Bilney took the bill and read it aloud ; but refusing, in the city council, to stand to that affirmation on oath, he was charged by the Mayor with equivocation, of a piece with his alleged shiftiness in certain money matters. The Mayor, Edward Reed, with the rest of the aldermen, who were also bystanders, were positive that if Bilney read the bill at all, he did it " softly ", that is, to himself, and not audibly to the people. When Dr. Pellis brought the bill before the council to be " exemplified " as having been publicly read by Bilney, the Mayor and aldermen refused to attest it as not according with their recollection of what had occurred. Reed, with the concurrence of all his colleagues but Curat, drew up a careful memorandum of what had taken place ; and held to it when a subsequent inquiry upon oath was made by the Lord Chancellor. What More's conclusion was does not certainly appear ; but he later wrote of Bilney as having made his peace with the Church. That, in a measure, was true ; but it no more necessarily involved a recantation than his previous abjuration before Tunstall. In his speech at the stake, recorded by Reed, Bilney acknowledges with regret certain faults and mistakes, but says not a word about the cult of saints and their shrines, about which he had been convicted. His sentence, of course, as a relapsed heretic was due, not to his preaching this or that, but to the breach of his penance by preaching at all without special licence. The truth seems to be that Bilney maintained his ground unwaveringly throughout. He would not, because he could not, recant opinions which he declared on oath that he had never held, or " return to the Church " which, in his own mind and conscience, he had never left. The law was such that, on the testimony of persons whose ears and prejudices, apart from any malice, might easily have deceived them, a man so little guilty as Bilney might be delivered over to death, neither his oath nor his character sufficing to save him.

One detail of the affair is significant. The Mayor, Edward Reed, was one of the burgesses who sat for Norwich in Parliament. On the Sunday before Michaelmas, according to Curat's deposition, Reed addressed his colleagues as follows :

" Brethren, so it is I must shortly go up to the Parliament, where I am sure I shall be inquired of concerning the death of Bilney. Wherefore I would desire you all to know your minds therein ; and that I might have a testimonial signed with your hands and sealed with the town seal, so that I might testify and verify the truth thereof." (Foxe, IV., Appendix.)

It is apparent that the House of Commons was following the proceedings of the Bishops with an attentive eye.

A few months after Bilney's execution Latimer, himself under vehement suspicion, wrote as follows to a correspondent :

" I am told that the Bishop " (Stokesley of London) " has informed the King that I defend Bilney and his cause against his ordinaries and judges. I did nothing of the kind, unless it were in admonishing judges to act indifferently. I have known Bilney a long time much better than did my lord of London, for I have been his ghostly father many a time. I ever found him meek and charitable, and a simple good soul not fit for this world, but if he has done anything contrary to Christian obedience, I do not approve it. How he ordered or misordered himself in judgment I cannot tell ; but I must wonder if a man living so charitably and patiently should die an evil death." (V., No. 607. Dec., 1531).

Meek and charitable, a simple good soul not fit for this world. Wolsey and Tunstall had shrunk from the thought of burning Bilney, and had strained the law in order to save him from the friars. But their wisdom departed with them, and other men were in their places.*

In November of the year Richard Bayfield was burnt at Smithfield, and John Tewkesbury followed him to the stake in December. These men must remain mere names so far as this narrative is concerned. In December, too, proceedings were begun against James Bainham, a barrister of the Middle Temple and son of a Gloucestershire squire and magistrate. It is in connection with Bainham's case that we hear most of the rigours alleged to have been suffered by persons accused of heresy while under detention in the household of Sir Thomas More. Our best informant on this much debated matter is More himself. He writes in the ' Apology ' of " the lies neither few nor small that many of the blessed brethren have made and daily yet make by me". As to the supposed flagellations, he mentions two incidents which really did occur, but had little really to do with heresy. In one case a youth in his service who had been perverted by a bad priest, attempted to pervert a younger lad. More, as a matter of domestic discipline, had the offender soundly birched. In the other case a man of unsound mind had been reported to him for indecent horseplay in church. More had him taken up by the constables, tied up to a tree outside his premises, and flogged " till he waxed weary and somewhat longer". The effect, he says, was salutary, and there were no more complaints. Apart from these cases, he says, " of all that ever came in my hand for heresy, as help me God, saving as I said the sure keeping of them — and yet not so sure

---

* " The second so-called martyr, though of greater renown, had not a much better claim to it " — the title of martyr, which the author has just denied to Thomas Hitton. " Little Bilney," as he was called, though he converted his ghostly father, Latimer, to his views at Cambridge, recanted, relapsed again and prevaricated, before he was finally burned at Norwich in 1531 ; but just before his death it seems perfectly clear (though Foxe would not believe it) that he again expressed abhorrence of the heresies he had maintained, and was reconciled to the Church once more." (Gairdner, ' The English Church in the Sixteenth Century,' pp. 129 - 30, cf. his ' Lollardy and the Reformation. I. 393 - 405). Of which it is perhaps enough to say that it was only in stature that little Bilney was small. Dr. Gairdner's reference to Bilney is of a piece with his consistent disparagement of all who, from Wyclif downwards, hazarded their lives for the cause of reform.

to disclose the whereabouts of her husband's books, and that in the hope, the vain hope, of forcing him to inform against others likeminded, he was racked in the Tower by More's order and in More's presence, I see no good reason to disbelieve her. Certainly, Bainham's own reported utterances at the stake suggest that, in his own mind, he had had exceptionally hard measure at the hands of the Lord Chancellor. (Foxe, IV., 705).*

The modern apologists who labour to acquit More of what they call "inhumanity" in dealing with heretics are really doing him no small injustice. He had a declared abhorrence of heresy, and no sentiment about the treatment of heretics. A heretic was a person to be reclaimed by persuasion, even harsh persuasion, or, failing that, to be exterminated by law. More's humanity went out, not to the heretic, but to the innocent faithful who might be led astray and eternally damned if the heretic were suffered to survive. Both More and the Bishops tried persuasion, as in duty bound ; but, that failing, they did as they were required by law, as well the law of the land as the law of the Church. That they felt no pleasure in having to enforce the law we know from their own solemn affirmation in response to the historic petition of the Commons in the following year.

Of Tewkesbury, mentioned above, Foxe relates that he was confined for a time in More's house, and kept, for six days without

---

* Dr. Gairdner says (ibid) : "We might well suspect" the "falsehood" of the rigours said to have been suffered by Bainham " from Foxe's own statement about Bainham's examination by the Bishop at More's house at Chelsea, where we read, 'They asked him whether he would persist in that which he had said, or else would return to the Catholic Church, — adding moreover many fair, enticing and alluring words, that he would reconcile himself, saying the time was yet that he might be received, etc.' That is to say both More and the Bishop of London endeavoured to win Bainham by gentle means wholly inconsistent with the alleged brutality." But, beyond allowing his house to be used for the purpose, More, as a layman, could take no part in the "examination by the Bishop"; and the "gentle means," the "fair, enticing and alluring words," were part of the ordinary procedure of the actual trial, and had nothing to do with the preliminary investigation carried out by More, as magistrate and Chancellor, in the Tower or elsewhere. And, as regards the alleged racking, "brutality" is hardly a word that would have been used by contemporaries, even the sufferer himself. It was, and was meant to be, extremely painful; but both Foxe and More agree that its effects might be no more than temporarily crippling.

release, in the stocks in the porter's lodge. The sceptic might ask,
What was a Lord Chancellor doing with a set of stocks in his
porter's lodge ? Yet it is from More himself, writing with somewhat
wry humour of the escape of George Constantine, that we hear
most about these stocks. " Some have said that when Constantine
was gotten away, I was fallen for anger in a wonderful rage. But
surely, thought I, I would not have suffered him go if it would
have pleased him to have tarried still in the stocks ; yet, when he
was neither so feeble for lack of meat but that he was strong enough
to break the stocks, nor waxen so lame of his legs with lying but
that he was light enough to leap the walls ; nor by any mishandling
of his head so dulled or dazed in his brain but that he had wit
enough when he was once out wisely to walk his way ; neither
was I then so heavy for the loss but that I had youth enough left
me to wear it out ; nor so angry with any man of mine that I
spake him any evil word for the matter, more than to my porter
that he should see the stocks mended and locked fast, that the
prisoner steal not in again. And as for Constantine himself, I
could him in good faith good thank. For never will I for my
part be so unreasonable as to be angry with any man that riseth
if he can when he findeth himself that he sitteth not at his ease."
(' Apology, ibid).

A useful sidelight is thrown upon all this in a letter written in
December by Stephen Vaughan, an impressionable person who
acted as Cromwell's agent in the Netherlands. In touch by correspondence with Cromwell and the Court, and, in person, with
Tyndale and other English refugees abroad, Vaughan was in the
position of the onlooker who sees most of the game. Cromwell
had given him a well-meant warning, and Vaughan replies (V.,
No. 574) :

" You say that George Constantine has been arrested, and will
perhaps accuse me of favouring Lutherans and their books, and
you advise me to apply myself only to the King's service. I am
surprised, for two reasons : first, that the Lord Chancellor, in
examining him and others brought up for heresy, always tries to
find some occasion of evil to be fastened upon me, which the

patient " (that is, the man under examination) " soon espies, and, trusting to escape, of pure frailty spares not to accuse the innocent. Secondly, in addition to his imminent peril, being a prisoner in my Lord's house, he was vehemently provoked, by the remembrance of his poor wife remaining here bewaished with continual tears, and the sharp and bitter threatenings, etc., to accuse whom they wished, rather than be tied by the leg with cold and — (?) iron like a beast, as appeared by the shift he made to undo the same and escape such tortures. Would God the King would look to these punishments, which threaten more hurt to the realm than the ministers who execute them conjecture ; for his subjects will be forced to leave the realm in great numbers, and live in strange countries, where they will practise not a little hurt to England. Instead of punishments, tortures and death ridding the realm of erroneous opinions, and bringing men into such fear that they will not be so hardy as to speak or look, be assured, and let the King be advertised from me, that he will prove that it will cause the sect in the end to wax greater, and these errors to be more plenteously sowed in his realm. Those who have most sowed those errors are those who have fled the realm. By driving men away, they will make the company in strange countries greater, and four will write where one wrote before. Advise the King to look to this matter, and not to trust to other men's policy, which threatens the weal of his realm. Let the King be assured that no policy nor threats can take away the opinions of his people until he fatherly and lovingly reforms the clergy, whence spring both the opinions and the grudges of the people."

Of himself Vaughan continues rather querulously :

" I hear everywhere how diligently the Lord Chancellor enquires concerning me of those whom he examines for heresy, and that others are also deputed to make like inquisitions." . . . " I hear that I have lost a most dear friend and special good master in you, and that you have excused yourself to the King for ever having advanced me, as you are greatly deceived in me. This was reported to me from my Lord Chancellor's mouth. If it is true, my troubles increase into a more bitter passion than ever. Nothing, however, can turn me from you, to whom I owe so much. I do not say it to win your favour, or to gape for gifts, having no need thereof ; nor, God willing, shall have, being able to get my living *partout*, as the Frenchman saith. I declare by this the earnest meaning of my heart, to which your exceeding merits have by force drawn me."

After references to some public matters, including the beheading of twelve pirates in Holland and the export of beer and " fair horses " from England, Vaughan concludes : " George Constantine came to Antwerp, after breaking from my Lord Chancellor, on the 6th of December. With him, nor with none other such, will I meddle, seeing that I am beaten with my own labours. Antwerp, 9th Dec., 1531.

I will get rid of your spermaceti before I leave the country."

Within a week of Vaughan's letter to Cromwell two events occurred in the Lord Chancellor's house at Chelsea. On December 15th, Bishop Stokesley opened his judicial examination of James Bainham : and, on the following day, the 16th, he passed sentence upon John Tewkesbury and handed him over to the Sheriffs, his burning at Smithfield following on the 20th. It was the seventeenth anniversary of the burning of Hunne's body.

Four months elapse — months of trial and tragedy for Bainham — and the ambassador Chapuys writes to the Emperor :

" The King is again soliciting the Estates " (that is, the House of Commons) " for an aid for the fortification of the Scotch frontier. Two worthy men dared to say openly that the fortification was needless, as the Scotch could do no harm without foreign aid, and that the best fortification was to maintain justice in the kingdom and friendship with the Emperor ; and to this end the Estates should petition the King to take back his wife and treat her well, otherwise the kingdom would be ruined, as the Emperor could do them more harm than any other, and would not abandon the rights of his aunt ; the discord which the cause was provoking would ruin the kingdom. These words were well taken by all present, except two or three, and nothing was concluded about the aid. The King was displeased, sent for the majority of the deputies, and made them a long speech in justification of his conduct in the divorce. He told them it was not a matter in which they ought to interfere " — (this, be it noted, some three years after the King is commonly supposed to have summoned the Parliament for the purpose of furthering it) — " and," continues Chapuys, " in a most gracious manner promised to support them against the Church, and to mitigate the rigours of the Inquisition which they have here, and which is said to be more severe than in Spain. It is true that he did not say this openly before all, but he made them understand it. Those who have conducted the affair have spoken more plainly ". (V., No. 989. May 2nd, 1532).

If Sir Thomas More, as Lord Chancellor, chose, or felt it his duty, to make his mansion at Chelsea the headquarters of this amateur Inquisition, house of detention and court-house conveniently in one, it is not surprising that fearsome tales of what went on beneath his roof were current among those whom he calls " the blessed brethren ", and even spread as far as Antwerp. Such tales would lose nothing in the telling ; but More's own admissions are sufficient to account for them.

" The Inquisition which they have here, said to be more severe than in Spain." Two days before Chapuys so wrote James Bainham, condemned by Bishop Stokesley in More's house, was burnt at Smithfield.

And within a fortnight of Bainham's execution, on May 15th, the Spirituality of England, under pressure from an anxiously orthodox House of Commons and King, surrendered their powers of independent legislation, of making laws, heresy laws or any other laws, at their own will and pleasure ; and on the following day, May 16th, Sir Thomas More, relieved at his own request of the office of Lord Chancellor, ceased to have any further responsibility, except of course as a county magistrate, for the discipline of heretics. On the same day the document embodying the ' Submission of the Clergy ' was presented to the King, five witnesses being specially summoned for the occasion. Four were titled members of the Royal Household ; the fifth is given as " Thomas Cromwell, Esquire ". (Wilkins, III., 755). Cromwell quietly takes the stage as More leaves it ; though it will be another year before observers become really aware of his hand upon events.

"Thomas Cromwell, Esquire " ; there is a world of historic irony in the words. Cromwell was neither lord nor knight, like his fellow-witnesses. He was still no more than member for Taunton and junior privy councillor. Not till about a month before (April 14th) had he been appointed, " during good conduct," to the very minor office of Master of the King's Jewels (V., No. 978, (13). His presence was a compliment to the will and address which, without much apparent troubling of the waters, had carried through a revolution. For this, the surrender by the spiritualty of their ancient rights of independent legislation, was, it might well be said, the real revolution of the reign ; and, as such, was resisted stoutly, if but little more than momentarily, by the prelates. It meant an inroad upon the most precious of the Church's ' liberties ', the invasion of the freedom confirmed to the Ecclesia Anglicana — understood as the hierarchy — by Magna Carta. It involved a more entire breach with the past than did the extrusion of the papal authority, the first definitive step towards which was not taken until a year later, in the Statute for the Restraint of Appeals (1533). That Statute, forbidding all appeals to Rome, applied to the whole field of jurisdiction an inhibition which had long been operative, through the acts " de Provisoribus ", over an important part of it. But the principle embodied in the ' Submission ' of 1532 was wholly new. The Submission conceded the claim of the laity to have a voice, through the King in Parliament, in the making and working of the ecclesiastical laws which governed them. The laity, in effect, were to be no more " subjects " but associates in the work of legislation. In their Submission the spiritualty undertook that they would no more meet in Convocation, nor enact or execute further canons, without the King's licence ; and that the provincial canons already enacted — that is to say, the law of the universal Church as embodied in the Constitutions of Canterbury and York should be subject to scrutiny and review by a mixed Commission of thirty-two, half of whom were to be " of the upper and nether House " of Parliament, and all of whom were to be

" chosen and appointed " by a layman, the King. A more complete overthrow of the mediaeval constitution as between spiritualty and temporalty could not well be imagined. It is obvious, too, that this claim of the Anglican laity to a co-ordinate voice in law-making could not well consist with that of the Sovereign Pontiff to be the sole, supreme and universal lawgiver. But the obvious is sometimes the last to be perceived ; and the laymen who made and imposed this claim were firmly orthodox, in full communion with the Holy See, and fully sensible of the hazards, political and commercial, of withdrawing from its obedience. How came it all about ?

Chapter VII

A MOVEMENT OF OPINION

For the answer we have to look to what we now call public opinion. Nowadays public opinion is formed mainly by Parliament and the Press ; for most of the first twenty years of Henry VIII's reign it was formed, or as some would say malformed, by the suppression of Parliament and the Press — in this context the foreign book press. It was allowed no " organs ", but, none the less, it was there and alive. I am not speaking of opinion among secret and sullen coteries of obscure sectaries, among whom the Wycliffite tradition lingered on, often in grotesque and contorted forms. The question is of opinion among London citizens of substance and standing, whose views would count in the shaping of events : the sort of men, thriving merchants and lawyers, who gathered in St. Paul's to hear Dean Colet preach. It is reasonable to suppose that Colet's scathing indictment of the state of the Church, delivered before Convocation in discreet Latin, was not only an expression of his own convictions, but a reflection of the opinions of the substantial citizens whose revered chaplain he had become. Their ill opinion was occasioned by what a later parliamentary document called the " evil examples and misuses of spiritual persons ", their tightfistedness, loose living, and the chartered criminality of the hordes of ne'er-do-wells in minor orders. Five years after Henry's accession the lay discontents focussed themselves upon the case of Richard Hunne. The fate of Hunne moved the populace, for, as Polydore Vergil tells us, he was known for his charities and never turned his back upon the needy. The City too was concerned, because Hunne was a member of one of the great City Companies, whose duty it was to see that their members had right. The efforts of the City, through its members in the Commons, to vindicate the credit of the City Coroner's Jury, to obtain the restitution of Hunne's property to his children, and to prevent the men indicted for his murder from eluding justice, are written large upon the records of the Parliament of 1515. Their failure left behind it a rankling sense of wrong, and a vivid apprehension of the sort of wrong that could be done under cover of the heresy laws. It brought home, too, the impotence of the laity in face of that " kingdom " within the kingdom against which Simon Fish was presently to inveigh. Fitzjames' asseveration, in his letter of appeal to Wolsey, that the citizens of London, such as were called to serve on juries, were so set in favour of heresy that no clerk could look for justice at their hands, was of course a mere libel ; the real heretics at that time were not the sort of people who were called to serve on juries or took their parsons to law. But the Bishop's words may be taken as marking his own sense that the feeling between laity and clergy in his diocese was as bad as could be. Or nearly : for there can be little doubt that his own success in defying it made it a degree worse. And Wolsey's long and arbitrary tenure of power as Chancellor and Papal Legate did not improve matters. His complaisance in supporting Fitzjames, and lending his influence to get Horsey out of the hands of justice, was an inauspicious beginning, not likely to be forgotten. An autocrat by temperament, the doggedness of the Commons on behalf of Hunne and against the criminous clerk in the Parliament of 1515 had given him an abiding distaste for parliamentary action ; and having advised the King to dissolve that Parliament, he made shift — with the single exception of the session of 1523, necessitated by an urgent need of money — to govern without one for the remaining fourteen years of his career. His foreign policy, with its recurrent French inclination, was unpopular in the City, and onerous to City purses. Magnifying to the uttermost his office as Legate, he impressed men's minds with the omnicompetence of the papal power, for everything except effective reform. In his last years he had to take action against a new form of contraband in which many besides heretics were interested. Wolsey's rise to power coincided with Luther's appearance upon the European stage. In due course Luther's doctrines and writings were condemned at Rome ; and Wolsey, urged, doubtless, by prelates like Nix

K   289 and Longland who were old hands at repression, could do no less than endeavour to counter them with ban and bonfire. But the ceremonial burning of prohibited books at Paul's Cross was less impressive than it might have been in an earlier day. Men of intelligence and affairs, who counted in the City, were conscious of living in a great new world of invention and discovery, and were able to conceive that novel ideas, even in religion, were not necessarily false or evil ; even to entertain the thought that the burning of people who held them, if not otherwise dangerous, might not be quite a civilised proceeding. The civic authorities of cities like London and Norwich, who, as required by law, obeyed the Bishop's mandate to attend the condemnation of heretics, and took delivery of their bodies for burning, must often have done so with mixed feelings. Certainly it would appear that at the execution of Bilney at Norwich the feelings both of the Mayor and of the mob were with the sufferer. And there was, too, a thing that no fellow, no plain-thinking Englishman at any rate, could understand : why the free circulation of the vernacular Scriptures should be catholic and commendable on the other side of the Channel and heretical and criminal on this. Certain unknown merchants answered the question for themselves in their own downright English way : by providing William Tyndale with the means to live and labour abroad, and to see his English New Testament through the foreign presses. Sir Thomas More and the authorities in London were well aware that Tyndale's activities could not be carried on without important financial backing of some kind. More tried to draw the secret from Constantine when the latter was a prisoner in his hands, late in 1531. Hall tells the story (Chronicle, 11, p. 162) :

" It fortuned one George Constantine to be apprehended by Sir Thomas More, which then was Lord Chancellor of England, of suspicion of certain heresies. And this Constantine being with More, after divers examinations of divers things, among other Master More said in this wise to Constantine :

' Constantine, I would have thee plain with me in one thing that I will ask of thee, and I promise thee I will show thee favour in all the other things whereof thou art accused to me. There is beyond the sea Tyndale, Joye, and a great many mo of you. I know they cannot live without help. Some sendeth them money and succoureth them ; and thyself, being one of them, haddest part thereof, and therefore knowest from whence it came. I pray thee who be they that thus help them ?

' My lord,' quod Constantine, ' will you that I shall tell you the truth ? '

' Yea, I pray thee,' quod my lord.

' Marry, I will ', quod Constantine ; ' truly ', quod he, ' it is the Bishop of London ' (Tunstall) — ' that hath holpen us ; for he hath bestowed among us a great deal of money in New Testaments to burn them ; and that hath (been) and yet is our only succour and comfort '.

' Now by my truth ' quod More, ' I think even the same ; and I said so much to the Bishop when he went about to buy them.'

More's superior shrewdness must surely have told him that Constantine's professedly candid admission was very far from being the whole truth. How came it that a penniless priest and scholar, leaving England with ten pounds in his pocket, the gift of his host and patron, the London merchant, Humphrey Monmouth, was able, with his assistant Roy, to live abroad for years, perfect his translation, print copies by the thousand, and arrange for their transit to sure hands in England ? Something more like the whole truth we learn from the German controversial writer Dobneck, called Cochlaeus, who came upon the trail of Tyndale's enterprise in its earliest stages. While having some printing of his own done at Quentell's press in Cologne, Cochlaeus, scenting an important secret, managed to get some of Quentell's compositors tipsily communicative, and so learnt that " two English apostates ", meaning Tyndale and Roy, had made some way with the surreptitious printing of a New Testament in English. On the city authorities, informed by Cochaeus, intervening, the two Englishmen gathered up the sheets already printed, and made their way up the Rhine to the Lutheran stronghold of Worms, where Tyndale was able to complete his work unmolested. And the costs, so

Cochlaeus learnt, were being supplied to any extent by English merchants, who meant to smuggle in the work when printed, and broadcast it secretly through the whole of England before the King or the Cardinal could be aware of it or forbid it. " Impensas abunde suppeti a mercatoribus Anglicis, qui opus excussum clam invecturi per totam Angliam latenter dispergere vellent, antequam Rex aut Cardinalis rescire aut prohibere possit ". (Hist. Johannis Coch. de Actis et Scriptis Martini Lutheri. Ellis, Original Letters, 3rd ser., vol. 2, p. 89).

Who were these English merchants ? All we know of them is that they were wealthy enough to make light of large monetary commitments, and few enough to keep a dangerous secret. It is quite unlikely that they were Lutherans, or heretics of any sort. They no doubt represented elements of City opinion which were opposed to Wolsey's regime, the Catholic anti-clericals who were to make their voices heard and their weight felt in the Parliament of 1529. They probably felt that some of the money which the Cardinal was trying to extract from them in benevolences and ' amicable loans ' might well be spent in helping Tyndale to carry through a work which would not only put the Gospel within reach of his countrymen, but, by its very nature, be a challenge to the sort of ecclesiasticism which they of the temporalty were resolved to end.

We should not expect to know by name more than a few of the men concerned in this kind of covert opposition ; but we do know the names of a few. There were the two London merchants George Robinson and George Elyot, who brought Simon Fish's ' Supplication of Beggars ' before the King. There was Humphrey Monmouth, the London cloth merchant, who sheltered and befriended Tyndale when Bishop Tunstall, whose countenance he had first sought and who sadly underestimated his suitor's stature, decided that he had no use for him. There was " one, Augustine Packington, a Mercer and Merchant of London ", " a man that highly favoured William Tyndale, but to the Bishop utterly showed himself to the contrary " : who, finding Tunstall at Antwerp and anxious to buy up all the copies of the English New Testament, obligingly undertook the business on his behalf, the purchase money finding its way into Tyndale's pocket for the production of new and better editions. As Hall sums up the transaction, " the Bishop had the books, Packington the thanks, and Tyndale had the money ". Finally, under date 1536, Hall tells us of another Packington, one Robert, " Mercer of London, a man of good substance, and yet not so rich as honest and wise. This man dwelled in Cheapside, at the sign of the Leg, and used daily at four of the clock winter and summer to rise and go to Mass at a church then called Saint Thomas Acres (but now named the Mercers' Chapel). And one morning among all other, being a great misty morning such as hath seldom been seen, even as he was crossing the street from his house to the church, he was suddenly murdered with a gun, which of the neighbours was plainly heard ; and by a great number of labourers at the same time standing at Soper Lane end he was both seen go forth of his house and also the clap of the gun was heard, but the deed-doer was never espied nor known. Many were suspected but none could be found faulty. Howbeit, it is true that, forasmuch as he was known to be a man of a great courage, and one that both could speak and also would be heard : and that the same time he was one of the burgesses of the Parliament for the City of London, and hath talked somewhat against the covetousness and cruelty of the Clergy, he was had in contempt with them ; and therefore most like by one of them thus shamefully murdered, as you perceive that Master Hunne was in the sixth year of the reign of this King." Here we have the case of a London merchant, a devout Catholic, a member for the City who commanded attention in the House and whose speeches against their ' covetousness and cruelty ' had so roused the feeling of the clergy as to make it likely, to his fellow-member Hall, that his unknown murderer had been one of them. (' Chronicle ', 11, pp. 278-9).

Another constituent of London opinion was that of the Inns of Court. The Bar was a conservative profession ; but its members had their own conservative tradition of opposition to the spirituality, and had evolved, out of their own inner consciousness and a colourable interpretation of Richard II's last statute of Provisors, what they called the Law of Praemunire, as an effective check on clerical pretensions. As practitioners of the Common Law they were professionally critical of the Cardinal's activities in Chancery. We hear of the " gentlemen of Gray's Inn " guying Wolsey in the interlude in which Simon Fish figured with distinction and to the detriment of his future. (Hall. ' Chronicle,' II., 79 and Foxe). And there was Simon Fish himself, with his broken career and his barbed and implacable pen. Of declared heretics we know only of James Bainham of the Middle Temple, who was pressed for information about others likeminded, but who defied More and Stokesley, and went to his death with sealed lips. More formidable were the less defiant, like Christopher Saint-German of the Inner Temple, who, cooing like a very dove of peace, deplored, and called pointed attention to, the ' Division between the Spiritualty and the Temporalty ', indicating its causes not uncertainly. There were " such as were learned in the law ", who were " appointed " by " the burgesses of the Parliament " as a drafting Committee in 1529. Among them was Edward Hall of Gray's Inn, member for Newark and author of the ' Chronicle ', a work which breathes throughout the spirit of the anti-clerical, and which has every appearance of representing the spirit then prevalent in the House of Commons. Among them, too, cognisant of, and no doubt sharing, both strains of opinion, mercantile and legal, was Thomas Cromwell, also of Gray's Inn, member for Taunton, and, from January, 1531, of the King's Council.

As to Cromwell's own opinions, what most strikes the student of his correspondence is the care he took to keep them to himself. If asked for his opinions in general, he would probably have replied blandly that they were really of no interest ; that he was a simple man of business ; and that his business was to give effect to the opinions of others, great or small, who might be good enough to command, and reward, his services. To a confidant, if he had one, he might have said, with that sudden illumination of his heavy countenance upon which Chapuys remarks, that if a man begins life as a vagabond and is in the way of ending it as King's vicegerent and peer of the realm, he is better without opinions, so long, at least, as his fortune is in the making. In that stage his opinions would be those of his client or patron for the time being ; and, his being usually the dominating intelligence, they were not unapt to coincide with his own. That he had opinions, and could act upon them when the time came with devastating effect, the country was very soon to learn. There can be no doubt that he shared to the full the anti-clerical sentiment general in the Commons, or that he regarded the ecclesiastical ' imperium in imperio ', with its independent legislature and judiciary, as an annoying relic which were better ended. Much has been written about his debt to his contemporary Machiavelli ; but Cromwell's own varied experience of life had left him little to learn, either of statecraft or other craft, from Machiavelli or anyone else. A conventional Catholic like Henry VIII and Wolsey, but more casual and more ' moral ' than either, he had no sentiment about Holy Church. He regarded it as a thoroughly worldly institution, legitimately to be exploited by cleverer worldlings like himself. As it was, it had brought too much grist to his own private mill to make him enthusiastic about reforming it. Change, what people called reform, would come ; but he was prepared to let it take its own time, and to bear a hand in directing it when the time came. His first political venture as Privy Councillor gives some indication of the trend of his thought. In the spring of 1531 he endeavoured, through his correspondent at Antwerp Stephen Vaughan, to establish some relations of amity between the King and William Tyndale. Vaughan wrote to the King giving his own favourable impression of Tyndale, and enclosing in ms. part of Tyndale's rejoinder to the attack upon him by Sir Thomas More. Cromwell delivered the enclosures, which the King promised to peruse at leisure ; but at his next ' repair ' to the Court, he found the King furious. Tyndale, down-right, resolute, independent of spirit, was too big a man for Henry, and Henry knew it. The King, in a tone which evidently alarmed Cromwell, instructed him to warn Vaughan against having anything further to do with Tyndale, the King regarding him as a seditious troublemaker, of whom the kingdom was well rid. The draft of Cromwell's instructions to Vaughan (see Merriman, ' Life and

Letters of Thomas Cromwell ', I., pp. 335-9) is perhaps the most untidy and embarrassed of all his drafts. The incident apprised him of the necessity of feeling the ground before venturing upon policies of his own. But it shows the direction in which his mind was working. Cromwell saw, more clearly than the King, that if the Divorce project were persisted in, it meant certain trouble with the Pope and the spiritualty ; and that it was time to be looking round for allies, and considering the means of enervating opposition. Important steps in the latter direction were taken in the parliamentary session of 1532. They were, very plainly, the handiwork of Cromwell.

Chapter VIII

THE SESSION OF 1532
'THE SUPPLICATION OF THE COMMONS AGAINST THE ORDINARIES'

In the latter months of 1531 the King and his coming adviser had to consider what to do with the Parliament. It had opened with one brisk six-weeks session in November and December 1529. In 1530 — the year of the ' liquidation ' of Wolsey and his possessions — it had never met at all. It held a second session in the spring of 1531, but only, with one exception, to deal with certain legal and mercantile measures in the nature of bye-laws and of no general interest. The one exception was the Act recording the King's pardon for his spiritual subjects of the province of Canterbury, and — the price of the royal clemency — the " grant " by their Convocation of a hundred thousand pounds, incorporating an acknowledgment of the King's Supreme Headship. On March 31st, the Houses were prorogued to October 14th, and then by a further prorogation to January 15th, 1532. As late as December 29th, Chapuys, referring to this last prorogation, wrote to the Emperor : " Parliament has been prorogued, as they do not know exactly what to discuss " (V. No. 614). The question of the hour was the King's divorce ; and with that, as the Commons were roundly told, they were not expected to meddle. Their sole concern with it was to receive a formal visit from Sir Thomas More " and divers lords of the spiritualty and temporalty to the number of twelve ", and to listen for half a day to the reading of " determinations " in the King's favour by sundry foreign universities ; which done, " the Chancellor said : Now you of this Common House may report in your countries what you have seen and heard, and then all men shall openly perceive that the King hath not attempted this matter of will or pleasure, as some strangers report, but only for the discharge of his conscience and surety of the succession

297

of his realm. This is the cause of our repair hither to you, and now we will depart " (Hall, ' Chronicle ', II., p. 195).

The Commons were glad enough to be dismissed to their " countries " with this or any other message. They were all men with important local affairs and interests, and, by the end of 1531, they had been kept within call of Westminster for two whole years with nearly nothing of any general consequence to do. It seemed as if their measures of the first session were as far as the King would allow them to go in taking order with the clergy ; and they saw no purpose in merely standing by. In fact, they were thinking of petitioning the King for a dissolution at the first opportunity.

But the M.P. for Taunton, Privy Councillor Cromwell, was thinking otherwise. The present House was his own ' point d'appui ' in politics. It had come in on a wave of anti-clerical feeling ; and Cromwell saw that just that feeling would be invaluable to the King if, by persistence in the Divorce project, he became involved in an outright quarrel with the Pope and with a spiritualty committed to the Pope's support. And not long before Chapuys wrote that " they ", meaning the Government, did " not know exactly what to discuss ", certain events had suggested a not unfruitful programme for the forthcoming session. Its chief measure, indeed, was concerned with certain first-fruits. And it shows how much of improvisation, how little of premeditated scheming and planning, marked these proceedings that this measure, the most important of the session and the first that tended to the prejudice of the Papacy, was not in contemplation a very few months before.

A few months before, the King, in anticipation of the October session — which was never held — had given " instructions to his trusty Councillor Thomas Cromwell, to be declared to the Council and undelayedly put in execution this Michaelmas term ". Seven of these related to exchanges of land between the King and certain heads of religious houses and colleges, profitable transactions in the arrangement of which Cromwell was a past master. These Acts of exchange, with two others, were duly passed in the spring session of 1532. Most of the other projects suggested were either dropped, or not carried beyond a first or second reading in that session. The only proposal having any ecclesiastical bearing perished stillborn. It was " for a Bill to be devised for every spiritual person holding promotion and resident without the King's licence in the Court of Rome, to divide his revenues into three parts : one for himself, the second for the reparation of manors, etc., the third for charity ". Of this nothing more was ever heard. (V., No. 394).

But shortly afterwards events occurred which seem to have suggested what proved to be the most significant measure of the forthcoming session. Wolsey's bishoprics of York and Winchester had been vacant for nearly a year, their ' temporalities ' accruing meanwhile to the King. However, on September 12th (1531), the King wrote to Clement VII " asking for the promotion of Dr. Edward Lee, his Almoner, to the archbishopric of York, " and that in the payment of Annates, consideration may be had to the great expense of his bulls " (V., No. 418). Also in September the King wrote to his envoys at Rome desiring them " to press his request to the Pope to promote Stephen Gardiner, his chief secretary, to the see of Winchester, and to urge his Holiness to consider, in the payment of the Annate, the recent expenses of the see in procuring bulls " (ibid., No. 419). Annates, or first-fruits, were the whole or part of a year's income of every benefice payable (in advance) by a newly appointed incumbent to the Roman Court. England was exceptional in confining the impost to bishoprics. The amount actually levied was to some extent a matter for negotiation, but in all cases it was considerable, and as much as could be got. Until the annates were paid, or security given for their payment, the sheaf of bulls giving effect to the appointment would not be despatched from Rome. It was officially computed in 1532 that since the second year of Henry VII, that is, within forty-five years, " the sum of eight hundred thousand ducats, amounting in sterling money, at the least, to eight score thousand pounds ", had been " paid for the expedition of bulls of archbishoprics and bishoprics ". It took a little time to arrange the matter in the case of Lee and Gardiner ; but on the 4th November Chapuys wrote : " A courier arrived here yesterday from

Rome, and has been sent back with all diligence. I think he only came about the payment for the two bishoprics, for which they demanded great sums at Rome, but at last have reduced it to 20,000 ducats " (V., No. 512). The amount would be about £80,000 in our money.

The simultaneous promotion of the King's secretary and the King's almoner, and their simultaneous quest for ready cash — they had, we learn from a letter of the King in the following March (ibid., No. 886) to borrow it from their friends* — gave rise to a good deal of talk about the Court ; and it occurred to someone, whom we should not be too rash in identifying as the latest courtier Thomas Cromwell, that something might be done with Annates by way of making them a useful bargaining counter in the King's pourparlers with the Pope. Accordingly a Bill was drawn impeaching annates as " intolerable and importable " — the latter a favourite word with Cromwell — and enacting that they shall " utterly cease." And it is further enacted that they shall not utterly cease, or cease at all, unless, " at any time on this side the beginning of the next Parliament ", the King, exercising the " full power and liberty " given him by the Act, should " declare, by the said letters patent, whether that the premises, or any part, clause or matter thereof, shall be observed, obeyed, executed, performed, and take place and effect, as an Act and Statute of this present Parliament, or not."

The reason given for this provision was not less remarkable than the provision itself.

" Forasmuch as the King's highness, and this his High Court of Parliament, neither have, nor do intend to use in this, or any other like cause, any manner of extremity or violence, before gentle courtesy or friendly ways and means first approved and attempted, but principally coveting to disburden this realm of the said great exactions and intolerable charges of annates and first-fruits, have therefore thought convenient to commit the final order and determination of the premises, in all things, unto the

---

* Among them friend Cromwell : see also V. 1285 (iv) and III. 841).

King's highness. So that if it may seem to his high wisdom and most prudent discretion meet to move the Pope's Holiness, and the Court of Rome, amicably, charitably and reasonably to compound, either to extinct and make frustrate the payments of the said annates or first-fruits, or else, by some friendly, loving and tolerable composition to moderate the same in such wise as may be by this realm easily borne and sustained : that then those ways and compositions once taken, concluded and agreed between the Pope's Holiness and the King's Highness, shall stand in strength, force and effect of law, inviolably to be observed ". (Gee and Hardy, p. 184).

In short, the intolerable and importable charges were not abolished, but their continued payment was made conditional upon the King's pleasure. Needless to say, nothing was done on either side towards the " friendly, loving and tolerable composition " so unctuously suggested. The only composition in which the King was interested was the composition of his marriage suit ; and the Act was designed to give him the means of playing upon the sensitive financial nerves of Pope and Cardinals. If they proved amenable, the Annates Act would remain a dead letter ; if not, the papal exchequer would suffer seriously. No sooner was the Act through Parliament than its purpose and discreet use as a bargaining counter were unblushingly explained to the English envoys at Rome in a letter from the King on March 21st (1532) (V.no. 886). Effective use was made of it as a bargaining counter early in the following year. Circumstances had made it urgent to get " the lady " married, and a Primate installed who would pronounce the marriage valid. Old Archbishop Warham's death in the previous August had precipitated events ; Cranmer was recalled from a mission abroad and designated as his successor. His bulls of appointment had to be got through as expeditiously and cheaply as possible. On January 31st (1533) Dr. Bonner — afterwards the Bonner of the Marian burnings — , wrote to a diplomatic colleague at Rome, having himself travelled post haste from Bologna. " Had a very bad passage," he says. " Arrived at Rye, and thence to Westminster, and had an interview with the King on the 25th. If the Pope could gratify the

King, he will do all that he can to please his Holiness. If not, the Pope will be in great danger here. As my lord elect of Canterbury, Dr. Cranmer, a man of singular good learning, virtue and all good parts, sends his bulls, it would be advisable that he should be gently handled in the charges, and especially the annates ; otherwise the matter of the annates, which is now only stayed by the King's goodness, will be determined to the disadvantage of the Court of Rome. They are to use all their efforts that the King's matter be committed to England ; and the King thinks that if it be skilfully handled, it may be accomplished. Has great reason for urging this, as divers things are now taken in hand ' beyond your expectation and mine.' He adds, ' I know well ye will marvel at these letters.' What the " divers things " were was soon to appear, and Bonner had evidently been given a shrewd inkling of them. On the very day of his interview with the King, Henry, recognising certain ' faits accomplis ' and taking the law into his own hands, went through a form of marriage with Anne Boleyn. The fact, for the moment, was kept a close secret, and all the circumstances of it have remained a secret ever since. And it was not until the following July, when the years of discussion with Rome had ended in an open duel and a papal excommunication was hanging over his head, that the King, sixteen months after its passing, put the Annates Act into operation by letters patent.

Cromwell of course, had taken care to see that the Annates bill looked as little like a mere bargaining counter as possible, and should stand as a workmanlike piece of legislation when its immediate diplomatic ends were served. He had to make timely provision for the situation which would arise if and when — and to his clear mind it was only a case of when — the King's patience and the Pope's forbearance alike gave out, and swords would be crossed in good earnest. When that time came the King would either have to surrender to a papal excommunication, or make good his recently assumed title with the help of Parliament, writing his Supreme Headship large upon the statute book. The Annates Act, pigeonholed for the time being, was Cromwell's blue-print of the sort of parliamentary action which would then be necessary. He plainly spared no pains in drafting it. Its phrasing is minute, rotund, lucid ; provision is made for every contingency. Annates, subject to the King's high wisdom and decision otherwise, shall " utterly cease " ; so long as bulls of appointment are obtained from Rome, the bishop-designate may remunerate the Roman secretariat to the extent of five per cent only of his net yearly income ; if " our said holy father the Pope," taking umbrage at the docking of his revenues, should withhold bulls and fulminate censures, arrangements are made by Act of Parliament, this Act to wit, for the consecration and functioning of Archbishops and Bishops notwithstanding. A copy of the Act was sent to Henry's envoys for discreet communiction to the Roman authorities. The Act was a polite, but plain, intimation to the Pope that England, in certain circumstances, would be prepared to get along without him. The King himself seems to have been a little frightened by his own audacity. His agents were instructed to say that his people had pressed for the Act, and that he could but yield to the importunities of his Parliament. What we know of the history of the bill in Parliament suggests that the truth was quite otherwise. Cromwell was none too sure of the fate of the measure in the House of Lords ; he wrote at the time to Gardiner : " This day was read in the Higher House a bill touching the Annates of Bishoprics ; for what end or effect it will succeed surely I know not " (Merriman, I. p. 343, Jan. 1532). It probably required some management to get it through the Commons. The Commons so far, insurgent as they were against their own prelates, had no quarrel with the Pope, and no desire to pick one ; it meant quarrelling with the Emperor, and with their own bread and butter derived from the all-important trade with Flanders. Furthermore, they had no special wish to spare the pockets of the prelates, against whose ' abusions ' they were, in this very session, petitioning the King. Part of the reason for remitting the whole matter to the King's decision may have been to smooth the passage of the bill by leaving the practical issue in more or less suspense. But the point to notice is that this Annates bill, the first that looked, even contingently, to the supersession of the Roman authority, was not in contemplation till three months before it was introduced, and not in operation till sixteen months

after its enactment. The fact shows how very tentative were the steps
that led to what is called the breach with Rome. It tends to show too
how mistaken is the notion — based upon inattention to chronology
and some specious imaginations of Cardinal Pole — that the so-
called breach was a long-headed and diabolic device of Cromwell's
to get Henry married to Anne and himself established in supreme
power. The breach was due to nobody's machinations ; it arose
out of the situation, which was none of Cromwell's making : a
deadlock between a wilful King infatuated with a woman who was
not his wife, and persuaded of the most exalted moral and political
grounds for insisting upon a divorce ; and a Pope acknowledged as
supreme judge, with no less cogent moral and political reasons for
inability to accede to the King's wish, feebly temporising, and cling-
ing to procrastination as to a rock of refuge. All Cromwell did was
to measure the situation, and bring to bear upon it, when the time
was ripe, an incisive mind and a decisive will. With him it had to be
one plain thing or the other ; he abhorred shilly-shallying of any
sort. While the King continued parleying with the Pope, Cromwell
stood aloof ; but when that stage passed with Henry's clandestine
marriage, he was ready with his plans ; and his master-plan was to
bring in Parliament. The King, standing alone, would have made a
poor showing against the perils, foreign and domestic, involved in an
open defiance of Rome ; but the King in Parliament was a power,
and could speak with the enemy in the gate. What Cromwell
brought the King, along with his own ability and resource, was the
alliance of a House of Commons* bent upon the redress of its
' griefs ' against the spiritualty, and ready, in return for the King's

---

* A sidelight is thrown upon the nature of Cromwell's ascendancy in the
Commons — a personal ascendancy supported by known Court favour — in
a statement made by Sir George Throgmorton when under examination in
October 1537 (L. and P. XII, pt. 2, no. 952). He had " conversed with Sir
Thos. Dyngley in the garden of St. John's about the Parliament matters.
Dyngley wondered that the Act of Appeals should pass so lightly, and Throg-
morton said it was no wonder, as few would displease my lord Privy Seal."
Cromwell did not become Privy Seal until July 1536 ; and when the Act of
Appeals was before Parliament three years earlier, he as yet held no important
office. In April of that year (1533) he was made chancellor of the exchequer,
then quite a minor post ; and he did not become officially important until
succeeding Bishop Gardiner as Secretary to the King in April 1534.

support, to go very far, little as it liked the divorce, in supporting King in the consequences of his re-marriage.

True that certain distinguished moderns have represented the ' griefs ' of the Commons as fictitious, fabricated by the Court, and foisted upon an obsequious and indifferent House. Against them is the authority of a historian who sat in the House and says the contrary : Edward Hall's picture conforming, moreover, with all we learn from the despatches of a close and accomplished observer, the imperial ambassador Chapuys. During the first three years of this Parliament the Commons had their own programme ; and it was only incidentally that it sorted with the King's policy and served the King's purpose.

The Annates Act, with its suspensory provisions, was mainly of interest to the Court ; but in two other measures of this spring session of 1532 the Commons took further steps towards the redress of their own special griefs. One dealt with a long-standing public mischief, the immunity of those elements of the criminal under world who found shelter in minor orders. It revived the temporary Act of 1512, of which the prelates in the Parliament of 1515, under the influence of the Abbot of Winchcombe and Bishop Fitzjames, had succeeded in the preventing the renewal (see above, pp. 136, 139). It deprived clerks below the degree of subdeacon of any privilege of clergy, and left them amenable to secular trial and punishment.

The second important measure was of more general interest. Archbishops possessed of right an appellate jurisdiction ; but the English Primates, apparently in virtue of their status as ' legati nati ' of the Holy See, claimed for their courts the right to entertain suits " devolved to them by way of querimony and complaint," wheresoever arising within their provinces.* For some cause, possibly quite trivial, a person in Machynlleth or Megavissey might be cited to appear in Bow Church and answer for himself before the Court of Arches, the apparitor who served the summons claiming twopence a mile, say five shillings in our money, for footing it to and fro. The hardships thus entailed upon the laity are pointedly set forth in the

* See notes on 23 Henry 8, c. 9, in Stephens' ' Ecclesiastical Statutes,' vol. 1.

preamble of the Act, providing " that no Person shall be cited out of the Diocese where he or she dwelleth, except in certain cases." It says :

" Where great number of the King's subjects, as well men, wives, servants, as other the King's subjects, dwelling in divers dioceses of this realm of England and of Wales, heretofore have been at many times called by citations, and other processes compulsory, to appear in the Arches, Audience, and other high courts of the archbishops of this realm, far from and out of the diocese where such men, wives, servants, and other the King's subjects been inhabitant and dwelling, and many times to answer to surmised and feigned causes, and suits of defamation, withholding of tithes, and such other like causes and matters, which have been sued more for malice and for vexation than for any just cause of suit.

" And where certificate hath been made by the summoner, apparitor, or any such light literate person, that the party against whom any such citation hath been awarded hath been cited or summoned, and thereupon the same party so certified to be cited or summoned, hath not appeared according to the certificate, the same party therefore hath been excommunicated, or at least suspended from all divine service ; and thereupon, before that he or she could be absolved, hath been compelled, not only to pay the fees of the court whereunto he or she was so called by citation or other process, amounting to the sum of two shillings or twenty pence at the least ; but also to pay to the summoner, apparitor, or other light literate person, by whom he or she was so certified to be summoned, for every mile being distant from the place where he or she then dwelled unto the same court whereunto he or she was so cited or summoned to appear, 2d., to the great charge and impoverishment of the King's subjects, and to the great occasion of misbehaviour and misliving of wives, women and servants, and to the great impairment and diminution of their good names and honesties : Be it therefore enacted . . . . . etc."

The Act was a moderate measure, in no way impairing the ordinary archiepiscopal jurisdiction. Citations might still issue to persons in any diocese in cases brought before the archbishop on appeal, or by letters of request from inferior judges ; in cases concerning the probate of wills ; and " for causes of heresy, if the bishop, or other ordinary immediate, thereunto consent, or if that the same bishop, or other immediate ordinary or judge, do not his duty in punishment of the same." Into the rights or wrongs of any further special privilege of citation claimed by the archbishops, the Act does not enter. It merely provides that any legal officer issuing citations in virtue of such a privilege and contrary to the Act, shall be liable to the complainant in double damages and costs, and also to the " forfeiture for every person so summoned " of " ten pounds sterling," say £300 of our money, half to go to the King and half " to any person that will sue for the same." The Act was quite in character with the three measures of the first session. All four provided reasonable remedies for the real grievances of the laity ; and none of them are properly to be regarded as " attacks upon the Church " except in the sense that they were carried by the laity, represented by the Crown in Parliament — an unimpeachably Catholic laity by the way — over the heads of Churchmen, meaning the hierarchy and their Convocations. In the hands of the Cardinal Legate, with his plenary powers, Church reform, admittedly needed, had failed to come to anything ; in the hands of the House of Commons which assembled upon Wolsey's fall, it was beginning to come to something quite appreciable.

But this was only a beginning. The Commons had much more in mind ; and their most important proceeding of the session was to draw up, in the form of a petition to the King, a comprehensive programme of reform, such as might provide ample work for another Parliament. This was the famous

' SUPPLICATION OF THE COMMONS AGAINST THE ORDINARIES,'

a document which, in view of the results to which it immediately led, must be regarded as amongst the most significant in our history. The ' Ordinaries ' were the prelates and ecclesiastical judges and administrators of every grade.

For a long time past students have been brought up upon the

notion — best expressed in the words of Dr. James Gairdner, who calendared the documents of this period (see ' Letters and Papers,' vol. V. Preface, p.xix ; and ' The English Church in the Sixteenth Century,' p.114), — that this Supplication of the Commons " really emanated from the Court ", and that the Commons, whose ostensible work it was, had so little interest in it and so little concern for what became of it that they followed up its presentation by a plea for the dissolution of Parliament. It is true that the Commons asked for a dissolution without waiting for the Ordinaries' answer to their complaints ; but to argue from this that their complaints were fictitious, a Court concoction put into their mouths, seems really quite unwarranted. In their Supplication they had put forward a long-term programme sufficient to occupy the time of more than one future Parliament of normal length. They had been tied to a plague-ridden metropolis for two and a half years ; the Parliament had already outlived the usual span. The Commons in 1532 would have been staggered at the suggestion that they should be detained for four more years at Westminster in order to put through their own programme or any other. Knights and burgesses, busy people with large local interests, had a natural wish to get home and attend to their own affairs. It is to be remembered that in that day service in Parliament was not a coveted distinction, to be attained at much cost and labour. It was, like service on juries then and since, an irksome public duty, to be discharged with as good a grace as possible, but not to be embraced with any enthusiasm. The Commons, we should gather from Hall's account, were surprised and disconcerted when the King, with some severe references to their obstinate blocking of his Wardships Bill, told them that, having made formal complaint against the Ordinaries, they must remain in session and abide their answer.

The sole evidence for the suggestion that the Supplication of the Commons " really emanated from the Court " lies in the fact that there remain in the Record Office certain " drafts, with corrections, in the handwriting of Thomas Cromwell ". But Cromwell, at this period at any rate, was not " the Court ". He was, of course, in

the confidence of the Court and the assiduous servant of the King
and Council. But he was equally in the confidence, and the assiduous servant, of the House of Commons : not at all the master of
it, as he made himself in later Parliaments. And there is Cromwell
himself to be considered. The attribution of puppetry either to
Cromwell or the Commons, this particular House of Commons,
has no real warrant. Cromwell's main interest was doubtless in
his own career ; but this is not to say that, as a public man, he
was without a sense of the public good, and opinions and convictions in regard to it. And there is nothing to show that his
opinions and convictions differed at all from those of Edward Hall
and others of the anti-clerical element in the House of Commons.
Hall, in his account of the Supplication, betrays no consciousness
that " it really emanated from the Court ", though he must have
known that its drafting was mainly or solely the work of Cromwell.
He says (Chronicle, II., p. 202) :

" After Christmas, the 15th day of January, the Parliament
began to sit ; and amongst divers griefs which the Commons were
grieved with, they sore complained of the cruelty of the Ordinaries
for calling men before them ex-officio, that is, by reason of their
office : For the Ordinaries would send for men and lay Accusations
to them of Heresy, and say they were accused, and lay Articles
to them, but no Accuser should be brought forth, which to the
Commons was very dreadful and grievous ; for the party so ascited
must either Abjure or be burned, for Purgation he might make
none.

" When this matter and other exactions done by the Clergy in
their Courts were long debated in the Common House, at the last
it was concluded and agreed that all the griefs which the temporal
men were grieved with should be put in writing and delivered to
the King ; which by great advice was done ".

Hall's intimate acquaintance with what occurred is shown by
the stress he lays upon the matter of heresy ; for the Supplication,
though it travelled over much other ground, was in the main an
indictment of the law and procedure in cases of heresy, and of
the " cruelty " or, in its own words, " the uncharitable behaviour

and dealing " of the Ordinaries, civil magistrates like More and bishops like Longland, Blythe, Nix and Stokesley, in administering it. In one important aspect it was the Commons' reply to the prelates who had rekindled the fires of Smithfield the year before, and, at that very moment, were about to send James Bainham to the flames. Hall regards the work of the Commons upon the Supplication as not less their own than was their work upon the reforming measures of the first session. It was, of course, of concern to " the Court ", because it was designed to lead to action, and no such action would be possible without the King's countenance and concurrence. Cromwell, in placing his final draft before the House, had to be in a position to assure his colleagues that, both as regards matter and manner, the Supplication would not be unfavourably received. He had to remember that, while he was a newcomer to the King's Council, there were veteran councillors like More and Gardiner, lately become Bishop of Winchester but still the King's chief secretary, who would be ready to pounce upon any expressions savouring of mere animus, and to remind the King of his royal privilege of defending the Faith, not least against covert attacks but thinly veiled under protestations of orthodoxy. That is why we have two complete versions of the Supplication, and not one.

That there were two complete versions and not one is patent to anyone who will compare the drafts preserved in the Record Office (V., No. 1016 (1), (2), (3) and (4)). It is patent to anyone who will compare (4) with (2) and (1), (1) being a fair and corrected copy of (2), and the ' Supplication ' in the final form in which it passed the House of Commons, was submitted to the King, and placed by him before the Bishops with a request for their answer. It is curious that this final version, which made history, has never been printed ; whereas the discarded draft, no more than an important curiosity of history, has been printed three times : by Froude in 1870, ' History ', I., pp. 208-19, Gee and Hardy, 1896, ' Documents Illustrative ', pp. 145-53 ; and by Merriman, 1902, ' Life of Thomas Cromwell ', I., pp. 104-11, this last giving a valuable record of Cromwell's final corrections.

310

A study of these papers makes it very clear that Cromwell is not merely correcting certain anonymous drafts, but devising and revising his own. Among them is a fragmentary draft which appears to be Cromwell's first attempt at getting his ideas for the 'Supplication' down on paper. He made a fresh start with the completed drafts which followed ; but this fragmentary paper, calendared as V. 1016 (3), is of interest for its opening paragraphs. The first goes straight to the point, and reads :

"Your most loving and obedient subjects the knights, citizens and burgesses in this present Parliament assembled shewen to your excellent Highness certain articles hereafter ensuing : Whereof they most humbly beseech your Grace to provide some remedy and reformation in this your most high court of Parliament as to your most excellent wisdom shall seem convenient." The second paragraph, in its original form, suggests that the Commons are conscious, and critical, of the fact that the prelates, with their place — until recently a predominant place — in the House of Lords, have a " liberty and a voice of assent " in secular legislation, whereas, in regard to ecclesiastical legislation touching the " bodies, possessions and goods " of laymen, the heresy laws in particular, the laity have no voice whatever. It reads :

" First, albeit that the spiritual lords of this Realm have a liberty and a voice of assent in the making of any your laws and statutes of this Realm, yet nevertheless they and the clergy of this Realm of themself and by themself in their Convocations do make laws and ordinances, Whereby, without your royal assent or the assent of any your lay subjects, they bind your said lay subjects in their bodies, possessions and goods," etc.

This cavil, so to call it, is dropped in the corrected version interlined by Cromwell, as shown in the photostat copy here reproduced. It reads :

" First, where the spiritual prelates, ordinaries and the clergy of this your most excellent Realm — (AND EMPIRE — the words " and Empire " are struck through) — have heretofore made, ordained and constituted divers laws, and also do daily make divers laws and ordinances without your royal assent or knowledge, or

311

the assent or consent of any of your lay subjects, with the which they have bound and daily do bind your said subjects in their bodies, possessions and goods : Which laws so by them made and put in execution be neither put in the English tongue nor yet published unto them ; by reason whereof your said poor, humble and obedient lay subjects daily incur into dangers, censures and pains contained in the same only by ignorance, and ben daily therewith vexed, troubled and put to importable charges against all justice, equity, reason and good conscience, to the diminishing and derogation of your Imperial Jurisdiction and Prerogative Royal."

This passage is reproduced in facsimile because it marks, so far as I am aware, the first appearance of what may be described, in an expressive Americanism of the day, as Cromwell's ' Big Idea ' : the idea of England as an " Empire " and of her King as possessing an " imperial " jurisdiction.* He seems himself to have hesitated about introducing it, striking out the words " and Empire " as above, but retaining the expression " imperial jurisdiction " at the end. This same expression occurs once in the original completed draft (V., 1016 (4) : Merriman, I., p. 105), but it disappears altogether from the final draft which was presented to the King and submitted to the prelates for their reply. It would seem indeed that the King was inclined to be a little shy of this innovating nomenclature. His modest kingdom, at that date, was not even a United Kingdom ; and he may have felt that in setting up for an Emperor he might be trenching provocatively on the style and dignity of the real Emperor of history and tradition, his unfortunate Queen's nephew Charles V., whom he was not a little anxious if possible to placate. A year later, when Henry had remarried and battle between the opposing forces was openly joined, the King's scruples had been overcome, and in the preamble of the statute for the Restraint of Appeals the kingdom appears as an Empire in all its fresh effulgence. " Where by divers sundry old authentic histories and chronicles " — the phrase would be comic if it had been less of a matter of faith to the man behind it — " it is

---

* Cf. Baumer, ' The Early Tudor Theory of Kingship,' p. 84.

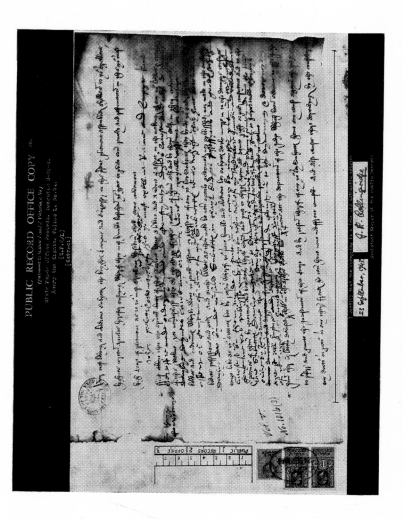

facing page 312

manifestly declared and expressed that this realm of England is an empire, and so hath been accepted in the world, governed by one Supreme Head and King, having the dignity and royal estate of the imperial crown of the same ", and so on and so on. The words " empire " and " imperial " were telling propaganda ; Cromwell's insinuation or contention was that the Crown of England acknowledged no suzerainty in, or allegiance spiritual or temporal to, any external or ' foreign ' power. That was the principle of all his legislation ; he carried through a revolution in the guise of a restoration ; there is, I think, as little doubt that he believed, as that the circumstances of the situation constrained him to believe, in his " divers sundry old authentic histories and chronicles ".

Leaving the fragment above noticed and turning to the two completed drafts, it is important to make clear that there are two, a prior and a final draft, the latter taking shape by a thorough recasting and revision of the former. This recasting and revision has gone so far that only three short paragraphs in the earlier version, and these dealing with minor matters, survive unaltered in the latter. And the object of the recasting and revision is fairly clear ; it is to make the ' Supplication ' more acceptable to the King, and less unacceptable to conservatives like Gardiner who were about the King. As to the ' Supplication ' having " really emanated from the Court ", a comparison of the prior and final drafts discountenances that notion entirely. The Calendar, however, gives no hint that these different documents are not one and the same. They begin and end in much the same way ; they are of some length, and travel over much the same ground. There was no apparent need to go through them, compare them, or look for differences and their significance. The numerous interlinear corrections were recognised as in the well-known handwriting of Cromwell ; and Cromwell being assumed, prematurely, to be " the Court " and the House of Commons a mere cypher, it seemed obvious to set down the ' Supplication ' as really emanating from the Court. This Dr. Gairdner does in his Preface to the fifth volume of the ' Letters and Papers ', p. xix (1880). He repeats the description, twice on one page, in his ' English Church in the

Sixteenth Century ', p. 114 (1904) ; and, no doubt, on Dr. Gairdner's great authority, the same statement is made in the introduction to the text of the Supplication — the prior and discarded text by the way — given in Gee and Hardy's Documents Illustrative of English Church History ', pp. 145 - 53 (1896)*. Dr. Pollard, in his ' Henry VIII ' (1905), gave some cogent reasons (p. 291) for qualifying Dr. Gairdner's view ; and that view is evidently at fault ; for the prior draft, on which the final version is clearly based, contains expressions, and in one important particular a whole type of treatment, which are not at all imaginable as emanating from the Court, that is to say, as having been approved or prompted by the King.

Two instances will suffice. The following quotations are from Dr. R. B. Merriman's ' Life and Letters of Thomas Cromwell ', pp. 104-11, which gives the text of the prior draft as itself corrected between the lines by Cromwell. Writing of the relations between temporalty and spiritualty, he speaks of " the very chief fountains, occasions and causes " of the " said seditions, factions, deadly

---

* M. Pierre Janelle, following Dr. Gairdner and like him citing the discarded version, writes : " The King, in getting his own way, had to appear to be carrying out the wishes of his people. So a petition was drawn up by one of the King's councillors, Thomas Cromwell, a new man, an ambitious adventurer and a politician on the Italian model ; and the House of Commons consented to present it and to pass it off as their own spontaneous work " : (il fallait que le roi, en imposant ses propres exigences, semblât se faire l'executeur des volontés populaires. Une petition fut donc rédigée par l'un des conseillers du roi, Thomas Cromwell, homme nouveau, aventurier ambitieux, politicien à l'italienne : et la Chambre des Communes consentit à la presenter, et à laisser croire qu'elle l'avait fait spontanément. " L'Angleterre Catholique à la veille du Schisme," p. 146.

More recently Dr. H. Maynard Smith (" Pre-Reformation England ") writes of the Supplication as having been " concocted at court," p. 49, n. 1, and " prepared by Cromwell and the king," p. 52.

If Dr. Gairdner and those who follow him on this matter are right, if the Commons really permitted a faked petition to be foisted upon them by " the Court," there was clearly no depth of servile complaisance to which they would not stoop. But, apart from the attribution of this petition to " the Court," I know no evidence whatever of the alleged servility of the Commons during these first years. And any but the most cursory examination of the extant drafts shows that attribution to be in substance mistaken. The King did not discourage, and was doubtless disposed to welcome, the move of the Commons ; but it was the Commons' own move, and Cromwell, in working upon the Supplication, was acting primarily for his colleagues in the Commons.

hatred and most uncharitable part-taking either part and sort " against the other. The King, for his own credit's sake, would never have allowed that the feeling between laity and clergy, strained though he must have known it to be, could properly be described, in a public document, by such words as ' deadly hatred '. Yet the words came naturally to the pen of Cromwell in endeavouring to express his own mind and the mind of the Commons. It was no exaggerated description of the feelings of men like the pamphleteer and barrister Simon Fish, or, on the other side, of the calumnious prelate Richard Fitzjames. And something not much less than deadly hatred is required to account for such incidents as those which the prelates themselves record in their ' Answer ' to the Commons : where they speak (Gee and Hardy, p. 174) of " divers of the clergy " having " sundry times been rigorously handled, and with much violence entreated by certain ill-disposed and seditious persons of the lay fee, so injured in their own persons, thrown down in the kennel in the open street at mid-day, even here, within this city and elsewhere, to the great reproach, rebuke and disquietness of the clergy and ministers of God's Church within this your realm, the great danger of souls of the said misdoers, and perilous example of your said subjects ".

In the final draft submitted to the King and the Bishops " the said seditions, factions, deadly hatred and most uncharitable part-taking " is watered down into " the said uncharitable variances and part-taking ".

A more striking example still. The prior draft has four paragraphs attacking the laws of heresy and the Ordinaries arbitrarily and harshly administering them. Cromwell first wrote :

" And furthermore, Where the said spiritual Ordinaries many times purposedly to revenge their inward greves and displeasures and to put their said laws in execution, their Commissaries and Substitutes, sometime for their own pleasures, sometime by the sinister procurement of other spiritual persons, use to make out process against divers of your said subjects and thereby compel them ", etc. Cromwell himself crossed out the words about revenging their inward griefs and displeasures, knowing, of course,

315

that no such words would have passed the King. Yet to Londoners like Edward Hall and Cromwell, who could remember what had happened less than twenty years before in the case of Richard Hunne, such words would be the first that came to mind in any indictment of the heresy laws. But the draughtsman had to be on his guard against them, and to remember that the King's very controversy with the Pope had made him the more determined stickler for orthodoxy and the laws that defended it. No words about revenge or anything like them appear in the final draft, in which, as we shall see, this matter about heresy was thoroughly recast in order not to offend the susceptibilities of the King, or play into the hands of a conservative opposition.

The ' Supplication ' in its final form, as passed and presented by the House of Commons, had, no doubt, the concurrence of the King ; but the known circumstances of its production preclude any idea that it " really emanated from the Court ", or was other than what it professed to be, the work of the House of Commons, put into shape, to the satisfaction both of King and Commons, by their man-of-all-work, ready writer, honest broker and mutual friend, M.P. and Privy Councillor Cromwell.

It covers two main, and ten minor, themes, the latter occupying rather more than half its length. Half of these concern the working of the spiritual courts. In the order in which they appear in the final draft, the complaints relate to : 1. Citations from distant dioceses, about which a remedial bill was then pending. (See above, pp. 305 - 7). 2. Excessive charges for legal instruments. 3. Delays and difficulties in obtaining probate. 4. Novel exactions for Tithes. 5. Vexatious suits for mortuaries. 6. Shortness of prescription held sufficient to establish title of clerks against laymen. 7. Rapacities in connection with institutions to livings. 8. Preferment of incompetent minors and the profits made out of it. And 10. Employment of clergy in " temporal offices " as " Stewards, Receivers, Auditors and Bailiffs ". Nearly all these matters of complaint are connected with clerical moneygrubbing in one form or other. The ' Supplication ' speaks in the preamble of the " evil examples and misuses of spiritual persons " ; but, to the layman, their vice of vices was always avarice. For some of the practices impeached by the Commons the prelates, in their reply, make out a plausible case ; others, to their credit be it said, they neither deny nor defend, acknowledging them to be " detestable in spiritual men ", and only urging that the clergy as a body cannot be held accountable for them. They do not explain why, with unfettered constitutional power to reform them in Convocation, they had left their reformation to a secular Parliament, while resenting and reprobating the interference of Parliament. They do not explain why they had left it to a layman like Simon Fish, with a pen dipped in scorn and vitriol, to denounce them. Or why, just twenty years after Dean Colet had pleaded with them on these very matters from the pulpit of St. Paul's, neither they, nor the Cardinal Legate with his plenary powers, had done one effective thing to set them right. And they were only now even acknowledging them when the hour of retribution had struck, and the work, their proper work which they had neglected to do, was being done for them and despite them.

The two main themes, occupying rather less than half the ' Supplication ', require fuller treatment. The first amounts to a claim that the King and his lay subjects — not the King alone, be it observed — should have a concurrent voice in ecclesiastical legislation, and that the clergy in Convocation should no longer make laws binding upon the laity without their " assent or knowledge ". Certain of the laws so made — the reference is apparently to the constitutions concerning clerical immunity — are alleged, " under the supportation of your Majesty ", to be " against your Jurisdiction and Prerogative Royal ". The other main theme relates to the heresy laws and their arbitrary execution. The two themes are connected because, chief among the arbitrary enactments which are the subject of complaint, were these same heresy laws. The Commons, complaining in 1532, found it convenient to forget that the Parliaments of Henry IV and Henry V had placed the whole civil administration at the disposal of the Bishops for the execution of Archbishop Arundel's heresy laws (see above p. 22). At the same time these Lancastrian Parliaments had provided certain safeguards for the liberty of the subject which the Bishops themselves had found it convenient to forget.

Hall, who knew, tells us that the subject matter of the ' Supplication ' was " long debated in the Common House ", and that " at the last it was concluded and agreed that all the griefs which the temporal men were grieved with should be put in writing and delivered to the King, which by great advice was done " (Chronicle, II., p. 202). The results of this debate and great advice are seen in the final form of the ' Supplication ', a general modification of Cromwell's original draft in the direction of moderation and sweet reasonableness. The Commons, at the cost of their real feelings and telling phrases, had to consider how their Supplication would look in the eyes of the King and other advisers less radical than Cromwell. They had, above all, to have the King with them. They had therefore to appear, not of course to be " attacking the Church ", but to be defending the King's " Jurisdiction and Prerogative Royal " and the " bodies, possessions and goods " of his humble, loving and obedient subjects. They must disclaim any intention " to take away from the said Ordinaries their authority to correct and punish sin, and in especial the detestable crime of heresy ". And they must so bowdlerise their initial treatment of the detestable crime, and so puddle it up with the unpopular jurisdiction for the correction of sin, as not to betray too evidently their own sense of the detestable way in which the crime was dealt with. It was dealt with in strict accord with the rules of the Canon Law ; but the procedure appeared to the Commons " dreadful and grievous ", in Hall's words, because it provided none of the safeguards for fair trial which Englishmen had learnt to regard as essential from the practice of the Common Law.

In the prior draft the Ordinaries' " authority to correct and punish sin ", the less grave, though the more intrusive and vexatious, branch of jurisdiction, is treated in a separate paragraph. The detestable crime occupies four following paragraphs ; and these show what Cromwell and the Commons really thought about those laws of heresy which Nix of Norwich and Stokesley of London, with the zealous assistance of Lord Chancellor More, had been so busily putting in execution. As part of the purpose of this enquiry is to exhibit the real mind of the people concerned in these affairs, I give, in modern spelling, the passage from Dr. Merriman's transcript of the prior draft (' Cromwell ', I, pp. 106-8).

" And Furthermore, Where the said spiritual Ordinaries, — (many times purposely to revenge their inward greves and displeasures and to put their said laws in execution), these bracketed words struck out by Cromwell himself — their Commissaries and Substitutes, sometime for their own pleasures, sometime by the sinister procurement of other spiritual persons, use to make out process against divers of your said subjects, and thereby compel them to appear before themselves to answer at a certain day and place to such articles as by them shall be of office afore themselves then purposed (proposed ?), and that secretly and not in open places ", — these last words interlined by Cromwell. The statute ' De Haeretico Comburendo ', 2 Henry, IV, c. 15, had safeguarded the accused both against secret inquisitions and against arbitrary and indefinite imprisonment before trial.— .... " and forthwith upon their appearance without cause or any declaration then made or shewed commit and send them to ward : Where they remain without bail or mainprise sometime half a year and sometime a whole year or more or (ere) they may in any wise know either the cause of their imprisonment or any name of their accuser : and finally their great costs, charges and expenses therein when all is examined and nothing can be proved against them, but they clearly innocent for any fault or crime that can be laid unto them in that part, ben set again at large without any recompense or amends in that behalf to be towards them adjudged.

" And also if percase upon the said process and appearance any party be upon the said matter, cause or examination brought forth and named either as party or witness, and then upon the proof and trial thereof not able to prove and verify his said accusation or testimony against the party so accused to be true, then the person so causeless accused is for the more part without any remedy for his charges and wrongful vexation to be towards him adjudged and recovered.

319

" Also upon the examination of the said accusation, if heresy be ordinarily laid unto the charge of the party so accused, then the said Ordinaries or their ministers use to put to them such subtle interrogatories concerning the high mysteries of our Faith as are able quickly to trap a simple unlearned or yet a well-witted layman without learning, and bring them by such sinister introduction soon to his own confusion. And forthwith, if there chance any heresy to be by such subtle policy by him confessed in words and yet never committed nor thought in deed, then put they without further favour the said person either to make his purgation and so thereby to lose his honesty and credence for ever : or else as some simple silly soul, precisely standing to the clear testimony of his own well-known conscience rather than to confess his innocent truth, to abide — (the extreme examination of death by the Fire ") : the bracketed words crossed out by Cromwell — the extremity in that behalf, and so is utterly destroyed.

" And if it fortune the said party so accused to deny the said accusation, and so put his adversary to prove the same untruly forged and imagined against him, then for the more part such witnesses as ben brought forth for the same be they but two in number, never so sore diffamed, of little truth or credence, adversaries or enemies to the party, yet they shall be allowed and enabled only by discretion of the said Ordinaries, their Commissaries and Substitutes, and thereupon sufficient cause to proceed to judgment, to deliver the party so accused either to the secular hands — (and so to be burned) : words in brackets crossed out by Cromwell — after abjuration without remedy ; and afore if he submit himself, to compel him when best happeneth to make his purgation and bear a Faggot to his extreme shame and utter undoing ".

Now in those days the Commons met in secret (or one might otherwise say private) session as a matter of course, and were jealous of leakages. They looked to Cromwell and his growing influence with the King to bring their purposes to effect ; and when the above was considered " by great advice ", it became plain to them that if Cromwell were to approach the throne with so downright an impeachment of the heresy laws and their administration, his credit with the King might very well be shaken. The King, no doubt, would be gratified by the Commons' solicitude for his sovereignty, but the Defender of the Faith might be disturbed, not to say antagonised and incensed, by an open attack upon the laws against heresy. On reflection, the King could be heard saying : " We take in very good part the tenderness of the Commons for Our Jurisdiction and Prerogative Royal ; but, Master Cromwell, what of this other matter ? You of the nether House are asking me, in effect, to abrogate the law of heresy, the only law there is. You are asking me to open the door wide to Tyndale and his like, the man I told you a year ago I would have nothing to do with, and told you to tell your man Stephen Vaughan to have nothing more to do with. I require you upon your allegiance to tell me who are behind all this. It may be that the prelates have too free a hand in arresting people on suspicion of heresy* ; that may need restraining ; but it is a very different thing from crippling their jurisdiction altogether. I marvel not a little — (always a phrase of menace in the mouth of the King or Cromwell) — that you, of my Council, should venture upon such a suggestion ".

And so, by great advice, the original draft was ingeniously modified : shortened, and diluted by an adroit admixture of matter drawn from an earlier paragraph dealing with the Church's minor — but more pervasive, intrusive and unpopular — jurisdiction for " the punishment of sin ", in which the penances imposed were " commonly ", as is alleged, redeemed for money. That the reader may judge, this earlier paragraph is here recited from Dr. Merriman's transcript :

" And where also many of your said most humble and obedient subjects, and specially those that be of the poorest sort, within this your Realm, ben daily convented and called before the said spiritual Ordinaries, their Commissaries and Substitutes, ex officio,

---

* In a despatch from Chapuys to Charles V on May 13th, 1532 occurs the following : " The King also wishes bishops not to have the power to lay hands on persons accused of heresy, saying that it is not their duty to meddle with bodies, and they are only doctors of the soul. The Chancellor (More) and the Bishops oppose him. He is very angry, especially with the Chancellor and the Bishop of Winchester, and is determined to carry the matter." V. no. 1013.

sometime at the pleasures of the said Ordinaries and Substitutes for malice without any cause, and sometime at the only promotion and accusement of their Summoners and apparitors, being very light and undiscreet persons, without any lawful cause of accusation or credible fame proved against them, and without any presentment in the visitation, ben inquieted, disturbed, vexed, troubled and put to excessive and importable charges for them to bear : and many times be suspended and excommunicate for small and light causes upon the only certificate of the proctors of the adversaries made under a feigned Seal which every proctor hath in his keeping : whereas the party suspended and excommunicate many times never had any warning, and yet, when he shall be absolved, if it be out of the court, he shall be compelled to pay to his own proctor twenty pence, and to the proctor which is against him other twenty pence, and twenty pence to the Scribe, besides a privy reward that the Judge shall have, to the great impoverishing of your said poor Lay Subjects ".

In the final draft the matter from this paragraph in the earlier, relating to the Church's minor jurisdiction over moral offences, is so worked in and worked up with matter from the four following paragraphs relating to the major issue of heresy as to blur and camouflage the outline of the latter, and make it difficult, in the final draft, to say whether any particular sentence refers to the lighter or graver category of offence. References to the commutation of penances for money, obviously concern the lighter ; but they are found mixed up with references to secret inquisitions and arbitrary imprisonment " without bail or mainprise ", — notorious illegalities to which Froude drew forcible attention long ago — which as obviously concern the process in heresy. The Commons manage to get in their stroke ; but its edge is deliberately dulled and blunted so as not to impinge too sharply upon the royal orthodoxy. And further to the same purpose, the Commons make solemn protestation, in the final draft, that " it is not intended to take away from the said Ordinaries their authority to correct and punish sin, and in especial the detestable crime of heresy ", affirming that if the laws against heresy are insufficient, they

" desire that there be devised and made more dreadful and terrible ".
They said this in order to make themselves right with the King ;
but there is no reason to doubt that they meant it. This House
of Commons, in which there was not a single known heretic or a
single known Lutheran, was as firm in the defence of the Faith
as the King himself ; but they meant that in future it should be
defended by a process less arbitrary, less open to abuse by malice
or caprice, less obscure to the subject laity, and less inconsonant
with ordinary secular canons of justice. Explicitly in the earlier
draft, implicitly in the final, the Commons indict the Ordinaries
as persons whom they had ceased to trust, administering a law
which might place any man's life and liberty at their mercy. Their
action shows that the shock to confidence which had been given
by the case of Richard Hunne subsequent happenings had done
nothing to repair. Every heresy trial was watched with suspicion
and distrust, every burning with a horrid doubt as to whether
the unfortunate at the stake had rightly been found guilty.

Events developed in their natural sequence. Action was taken,
first and immediately, upon the part of the ' Supplication ' in which
the King wholeheartedly concurred, that relating to his ' Jurisdiction and Prerogative Royal '. It was not until two years later
(1534) that the matter in which the Commons were mainly interested was dealt with, and a new Heresy Act, repealing Henry IV's
' De Haeretico Comburendo ', took the power of direct arrest out
of the Bishops' hands. The preamble of this Act, 25 Henry VIII,
c. 14, reproduces pretty exactly the position taken by the Commons
in the prior draft of their ' Supplication ' in 1532 ; the common
draughtsmanship is unmistakable. For the production of this
prior draft, or of an Act based upon it, the time was not ripe in
1532, or, in other words, the King's mind, on this head, was not
sufficiently interested or persuaded. Cromwell, with his following
in the Commons, knew where he was going, but he had to move
carefully. It is important to note these marks of time. The next
two years were to add greatly to the strength of Cromwell's position,
and to the King's dependence upon his decision and resource.

Here may be given, in full, the ' Supplication of the Commons ' in its final form, as laid before the King and by him before the Bishops. About three-fifths of its text has been known through extensive quotations in the ' Answer of the Ordinaries ' printed by Gee and Hardy (' Documents illustrative ,' pp. 154 - 76). The following transcript is from the Record Office ms., No. 22 in P.R.O. Theological Tracts, Vol. 1, calendared in L. and P., Henry VIII, V. as No. 1016 (1), this being a fair copy of No. 1016 (2). The heads of complaint are numbered for convenience of reference. If section 2 (pp. 325 - 7) be compared with the paragraphs relating to heresy in the earlier draft (above, pp. 319 - 20), the extent and purpose of the revision will become apparent.

" In most humble wise shewen unto your excellent Highness and most prudent wisdom your faithful, loving and most humble and obedient subjects the Commons in this your present Parliament assembled : That where of late, as well through new fantastical and erroneous opinions growen by occasion of seditious and over-thwartly framed books compiled, imprinted and made in the English tongue in the parts of beyond the sea, contrary and against the very true Catholic and Christian faith, and published and sold within this your Realm : as also by the uncharitable behaviour and dealing of divers Ordinaries, their Commissaries and Substitutes in the common and often vexation of your said subjects in the spiritual courts of this Realm : and also by other evil examples and misuses of spiritual persons, much discord, variance and debate hath risen, and more and more daily is like to increase and ensue amongst the universal sort of your said subjects, as well spiritual as temporal, either against other, in most uncharitable manner to the great inquietation and breach of your peace within this your most Catholic Realm : Some special particular griefs whereof, which most principally concern as well your Highness and Jurisdiction Royal as your said Commons and Lay Subjects : And which are, as they undoubtedly suppose, part of the chief fountains, occasions and causes that daily breedeth, fostereth, and nourisheth and maintaineth the said uncharitable variances and part-taking, either part and sort of your said subjects spiritual and temporal against the other, hereafter followingly do ensue :

First, the prelates and other of the Clergy of this your Realm, being your subjects, in their Convocations by them holden within this your Realm, have made and daily make divers fashions of laws and ordinances concerning temporal things : and some of them be repugnant to the laws and statutes of your Realm, not having ne (nor) requiring your most royal assent to the same laws by them so made, nor any assent or knowledge of your lay subjects is had to the same, nor to them published and known in the English tongue : Albeit divers and sundry of the said laws extend in certain cases to your excellent person, your liberty and prerogative royal, and to the interdiction of your lands and possessions : and some likewise to the goods and possessions of your lay Subjects, declaring the infringers of the same laws so by them made not only to incur into the terrible censures of excommunication, but also into the detestable crime and sin of heresy : by the which divers of your most humble and obedient lay subjects be brought into this Ambiguity, whether they may do and execute your laws according to your Jurisdiction Royal of this your Realm for dread of the same pains and censures comprised in the said laws so by them made in their Convocations, to the great trouble and inquietation of your said humble, loving and obedient lay subjects : and as they suppose, under the supportation of your Majesty, the same laws so made are against your Jurisdiction and prerogative Royal.

II. Also divers and many of your said most humble and obedient subjects, and specially those that be of the poorest sort, within this your Realm, ben (be) daily convented and called before the said spiritual Ordinaries, their Commissaries and Substitutes, ex officio, sometime at the pleasures of the said Ordinaries, their Commissaries and Substitutes, for displeasure, without any probable cause : and sometime at the only promotion and suggestion of their summoners and apparitors being very light and undiscreet persons, without any other lawful accusation or credible fame first proved against them, and without any presentment in the Visitation or other presentment according to your laws : and sometime, upon their appearance ex officio at the only will and pleasure of the Ordinaries, their Commissaries and Substitutes, they be

325

committed to prison without bail or mainprise : and there some lie, as it is reported, half a year and some more or (ere) they can come to their declaration : And when there is none accuser, nor common fame lawfully proved, nor any presentment in the Visitation, yet divers so appearing ex officio shall be constrained to answer to many subtle questions and interrogatories only invented and exhibited at the pleasure of the said Ordinaries, their Commissaries and Substitutes : by the which a simple, unlearned, or else a well-witted layman without learning sometime is and commonly may be trapped and induced by an ignorant answer to the peril of open penance to his shame, or else to redeem the same penance for money, as it is commonly used. And if it rest upon witnesses, be they but two in number, never so sore defamed, of little truth or credence, adversaries or enemies to the party, yet in many cases they may be allowed only by the discretion of the said Ordinaries, their Commissaries and Substitutes, to put the party accused or infamed ex officio to open penance, and then to redemption for money : So that every your subjects, upon the only will and pleasure of the Ordinaries, their Commissaries and Substitutes, without any accuser, proved fame or presentment, sometime is and may be infamed, vexed and troubled to the peril of their lives, their shames, costs and expenses.

And it is not intended, most dread Sovereign Lord, by your most humble and obedient lay subjects, to take away from the said Ordinaries their authority to correct and punish sin, and in especial the detestable crime of heresy : for if the laws for punishment thereof be insufficient or too little punishment, your said humble and obedient lay subjects desire that with the assent of your Highness there may be devised and made more dreadful and terrible laws for the repress of the same than hath been in times past : so that some reasonable declaration may be known to your people how they may if they will eschew the peril of heresy ; and also that some charitable fashion and mean may be devised by your most excellent wisdom for the calling of any your subjects before them, so it shall not stand in the only will and pleasure of the Ordinaries, their Commissaries and Substitutes, to call any person ex officio at their own imaginations without lawful accusation, proved fame by honest witnesses, or presentment in the Visitation or other lawful presentment according to your laws ; or by such other charitable mean as shall be thought by your most excellent wisdom reasonable in that behalf for the quietness of your subjects.

III.   Also divers and many of your most humble and obedient lay subjects be originally ascited to appear out of the diocese that they dwell in, and many times be suspended and excommunicate for small and light causes upon the only certificate devised by the proctors of the adversaries made under a pretensed seal of an archdeacon, which any proctor hath at his pleasure : whereas the party suspended and excommunicate many times never had any warning ; and yet, when he shall be absolved, if it be out of the court, he shall be compelled to pay to his own proctor twenty pence, and to the proctor which is against him other twenty pence, and twenty pence to the scribe, to the great impoverishing of your said poor lay subjects.

IV.   Also your said most humble and obedient subjects find them grieved with the great and excessive fees taken in the said spiritual courts, and in especial in the said courts of the Arches and Audience, where they take for every citation 2/6 : for every Inhibition 6/8 : for every proxy 16d : for every certificate 16d : for every libel 3/4 : for every answer to any libel 3/4 ; for every act, if it be but two words, in the Register 4d ; for every personal citation or decree 3/4 : for every sentence or judgment, to the Judge 26/8 : for every testimonial upon any such sentence or judgment 26/8 : for every significavit 12/- : for every commission to examine witness 12/-. And also there is exacted for serving their process after the rate of the miles, for every mile 2d.

V.   Also in probate of testaments, notwithstanding the last statute thereof made, there is invented new fashions to charge your subjects for probate of testaments, that is to say, long delays and tracts or (ere) the proof thereon can be admitted ; and also some-time the executors be put to travel to far places out of the shires they dwell in, although the probate thereof belong not to the prerogative.

VI.   And likewise, sithen the statute made for Mortuaries, there is exacted and demanded of your subjects in divers parishes of this your Realm other manner of Tithes than they have been accustomed to pay this hundred years past : And in some parts of your Realm there is exacted double tithes, that is to say, 3d or 2½d for the acre over and beside the tithe for the increase of the cattle that pastureth the same land : and daily vexation by citation for the same.

VII. And where any Mortuary is due after the rate of the statute, sometime curates, before they will demand it, will bring citations for it, and then will not receive the mortuary till he may have such costs as he sayeth he hath laid out for suit for the same ; when indeed, if he would have charitably first demanded it, he needed not to have sued for the same and should have had it with good will.

VIII. And if any spiritual person hath obtained the possession of any profit for the term of thirty or forty years against any lay person, albeit that such profit began sometime by sufferance and sometime by devotion, yet it is said that prescription in their law of such little term of thirty or forty years maketh for them a good title against every lay person : which things be used to the importable charge and vexations of your subjects, and necessary to have some charitable reformation.

IX. And also, whereas divers spiritual persons, being presented as well by your Highness as by other patrons within this your Realm to divers benefices and other spiritual promotions, the said Ordinaries and their ministers do not only take of them for their Letters of Institution and Induction many great and large sums of money and rewards, but also do long delay them without reasonable cause before they will admit, institute and induct them, by cause they will have the profits of the benefice during vacation unless they will pact and covenant with them by temporal bond after such fashions and conditions as they will : whereof some bonds contain that the Ordinaries should have part of the profits of the said benefice after their institution, so as they, being once presented or promoted as is aforesaid, ben by the said Ordinaries sometime uncharitably handled, not only to the hurt of the lay patrons, but also to the hindrance and impoverishment of their clerks by them presented : which your said subjects suppose, not only to be

328

against right and good conscience, but also seemeth to be simony and contrary to the laws of God.

X. And also the said spiritual Ordinaries do daily confer and give sundry benefices unto certain young folk, calling them their nephews or kinsfolks, being in their minority and within age, apt ne (nor) able to serve the cure of any such benefice : whereby the said Ordinaries do keep and detain the fruits and profits of the same benefices in their own hands ; and so the cures and other promotions given unto such Infants ben only employed to the enriching of the said Ordinaries, and the poor silly souls of your people and subjects which should be taught in the parishes given aforesaid, for lack of good curates do perish without good example, doctrine, or any good teaching.

XI. And also where a great number of holy days, which now at this present time with very small devotion be solemnised and kept throughout this your Realm : upon the which many great, abominable and execrable vices, idle and wanton sports, and plays of the stage (written in above line), ben used and exercised : which holy days, if it may stand with your gracious pleasure, and specially such as fall in the harvest, might by your Majesty, by the advice of your most honourable Council, prelates and Ordinaries, ben made fewer in number : and those that shall hereafter be ordained to stand and continue might and may be the more devoutly, religiously and reverently observed to the laud of Almighty God and to the increase of your high honour and fame.

XII. Also divers and many spiritual persons, not contented with the convenient living and promotion of the Church, daily intromit and exercise themselves in secular offices and rooms, as Stewards, Receivers, Auditors, Bailiffs and other temporal offices, withdrawing themselves from the good contemplative life that they have professed in the service of God, not only to the great damage of all your said subjects, but also to the perilous example of your loving and obedient subjects.

IN CONSIDERATION WHEREOF, most gracious Sovereign Lord, and forasmuch as there is at this present time, and by a few years past hath been, much misdemeanour and violence on the one part and much default and lack of patience, sufferance, charity and goodwill on the other part, a marvellous discord of the goodly quiet, peace and tranquillity that this your Realm heretofore hath been in, ever hitherto through your politic wisdom in most honourable fame and catholic faith inviolably preserved : It may therefore, most benign Sovereign Lord, like your excellent goodness, for the tender and universally indifferent zeal, benign love and favour that your Highness beareth toward both the said parties, the said articles, if they or any of them shall be by your most clear and perfect judgment thought any instruments or causes of the said variance and disorder, or those and all other occasions whatsoever accompted by your Highness to make toward the said factions deeply and weightily after your accustomed ways and manner searched, weighed and considered, graciously to provide, by the assent of the said prelates and other the temporal nobles of this your Realm with the Commons in this your most high Court of Parliament assembled, all violence and uncharitable demeanours on both sides utterly and clearly set apart, some such necessary and behoveful remedies, laws and ordinances as may effectually declare and establish not only those things which to your Jurisdiction and prerogative Royal justly appertaineth, but also reconcile and bring into perpetual unity your said subjects spiritual and temporal.. Whereunto your said Commons most humbly, heartily and entirely beseech your Grace, as the only Sovereign Lord, protector and defender of both the said parties, in whom and by whom the only and sole redress, reformation and remedy herein absolutely resteth and remaineth : By occasion whereof all your said Commons in their consciences surely accompt that besides the marvellous fervent love that your Highness shall thereby kindle and ingender in their hearts towards your Grace, ye shall do the most princely feat, and shew the most honourable and charitable precedent, ensample and mirror, that ever did Sovereign Lord upon his subjects : and therewithal merit and deserve of our merciful Lord eternal bliss : Whose goodness grant your Grace in most godly, princely and honourable estate long to reign, prosper and continue as the Sovereign Lord over all your said most humble and obedient subjects ".

Chapter IX

THE 'ANSWER' OF THE ORDINARIES AND THEIR "SUBMISSION"

THE MEDIAEVAL ORDER AT AN END

The ' Answer ' of the prelates was masterly in its way ; their best minds had plainly been engaged upon it. Its firmness of tone upon the two main issues disconcerted and displeased the King, who had looked for something more in the way of submission. He was especially " discontent " because his own Secretary, Dr. Stephen Gardiner, whom he had lately preferred to the bishopric of Winchester, had had a chief hand in the drafting of the reply. Gardiner, having " heard, to his great discomfort, what opinion the King has conceived of him," wrote a justificatory letter, in manly contrast with the idolatrous adulation with which Majesty was commonly approached (V. no. 1019). The reply, of course, must be read as that of the prelates as a body.

They begin by adverting, in a tone of pained surprise, to the alleged estrangement between themselves and the laity. They protest that there are no hard feelings upon their side, " assuring your Majesty that in our hearts and conscience there is no such discord, debate, variance, or breach of peace on our part against our brethren in God and ghostly children, your subjects, as is induced in this preface ; but our daily prayer is and shall be that all unity, concord and peace may increase among your Grace's true and faithful subjects, our said ghostly children, whom, God be our witness, we love, have loved, and shall love ever with hearty affection : never intending any hurt or harm towards any of them in soul or body ; and never enterprised anything against them of trouble, vexation or displeasure ; but only have, as we dare surely affirm, with all charity, exercised the spiritual jurisdiction of the Church, as we are bound of duty, upon certain evil-disposed persons infected and utterly corrupt with the pestilent poison of heresy ; and to have had peace with such, had been against the gospel of our Saviour Christ, wherein he saith, ' Non veni mittere pacem sed gladium " (I came not to send peace but a sword). (Gee and Hardy, p. 155).

The prelates appear to be unconscious throughout that the real matter at issue between themselves and the Commons was this same law of heresy, and their " uncharitable behaviour and dealing " in the use of it.

As regards the minor heads of complaint, the prelates, while saying what could be said in explanation or justification of current practice, neither deny nor defend what was notorious and indefensible : even allowing that the graver abuses, supposing them to exist, are " detestable in spiritual men." They plead however, after More's fashion, that the whole body of the clergy cannot be held answerable for the misdeeds of the misdoers. As to the petty vexations of the spiritual courts and their petty officials, a source of universal irritation, they virtually plead guilty, while ascribing them, not to their own slackness and indifference to reform, but to something mysterious and inscrutable in the ways of Providence. The passage is remarkable as indicative of a type of mind.

" Where they say that divers and many your Grace's obedient subjects, and especially they that be of the poorest sort, be daily called before us, the special ordinaries or commissaries and substitutes ex officio ; sometime at the pleasure of us, the said ordinaries or commissaries and substitutes, for displeasure, without any probable cause, and sometime at the only promotion of our summoners, being light and indiscreet persons, without any credible fame first proved against them, and without any presentment in the visitation or lawful accusation :

" To this we, your Grace's said orators, do answer and say, — and first we most humbly desire your highness by your high wisdom and learning to consider that albeit, in the ordering of Christ's people your Grace's subjects, God of his special goodness assisteth His Church, and inspireth by the Holy Ghost, as we verily trust, such wholesome rules and laws as tend to the wealth of His elect flock, the increase and augmentation of His faith, honour and glory — yet, upon consideration to man unknown, His infinite wisdom leaveth and permitteth men to walk in their infirmity and frailty. So that we cannot, nor will, arrogantly presume of ourselves, as though, being in name spiritual men, we were also all, in all our acts and doings, clean and void from all temporal affections and carnality of this world, in that the laws of the Church made for spiritual and ghostly purpose be not sometimes applied to worldly intent : which we ought and do lament (as becometh us) very sore. Nevertheless, inasmuch as the evil acts and deeds of men be the more (mere ?) defaults of those particular men, and not of the whole order of the clergy, nor of the laws wholesomely by them made, our request and petition shall be, with all humility and reverence, that all laws well made be not therefore called evil because at all times, and by all men, they be not well executed ; and that in such defaults as shall appear, such distribution may be used as St. Paul speaketh of : *ut unusquisque onus suum portet*, and remedy to exhibit to reform the offenders ; unto the which your highness shall perceive as great towardness in your said orators as can be required upon declaration of the particulars and special articles in that behalf. And other answer than this cannot be made in the name of your whole clergy, considering that, in many of the particularities which be alleged as defaults, if the whole clergy should confess or deny them, they be not all true or all false generally in the whole ; for though *in multis offendimus omnes*, as St. James saith, yet not *in omnibus offendimus omnes* ; and the whole number can neither justify nor condemn particular acts to them unknown but thus. He that calleth a man ex officio for correction of sin doeth well. He that calleth men for pleasure and vexation doeth evil. Summoners should be honest men. If they offend in their office they should be punished. To prove first the same, before men be called, it is not necessary. He that is called according to the laws ex officio or otherwise cannot complain. He that is otherwise ordered should have, by reason, convenient recompense and so forth ; that that is well to be allowed, and misdemeanour, when it appeareth, reproved." (pp. 160 - 2).

All the above concern matters of practice ; and with regard to them the prelates show no indisposition towards reform, the need of which is sufficiently acknowledged. A stiffer tone pervades the lengthy passage in which Archbishop Warham, speaking in his own person, maintains the privileges of the archiepiscopal courts, especially his own Court of Arches. He has recently cut down its scale of fees, a reform for which the Commons have given him no credit. He urges that his courts have been an invaluable training-ground for the doctors of civil law who are essential to the diplomatic service. " For the space of four hundred years or thereabouts " " it hath appertained to the Archbishops of Canterbury and York," as ' legati nati ' of the Holy See, " to have spiritual jurisdiction over all them your Grace's subjects dwelling within their provinces, and to have authority to call them before them by citation, not only in spiritual causes devolved to them by way of appeal, but also by way of querimony and complaint." This privilege is imminently threatened by a bill then before Parliament (see above pp. 305 - 7), " and forasmuch as the spiritual prelates of the clergy, being of your Grace's Parliament, consented not to the said Act, for divers great causes moving their consciences," . . . . . " we most entirely and most humbly beseech your Grace that, of your superabundant goodness and absolute power, it may please the same to set such an order and direction in this behalf as we may enjoy the privileges of our churches, lawfully prescribed and admitted so long " . . . . in short, to withhold the royal assent to the pending bill. (pp. 167 - 8).

Stiffer still, to the point of inflexibility, is the attitude of the prelates towards the matters of principle involved in the first two articles of the Commons' complaint.

As regards the laws for the repression of heresy, the Commons' somewhat oblique attack had lent itself to an oblique defence. The prelates do not defend the heresy laws directly, or, in fact, defend them at all. On this matter they were misled by the apparent strength of their position. The " determination of Holy Church " with regard to heresy was so strongly entrenched behind the confirming and co-operating statutes of Henry IV and Henry V as to

334

appear impregnable. There seemed to be no moral or political need to justify or defend it. The prelates maintain their position at every point. As regards arbitrary citation, "without lawful accusation, proved fame by honest witness, presentment in the visitation or other lawful presentment," "your said orators answer that a better provision cannot be devised than is already devised by the clergy, in our opinion ; and if any default appear in the execution, it shall be amended upon the declaration of the particulars and the same proved." (p. 165).

As regards arbitrary imprisonment, "we use no person before conviction but for sure custody, only of such as be suspected of heresy, in which crime, thanked be God, there has fallen no such notable personage, in our time, or of such qualities as hath given occasion of any sinister suspicion to be conceived of malice or hatred to his person other than the heinousness of that crime deserveth. Truth it is that certain apostates, friars, monks, lewd priests, bankrupt merchants, vagabonds, and lewd idle fellows of corrupt intent, have embraced the abominable and erroneous opinions lately sprung in Germany, and by them some seduced in simplicity and ignorance. Against these, if justice has been exercised according to the laws of the Church, and conformably to the laws of this realm, we be without blame. If we have been too slack and remiss, we shall gladly do our duty from henceforth. If any man hath been under pretence of this particularly offended, it were pity to suffer any man wronged ; and thus it ought to be, and otherwise we cannot answer, no man's special case being declared in the said petition." (p. 162).

As regards the acceptance of tainted testimony, it is defended precisely in the fashion of Sir Thomas More. (See ante pp. 31 - 2). "The Gospel of Christ teacheth us to believe two witnesses ; and as the cause is, so the judge must esteem the qualities of the witness, and in heresy no exception is necessary to be considered if their tale be likely ; which hath been highly provided lest heretics, without jeopardy, might else plant their heresies in lewd and light persons, and, taking exception to the witness, take boldness to continue their folly. This is the universal law of Christendom and hath universally done good. Of any injury done to any man thereby, we know not." (p. 164).

As to the Commons' desire that " some reasonable declaration may be known to your people how they may (if they will) avoid the peril of heresy," the prelates answer summarily that " there can be no better declaration known than is already by our Saviour Christ, the apostles, and the determination of the Church, which if they keep they shall not fail clearly to eschew heresy." (p. 165).

To the Commons' protestation " that it is not intended by them to take away from us our authority to correct and punish sin, and especially the detestable crime of heresy : To this your said orators answer, in the persecution of heretics we regard our duty and office whereunto we be called, and if God would discharge us thereof, or cease that plague universal — as by your mighty hand, and directing the hearts of princes, and specially of your highness (laud and thanks be unto Him), His goodness doth commence and begin to do, — we should and shall have great cause to rejoice, as being our authority therein costly, dangerous, full of trouble and business, without any fruit, pleasure or commodity worldly, but a continual conflict and vexation, with pertinacity, wilfulness, folly and ignorance, whereupon followeth their bodily and ghostly destruction, to our great sorrow and lamentation." (p. 164).

Rebutting the allegation of " violence " — which had not in fact been made — " we ascertain your Grace, as touching the violence which they seem to lay to our charges, albeit divers of the clergy of this your realm have sundry times been rigourously handled, and with much violence entreated by certain ill-disposed and seditious persons of the lay fee, so injured in their own persons, thrown down in the kennel in the open street at mid-day, even here within your city and elsewhere, to the great reproach, rebuke and disquietness of the clergy and ministers of God's Church within this your realm, the great danger of souls of the said misdoers, and perilous example of your said subjects : Yet we think verily, and do affirm the same, that no violence hath been so used on our behalf towards your said lay subjects in any case ; unless they do esteem this to be violence, that we do commonly use, as well for the health of their souls as for the discharge of our duties, in taking, examining and punishing of heretics according to the law : wherein we doubt not but that your Grace and divers of your Grace's subjects do right well perceive and understand what charitable demeanour and entreaty we have used with such as have been before us for the same cause of heresy, and what means we have devised and studied for favour and safeguard specially of their souls ; and that so charitably (as God be our judge) and without all violence as we could possibly devise." (p. 174).

In all this there is not a syllable of concession. There seemed no call or occasion for any concession. The prelates were misled into taking the Commons' zeal against heresy for satisfaction with the laws of heresy ; to point out that the matters of complaint, arbitrary citation, arbitrary imprisonment and the rest, were incident to the laws of heresy seemed sufficient justification. Their feet planted upon an assured legality, the Bishops had no sensation of the quaking ground around them. From the penal laws upon which they took their stand opinion had recently and rapidly been receding. Living their own life, and a life gravitating mainly about Westminster and the Court, they seem to have had little notion of what people were thinking east of Temple Bar. They had no idea that draft bills for the parliamentary reform of the heresy laws were already on the anvil, or that one such bill* would be on the

---

* The preamble of one such draft — calendared L. and P. VI, no. 120 (2), and under date 1533, though it seems better suited to the situation prevailing in 1532 . . . , after reciting certain provisions of the existing statute (2 Henry IV, c. 15) giving the ordinaries power to arrest upon suspicion, proceeds as follows :
" ; . . . . . as in the same Act more plainly doth appear : The said Diocesans, Ordinaries and Commissaries, the accomplishment and fulfilling of their un-charitable minds, desires and pleasures more highly preferred than the just and true execution of the said Act and quietness of the King's subjects, perversely and uncharitably hath and do arrest and convent before them such as other (either) doth preach, speak or reason against their detestable and sinful living, or by the King's laws or otherwise them grieve, vex, trouble or displease : and them in prison do keep under the colour and name of heresy, until such time as by the said diocesans, Ordinaries, commissaries or their ministers enquiry is made of the living and conversation of the persons so arrested and convented ; that thereby may be gathered and made feigned articles for them to be examined of, and so perforced either to abjure and remain in perpetual prison, or else to be burned and utterly cast away for ever ; without that the said Diocesans, ordinaries or their commissaries hath any proves or witness in that behalf but

statute book within two years. They even thought, and said — on the eve of the execution of James Bainham — that their endeavours for the extirpation of heresy had already all but achieved their purpose. To the suggestion of the Commons for even more stringent heresy laws provided their effect is made known to the laity, " your said orators answer, this is undoubtedly a more charitable request than (as we trust) necessary, considering that by the aid of your highness, the pains of your Grace's statutes already made freely executed, your realm may be, in short time, clean purged from the few small dregs that do remain, if any do remain." (p. 165).

The prelates' implied ' non possumus ' to the Commons in the matter of the heresy laws was preceded, in the first section of their Answer, by an equally firm ' non possumus ' to the King himself. They roundly deny that any of their constitutions encroach upon the King's prerogative, or " extend to the interdiction of your lands and possessions." They say the King himself knows better. They deny that their laws " extend to the goods and possessions of your said lay subjects " except in one particular. " We remember no such ; and yet, if there be any such, it is but according to the common law of the Church, and also to your Grace's laws, which determine and decree that every person, spiritual or temporal, condemned of heresy shall forfeit his movables and immovables to your highness, or to the lord spiritual or temporal that by law hath right to them." (p. 159)'.

Then the Commons had complained — and this was the other

by their own uncharitable suspicion that such persons as they in manner aforesaid hath and do detain in prison do preach or inform anything, or any book do write or make, contrary to the Catholic Faith and determination of Holy Church : And without that the said Diocesans, ordinaries or commissaries safely hath or doth keep in prison, or hath, doth or will suffer in any wise the said persons so arrested to make their purgation : And without the said diocesans, ordinaries or commissaries do finish and determine such manner of business within three months " — as required by the statute — " but some of the said matters they keep depending more than four months, ten or twelve months and more (with the bodies of the parties in prison) unfinished and undetermined, to the extreme impoverishing and undoing of the King's subjects within this his Realm." (From the Record Office ms.).

Here we see plainly the chain of causation : the lay outcry against clerical greed and dissoluteness ; the answering cry of Heretic, Heretic ; and the lay uprising against the laws (and illegalities) which made that cry formidable.

main matter of principle raised in their ' Supplication ' — that the clergy in their Convocations enacted laws " concerning temporal things " " not having nor requiring your most royal assent to the same laws so by them made, neither any assent or knowledge of your lay subjects." The pretension of the laity to " a voice of assent " in ecclesiastical legislation the prelates merely ignore, doubtless as too presumptuous for attention. The like claim on behalf of the King they meet with a ceremonious but firm refusal. Why, it may be asked, was it made at all ? The royal assent to acts of Convocation was not a burning question. It had never in fact been raised at all ; the sovereigns had had other means of ensuring that the proceedings of Convocation should be acceptable to themselves. Moreover, at this time the legislative powers of Convocation had been almost in abeyance for over a century ; the last important occasion of their exercise had been the passage of Archbishop Arundel's constitutions against heresy in 1407. What then was the object of Cromwell and the Commons in this opening gambit of their ' Supplication ' ? It was, apparently, to raise the issue of sovereignty once for all, and, by playing upon the King's most sensitive nerve, to make sure of his support in their action against the hierarchy.

The claim once made, the prelates met it, to their honour be it said, with unequivocal candour.

" Forasmuch as we repute and take our authority of making of laws to be grounded upon the Scripture of God and the determination of Holy Church, which must also be a rule and square to try the justice and righteousness of all laws, as well spiritual as temporal, we verily trust that in such laws as have been made by us or by our predecessors, the same being sincerely interpreted and after the good meaning of the makers, there shall be found nothing contained in them but such as may be well justified by the said rule and square. And if it shall otherwise appear, as it is our duty, whereunto we shall always most diligently apply ourselves, to reform our ordinances to God's commission, and to conform our statutes and laws, and those of our predecessors, to the determination of Scripture and Holy Church, so we hope in God, and shall daily pray for the same, that your highness will, if there appear cause why, with the assent of your people, temper your Grace's laws accordingly ; whereby shall ensue a most sure and perfect conjunction and agreement, as God being *lapis angularis* to agree and conjoin the same.

" And as concerning the requiring of your highness's royal assent to the authorizing of such laws as have been by our predecessors or shall be made by us, in such points and articles as we have by good authority to rule and order by provisions and laws, we, knowing your highness's wisdom, virtue and learning, nothing doubt but that the same perceiveth how the granting thereunto dependeth not upon our will and liberty, and that we, your most humble subjects, may not submit the execution of our charges and duty, certainly prescribed by God, to your highness's assent ; although, of very deed, the same is most worthy for your most princely and excellent virtues, not only to give your royal assent, but also to devise and command what we should, for good order and manners, by statutes and laws provide in the Church. Nevertheless, considering we may not so, nor in such sort, restrain the doing of our office in the feeding and ruling of Christ's people your Grace's subjects, we — most humbly desiring your Grace, as the same has done heretofore, so from henceforth to show your Grace's mind and opinion unto us, what your highness's wisdom shall think convenient, which we shall most gladly hear and follow if it shall please God to inspire us so to do — with all submission and humility beseech the same, following the steps of your most noble progenitors, and conformably to your own acts, to maintain and defend such laws and ordinances as we, according to our calling and by the authority of God, shall, for His honour, make to the edification of virtue and the maintaining of Christ's faith, whereof your highness is defender in name, and has been hitherto in deed, a special protector." (pp. 157 - 8).

Here was the ' articulus stantis vel cadentis Ecclesiae,' the principle by which the Church stood or fell, as the Middle Ages accounted it. Its affirmation by the prelates was courteous but uncompromising. They could say no other. Their freedom, within the framework of the universal Canon Law, to make spiritual laws both for clergy and laity independently of any sort of secular assent was the most precious of the " liberties " assured to the Ecclesia Anglicana — which meant the clerical order and primarily the prelates — by Magna Carta. It had never hitherto been called in question. Convocational action unacceptable to the Crown or the Common Law had been countered in various ways as occasion arose ; but never by challenging the power of the Convocations to legislate freely in their own right. For the Commons to call it in question at that time of day was perhaps a pardonable solecism, which the amply learned Defender of the Faith could be trusted to dismiss as such. The Commons' claim upon the King's behalf was less presumptuous perhaps, but not more tenable, than their like pretension on behalf of the laity. They had, however, presented the prelates with a useful opportunity. The latter, rather more than a year before, had been ruffled and surprised into an acknowledgment of the King's Supreme Headship ; but they had saved their consciences by appending to it a qualification, ' quantum per Christi legem licet,' so far as the law of Christ allows. Some, like their friend the imperial ambassador Chapuys, had been sceptical of the value of that reservation : " no one now," Chapuys had written, " will be so bold as to contest with his lord the importance of this reservation " (V. no. 105). Here was the opportunity to show that they had been in earnest, and to tell the King, with profound respect, that by the law of Christ — " the Scripture of God and the determination of Holy Church," the " rule and square to try the justice and righteousness of all laws . . . . . ," there were concessions which they could not make, positions which they could not cede. On the matter in question, they could trust the King's " wisdom, virtue and learning " to acknowledge that they were in the right.

As to any suspicion or idea that the King was behind the Commons ' Supplication,' or that the document " really emanated from the Court," they were entirely innocent of it ; and they themselves, many of them, were familiars of the Court.*

---

* Eminent among them was the King's secretary, Bishop Stephen Gardiner. Misled, like other scholars, by the defective calendaring of these documents, Bishop Stubbs wrote (' Seventeen Lectures,' p. 281) : " The old antagonism

341

THE 'ANSWER' OF THE ORDINARIES

It was on the 18th March (1532), Hall tells us, that " the Common Speaker, accompanied with divers Knights and Burgesses of the Common House, came to the King's presence, and there declared to him how the temporal men of his Realm were sore aggrieved with the cruel demeanour of the Prelates and Ordinaries, which touched both their bodies and goods ; all which griefs the Speaker delivered to the King in writing, most humbly beseeching his Grace to take such an order and direction in that case as to his high wisdom might seem most convenient.

" Further, he beseeched the King to consider what pain, charge and cost his humble subjects of the nether House had sustained syth the beginning of this Parliament, and that it would please his Grace of his princely benignity to dissolve his court of Parliament, that his subjects might repair into their countries.

" When the King had received the Supplication of the Commons, he paused awhile and then said :

' It is not the office of a King, which is a Judge, to be too light of credence, nor I have not, nor will not, use the same ; for I will hear the party that is accused speak or (ere) I give any sentence. Your book containeth divers Articles of great and weighty matters, and, as I perceive, it is against the Spiritual persons and Prelates of our Realm ; of which thing you desire a redress and a reformation, which desire and request is mere contrariant to your last Petition ; for you require to have the Parliament dissolved and to depart into your countries, and yet you would have a reformation of your griefs with all diligence. Although that your pain have been great in tarrying, I assure you mine hath been no less than yours, and yet all the pain that I take for your wealths is to me a pleasure ; therefore, if you will have profit of your complaint, you must tarry the time or else to be without remedy.

' I much commend you that you will not contend nor stand in strife

of the Commons to the spiritual courts was utilised, and an address drawn up by the king's secretaries was put in their hands to be delivered to the king as the prayer of the Commons." But what Gardiner drafted, or had a main hand in drafting, was not the Supplication of the Commons but the prelates' " Answer " to it, and that in such reverential but uncompliant terms as to draw upon himself the King's displeasure.

with the Spiritual men, which be your Christian brethren ' — the King professes to regard the Commons ' Supplication as in the nature of an eirenicon — ' but much more methinketh that you should not contend with me that am your Sovereign Lord and King, considering that I seek peace and quietness of you.' (Chronicle II. pp. 202 - 3). And he therewith proceeds to rate the Commons for their obstinacy in refusing to follow the Lords in the acceptance of his Wardships Bill.

For some reason it was not until April 12th that Archbishop Warham brought the ' Supplication ' before the Houses of Convocation ; and about a fortnight was spent in careful consideration of their answer. It was presented to the King a few days before the end of the month. The King and his henchman in Parliament and the Council, Cromwell, were not long in making up their minds about it. To the article which especially concerned the King, that touching his " Jurisdiction and Prerogative Royal,' the prelates had returned a respectful but decided No ; and Cromwell would not fail to point out that, while declining to submit their own constitutions to the King's assent, the prelates, in the same breath, were moving him to withhold his assent from a bill for the redress of one of the lay grievances then pending in Parliament.

" The last day of April," Hall's story goes on, (ibid, ii., p. 209) " the Parliament sitting, the King sent for Thomas Audley, Speaker of the Common House, and certain other, and declared to them how they had exhibited a book of their grieves the last year " (that is, in the last month, before the end of March) " against the Spiritualty : which, at their requests, he had delivered to his spiritual subjects to make answer thereto ; but he could have no answer till within three days last past : which answer he delivered to the Speaker, saying, ' We think their answer will smally please you, for it seemeth to Us very slender. You be a great sort of wisemen ; I doubt not but you will look circumspectly on the matter, and We will be indifferent between you.' "

With that encouragement to critical debate the Commons retired. What course their debates took we are not informed. In any case they were not prolonged. Within a week or so the King and

Cromwell had decided to bring matters to an issue by repeating the expedient which had proved so effective the year before in the enforced acknowledgment of the Supreme Headship. It was to present the prelates with a set of cut and dried propositions to which their assent was peremptorily required. Accordingly on May 10th Dr. Edward Fox, a member of Convocation but also King's Almoner, brought before Convocation three staggering demands : first, that they should only assemble by the King's writ : second, that they should not in future enact or execute any constitutions without the King's licence and assent : and thirdly, that they should submit all constitutions made in time past to the arbitrament of a mixed Parliamentary Commission, who should have power, by a majority, to annul all such as were held " not to stand with God's laws and the laws of the Realm."

Immediately the swift tragi-comedy of the year before was re-enacted. There were a few days of distracted consultations, comings and goings, references at home to the invalid Fisher of Rochester — the one tower of moral strength they had among them, — desperate and unavailing suggestions of compromise, chief among them that the concessions demanded should apply only to the King and his natural life. Meanwhile, within these few days, the King was fingering critically the episcopal oaths, and well perceiving, as he said, that the Bishops, swearing fealty to the Pope, " be but half our subjects, yea, and scarce our subjects," was requiring the Commons " to invent some order " in the matter (ibid. p. 210). Meanwhile, also, the plague at the moment was growingly rife in London ; King, prelates and all concerned had to think of their bodies as well as their souls, and prorogation was imperative. In short — and its whole shrift was very short, — on Wednesday, April 15th, five days after the royal ultimatum, Convocation gave in, prelates and proctors surrendering at discretion.

Of all the Bishops present and voting the one out-and-out dissentient was John Clerk of Bath and Wells. How far they realised the import of what they had been brought to do it is not easy to say. Perhaps none of them, except possibly Fisher, who was above all things a man of principle, understood that, so far as

344

England was concerned, they had written Finis to the great story of the Middle Ages, laid their mediaeval imperium at the feet of the Crown, and made a final cession of powers which, by the law of Christ, they had claimed as inalienably their own. Some must have realised that if the subjection of spiritual authority within the realm were to be followed by the rejection of any spiritual authority beyond the realm, their power to make head against it was at an end. Opposition would smack of treason ; and politician-prelates like Gardiner saw that they would have to frame their minds accordingly. The cause of their surrender they could not well disguise from themselves. They had suddenly found that, formidably attacked, they had no backing anywhere, and that, for reasons of his own, the King, upon whose support they had confidently leaned, was hand in glove with the insurgent Commons. One at least must have known why opinion, especially in London, had turned against them, and, when not actively hostile, was indifferent to their fate. Bishop Standish of St. Asaph was none other than the " one poor friar " who had had to throw himself on the King's protection when himself charged with heresy in the Convocation of 1515 (see above pp. 145 - 52). One can but wonder whether Standish, in the bitterness of his spirit, forbore the temptation to tell his brother prelates that, before joining battle with the lawyers over the criminous clerk and helping Fitzjames to save his wretched chancellor from justice, they would have done well to look ahead and count the cost.

Cromwell saw to it that the terms of the surrender, presently to be embodied in an Act of Parliament, left nothing to be desired in the way of explicitness.

" We your most humble subjects, daily orators and bedesmen of your clergy of England, having our special trust and confidence in your most excellent wisdom, your princely goodness and fervent zeal to the promotion of God's honour and Christian religion, and also in your learning, far exceeding, in our judgment, the learning of all other kings and princes that we have read of, and doubting nothing but that the same shall still continue and daily increase in your Majesty,

First, do offer and promise, *in verbo sacerdotii*, here unto your highness, submitting ourselves most humbly to the same, that we will never from henceforth enact, put in ure, promulge, or execute any new canons or constitutions provincial, or any other new ordinance, provincial or synodal, in our Convocation or synod in time coming, — which Convocation is, always has been, and must be, assembled only by your highness' commandment of writ — unless your highness by your royal assent shall license us to assemble our Convocation, and to make, promulge and execute such constitutions and ordinances as shall be made in the same ; and thereto give your royal assent and authority.

Secondly, that whereas divers of the constitutions, ordinances and canons, provincial or synodal, which have been heretofore enacted, be thought to be not only much prejudicial to your prerogative royal, but also overmuch onerous to your highness' subjects, your clergy aforesaid is contented, if it may stand so with your highness' pleasure, that it be committed to the examination and judgment of your Grace and of thirty-two persons, whereof sixteen to be of the upper and nether House of the temporalty, and other sixteen of the clergy, all to be chosen and appointed by your most noble Grace. So that finally, whichsoever of the said constitutions, ordinances or canons, provincial or synodal, shall be thought and determined by your Grace and by the most part of the said thirty-two persons not to stand with God's laws and the laws of your realm, the same to be abrogated and taken away by your Grace and the clergy ; and such of them as shall be seen by your Grace, and by the most part of the said thirty-two persons, to stand with God's laws and the laws of your realm, to stand in full strength and power, your Grace's most royal assent and authority once impetrate and fully given to the same " (Gee and Hardy, pp. 176 - 8).

In the Act of Submission (1534) it is made clear that any vacancies caused by death among the thirty-two laymen or clergy of the Commission the King is to fill up by nomination from " the said two Houses of the Parliament." It is to be purely a Parliamentary Commission, with the King appointing, presiding, and giving, when need be, a casting vote. Mercifully, it perished in embryo.

In a former passage (above, pp. 241 - 2) I hazarded a suggestion that the 'Supreme Head' idea was really Cromwell's. I feel less hesitation, indeed none at all, in attributing this latest development to the same source. For consider what it meant. The Canon Law of the Church Universal, so far as it is recited or reflected in the provincial constitutions of Canterbury and York — assumed to be the whole law that counts* — is to be submitted to the arbitrament of an English Parliamentary Commission, which is to have power to bind or loose, retain or reject, according as its august content shall be deemed by a majority to stand or not with God's laws and the laws of this realm. A proposition so sacrilegious in its audacity, so bluntly assertive of an ecclesiastical nationalism, so profoundly uncatholic as the word catholic was then understood, could have had its birth nowhere but in the masterful and unmannerly brain of Thomas Cromwell. How came it that the King, who was nothing if not catholic, fell in with it so readily? The answer is perhaps to be found in his inflated sense of sovereignty, which seems to have acted as a sort of solvent and absorbent of every other sense. As we have seen (above, p. 153), he had already given pointed expression to it in the course of the bickerings with Convocation in 1515. " By the ordinance and sufferance of God We are King of England, and the Kings of England in time past have never had any superior but God only. Wherefor know you well that We will maintain the right of our Crown and of our Temporal jurisdiction as well in this point as in all others." Henry's foible was to be taken for every inch a King, even to the compass of his personable calves. It had grown upon him in the intervening years ; and in these last days Cromwell, investing him with a Supreme Headship and a lordship of Convocation, was offering him on a platter a surfeit of sovereignty, knowing that his ' imperial ' stomach would digest it all. Many writers and historians, from Cardinal Pole onwards, have regarded the King and Cromwell as playing a deep, double game, directed from the outset to the repudiation of the papal authority. So it

---

* This may need stressing, in view of certain expressions in Chap. IV. of the Report of the Archbishops' Commission on Canon Law, just published).

might well seem in the light of events. But to the actors upon the great stage the light of events is only vouchsafed in a very limited degree* ; and if simple motives will account for what they do, those simple motives may well be the true ones. The King, it must be remembered, had himself no quarrel with the clergy ; and the action which he took at their expense and at the instance of the Commons was sufficiently commended to him as tending to the enlargement of his sovereignty and the replenishment of his purse. And the same straightforward explanation applies to Cromwell. He was simply a consummate man of business who, launched into politics, found a situation and an opportunity, and proceeded, with a firm and intrepid grasp of realities, to make what he could of both. A London citizen, he shared to the full the feeling of his fellow-citizens, and of his colleagues in the Commons, that the wealth and power of the clerical order had increased, was increasing, and ought to be diminished. If its diminishment spelt fortune for himself, riches for the Crown, and an easier passage for the King's policies, the Divorce and what not, that was so much to the good. Of course he was at pains, like any other intelligent politician, to forecast the course of events and to plan accordingly. And his distinction is that when the time was ripe his measures were not hand-to-mouth expedients, but integral parts of an ordered plan, based upon a principle which was not without virtue, and which men in general could understand and apply. It is the more strange that he should rank, in the eyes of so much of what ranks as history, as merely or mainly an intriguer and a destroyer. The work of few has stood more solidly.

May 15th, 1532, the date of the Submission, is a landmark. From one point of view, it marks the retreat and capitulation of a great Order. From another and wider, it meant that that Order

---

* " It is so much easier, in discussing the causes and stages of a political contest, to generalise from the results than to trace the growth of the principles maintained by the actors, that the historian is in some danger of substituting his own formulated conclusions for the programme of the leaders, and of giving them credit for a far more definite scheme and more conscious political sagacity than they would ever have claimed for themselves." Stubbs, Const. Hist. 11, pp. 557 - 8.

was relieved of sole responsibility, and that a share of it was being taken over by the laity, represented by the Crown in Parliament. That was, and remains to this day, the constitutional principle of the reformed Church in England, the Church of England as it is significantly called.* The principle was accepted, under pressure

* Unfortunately the tradition was not continuous. While Henry lived, from 1534 onwards, the Royal Supremacy was a constitutional fact which nobody argued. It meant the Supremacy of the King in Parliament, or, alternatively, of the King in Convocation, subject to the overriding authority of Parliament. And the King himself being a Member, and the one indispensable Member, of any Parliament, the old debate as to whether the Supremacy, as originally conceived, was royal or parliamentary, becomes largely unreal. Parliament, as authoritatively defined by legists, " means the King, the House of Lords, and the House of Commons ; these three bodies acting together may be aptly described as the ' King in Parliament,' and constitute Parliament " (Dicey, ' Law of the Constitution,' p. 37). Not one single act was done by virtue of the Supremacy in Henry's reign except by authority either of (a) the King in Parliament, or (b) the King in Convocation, or (c) both acting in conjunction. (A) is illustrated by all the ecclesiastical statutes from 1534 onwards ; (b) by the royal ordinance for the observance of holy days issued August 11, 1536 by letters patent under signet, the enacting words of which are " it is therefore by the king's highness' authority as supreme head on earth of the Church of England, with the common consent of the prelates and clergy of this realm in Convocation lawfully assembled and congregate, among other things decreed, ordained and established," etc. (Report of Royal Commission on Ecclesiastical Courts, 1883, p. xxvii) ; (c) by the preamble of the Six Articles Act of 1539, which states that " after a great and long, deliberate, and advised disputation and consultation had and made concerning the said articles, as well by the consent of the king's highness, as by the assent of the Lords spiritual and temporal, and other learned men of his clergy in their Convocation, and by the consent of the Commons in this present Parliament assembled, it was and is finally resolved," etc. (ibid. Historical Appendix iv, p. 117, cf. Gee and Hardy, p. 305).

The powers of visitation and injunction exercised by Cromwell as Vicegerent were all provided for in the Supremacy Act of 1534. That Act merely extended the King's sovereignty to the ecclesiastical sphere ; but, like all sovereignty in this country, it was, as in other spheres, constitutional, not solely personal.

But not long after Henry's death there begins to emerge the notion that the Supremacy was some mystic endowment of the royal person which the King's colleagues in Parliament were to share only on sufferance or not at all. This aberration of doctrine, developed to the extreme by Stuart pedants and pulpiteers, was only extirpated at, and by, the Revolution of 1688, having helped to involve the country meanwhile in Civil War, regicide, the temporary supersession of Parliament, military government, and an attempt to subvert the Reformation settlement by a royal assumption of dispensing power.

The King and Cromwell, with all their faults, were statesmen ; the Supremacy had been, and could only have been, established by Parliament, and neither ever thought of cutting loose from Parliament. Henry was very much a King ; but he told Parliament himself, in 1543, that never was he so much a King as when King in Parliament. " We be informed by my judges that we at no-time stand so highly in our Royal estate as in the time of Parliament, wherein We

of course, by a wholly catholic prelacy, on the demand of a very catholic King, at the instance of a House of Commons expressly protesting itself catholic : all being at the time in full communion with the Pope. It was a new experiment in catholicity, like Christianity itself. Of it might have been said, as of the original experiment, " If this counsel or this work be of men, it will come to nought." There are who would persuade us that it was wholly of men, and of the worst that was in men ; but of that its survival in ever-growing strength is a sufficient refutation. Though the rain descended, and the floods came, and the winds blew, it fell not, because it too, as its sons believed, was founded upon a rock. The new order, in its inception,* had very little to do with Anne Boleyn or the Divorce, and nothing at all to do with certain extremities of action which were to darken the coming period of the reign. But it had everything to do with the determination of an adult laity to have a voice in the making of the laws which governed them, and to have done with clerical domination and the incubus of prelates like Bishop Fitzjames. No longer mere " subjects " of the clergy, they claimed their own share of responsibility ; and have exercised it ever since, not unfaithfully, through the Crown in Parliament, and latterly also through Houses of Laity established by an Enabling Act of Parliament.

as head and you as members are conjoined and knit together in one body politic " (Tanner, Const. Doc. p. 582).

The first impulse towards statutory reform came from the uprising of the laity in the Commons against the arbitrary nature and action of the ecclesiastical laws ; and it is not to be supposed that the Commons intended to vest a like arbitrariness, but even more formidable and irresponsible, in the King's person. There is documentary proof that they had no such intention, and their subsequent conduct shows it.

* For another view, succinctly expressed, cf. Dr. Gairdner in Dictionary of English Church History, p. 272, art. Heresy : " The Reformation here began with a royal despotism which wilfully stirred up heresy to help in destroying that supreme power at Rome on which existing church order depended."

Chapter X

SOME LINKING PASSAGES, AND A SUMMING-UP

This inquiry is not designed to extend beyond the point to which events may be said to have been discernibly influenced by what had happened in, and in connection with, the case of Richard Hunne. Within nine months of the time now reached, they began to be governed by a very different event, the clandestine marriage of Henry and Anne Boleyn, entailing action by the Crown in Parliament against papal jurisdiction, papal claims, and any in England who were disposed to favour, or resolute to maintain them. That is another, and in the main a self-contained, story ; and it is beyond the scope of this book. But the following summary may be useful to the reader as linking what has been told in detail of the first three years of the Parliament with the events, much more rapid and momentous, which took place in the last three.

On May 16th (1532) Archbishop Warham presented to the King the document embodying the ' Submission of the Clergy,' accepted by Convocation on the previous day. " Thomas Cromwell, Esquire " and four titled personages of the Court were specially summoned as witnesses of the ceremony. On the same day Sir Thomas More received the King's gracious permission to resign the Chancellorship, in which he had succeeded Wolsey two and a half years earlier. More, in entering upon office, had had some hard things to say about Wolsey ; but Wolsey was no sooner dead, a year later, than his own world began to crumble ; the clergy were stricken with the blow of praemunire, and having to ransom themselves by an enormous fine and the recognition of the King's Supreme Headship. Chapuys wrote at the time : " There is none that do not blame this usurpation except those who have promoted it. The Chancellor is so mortified at it that he is anxious above all things to resign his office " (V. no. 112). He remained, however, pursuing his legal work faithfully, but deprived of all political influence by his steadfast disapproval of the King's divorce project. After another year came another blow. The Commons had formally impeached the Ordinaries, the Bishops and their legal officers, and had attacked their Courts and Convocations. Whether More was consulted in the framing of their Answer we do not know. It was natural that he should have been ; and the Answer, both in matter and manner, reflected faithfully what we know to have been the mind of More on all the issues in debate. Its summary rejection as regards its most vital article, the surrender by Convocation of its independent powers, the subjection of the Canon Law to the scrutiny of a parliamentary commission, all must have been felt by More as a grievous shock. He felt that he could no longer go on ; and the King, with the benignity which he knew so well how to assume, was pleased to release him. Writes Chapuys again (May 22nd) : " The Chancellor has resigned, seeing that affairs were going on badly, and likely to be worse, and that if he retained his office he would be obliged to act against his conscience or incur the King's displeasure, as he had already begun to do, for refusing to take his part against the clergy. His excuse is that his emolument (traictement) was too small, and that he was not equal to the work. Everyone is concerned, for there never was a better man in the office " (V. no. 1046). More was not built for politics, but he was not lacking in courage ; and had he foreseen, more certainly than he did, the imminence of sterner storms to come, he might have felt it his duty to remain on the bridge. As it was, his one feeling was of intense relief at being quit of office, and free to devote himself to his prayers, his family, and his literary and other efforts to make head against heresy. His withdrawal removed a silent reproach from the royal presence, and a possible embarrassment from the path of Cromwell.

For the next three months it is the pathetic figure of the aged Archbishop that occupies the stage. Warham held a key position in Henry's plans. For a long time the King, appealing to the decrees of certain Councils, had contended that by right law ecclesiastical suits should be heard and determined in the province within which they arose, and that, consequently, the proper judge in his matrimonial suit was the Archbishop of Canterbury. But Warham of late had been showing signs of restiveness. Constitutionally timid, the thought of his own final account was beginning to prevail over other fears. In February, well before the date of the Submission, he had executed a formal instrument repudiating all that had been done in Parliament to the prejudice of the Apostolic See and of his own Church of Canterbury. It was by no means certain that if the King's case was brought before him he would consent to entertain it in face of a papal inhibition, still less pronounce the obliging sentence required. Now over eighty, he had spoken of himself, in the ' Answer ' to the ' Supplication,' as " a man spent, and at the point to depart this world." But he was an unconscionable time in dying ; and Cromwell, whose instinct was to keep things moving, was no doubt chafing at the delay. It is worry that kills ; and, adopting an expedient which had been the beginning of the end of Wolsey, an attempt was made to hasten matters by involving the Archbishop in a charge of ' praemunire.' The charge was as preposterous as such charges usually were. The alleged offence was fourteen years old. In 1518 Warham had consecrated Standish to the see of St. Asaph before ascertaining that the latter had exhibited his bulls of appointment to the King with a view to the restitution of his temporalities. The Archbishop met the charge with unwonted spirit. There survives in the Record Office a draft of a speech prepared by him or his chaplains apparently for delivery in the House of Lords (V. no. 1247). It is a masterly appeal to reason and history, the spirit of Becket flaring up once again before flickering out. The Archbishop denies utterly that his action in the case of Standish or any other such case can be blameworthy, let alone criminal. To admit the principle of the charge would be to allow that the exercise of the pastoral office could be held up indefinitely at the whim of any temporal ruler. He, Warham, " would rather be hewn in pieces than confess this article, for which St. Thomas died, to be a praemunire." The speech is further remarkable for its conclusion, which shows that a moment of clairvoyance had been vouchsafed to the old Primate in his last days. He, like Wolsey before him, had been offered the

M

help of lay counsel for his defence. He replies drily and pointedly as follows :

" And where it pleaseth you, my Lord, to assign to me lay counsel : my Lord, I will not refuse their counsel being good, albeit for two causes I think they shall little profit me. One, for laymen have always used, and be accustomed to advance their own laws rather than the laws of Holy Church ; as your Lordships may see that laymen daily encroacheth upon the laws and liberties of the Church by praemunires and prohibitions ; whom Christ rebuketh in the Gospel, saying, ' Wo worth ye that break the law of God for the maintaining of your own laws. Wo vobis qui transgredimini legem Dei propter traditiones vestras.' And in this behalf I understand that such temporal learned men as have been assigned of counsel with spiritual men lately in cases of praemunire (as it was surmised), for the advancing of their temporal laws and for the derogation of the laws of the Church, have counselled them and induced them to confess and grant a praemunire. Whereto peradventure they would advise me in likewise, which if I were so minded to confess, I needed not to have their counsel " (from the ms. V. no. 1247).

The passage shows that the bluff of praemunire was wearing thin, and that even the harassed prelates were beginning to see through it. The charge went no further, the promoters not wishing to have their bluff called, and themselves disconcerted by having to produce the hobgoblin statute in open court.

Other artifice was unnecessary, death coming to the old Archbishop on August 22nd.

There was an immediate acceleration in the pace of events. Within hardly more than a week (September 1st) Anne Boleyn was created ' Marquess ' of Pembroke and endowed with handsome estates. Within the same month (September 30th) Dr. Nicholas Hawkins was given his credentials for replacing Dr. Cranmer, Archdeacon of Taunton, " quem nuper revocavimus," whom We have lately recalled, at the court of the Emperor. Dr. Cranmer, a diplomat-divine of Lutheran leanings, and an ingenious and industrious promoter of the Divorce, had been already marked down as Warham's successor. In order to advertise to the world their perfect accord as against Pope and Emperor, an elaborate meeting between Henry and Francis I on French soil had for some time been projected ; and duly took place, with ceremonious pageantry, in the latter part of October. It had been intended that the new Marquess should accompany the King in some state ; but the arrangements for this had to be countermanded because no reputable lady of the French Court could be found willing to receive her. Anne had her moment, however. On Sunday the 28th, the day but one before their leavetaking, the two sovereigns supped sumptuously together at Calais.

" After supper came in the Marchioness of Pembroke, with seven Ladies in masking apparel, ... The Lady Marquess took the French King, and the Countess of Derby took the King of Navarre, and every Lady took a Lord, and in dancing the King of England took away the ladies' visors, so that there the ladies' beauties were shewed ; and after they had danced awhile they ceased, and the French King talked with the Marchioness of Pembroke a space ; and then he took his leave of the Ladies, and the King conveyed him to his lodging." On the 30th " the two Kings departed out of Calais and came near to Sandyngfeld, and there alighted in a fair green place, where was a table set ; and there the Englishmen served the Frenchmen of wine, Ypocras, fruit and spice abundantly. When the two Kings had communed a little, they mounted on their horses, and at the very entering of the French ground they took hands, and with princely countenance, loving behaviour and hearty words, each embraced other and so there departed."

And here at this point, if it be not beneath the dignity of History to say so, the Clerk of the Weather, as more than once has happened with us, decided to take a hand in the great game. A sudden, fierce gale blew up and swept the Channel for a fortnight. Seagoing was impossible ; La Manche became the sleeve of fate. Hall thus depicts the seascape as viewed from Calais and the continental seaboard :

" When the King was returned to Calais, many gentlemen took ship to sail into England, but the wind was so contrariant that divers of them were driven back again into Calais, and divers into

Flanders ; and in November rose such a wind, of the North and North-west, that all the ships in Calais haven were in great jeopardy, and in especial the hoys ; at which season was such a spring tide that it brake the walls of Holland and Zeeland, and drowned divers towns in Flanders, in so much that the water rose three feet above the wharf where the Quay stood in Antwerp ; this storm continued till the fourth day of November, but for all that the wind changed not. The eighth day rose such a wind, tempest and thunder that no man could conveniently stir in the streets of Calais ; much lamentation was made for them that had taken ship into England, for no man knew what was become of them. On Sunday the weather was fair ; the King caused his bed and other things to be shipped, and intended to depart ; but suddenly rose such a mist that no Master could guide a ship, and so he tarried that day. On Tuesday at midnight he took ship, and landed at Dover the morrow after, being the fourteenth day of November, ..." (Chronicle ii, pp. 220 - 1).

All these days the King and Anne were thrown together in intimate association, with nothing to do. Henry, so he later averred, had been advised by Francis to marry his favourite out of hand ; but he was nothing if not cautious, and statesman enough to know the hazards of such a course. Anne, at the -moment, may have been less inclined to circumspection. Hitherto it would seem that, despite some rumour and scandal, she had kept the King's passion simmering by holding him off. By this time she may have thought her prospects secure enough to justify risks. Her new dignity, a renewed draught of the lively French atmosphere she had breathed in youth, the exhilaration of the recent festivities, a spice perhaps of the ' esprit gaulois,' may have gone to her long and, as some said, lovely head. Be that as it may, the storm, in due course, blew itself out ; and in due course, some two months after his return, the King found it necessary to recognise certain ' faits accomplis ' by going through a form of marriage with Anne.

To this day no one knows for certain when, where, or by whom the marriage, so-called, was solemnised. The date later given out was on or about January 25th, St. Paul's Day. For a time the event had to be kept a close secret ; no inkling of it could be allowed to reach the Roman Court before the bulls for the appointment of Dr. Cranmer, whose task as Archbishop would be to pronounce the marriage valid, had been duly obtained. To get the bulls put through expeditiously and cheaply, the permissive proviso of the Annates Act was brought into play, and the power given to the King by Parliament NOT to put the Act into operation was dangled like a carrot before the Roman authorities. Meanwhile, as early as February 8th, the faithful Chapuys had conveyed to the Emperor the Queen's acute apprehension at the hasty appointment of Cranmer, advised that the bulls should be withheld until the position was clearer, and written that ' if the Pope knew the report that was current here about the new Archbishop being a Lutheran, he would not be too hasty to admit and confirm him (VI. no. 142). It was, however, easy for Henry's agents abroad to convey the impression that their efforts for the Divorce were not really of their own volition; and Cranmer was among those who seem to have done so.* Besides, the hope of continuing to receive the Annates from England was a strong argument for not disobliging the English King, and for giving the dubious Archbishop-designate the benefit of any doubt. The bulls were despatched ; Cranmer was consecrated on March 30th ; within ten days the clandestine marriage was an open secret ; and on April 11th the new Archbishop wrote to the King praying his permission to hear and determine his cause of matrimony : a prayer which, after a still more obsequious repetition by " the most principal minister of Our spiritual jurisdiction," the King was graciously pleased to grant.

Meanwhile Parliament was occupied with one of the most remarkable measures that ever reached the statute book, the Act for the Restraint of Appeals. It was at once declaratory and

---

* Friedmann (' Anne Boleyn,' W. I. 179, n. 1) quotes from the Vienna Archives a letter from Granvelle to Chapuys, dated Sept. 26, 1535 :
" Je mesbahys fort des termes estranges que comme lon a entendu du couste de Rome tient larchevesque de Canturbery mesmes en laffaire des Royne et Princesse, actendu que durant le temps quil estoit resident en ceste court il blasmoit mirablement ce que le Roy dangleterre son maistre et ses autres ministres faisoient en laffaire du divorce encontre les dictes Royne et Princesse."

retrospective. It declared the law of the constitution to be such and such, and invalidated processes begun, among others by the King and Queen, on the secure assumption that the law of the constitution was in fact quite otherwise. On the strength of " divers sundry old authentic histories and chronicles," it affirmed " this realm of England " to be " an empire — governed by one supreme head and king, having the dignity and royal estate of the imperial crown of the same " . . . . . that part of the " body politic, called the spiritualty, now being usually called the English Church," being " sufficient and meet of itself, without the intermeddling of any exterior person or persons, to declare and determine " all spiritual causes. It enacts " that all causes testamentary, causes of matrimony and divorces, rights of tithes, oblations and obventions (the knowledge whereof by the goodness of princes of this realm, and by the laws and customs of the same, appertaineth to the spiritual jurisdiction of this realm) already commenced, moved, depending, being, happening, or hereafter coming in contention, debate or question within this realm . . . . shall be from henceforth heard, examined, discussed, clearly, finally and definitively adjudged and determined within the king's jurisdiction and authority, and not elsewhere." (Gee and Hardy, pp. 187 - 90).

In these enacting words two things are to be observed. First, there is no mention of the very important branch of jurisdiction concerning rights of patronage, the reason of course being that processes and appeals to Rome in regard to these had long been barred by the old Statutes of Provisors, which had reference to rights of patronage and nothing else. What this new Act did was to extend to the whole field of jurisdiction an inhibition which had long applied, on paper at least, to one important part of it. As to the suggestion that " divers and sundry inconveniences and dangers " had " arisen and sprung by reason of appeals sued out of this realm to the see of Rome in causes testamentary, causes of matrimony," etc. because they were " not provided for plainly " by the Statutes of Provisors, it is mere propaganda, a pure ' suggestio falsi ' ; since the Statutes of Provisors neither had, nor made, any reference to these matters. It has the same relation to truth as the broader suggestion that the Statutes of Provisors were designed to defend the King's prerogative by barring all appeals to Rome, instead of one particular category of appeals. It is strange that preambular propaganda of this kind — and there is a good deal of it in Cromwell's drafts — should ever have been taken at its face value. One can only respectfully insist that, in a matter of plain historical fact, a perversion of the truth does not become other than it is for being put, and even put repeatedly, into the mouth of Parliament.

Secondly, we have to observe the words which point to the immediate purpose of the Act, and make it retrospective : the words " already commenced, moved, depending, being, happening." They were designed to invalidate, by the law of Parliament, the Queen's long-pending appeal to Rome, and to render anyone doing an act in furtherance of that appeal liable to the penalties of ' praemunire.' The immediate object was to leave Queen Katherine no recourse but to the court which the new Primate, appointed for the purpose, was to open at Dunstable ; and to leave her no appeal from that court but to the Upper House of Convocation, which, by resolutions adopted as this very time, had prejudged the case against her. Such was the statute to which, after five years' prate of justice, the last gentleman in Europe was to append the time-honoured words, ' Le Roy le veult.' In a manful colloquy with the King, Chapuys ventured upon a strong remonstrance, protesting that " laws were prospective and not retrospective " (VI. no. 351). The true word about the statute has been said by Henry's stoutest and most ingenious apologist. Writing in the tradition of that Protestant chivalry which was presently to emerge, Froude says (History, 1. pp., 434 - 6) :

" It is open to the censure which we ever feel entitled to pass upon a measure enacted to meet the particular position of a particular person. . . . . Our instincts tell us that no legislation should be retrospective, and should affect only positions which have been entered into with a full knowledge at the time of the condition of the laws.

" The statute endeavours to avoid the difficulty by its declaratory form ; but again this is unsatisfactory ; for that the Pope possessed some authority was substantially acknowledged in every application which was made to him ; and when Catherine had married under a papal dispensation, it was a strange thing to turn upon her, and to say, not only that the dispensation in the particular instance had been unlawfully granted, but that the Pope had no jurisdiction in the matter by the laws of the land which she had entered.

" On the other hand . . . . .

" Yet, if we allow full weight to these considerations, a feeling of painful uncertainty continues to cling to us ; and in ordinary cases to be uncertain on such a point is to be in reality certain. The state of the law could not have been clear, or the Statute of Appeals would not have been required ; and explain it as we may, it was in fact passed for a special cause against a special person ; and that person a woman."

The simple explanation was that the King, impelled by his afflicting conscience, was behaving as he did in order to make good his case that, having all along been a bachelor, he was not a bigamist, and that his marriage with Anne had been good, like everything else he thought and did. One of the most appalling egoists in history, he had to be right though the heavens fell. Taken for all in all, the affair was abominable ; but nearly all the men of consequence in that Catholic generation, from the King downwards, were blind, or from fear or interest or party spirit turned a blind eye, to its baseness ; in so much that the tiny few who saw it for what it was and stood out against it to the last, appear before posterity as saints and martyrs. The whole business of the Divorce shows how generally, on its moral side, mediaeval Catholicism had gone to seed. Yet it is open to its apologists, in this age of divorces while you wait, to insist that other things have gone to seed as well. It is not for us to be over-ready to cast stones.

The remarkable thing about this Statute of Appeals is its scope and range. Regarded as a means of invalidating the Queen's appeal, it would be like using a sledgehammer to crack a nut. Cromwell's mind, which was not at all a common mind, looked far beyond that immediate object. He saw, and was the first to see, that in England at any rate the Mediaeval order, with its balance of magistracy between spiritualty and temporalty, Pope and King, was foundering

360

in the welter of the Divorce ; and that the task in hand was to design and construct, from the keel upwards, a new vessel of state, the self-contained and self-determining State as we moderns know it, based, not upon a theory, but upon the fact of Sovereignty, and symbolised by the ' Imperial ' Crown, owning no obeisance to the triple crown of Rome or any other. And the Statute of Appeals is Cromwell's essay in laying the keel. Events proved that his design of the State-to-be was on the whole sound, though its lay-out included some elements of make-believe to which it is unprofitable to shut one's eyes. For instance, the penalties for infraction were those " ordained and provided by the Statute of Provision and Praemunire," a title previously unknown to the statute book. The reference is to 16 Richard 11, c. 5, ' Concerning Provisors and others,' which is wrested from its proper purpose and to the purposes of the new despotism by distorting its title and perverting its text. Again, " divers sundry old authentic histories and chronicles " appears a queer sort of basis on which to re-found a constitution, though there was really more in it than might appear at first sight. Cromwell's antique material was, so far as it went, a witness against the innovating Papacy of recent centuries. It served its turn as a warrant for reversion.

The passage of the Bill marks a critical point, and a turning point, in the history of this Parliament, already over three years old. It had no easy passage, even in the Commons. Its evident purpose was an offence to the generous instincts of the House. They had recently been overhauling the ecclesiastical courts ; and they had no wish to add to the authority of the prelates, or to devolve upon their courts the profitable litigation which had hitherto gone over their heads to Rome. The mercantile element saw in the Bill the first decisive motion against the Pope, with whom they themselves, and the Commons in general, had no particular quarrel : and they were apprehensive of its effect upon relations with the Emperor and their own trade with Flanders. On the other side the Government party, known then as " the King's servants," was strong, and strongly led by the member for Taunton, Privy Councillor Cromwell, long a powerful influence in the House, and now suddenly beginning to be recognised, by observers like Chapuys, as " powerful with the King " (VI. no. 351).

Seven years of controversy had furnished Cromwell and his supporters with an ample armoury of debate. They could urge the vexatious delays and charges attendant upon appeals to Rome ; the interminable vacillations of the Roman Court in dealing with the King's own suit ; the Pope's political subservience to the Emperor ; his fear of his own shadow and of the Emperor's soldiery ; the King's unquiet conscience, his Grace being publicly chidden by Court preachers for having lived in sin for a quarter of a century with a Queen who, according to Leviticus and some respectable Universities, had never really been his wife at all ; his natural desire for a male heir ; the necessity of an undisputed succession if the nation was not to be haunted by the spectre of another civil war ; the fact that the papal claims to jurisdiction were the product of quite recent centuries, the truth being that " no worldly laws, ordinances, jurisdiction or authority of any person, at the beginning of the Catholic Faith nor long after, was practised, experimented or put in execution within this realm but only such as was ordained, made, devised and depended of the Imperial Crown of the same." On occasion former Kings and Parliaments had stoutly withstood those claims : and the present Parliament " were marvellously to be noted both negligent and unnatural to their commonweal and to the privilege of their Realm and Native Country if they should not as well now foresee and purvey for the maintenance and supportation of the Imperial dignity, jurisdiction spiritual and temporal, of this Realm, as their predecessors have done in time past."* With such arguments the bill was pushed through. Henceforward the Commons had to follow the logic of their own decision, and to go the whole way with the King and Cromwell. So far the forms of courtesy had been observed ; the Statute of Appeals still speaks respectfully of the See of Rome and the Court of Rome. The year after (1534), in the three statutes which severed the legal

* The words in inverted commas are taken from one of the original drafts of the Statute in the Record Office, no. 3 in State Papers, Henry VIII, N fol. : cf. L. and P. VI, no. 120 (7).

strands attaching England to the Papacy, the phrase has become personal and opprobrious ; it is " the Bishop of Rome, otherwise called the pope." The fight was on, and the gloves were off.

Cromwell and the King — the order is not inappropriate, for the King, by marrying Anne, had put himself in the hands of Cromwell and become committed to the line of action which Cromwell, foreseeing the issue, had been meditating and preparing, — having got their ad hoc Primate and their ad hoc Act of Parliament, lost no time in putting both to use. On Saturday, May 10th, Cranmer opened his court at Dunstable, a few miles from Ampthill where the Queen was residing, and at a discreet distance from London and its ribald mobs. On Monday the 19th, with all the splendid pageantry of the River, Anne was escorted from Greenwich to the Tower, where she was to lodge until the eve of her Coronation. Meanwhile the court which was to decide that the Queen was an unmarried widow and no queen, was in session at Dunstable, divines and canonists reviewing once more the legal intricacies, the old and threadbare indecencies of the case. Katherine remained at Ampthill, ignoring the citation, the court and everything to do with it. On Friday the 23rd the Archbishop, declaring her contumacious, proceeded to sentence, pronouncing her marriage with Henry null and void. Five days afterwards, on Wednesday the 28th, after an inquiry at Lambeth as secret as the alleged marriage itself, he pronounced the King and Anne Boleyn to have been duly married. On Saturday the last day of May, with all the civic pageantry which the King could order and the City Companies devise, Anne was conducted in gorgeous procession from the Tower to Westminster. And on the following day, Whitsun Day, June 1st, her own chapter of tragedy begins with her solemn coronation in the Abbey.

It might have been plain to everyone, and must have been plain to a man of the world like Cromwell, that a King so avid of popularity as Henry VIII could not long retain his infatuation for a woman for whom he could command everything but respect.

The defiance of Rome involved in these proceedings was not to be borne. On July 11th Pope Clement formulated a delayed-action bull of excommunication against the King of England. And two days earlier (July 9th) the King, for his part, had issued letters patent putting into operation the Annates Act, and cutting off from Rome the death-and-succession duties leviable upon English bishoprics. These were the opening exchanges in a battle of wills and wits which, under Cromwell's generalship, was to be sharp, short and decisive, and fought to a decision within the three remaining years of this historic Parliament.

August was uneventful, a month of expectation. Early in September the disappointing mite for whom so much had been risked was born ; and christened Elizabeth.

To sum up. I have endeavoured, in this book, to establish the truth in the case of Richard Hunne. Of the popular belief about that case there has never been any question ; but it was shared as a sober conviction by men of weight and substance, men constituting the sort of responsible opinion which found voice in Parliament. Hunne had been a liveryman of the City ; and the City, through its membership and influence in the House of Commons, made his cause its own. Throughout the two sessions of the Parliament of 1515 the Commons fought a running battle with the prelates, who held a majority in the House of Lords. The endeavour of the Commons was to save the dead man's family from penury by obtaining the restitution of his property, forfeited by his condemnation to the Crown ; to vindicate the integrity of Coroner Barnwell's jury against the aspersions of Bishop Fitzjames ; and to see that under cover of the cloud of dust raised in Parliament and Convocation over the criminous clerk in general, the particular clerk Horsey, indicted for the murder of Hunne, should not succeed in eluding trial. By strong leadership and skilful manoeuvering, with the votes of his brother-prelates and Wolsey's influence with the King, Fitzjames defeated these endeavours. It was as costly a victory as ever man won. Hunne's children were left in beggary ; and Horsey, pleading not guilty and having his plea allowed by the Crown, was released, and long survived on comfortable preferments in the west. Fitzjames died in 1521, long before he could learn the cost of his victory. Even Wolsey, dying nine years later, did not quite live to learn its cost. But, less fortunate, Archbishop Warham and most of his colleagues did live to learn it, and rue it bitterly. As for the City and the Commons, their feelings in defeat may be best gathered from the sequel, fourteen years later. In their eyes the whole of the prelacy, by their united support of Fitzjames in the successful effort to save his chancellor, had made themselves accessory to an unpunished crime. On the day the 1515 Parliament ended Wolsey, Archbishop of York, succeeded Warham as Lord Chancellor. Retiring from the lost field with an exasperated sense of impotence, the Commons asked themselves the question later put into fierce words by the brilliant young barrister Simon Fish : What justice could laymen look for with a great ecclesiastic as Lord Chancellor, and bishops and abbots dominating Parliament ? Any priest could do what he liked with any layman while " the captains of his kingdom " were in civil control. Upon none had the proceedings of 1515 more effect than upon Wolsey himself. Writing on Wolsey's death, Hall has one pregnant sentence (Chronicle, 11, p. 183) : " He hated sore the City of London and feared it." He feared it, among other things, because, in the matter of Hunne, he had made himself a principal party to a wrong which the City had not forgotten and would not forgive. Wolsey was sensible enough of the need of reform ; but, ' capax imperii nisi imperasset,' he meant to reserve it to himself when papal Legate a latere, as he was presently to become. His dread was lest Parliament, in the ugly temper of the Commons in 1515, should take it out of his hands, overthrowing the constitution in the process. In that fear, and with one brief exception in 1523, he kept the hatches battened down upon parliamentary action for the remaining fourteen years of his career, regardless of any explosive gases that might be accumulating beneath. They were fateful years, in which two very dissimilar persons appeared in the field of high politics. One was Luther ; and the Lutheran revolt, igniting Germany, was sending dangerous sparks across the Channel, which the Bishops were busy in trying to tread out. The other was a sister of one of the King's mistresses, Anne Boleyn, who took the royal fancy, not only as a piquant toy, but as the possible mother of a legitimate male heir if only his marriage with his admirable but ageing Queen could be legally annulled. In his endeavours to that end his conscience and his passions were inextricably engaged ; and for those who had eyes to see, the King's distress of conscience, and his conscienceless courtship of his Queen's rival, portended, sooner or later, a weakening of the bond between Crown and Spiritualty which had saved the latter from going under in the earlier wave of Wycliffite reform. Men — perfectly good Catholic men who had had more than enough of clerical domination — were beginning to look up and lift up their heads ; " all men mused in their hearts " as to when and how a change would come.

It came with the fall of Wolsey and the revival of Parliament. When the Commons met again in November, 1529, they had many old scores to settle, not so much with Wolsey as with his whole Order. Not least among their memories of wrong was the case of Richard Hunne, and the defeat of justice in connection with it. If the tale of Hunne had been the mere cock-and-bull story that More and those who read him uncritically would have us believe, it would long ago have blown over. It had not blown over. It had held its place in the public mind as a vivid and vengeful memory. How vivid is shown by the laborious effort of Sir Thomas More, writing in 1528, to put some tolerable face upon it. How vengeful, by the determined and implacable temper in which the Commons, immediately on their assembly in 1529, " began to common of their griefs wherewith the spiritualty had beforetime grievously oppressed them " (Hall, 11, p. 166) ; and, first of all, to deal drastically with the old irritant concerning mortuaries, his lone attempt at redressing which had brought Hunne into such grievous trouble. This was the opening stroke in something like a vendetta which reached its bitterest in the ' Supplication against the Ordinaries ' in the session of 1532.

In this Parliament two streams of circumstance, diverse both in origin and object, became united in fortuitous confluence. They were, on the one hand, the disaffection of the laity towards the clergy, and especially the bishops and their legal officers big and little : and, on the other, the dissatisfaction of the King with his marriage, and his determination to have it annulled. The King, at the outset, had no particular quarrel with the clergy : and the Commons, so far from having anything against the Queen, were strongly in sympathy with her in her unhappy fortune.* Would there emerge some co-ordinating brain and will capable of

---

* A learned friend asks what was the evidence for the Commons' sympathy with the Queen. Some of it has been given in Appendix 2, p. 379, relating to an incident that took place in the House on April 30, 1532. It seems to have been the policy, at any rate in the earlier stages, to keep the Commons out of the Divorce affair, a circumstance in itself significant. On this one recorded occasion on which the Queen was mentioned in debate, the feeling for her was such that the King had to come down and tell members to hold their tongues, because the matter " touched his soul."

Hall's graphic account of what happened a year earlier also shows that there was a felt necessity for conciliating opinion in the House and tuning it in the country.

" While the Parliament sat, on the xxx day of March (1531) at afternoon, there came into the common house the lord Chancellor (More) and divers lords of the spiritualty and temporalty to the number of xii ; and there the lord Chancellor said : ' You of this worshipful house I am sure be not so ignorant but you know well that the king our sovereign lord hath married his brother's wife : for she was both wedded and bedded with his brother prince Arthur, and therefore you may surely say that he hath married his brother's wife ; if this marriage be good or no, many clerks do doubt. Wherefor the king like a virtuous prince willing to be satisfied in his conscience, and also for the surety of his realm, hath with great deliberation consulted with great clerks, and hath sent my lord of London here present to the chief Universities of all Christendom," etc., etc.

There followed the reading, " word by word," of the " determinations " of eight foreign Universities. And

" After these determinations were read there were showed above an hundred books drawn by doctors of strange Regions, which all agreed the King's marriage to be unleful : which were not read for the day was spent. Then the Chancellor said : " Now you of this common house may report in your countries what you have seen and heard : and then all men shall openly perceive that the king hath not attempted this matter of will or pleasure, as some strangers report, but only for the discharge of his conscience and surety of the succession of his realm. This is the cause of our repair hither to you, and now we will depart."

" When these determinations were published, all wise men in the Realm much abhorred that marriage ; but women, and such as were more wilful than wise or learned, spake against the Determination, and said that the Universities were corrupt (ed. ?) and enticed so to do, which is not to be thought." (Chronicle, II, 185, 195).

Between them women generally and " wilful " men were a fairly formidable opposition.

There was, further, the difficulty Cromwell had in getting the statute for the Restraint of Appeals, designed to scotch the Queen's appeal to the Pope, through the House in the spring of 1533

combining the diverse aims in a workable and coherent policy which King and Commons could pursue together in necessary dependence upon one another ? The hour found the man in Thomas Cromwell. Cromwell, in Parliament as in business, had to make himself from nothing at all. He acquired merit and influence at once by speaking up for his fallen patron, by identifying himself with the prevailing purpose of the House, and by evident powers of leadership. As a layman and a Londoner, with an extensive and peculiar knowledge of ecclesiastics, he was in full accord with his colleagues in the Commons in their resolve to bring the clergy, in all that concerned " the bodies, goods and possessions " of the laity, into subjection to the will and law of the Crown in Parliament. This, with the Commons, was the end in itself. With Cromwell, in close touch with the King and cognisant of his character and purposes, it was also a means to an end. For if the King failed to secure a favourable sentence at Rome and matters proceeded to a rupture, it was important to have any clerical opposition immobilised beforehand. Cromwell, as the King's servant and Councillor, had to fall in with the project of the Divorce ; but there is no evidence that, prior to the event, either he or his supporters in the Commons, any more indeed than the King himself, either favoured or worked for a breach with Rome. Pole's later lucubrations are not evidence, though plausible as inferences from the accomplished fact. Cromwell was not given to views of any sort. He was always the attorney of genius, providing for his own affairs sufficiently by his masterly handling of other people's. If a breach came — and it seemed more and more likely as time went on — he held himself ready to deal with it as part of the day's work, and to put through the consequential measures, mainly administrative and financial, required to keep the Church and Kingdom going independently of the Holy See. Broadly speaking, it would not be greatly untrue to say that during the earlier half of the life of this Parliament he acted mainly as factor for the Commons, managing the King ; and that, during the latter half, he was acting wholly as factor for the King, managing the Commons. But in different degrees, the one dispassionate and clear-brained person, he was managing them all throughout. And as private member and a very minor court official, devilling indefatigably for both Commons and King, he was careful that none of them should know to what extent they were being managed. The purpose of the Commons was to bring the clergy to book : that of the King and Cromwell was to bring them to heel : and so long as the King remained an obstinate litigant in the Roman Court, matters could go no further. A new situation arose when the death of Warham in August 1532 opened to the King the prospect of being able, through a new Archbishop, to take the law into his own hands and fashion it to his liking. Hitherto, for years, there had been constant appeals to, and respect for, law ; but within five months, so precipitate was now the course of affairs, it had become imperative that Henry, law or no law, should go through a form of marriage with Anne Boleyn. And Cromwell, not unprepared for the event, at once comes forward with plans for conjuring order out of confusion, and first of all with the Statute of Appeals. And they were real plans, not just make-shift expedients. They were based upon a principle, that of the realm of England as an ' Empire,' its monarch possessing an ' imperial ' jurisdiction, and feudatory to none. Going behind the compilations of the Canon Law by which the papal authority was implemented, and which, in origin, were no more distant from Cromwell's day than is Cromwell's from our own, he found his principle, apparently, in Bracton and the fathers of the English Common Law.* Wherever he found it, his drafts, tentative and

---

* When Henry affirmed, to the prelates in 1515 (above, p. 153) that ' By the ordinance and sufferance of God we are King of England, and the Kings of England in time past have never had any superior but God only,' he may have been looking back to Bracton. Cromwell at any rate knew Bracton well enough to appreciate his uses as a source of propaganda. Professor Merriman (' Thomas Cromwell, I, pp. 122 - 3) quotes a letter written by Sir Thomas Denys in 1538 in which the writer ' tells how Cromwell three years earlier had advised him to " rede in a boke called Bratton (Footnote. Henry de Bracton's De Legibus et Consuetudinibus Angliae) nott unwrittyn his cccc yeres where he doth call the Kinges grace Vicarius Christi . . . . wherefore I do rekyn a papiste and a traitour to be one thing " (Calendar, XIII, I, 120).

The reference for the ' Vicarius Christi ' passage is De Legibus (Rolls Ser.) I, 38. Cf. II, 174.

Bracton had laid it down (I, 38) that ' the King should not be under man,

final, show that he embraced it with the ardour of a discovery. To him it was not a notion or a slogan but a creed, as near a thing to a religion as he ever attained. It was because he believed in it, and put a strong intelligence and a firm will behind it, that he made it prevail. And his religious hold upon it goes far to account for what seems his cold-blooded ruthlessness in dealing with opposition. For the obstinate malcontent, the rebel who set himself against the royal will and the will of Parliament — and the two from henceforth were to be one — was a political heretic ; and Cromwell regarded him exactly as the persecuting prelate regarded the more ordinary sort of heretic, as a person to be reconciled and reclaimed if possible, or otherwise to be exterminated by process of law, the law, if need be, being made accordingly. The determination of the King in Parliament was to be as absolute as the determination of Holy Church ; and the political heretic, like the common heretic, was entitled to the rigour of the law, no more and no less. This rigorist spirit in Cromwell comes out notably in his handling of the great test case of Sir Thomas More. In March 1534 Parliament passed a Succession Act settling the crown upon the issue of Henry and his " most dear and entirely beloved wife Queen Anne," and providing for a corporal oath to maintain " the whole effects and contents of this present Act." The oath was tendered to More and Fisher. More declared his willingness to swear to the body of the Act settling the succession, for this he admitted to be within the competence of Parliament. The Act, however, included a lengthy preamble in which the King is prayed to enact " that the marriage heretofore solemnised between your Highness and the Lady Katherine, being before lawful wife to Prince Arthur, your elder brother, which by him was carnally known, as does duly appear by sufficient proof in a lawful process had and made before Thomas, by the sufferance of God now Archbishop of Canterbury and Metropolitan and Primate of all this realm, shall be, by authority

---

but under God and the law.' The qualification ' and the law,' on which Bracton solemnly insists, gave no pause to Henry and Cromwell who, through a very peculiar conjunction of circumstances, were able to get the law made for them as they went along.

of this present Parliament, definitively, clearly and absolutely declared, deemed and adjudged to be against the laws of Almighty God, and also accepted, reputed and taken of no value nor effect, but utterly void and annulled ; and the separation thereof, made by the said Archbishop, shall be good and effectual to all intents and purposes ; any licence, dispensation, or any other act or acts going afore, or ensuing the same, or to the contrary thereof, in any wise notwithstanding." To the preamble, containing this and much else, More refused to swear. From motives of policy and doubtless worthier motives Cranmer wrote to Cromwell urging that the Government, that is to say the King and Cromwell, should accept More's oath as he was willing to take it. And Cromwell replied upon the King's behalf rejecting the suggestion. The oath had to be " to the whole effects and contents " of the Act ; and an oath to the Succession apart from the preamble " might be taken as a confirmation of the Bishop of Rome's authority, and a reprobation of the King's second marriage " (VII. nos. 499, 500). The preamble, in fact was the touchstone of political orthodoxy, and Cromwell would not have the law strained to circumvent it, even for the sparing of More. And More, we cannot doubt, was well able to understand his attitude. Six years before, Bishop Tunstall, from motives both of policy and humanity, had strained the law in order to save ' little Bilney ' from the stake in spite of himself, accepting a form of abjuration " so strange that the like hath been very seldom seen, if ever it were seen before." " Whereof," had written More in the same chapter of the ' Dialogue ' (bk. 3, chap. 5), " I never saw the like, nor in so plain a case never would, were I the judge, suffer the like hereafter." And now More, refusing the oath to " the whole effects and contents " of the Act, incurred the penalties of misprision of treason and suffered over a year's imprisonment in the Tower through encountering in Thomas Cromwell the same rigorist spirit which he himself had shown in the case of Bilney. The same hard temper of the inquisitor, bent upon applying tests of orthodoxy, appears in Cromwell's later examination of More under the Treasons Act, passed, along with the Supremacy Act, in the second session of 1534. Even the procedure was borrowed from the process in heresy, the accused being subjected to a searching catechism in order to make him convict himself out of his own mouth. In vain was the net spread in the sight of More, who knew the procedure inside out. The new Treasons Act had the sweep and range of all the legislation devised by Cromwell, but its immediate purpose was expressed in a couple of lines. It was made treason to deprive " the King's most royal person, the Queen's, or their heirs apparent " " of their dignity, title, or name of their royal estates," : in effect, to deny the King's Supreme Headship as declared in the concurrent Supremacy Act. More's view of the Supremacy was well enough known ; but for its expression to be treasonable within the terms of the new Act, the derogatory words had to be uttered " after the first day of February " 1535. More, though prepared for martyrdom, held it to be no part of the duty of a Christian to throw his life away ; and, when examined on the question of the Supremacy in May, he declined to open his mouth upon the subject.

" Now I have in good faith discharged my mind of all such matters," he averred, " and neither will dispute Kings' titles nor Popes' ; but the King's true faithful subject I am, and will be, and daily I pray for him, and all his, and for you all that are of his honourable Council, and for all the realm. And otherwise than this I never intend to meddle."

' But, said Cromwell (R. W. Chambers, ' Thomas More,' p. 324), the King was merciful, and would wish to see More take such conformable ways that he might be abroad in the world again among other men :

" Whereunto I shortly . . . . . . answered . . . . . . that I would never meddle in the world again, to have the world given me, ... but that my whole study should be upon the passion of Christ, and mine own passage out of this world."

Still pressed to declare himself, he was reminded by Cromwell that when doing his duty as civil magistrate in examining heretics under the Lancastrian laws, he himself had put such interrogatories to the accused, and insisted upon a plain answer. More does not contest this, only pointing out that the subject-matter of his questioning

372

had been the papal authority, a thing then acknowledged in all realms, and not merely in one. Both More and Cromwell realised that their positions, the one in maintaining the old dogma of the Church, the other in maintaining the new dogma of the State, were not very dissimilar. The two men understood one another very well. More had nothing hard to say of his judges, who had been his colleagues and friends. He only speaks with scornful severity of the reptile Solicitor-General Rich, who had contributed the touch of perjury necessary to clinch the case against him. Of the rest he had probably most respect for Cromwell, who at least believed in something, even if it was nothing more exalted than the all-compassing State. There was perhaps something of a noble justice as well as of a noble charity in More's farewell words to Cromwell and the Commissioners : (ibid. p. 342) :

" More have I not to say, my Lords, but that like as the blessed apostle St. Paul, as we read in the Acts of the Apostles, was present, and consented to the death of St. Stephen, and kept their clothes that stoned him to death, and yet be they now both twain holy saints in Heaven, and shall continue there friends for ever, so I verily trust, and shall therefore right heartily pray, that though your Lordships have now here in earth been judges to my condemnation, we may yet hereafter in Heaven merrily all meet together, to our everlasting salvation."

And so there passed out, behind the axe reversed, an altogether lovely, humble and triumphant soul, judged but unjudging.

APPENDIX I. (see p. 176)

This conclusion accords with all that Chapuys, almost our only informant, tells us beforehand as to the dispositions of the Court circle in regard to the forthcoming Parliament.

Reporting to the Emperor on September 1st he writes :

" The cause of this misunderstanding between the King and the Cardinal can be no other but the utter failure of the measures taken in order to bring about the divorce : on which failure those parties who for a long time have been watching their opportunity to revenge old injuries and take the power out of the Cardinal's hands, have founded their attacks to undermine his influence with the King and get the administration of affairs in their own hands.

" The people who have thus sworn the Cardinal's ruin I shall name in my next despatch, when I have obtained more credible information on this point."

And on September 4th :

" Parliament is to meet at the end of this month, some say to hear certain complaints against the administrators of justice and of the finances of the kingdom, in which they say much abuse and defalcation have prevailed in former times. The whole of this, as I am given to understand, is for the purpose of taking away the seals from the Cardinal, which could not well be done according to the use and custom of this country without Parliament or the Estates General of this kingdom assembling to sanction the measure." (A foreigner's mistake : which, nevertheless, points to the intended use of Parliament as a means of overthrowing the Cardinal).

On September 21st :

" It is reported that the real cause of this Parliament having been convoked for the 2nd of November is, independently of others specified in my despatch of the 4th of September, to investigate the conduct and examine the accounts of all those functionaries who have been connected with the finances of the country. Others add that a motion will be made to abolish the Legatine Office in England, and prevent the Pope from appointing or sending in future legates to this country " (ibid. no. 158).

Finally on October 25th, five days before Wolsey's condemnation in the King's Bench and nine before the opening of the Parliament, Chapuys wrote :

" The Cardinal through all his misfortunes kept a brave face until the day of St. Luke (Oct. 18th) when all his bravadoes turned suddenly into bitter complaints, tears and sighs, which are unceasing day and night. The King hearing of this, either moved to pity, or perhaps thinking it inconvenient that the Cardinal should die before making a full disclosure and confession of all his acts, has lately presented him with a ring by way of consolation. He is now living at a place about ten miles from London, with a very small train indeed . . . . People say execrable things of the Cardinal, all of which are to come to light before next Parliament : for it may be supposed that, whatever be the end of this matter, those who have raised this storm against the Cardinal will not rest until they have entirely done for him, knowing full well that were he to recover his lost ascendancy and power their own lives would be in jeopardy." (Spanish Calendar, nos. 132, 135, 158 and 194).

And three weeks earlier (Oct. 4th) the French ambassador du Bellay had written :

" I forgot to tell you I see plainly that by this Parliament the Cardinal will be utterly undone (par ce Parlement le Cardinal s'en va totalement) : I see no chance to the contrary " (Le Grand, 111, 363 - 4).

Mens' minds were full of the fall and fate of the Cardinal ; and there is little to show that in August, 1529, when the order was given for the summoning of Parliament, either the King or anybody else was looking very much beyond it.

With these passages compare Fisher, ' History of Europe,' II, pp. 516 - 7 : " With a great flash of political insight Henry summoned Parliament to assist him in his conflict with the papal see."

Was it really so ? With the ending of Wolsey's one-man rule and its financial shifts, the speedy summoning of Parliament was in any case inevitable if the King's Government was to be carried on. Henry's superb egotism doubtless led him to assume that any Parliament he might be pleased to summon would take his own view of the merits of his case, and further his wishes as a matter of course. In any such assumption his political insight was very much at fault. Certain passages in the diplomatic correspondence enable us to see what was in the mind of the respective parties to these affairs. They were by no means all of one mind. About a fortnight after the order for the issue of the writs (August 23rd, 1529) the French ambassador du Bellay wrote : " What people here are thinking about is of holding the Parliament this winter, and then acting by their own authority in case of failure on the part of our Holy Father to adjudicate and render justice in the matter of the divorce now afoot " (Le Grand, ' Preuves de l'historie du Divorce,' III, 342). And writing some four months later (Dec. 13th) with the first session of the Parliament closing and its reforming measures fresh in mind, Chapuys wrote :

" The reform about which I wrote to your Majesty* is partly

---

* The reference is to an earlier despatch of Nov. 8th, in which Chapuys gives an account of the Lord Chancellor's speech at the opening of Parliament. It is concerned mainly, as is Hall's entirely, with the Cardinal and his offences ; but Chapuys adds :

" The Chancellor then went on to say that of all matters of State those concerning ecclesiastics needed most reform, especially in England, and that reform the King intended to undertake at once." (Spanish, Calender, no. 211).

This, in Chapuys' narrative, reads like a rather perfunctory postscript to the speech, and may mean no more than that the Government were aware of the temper of the new Parliament, and not undisposed to meet it half way. Whatever was said upon the matter was so slight as to make no impression upon Hall, whose account contains no reference to it.

owing to the anger of these people at his Holiness' advocation of the divorce case to Rome. Although many causes are assigned for it, there can be no doubt that this last is the real one, and that, having begun the said reform, they will go on with it as quickly as they can, and this for many evident reasons. First of all because they will get large sums of money by the sale of Church property, and a judicious investment of the same. Secondly, because nearly all the people here hate the priests, they may perhaps gain them over and persuade them to consent to this marriage, and declare that the Pope has no power to grant dispensations in marriages or in other matters, and that no more of their substance shall go to Rome in future (ibid. no. 232).

Chapuys, it must be insisted, is here reporting the mind of the King and the Court, which he was specially concerned to ascertain. It was not necessarily, and not actually, the mind of the newly elected House of Commons.

This despatch of Dec. 13th seems to give the clue to what really happened. It is much more than a mere adumbration of the line of action subsequently taken, as events developed, by the King and his henchmen in the Council. And its date is very significant : it was not written until almost the close of the first six-weeks session of the new Parliament. In the previous August the peers, spiritual and temporal, who advised the issue of the writs, had doubtless assumed that whatever anti-clerical feeling there might be was directed, not against the hierarchy as a body but, like their own animosity, against the Cardinal Legate. Parliament had to be summoned, therefore, not only for necessary supply, but as the ready and essential means of putting an end to Wolsey and his overweening Legacy. But, when the newly-elected Commons assembled in November, any feeling they may have had against Wolsey had had its edge turned by the proceedings already concluded against him in the King's Bench. And their feeling against the hierarchy as a body at once declared itself, during the weeks that followed, with such strength and spontaneity as to open the eyes of King and courtiers to the possibilities of the Parliament as a means of spoliatory pressure upon the clergy and even, if need be, of minatory pressure upon the Pope. But there is nothing to show that such long-headed and sinister anticipations were shared at the time by the House of Commons itself. There is no evidence that the House, in its initial measures of reform, had any ulterior purpose of spoliation, or of an attempt to press the clergy to conform themselves to the King's wishes in the matter of the divorce. The evidence, in fact, is all the other way. Writing within a fortnight after the close of the first session Chapuys records that the King had already made an attempt to sound the House as to its willingness, in Dr. Fisher's words, " to assist him in his conflict with the papal see " : the result was disconcerting. " I am told besides," he wrote, " that the King has particularly tried to feel the pulse of this present Parliament, and see whether there was any way of making its members declare in his favour ; but he has not found one foolish enough to bring forward the motion, and for that reason the plan has been abandoned " (ibid. no. 241, p. 387). Nine months later a more formal and deliberate attempt was made to take soundings in the same direction ; with no better result. On October 15th (1530) Chapuys writes :

" The King . . . . . . called together the clergy and lawyers of this country to ascertain whether, in virtue of the privileges possessed by this kingdom, Parliament could and would enact that, notwithstanding the Pope's prohibition, the cause of the divorce be decided by the archbishop of Canterbury. To this question the said clergy and lawyers, after having studied and discussed the affair, have deliberately answered that it could not be done. On hearing which answer the King was very angry, and adopted the expedient of proroguing Parliament till the month of February, in the hope, as may be supposed, that in the meanwhile he may hit upon some means of bringing over to his opinion the said lawyers as well as some members of his Parliament, — with whose power he is continually threatening the Pope, — and see whether by compulsion or persuasion he can ultimately gain his end " (ibid. no. 460, p. 758).

Chapuys here enables us to explain how it was that, after six weeks of concentrated activity in the last two months of 1529, the Parliament never met at all for business during the whole twelve months of 1530. The reason was that the one business the King had at heart the Parliament, at that stage, would do nothing to further. The plain truth was that this Parliament, actively anti-clerical from the outset, was, for not much less than half its duration, passively pro-papal as regards the King's " great matter." This came out remarkably some eighteen months later still (April 30th, 1532). The King had called upon the Commons for an aid to fortify the Scottish border. In the ensuing debate one of the members for Westbury, Thomas Temys, rose and declared that the Scots could do nothing without foreign help, and moved that, as the best means of safeguarding the kingdom against menace from abroad, the King should be petitioned to take back his wife and treat her as became her station. The motion, whether carried or not, was received with a degree of favour that called for the royal notice. On " the last day of April " (1532), says Hall, the King sent for the Speaker and " certain other " of the Commons. He handed to them the " Answer " of the Ordin-aries to their recent " Supplication," saying (Hall) " We think their answer will smally please you, for it seemeth to us very slender " ; and he then went on to rebuke the Commons for their temerity in discussing his relations with his Queen. " Farther the King said that he marvelled not a little why one of the Parliament house spake openly of the absence of the Queen from him : which matter was not to be determined there, for he said it touched his soul," etc. (Hall, II, pp. 209 - 10. L. and P., V. 989). So here, nearly three years after the decision to summon Parliament, we have the King, on one and the selfsame occasion, encouraging the anti-clerical Commons in their action against the Spiritualty, and taking them to task for what was virtually their pro-papal attitude in standing by the Queen, whose cause the Pope, impelled by the Emperor and his own conscience, was refusing to throw over. In view of all this, what becomes of Henry's " great flash of political insight " ? It was only by gradual and cunning indoctrination, careful nursing, and a steady play upon the chord of nationalism, that this Parliament was brought, half way through its career, to act decisively against the Queen and the Pope. The insight and

379

address which achieved this feat of management were those, apparently, of Thomas Cromwell. It is not clear that the King did anything towards the result except, in January 1533, by lawlessly marrying Anne Boleyn, and so getting himself into the sort of hole from which only Parliament, by altering the law, could get him out. When the Commons brought themselves to do this, in the Act for the Restraint of Appeals, it was with a sense of misgiving, and of having to make a dubious decision between a choice of evils. It is questionable whether, even then and with all his efforts, the King could have gained over the Commons had he not been able to play upon the lively fears of an uncertain succession and the memories of dynastic civil war.

The King, in fact, misjudged his people greatly if, in the summer of 1529, he imagined that the country would return a Parliament which would help him actively to put away his wife, and dethrone the Queen in favour of an upstart beauty who, as her hopes and insolence grew and became known, could not stir abroad in public without risk of being mobbed.

Another sentence in the same context calls for notice. " At the very opening of the Seven Years Parliament clergy and laity were cowed by learning that having connived at Wolsey's legatine commission they had exposed themselves to the dire penalties of Praemunire." (Fisher, ' History of Europe,' II, pp. 518 - 9). This is too rough an approximation to the truth to be otherwise than misleading. It was not at the very opening of the Parliament but a good twelvemonth afterwards that action was taken against the clergy as a body. Wolsey was condemned in the King's Bench on the 30th October, 1529, four days before the Parliament met. It was realised at once that INDIVIDUALS who had had personal dealings with him as Legate lay open to the praemunire charge. Chapuys wrote on November 8th : " It is even reported that whoever in this country has treated or negotiated with him as such papal Legate, and even favoured or consented to such negotiations as regards dispensations for marriages, legitimisations of bastards and so forth . . . . . will be subjected to the same penalty " (Spanish Calendar, no. 211). Months later, in June, 1530, we have

380

" memoranda of indictments " against certain individual dignitaries who are the subject of proceedings (see p. 221) ; but it is not until October that we have, in a letter from Cromwell, the first obscure hint of an intention to bring the whole body of the clergy within the scope of the charge. The first overt act in that direction was the filing of an indictment in the King's Bench in December (1530) against the clergy as a body.

The character of the project and its belated appearance point to some new influence in the royal counsels ; and though, apart from his membership of the House of Commons, Thomas Cromwell had as yet no official status, not even that of a Privy Councillor, there can be, I think, little doubt as to whose influence it was. The plan was no sooner well under way than Cromwell, in January, 1531, was sworn of the Privy Council.

As to the guilt of the laity, it was first mooted by the laity themselves, when the House of Commons, in the spring session of 1531, refused to pass the Bill for the pardon of the clergy without a similar bill of indemnity on their own behalf. Though they were, as the King later told them, " a great sort of wise men," they could see no argument for the guilt of the clergy which the King's lawyers, with equal force, could not bring to bear against the laity ; and they decided to take no risks (see pp. 250 - 2).

BIBLIOGRAPHY

Arnold, Richard, *Chronicle*, ed. Douce, 1811.

Baumer, F. le van, *The Early Tudor Theory of Kingship*. (New Haven, 1940).

Blythe, Geoffrey, Bishop of Lichfield and Coventry, *Ms. Register*.

Bracton, Henricus de, *De Legibus et Consuetudinibus Angliae*, Rolls ser. (London, 1878).

Brewer, J. S., *The Reign of Henry VIII from his accession to the death of Wolsey*, ed. J. Gairdner, 2 vols. (London, 1884).

Burnet, Gilbert, *The History of the Reformation of the Church of England*, ed. Pocock, 7 vols. (Oxford, 1865).

Collier, J., *Ecclesiastical History of Great Britain*, ed. Lathbury, vol. iv. (London, 1852).

Coulton, G. C., *Mediaeval Studies*, 1st ser. (London, 1915). *Sectarian History*, (Taunton, 1937).

Cavendish, George, *Life of Cardinal Wolsey*. (London, 1852).

Cecil, Algernon, *A Portrait of Thomas More, Scholar, Statesman, Saint*. (London, 1937).

Chambers, R. W., *Thomas More*. (London, 1935).

Church Quarterly Review, Oct., 1900 and Jan., 1901, *Dr. Gasquet and the Old English Bible*). (By the present writer).

Coke, Edward, *Institutes*, vol. III.

Creighton, Mandell, *Cardinal Wolsey*. (London, 1888).

Davis, E. Jeffries, *The Authorities for the Case of Richard Hunne* (1514 - 15), English Historical Review, vol. 30, July, 1915. *Victoria History of London. Ecclesiastical History*, 1521 - 47, p. 237.

Deanesly, Margaret, *The Lollard Bible and other Mediaeval Biblical Versions*. (Cambridge, 1920).

Dixon, R. W., *History of the Church of England from the abolition of the Roman Jurisdiction*. (London, 1878).

Ecclesiastical Courts, Royal Commission on, 1883, *Report*, 2 vols. (London, 1883).

Ellis, Henry, *Original Letters illustrative of English History*, 3rd ser. (London, 1846).

The Enquirie and Verdite of the Quest panneld of the death of Richard Hune wich was founde hanged in Lolars tower.
(Only three or four copies are known to exist ; two (one imperfect) in the British Museum, one in the library of Corpus Christi College, Cambridge, and part of one in that of St. Paul's Cathedral. Miss E. Jeffries Davis, E.H.R., July, 1915).

Erasmus, Desiderius, *Epistolae*, ed. P. S. Allen, vol. VI. (Oxford, 1908). *Life of Dr. Colet, writ by Erasmus Roterdamus*. (Cambridge, 1661), (Bodl. Mason, AA, 212 (4).

382

Fiddes, Richard, *Life of Cardinal Wolsey*, 2nd ed. (London, 1726).

Fish, Simon, *The Supplication of Beggars*, ed. Furnivall, E.E.T.S., 1871.

Fisher, H. A. L., *Political History of England*, 1485 - 1547. (London, 1906). *History of Europe*, 2 vols. (London, 1943).

Fitzjames, Richard, Bishop of London, *Ms. Register.*

Forshall and Madden, ed. *The Holy Bible in the earliest English versions made from the Latin Vulgate by John Wycliffe and his followers* ; edited by the Rev. Josiah Forshall and Sir Frederick Madden, 4 vols. (Oxford, 1850).

Foxe, John, *Acts and Monuments*, 4th ed., ed. Pratt, 8 vols. (London, 1841).

Friedmann, Paul, *Anne Boleyn*, 2 vols. (London, 1884).

Froude, J. A., *History of England*, vol. I. (London, 1893).

Fuller, Thomas, *The Church History of Britain*, ed. J. S. Brewer, 3 vols. (Oxford, 1845).

Gabel, Leona C., *Benefit of Clergy in England in the Middle Ages.* Northampton. 1929).

Gairdner, James, *The English Church in the Sixteenth Century from the accession of Henry VIII to the death of Mary.* (London, 1902). *Lollardy and the Reformation in England*, 4 vols. (London, 1908 - 13). Art. *Thomas Cromwell*, in D.N.B.

Gasquet, F.A., *The Old English Bible and other Essays.* (London, 1897). 2nd ed. (London, 1908).

Gee and Hardy, ed. *Documents illustrative of English Church History.* (London, 1896).

Gibson, Edmund, *Codex Juris Ecclesiastici Anglicani*, 2 vols. (London, 1713).

Henry VIII, Reign of, Letters and Papers Foreign and Domestic, ed. J. S. Brewer, and James Gairdner, 1514 - 34. *Calendar of State Papers, Spanish*, 1529 - 33.

Holdsworth, W. S., *History of English Law.* (London ,1938 - ——).

Hall, Edward, *Chronicle*, with an introduction by Charles Whibley, 2 vols. (London, 1904).

Janelle, Pierre, *L'Angleterre Catholique à la veille du Schisme.* (Paris, 1935).

Keynon, F. G., *Our Bible and the Ancient Manuscripts.* (London, 1895).

Le Grand, J., *Histoire du Divorce de Henry VIII, roy d'Angleterre et de Catherine d'Arragon, avec —— les preuves.* (Paris, 1688).

Maitland, F. W., *Roman Canon Law in the Church of England.* (London, 1898).

Makower, Felix, *The Constitutional History and Constitution of the Church of England.* (London, 1895).

More, Sir Thomas, English Works, vol. 2. *The Dialogue concerning Tyndale*, ed. Dr. W. E. Campbell, with modern version. (London, 1931). *The Supplycacyon of Soulys agaynst the supplycacyon of Beggars.* (London, Rastell, 1529). *The Apologye of Syr Tho. More.* (London, Rastell, 1533).

Ogle, A., *The Canon Law in Mediaeval England : an examination of William Lyndwood's ' Provinciale' in reply to the late Professor F. W. Maitland.* (London, 1912). See ante. *Church Quarterly Review.*

BIBLIOGRAPHY

Ollard and Crosse, ed. *A Dictionary of English Church History*, art. Courts. (London, 1912).

Jacobs, G., *New Law Dictionary*, 8th ed. 1762.

James, Dr. M. R., *Catalogue of the Library of Corpus Christi College, Cambridge*.

Keilwey, Robert, *Reports d'ascuns cases qui ont evenus aux temps du roy Henry le septième —— et du roy Henry le huitième. Seligés hors des papieres de Robert Keilwey —— par Jean Croke.* (London, 1688).

Lodge and Thornton, ed. *English Constitutional Documents*, 1307 - 1485. (London, 1935).

Lords, House of, *Journals*, 1515

Lupton, J. H., *Life of John Colet*. (London, 1887).

Lyndwood, William, ' *Provinciale* ' (*seu Constitutiones Angliae*). (Oxford, 1679).

Merriman, R. B., *Thomas Cromwell*, 2 vols. (Oxford, 1902).

Muller, J. A., *The Letters of Stephen Gardiner*. (Cambridge, 1933).

Nelson, William, *Rights of the Clergy*. (The Savoy, 1715).

Notes and Queries, 5th ser. X, 241 - 2.

Pickthorne, Dr. K. W., *Early Tudor Government*, 2 vols. (Cambridge, 1934).

Pole, Reginald, Cardinal, *Apologia ad Carolum V*. (Brixiae, 1744).

Pollard, Dr. A. F., *Wolsey*. (London, 1929). *Henry VIII*. (London, 1902). *The Evolution of Parliament*. (London, 1934).

Roper, William, *The Life and Death of Sir Thomas More*. (London, 1729).

Rymer, Thomas, *Foedera*, vol. VI. (London, 1726 - ——).

Saint German, Christopher, *A treatise concerning the division between the Spiritualty and Temporalty*. (London, 1530).

Smith, H. Maynard, *Pre-Reformation England*. (London, 1938).

Stephens, A. J., *Ecclesiastical Statutes*, 2 vols. (London, 1845).

Stubbs, William, *Seventeen Lectures on Mediaeval and Modern History*. (Oxford, 1886). 3rd edition (Oxford, 1900). *Constitutional History of England*, 3 vols. (Oxford, 1880).

Tanner, J. R., *Tudor Constitutional Documents*, 1485 - 1603. (Cambridge, 1922).

Tyndale, William *Answer to Sir Thos. More's Dialogue*. (Parker Society).

Van Dyke, Professor, Art. on *Pole's Apologia* in American Historical Review, vol. IX, July, 1904.

Vergil, Polydore, *Anglicae Historiae*. (Basel, 1555).

Warham, William, Archbishop, *Register*, Heresy trials in.

Waugh, F. W., Art. on *The Great Statute of Praemunire*, in English Historical Review, vol. 37, 1922.

Wilkins, David, *Concilia*, vol. III. (London, 1737).

Wriothesley, Charles, *Chronicle of England during the reigns of the Tudors*, 1485 - 1559, Camden Society. (London, 1875).

Wyclif, John, *Trialogus*, ed. G. Lechler. (Oxford, 1869).

Wycliffite Bible, Introduction (Forshall and Madden), ms. no. 116. Corpus Christi College, Cambridge, Ms. No. 147.

INDEX

Charles V, Emperor (1500 - 58), 177, 178, 205, 224, 256, 257, 312, 321 n, 354, 362, 374, 376, 379

Cheapside, 293

Chelsea, More at, 261, 281 n, 284

Chichester, See of, 221, 223

Christ's Church, Oxford, 183, 212, 213

Church Quarterly Review, 117

' Circumspecte agatis,' 60

Citations Act, 305 - 7

City of London, 34, 67, 83, 86, 180, 288, 289, 364, 365

Civil Law, 30

Clement VII, Pope (d. 1534), 177, 217, 217 n, 255, 299, 362, 363.

Clerk, John, Bishop of Bath and Wells (d. 1541), 221, 344

Cochlaeus (Dobneck) (1479 - 1552), 291

Coke, Edward (1552 - 1634), 54,

Colchester, 211

Colet, John, Dean of St. Paul's (1467 ? - 1519), 35 - 7, 43, 45 n, 46, 59, 62, 288, 317.

Common Law, 52 - 3, 235, 318, 369

Commons, House of, 1515, Conflict with the prelates in Parliament over the case of Hunne, 134 - 57 : Keilwey's Memorandum, 144 - 54 ; 1523, Sir Thomas More, Speaker, 91, 181 : Thomas Cromwell a member ; his satiric summary of proceedings, 181 - 3 : 1529, Cromwell M.P. for Taunton, 186 : the anti-clerical measures of the first session, and Cromwell's part in them, Nov. 3rd to Dec. 17th, 194 - 208 : 1531, the Commons and the Acts of Pardon, 250 - 2 : Session of 1532, Annates Act, 299 - 304, 357, 364 : Citations Act, 305 - 7 : the ' Supplication of the Commons against the Ordinaries,' 307 - 30 : not a Court concoction, 307 - 16 : Text of the ' Supplication,' 323 - 30 : 1533, Act for the Restraint of Appeals 357 - 62 : attitude of the Commons towards the Divorce project, 367 n, and Part II, Appendix II

Compton, Sir William (1482 ? - 1528), 197

Constantine, George, (1501 - 59), 282, 284, 290 - 1

Convocation of Canterbury, 13, 49, 84, 109, 121, 288, 359 : protests against the use of writs of praemunire in stay of Courts Christian within the realm, 1434, 1447, 52 - 4, 56, 236 : 1512, Dean Colet's sermon before, 35 - 7 : 1515, Abbot Kidderminster, in opening sermon, denounces the Criminous Clerks Act, 141 - 7 : Friar Standish charged with heresy in, 148 - 54, 156 : 1531, Praemunire and Supreme Headship, 227 - 52 : Convocation and heresy, 22, 148 - 51 ; Tracy, 63 - 5 : Bilney, 265 - 77 : 1532, the ' Answer ' to the Commons' ' Supplication against the Ordinaries,' 331 - 43 : the instrument of ' Submission ' ; legislative independence at an end, 344 - 6

Convocation of York, 221 - 2, 249

Corpus Christi College, Cambridge, 117, 127, 129, 131

Coulton, Dr. G. C., 117 n

Courts Christian, 237

Coventry, Heresy trials at, 121 n : Little Park at, 122 n

Cranmer, Thomas, Archbishop of Canterbury (1489 - 1556), Ambassador to Emperor, 301 - 2 : Archbishop, 357, 359 : gives sentence against Katherine at Dunstable, 363 : intercedes for More, 371.

Creighton, Bishop Mandell, (1843 - 1901), 15

Creke, John, 182

Crome, Edward, (d. 1562), 275

Cromwell, Thomas, M.P. for Taunton (1485 ? - 1540,) Early career, 180 - 3 : Wolsey's agent in suppression of religious houses, 183 : anxieties on Wolsey's fall, 184 - 6 : enters 1529 Parliament as member for Taunton, 186 : his powers and place of leadership in the Commons, 191 - 3 : Cardinal Pole on, 205 - 6 : his usefulness to the Court as ex-agent of Wolsey, 209 - 15 : his covert part in the transactions which led to the charge of praemunire against the Clergy, and their acknowledgement of the Supreme Headship, 215, 221 - 7 ; sworn of the Privy Council, Jan. 1531, 227 : the King's confi-

INDEX